Road Traffic Law Handbook

Road Traffic Law Handbook

Katie Dawson

BCL, Barrister-at-Law

Bloomsbury
Professional

Published by
Bloomsbury Professional
Maxwelton House
41–43 Boltro Road
Haywards Heath
West Sussex
RH16 1BJ

Bloomsbury Professional
The Fitzwilliam Business Centre
26 Upper Pembroke Street
Dublin 2

ISBN 978 1 84766 719 9
© Bloomsbury Professional 2010

British Library Cataloguing-in-Publication Data
A catalogue record for this book is available from the British Library

Typeset by Lonsdale Law Publishing

Printed and Bound in Great Britain by Hobbs the Printers Ltd

Introduction

According to the provincial laws of New Brunswick, Canada, it is illegal to drive on the road. In Dublin, Illinois, it is illegal to drive your car through a playground. In Moscow, it is illegal to drive a dirty car and in Denmark it is illegal to start a car while someone is underneath the vehicle. In Glensdale, California, it is illegal to jump from a car travelling at 65mph. In Alabama, it is illegal to drive a vehicle whilst blindfolded. In Bangkok, Thailand, it is illegal to drive shirtless. In London, it is illegal for cabs to carry rabid dogs or corpses and it is also illegal to flag down a taxi if you have the plague. In Germany, it is illegal to run out of petrol on an Autobahn. In Quebec, it is illegal to turn right on a red light at any time. In Beijing, drivers of power-driven vehicles who stop at pedestrian crossings are liable to a fine of up to five yen.

While Ireland does not have any Road Traffic laws as bizarre as some of the above, there are a very large number of offences an individual can commit on our roads. An exhaustive list of all Road Traffic offences is beyond the scope of this text. Instead, I have outlined some of the most common offences dealt with by Irish courts. For each offence, I have given an overview of the applicable law, set out the key elements of the offence, possible defences, some brief analysis and the penalties which apply.

This text does not contain complete analysis of every single section and subsection of Road Traffic legislation. There have been 11 separate Road Traffic Acts since the Principal Act of 1961 and hundreds of statutory instruments. In this Author's opinion, our legislature should give serious consideration to the drafting of a new bill which would consolidate the various provisions contained in the present Road Traffic Acts.

However, in the absence of any consolidated Road Traffic Act, the purpose of this handbook is to provide practitioners with an easy, accurate and up-to-date reference setting out the categories of offences routinely before the courts and the applicable penalties and disqualification periods. It deals with the main categories of offences, including an up-to-date list of penalty point offences and fixed charge penalty offences. It also refers to some relevant case law, particularly in respect of drink driving offences and covers the main offences contained in the Road Acts 1961 – 2006, while also setting out the main provisions of the Road Traffic Act 2010.

References to the Principal Act refer to the Road Traffic Act 1961. It is to be assumed that any reference to a vehicle, relates to a mechanically-propelled vehicle (mpv) unless otherwise stated; similarly any reference to an 'owner' should be taken to mean 'registered owner' unless a differentiation is made.

All information contained is correct as of November 2010. Given the very large number of Acts, Regulations, Bye Laws and EU directives covering the area of Road Traffic offences, it is hoped that all the information contained herein is correct; however any errors which have occurred are my own. I would like to sincerely thank Pauline Walley SC for her invaluable advice in respect of this handbook.

This book is dedicated to my parents, Tom & Pauline.

Katie Dawson BL

Table of Contents

Table of Cases

Table of Legislation

EUROPEAN LEGISLATION

STATUTORY INSTRUMENTS

CHAPTER 1

Prosecution of Offences,
Set-Aside Applications and Appeals

The principal piece of legislation governing Road Traffic Law is the Road Traffic Act 1961. There have however been a further 11 Road Traffic Acts which have amended the principal act (including the new Road Traffic Act 2010[1]), and a myriad of Statutory Instruments.

The main categories of road traffic offences which are dealt with by the courts can be summarised as follows:

- speeding offences.
- driving licence offences.
- tax certificate & NCT test offences.
- insurance offences.
- duties and obligations at scene of accident.
- dangerous driving.
- taking vehicle without authority/unauthorised interference.
- drink/drug driving.
- fixed charge offences.
- penalty points offences.

While a defendant may receive a charge sheet, or more usually a summons in respect of just one road traffic offence, it is more common for individuals who find themselves summoned to court to have accrued numerous road traffic charges, particularly when charged with no insurance and/or no driving licence and/or no tax/NCT offences. In such cases, defendants are often charged with the substantive offence (i.e. having no valid licence/no valid insurance) and also with other related offences of failing to produce/failing to display. This chapter

---

[1] Which was signed into law by the President on 20 July 2010.

outlines the general procedure in respect of the prosecution of road traffic offences, general defences which might apply and general comments in respect of advising and representing defendants.

Road traffic offences are generally prosecuted in the District Court, with the exception of more serious offences, which may be tried on indictment (for example – Dangerous Driving causing serious harm or death). Road traffic offences are prosecuted either by means of a charge sheet, or more generally by means of a summons. In practice, most Road Traffic matters are dealt with by way of a summons. It is not proposed to address the provisions in respect of the instituting of proceedings except to say that the prosecution must adhere to all statutory provisions in respect of the summons and charge sheet procedures.

CHARGE SHEET PROCEDURE

Under the charge sheet procedure, a defendant is arrested (without warrant) and brought to a Garda station where he/she is charged, cautioned and given a copy of their charge sheet. (See Order 17, District Court Rules 1997).[2] A defendant is either given station bail and a remand date to appear before the District Court or they are remanded in custody to the next sitting of the District Court. In respect of a defendant who is before the court either:

(a) on Station Bail,[3] or

(b) in Custody,[4]

evidence must be given to the court, on the first date, of Arrest, Charge and Caution, either by the prosecuting Garda, or by way of a certificate,[5] or the complaint will not be properly before the court.

SUMMONS PROCEDURE

Under the summons procedure, the Prosecuting Garda applies for the summons, either to a District Court Judge[6] or, in most cases, to a

---

[2] S.I. No.93 of 1997.
[3] See s.31, Criminal Procedure Act 1967 (as amended by s. 3, Criminal Justice (Miscellaneous Provisions) Act 1997).
[4] See s.51, Criminal Justice Act 1951 (as amended by s. 26, Criminal Justice Act 1984.
[5] See s.6, Criminal Justice (Miscellaneous Provisions) Act 1997.
[6] See s.10, Petty Sessions (Ireland) Act 1851.

District Court Clerk.[7] This application constitutes the making of the complaint.[8] The summons issued is given a return date and is served on the defendant.

Practitioners should ensure that all relevant procedural requirements have been followed, particularly in respect of:

(a) an application for the issuing of a summons (including time limits);

(b) contents of the summons – (i.e. statement of charge); and

(c) service of the summons (including time limits for service and requirements of proof of service).[9]

However, practitioners should also note that technical defects and discrepancies in a summons will not usually prove fatal, the purpose of a summons is to secure a defendant's attendance in court:[10] invalidity of summons or a technical defect on the face of the summons will often relieve a defendant of his/her obligation to attend court; however, if they do attend court (otherwise than to challenge validity of summons),[11] his/her appearance will remedy the technical defect and the case can proceed on the basis of the complaint being read out in court.[12]

Once the State can show compliance with the provisions of section 22 of the Courts Act 1991 and Orders 10 and 15 of the District Court Rules 1997, there is a rebuttable presumption that service shall be deemed good, unless and until the contrary is shown;[13]

(a) where service is by Registered Post: upon proof that a copy of the summons was personally placed in an envelope and that

---

[7] See s.1, Courts (No.3) Act 1986 and also O. 15, Rules of District Court 1997 – S.I. No.93 of 1997 (as amended by the District Court (Summonses) Rules 2005 – S.I. No.167 of 2005.

[8] The complaint is a statement of the facts constituting the offence and can be made orally or in writing – see also outline of summary proceedings set out by Gannon J in *DPP v. Sheeran* [1986] I.L.R.M. 579.

[9] See O. 10, Rules of District Court and s.22, Courts Act 1991.

[10] See decision of Henchy J in *DPP v. Clien* [1983] I.L.R.M. 76.

[11] See *Francis McGirl v. District Justice Donal McArdle* [1989] I.R. 596 and also *Michael Flaherty v. District Judge Timothy Crowley* [1999] IESC 28; *Coughlan v. Judge Patwell* [1993] 1 I.R. 31; *Robert Payne v. District Judge John Brophy* [2006] IEHC 34.

[12] See *Application of Richard Tynan* [1969] I.R. 1; *DPP v. Clien* [1981] I.L.R.M. 465; *Finnegan v. Clifford* [1996] 1 I.L.R.M. 446.

[13] See s.22(2) of the Courts Act 1991.

the envelope was addressed, recorded, prepaid and sent or was delivered in accordance with these provisions.[14]

(b) where service is by way of Personal Service on the defendant: upon direct oral evidence being given to the court by the Garda who served the summons on the defendant.[15]

Often a summons will be served on the address of the registered owner or the address given by the user/owner when stopped. Defendants should be advised that if they change their address, then they have an obligation under Article 9 of the Road Vehicles (Registration and Licensing) (Amendment) Regulations, 1992,[16] to notify the Motor Tax Office of their new address.

However, notwithstanding the presumption that service is good, it is open to a Judge, where a defendant is not present in court, to either adjourn the matter to allow a Garda to take further steps to notify a defendant of the summons, or strike the matter out if concerned that service is not good.[17]

PROSECUTION OF OFFENCES UNDER ROAD TRAFFIC LEGISLATION

Without setting out the general rules of evidence, in detail as in all cases, it will be necessary for the prosecution to prove all requisite elements of the offence. Essential elements of most, if not all, Road Traffic Act offences will include evidence as to:

(a) *Identity of the accused*
Evidence should be adduced that the defendant was;

(i) The user of vehicle at the time of alleged offence.

(ii) Where applicable, the defendant was the registered owner of vehicle at time of alleged offence.[18]

---

[14] See O. 10, rule 13(2)(a), S.I. No.93/1997 (as amended).
[15] See O. 10 rule 13(2)(b) of the District Court Rules 1997.
[16] S.I. No.385/1992, Road Vehicles (Registration &Licensing) Regulations 1992.
[17] A full examination of the charge sheet and summonses processes are beyond the scope of this text. For further information on the commencement of summary proceeding see Chapter 13 – The District Court and the Initiation of Criminal Proceedings of Dermot Walsh's book on Criminal Procedure.
[18] For what constitutes a Registered owner see article 1(5) of S.I. No.585/1992 – Road Vehicles (Registration &Licensing) Regulations 1992 as amended by article 2 of S.I. No.213/2004 – Road Vehicles (Registration & Licensing) (Amendment) Regulations 2004.

(b) *Locality of the offence*

The District Court has local and limited jurisdiction - generally an offence, if tried summarily, must have been committed within same District Area.[19] Although a defendant can be prosecuted within the District Area (if different) where:

(i) The defendant was arrested for this offence; and

(ii) The defendant resides and/or carries out his/her business.

(c) *Location of the offence being in a public place*

This is an essential element in the majority of road traffic offences and, where applicable, the prosecution must adduce positive evidence that the offence took place in a public place. If a Garda fails to give evidence that location was a public place, a direction can be sought at close of prosecution case.

(d) *Vehicle involved was a 'Mechanically-propelled vehicle'*

The majority of offences set out in this book refer to a vehicle relate to the use of a mechanically-propelled vehicle (MPV), unless otherwise stated.[20] Where the offence relates to a MPV – it is for the prosecution to prove that the alleged vehicle was a MPV and direct evidence to that effect should be adduced.

(e) *Incident involved a contravention of Road Traffic Legislation (including regulations and bye-laws made under the provisions of Road Traffic Acts)*

Very clearly, evidence must be adduced that a particular offence occurred. The summons (or charge sheet) should set out the sections of Road Traffic Acts and regulations/bye laws which have been contravened.

Many offences relate to an allegation that an individual was 'driving or attempting to drive'; whilst a summons can allege both offences, an individual can only be found guilty or either driving or attempting to drive in respect of a particular summons and not both.

---

[19] See s.79, Courts of Justice Act 1924 (as amended) and O. 13, District Court Rules 1997.

[20] For further statutory guidance as to what constitutes a MPV – see s.3, Road Traffic Act 1961.

Generally speaking, it is not open to the court to find a defendant guilty of an alternative offence to that set out in charge sheet/summons, however there are exceptions specifically set out in law. In respect of a dangerous driving charge[21] it is open to the Judge/Jury to substitute the lesser offence of careless driving[22] and to convict a defendant of the lesser offence.[23]

(f) *Comply with the particular forms of proof or evidence required by statute*

Very clearly, where statutory provisions in respect of a partiular offence set out specific procedures and/or prescribe a particular form by which such evidence should be adduced, then the prosecution must fully comply with all statutory procedures and a failure to so do may be fatal to prosecution case. See for example, section 21 of the Road Traffic Act 2002.[24]

In respect of speeding offences, practitioners should be familiar with PART II of the Road Traffic Act 2004. The prosecution must prove that a particular speed limit applied to the location of the offence. In the case of any prosecution of an individual for an alleged offence of speeding, prosecution should also be in a position to prove that the speed limit (other than ordinary speed limit) was properly signposted and also produce certified copy of Bye-Law or Road Works order (where applicable).[25]

(g) *Garda exercised lawful authority in investigation of an offence*

Where a Garda has exercised his powers to:

(i) stop a defendant.[26]

(ii) search/examine/inspect a vehicle.[27]

(iii) detain/remove/immobilise a vehicle.[28]

(iv) demand information.[29]

---

[21] See s.53, Road Traffic Act 1961 (as amended) and Chapter 8.
[22] See s.52, Road Traffic Act 1961 (as amended) and Chapter 8.
[23] It is also possible for a court to substitute a s.49, Road Traffic Act 1961 Drink driving charge (driving or attempting to drive) for a s.50, Road Traffic Act 1961 Drink driving charge (in charge of a vehicle with the intention of driving/attempting to drive) or vice versa – see chapter on drink driving offences).
[24] As amended by s.15, Road Traffic Act 2004 and s.17, Road Traffic Act 2006.
[25] See Chapter 3 in respect of speeding offences.
[26] See s.109, Road Traffic Act 1961 (as amended).
[27] See s.20, Road Traffic Act 1961 (as amended).
[28] See s.41, Road Traffic Act 1994 (as amended).
[29] See s.107, Road Traffic Act 1961 (as amended).

    (v)   demand production of documentation.[30]

    (vi) demand a sample be provided under drink/drug driving legislation.[31]

    (vii) arrest a defendant.[32]

The prosecution should adduce evidence that the Garda was exercising his lawful authority in exercising any of above powers, including what opinion the Garda formed, the basis on which the Garda formed their opinion as well as setting out the statutory basis on which each power/authority was being exercised.

GENERAL DEFENCES APPLICABLE TO ROAD TRAFFIC OFFENCES

Apart from the specific defences that may arise in respect of particular offences, there are certain general defences which will apply in most, if not, all cases. These are:

    (a) no case to answer – evidence adduced by the prosecution does not disclose an offence and/or does not establish the offence the defendant charged with;

    (b) proceedings are statute barred as complaint is not made within the statutory time limit.

Although the defence does not need to prove that the time limit for making of the complaint/application for the summons had expired – (same knowledge is entirely within the knowledge of the prosecution), if the defence believes a matter is statute barred, then they must raise this with the court and request that the court carries out an inquiry in respect of same.[33]

The general time limit for the commencement of summary prosecution is six months. The complaint/application for the summons must be made within six months of the date of the alleged offence.[34]

Therefore, relevant dates to consider are:

---

[30] See for example, s.69, Road Traffic Act 1961 (as amended) – lawful demand to produce certificate of insurance within 10 days.

[31] See for example s.12, Road Traffic Act 1994 or s.4, Road Traffic Act 2006.

[32] Many of the provisions of the Road Traffic Acts – (for example s.49(8) or s.50(10), Road Traffic Act 1961 (as amended)) allow for Gardaí to arrest an individual without warrant if in the Garda's opinion they have committed or are committing an offence under that particular section.

[33] See *Duff v. Mangan* [1994] 1 I.L.R.M. 91;

[34] See s.10(4) Petty Sessions Act 1851, as amended by Pt.II of the Schedule to the Statute of Limitations Act 1957.

(a) the alleged date of offence. Practitioners should note that the relevant date is the date when the offence is complete: for example, where a lawful demand is made to produce documents within 10 days, the offence is not complete until a 10 day period has expired without documents having been produced), and

(b) the date on which either the complaint is made before the appropriate District Court Judge [charge sheet procedure]/or an application for summons is made before the appropriate District Court Clerk [summons procedure].

It is important to note that the relevant issue to be considered by the court is whether the original complaint/application for a summons was made within six months. In circumstances where a matter is struck out at any stage prior to a dismissal/conviction at hearing, it is open to the prosecution to issue a fresh summons.[35] Indeed, where the offence is triable on indictment, a dismissal made by a District Court Judge – prior to matter being sent forward to Circuit Court will not be a bar on a fresh summons issuing.[36] An issue of delay may, however, arise in circumstances where some time has passed before fresh summons issues.

A general time limit does not apply where a 'special time limit' has been provided under relevant Road Traffic Act legislation – for example, section 64 of the Road Traffic Act 1961 or summary offences under EC regulations. Time limits do not apply to Road Traffic Act offences which are triable on indictment, even if they are actually tried summarily.[37]

In the case of fixed charge offences, a six-month time limit applies, however, court proceedings shall not be instituted where a 56 day notice period has not yet expired and the specified payment, and completed notice (where applicable) is made during the notice period.[38]

More Specific Defences Which Might Apply to Road Traffic Offences

(a) Delay in instituting/prosecuting summary proceedings

There is very considerable case law in the area of delay and it is not proposed to repeat or reference to same here. It is established that a defendant has a constitutional right to a trial in due course of law

---

[35] See *DPP v. McKillen* [1991] 2 I.R. 506.
[36] See Pt.III, Criminal Justice Act 1999.
[37] See s.7, Criminal Justice Act 1951.
[38] S.103(8)(e), Road Traffic Act 1961 (as amended).

(Article 40.3) – which includes a trial with reasonable expediency. It is therefore open to a defendant to raise an issue of delay and seek for proceedings to be dismissed where the prosecution has not issued, or prosecuted, proceedings with reasonable expediency.

However, in such cases the onus is on the defence to show firstly, that an unreasonable/unexplained delay has occurred, and secondly, that same delay has been prejudicial to the defendant. Factors which will be considered include:

(a) length of the delay;

(b) reason advanced for the delay which has occurred;

(c) nature of charges; and

(d) whether the defendant has spent time in custody waiting a hearing date.

A defendant is unlikely to succeed if he/she has contributed to the delay which has occurred through attempting to avoid service or failing to attend court.

(b) Accused can rely upon a statutory defence/statutory exemption to charge

It is often a defence to a charge under the Road Traffic Acts if:

(a) the owner of the vehicle can demonstrate that he/she were not driving the vehicle and that the vehicle was being driven without his/her consent.

(b) the user of the vehicle can demonstrate that he/she were not the owner of the vehicle and were driving same vehicle as an agent/servant of the owner and under the express order of the owner.

(c) the defendant can rely on a statutory exemption.

Again, where a defendant is seeking to rely on a specific defence or a statutory exemption, the onus is on the defence to demonstrate that the same defence/exemption applies to the circumstances of case.

(c) No case to answer

The prosecution has failed to adduce evidence of an essential ingredient of offence (for example):

(a) that the offence took place in public place;

(b) that a lawful demand was made of the defendant to produce documentation within 10 days;

(c) the prosecution evidence does not establish the offence with which the defendant is charged.[39]

In most circumstances, road traffic offences are prosecuted in the name of the DPP and a prosecuting Garda or solicitor will attend court on behalf of the DPP. Even in cases where a solicitor is instructed to appear on behalf of the DPP (and this is not common in respect of minor RTA offences), the prosecuting Garda should be in court on the hearing date to give oral evidence in respect of the offences. Where matters are contested, it is not sufficient for them to have instructed another Garda to appear on his/her behalf instead; the rule against hearsay evidence will clearly apply, and positive evidence of an offence having been committed must be adduced.

Practitioners should also be aware that whilst the general burden of proof is on the prosecution to prove all the elements of an offence, and generally speaking there is no obligation on a defendant to adduce evidence in his defence; there are a number of exceptions to this legal principle.

(1) Rebuttable presumptions of law

There are a large number of road traffic offences which clearly set out rebuttable presumptions of law; thereby shifting the burden of proof from the prosecution to the defence. This is most commonly set out in statute as follows – 'unless and until the contrary is shown it is presumed that...' or 'it shall be presumed, until the contrary is shown by the defendant that...'.

For example, where it is alleged that a defendant was driving without proper documentation, Driving Licence, Insurance Certificate, Tax Disc, NCT test, DOE cert – there is an obligation on the defendant to produce documentation either at his/her Garda station within 10 days, and/or in court to disprove a rebuttable presumption that they were driving vehicle without the requisite documentation.

(2) Obligation on a defendant to show he/she comes within statutory exception/exemption

For example, article 11, EC (Compulsory Use of Safety Belts and Child Restraint Systems in Motor Vehicles) Regulations[40] sets out

---

[39] Although in some cases Judge/Jury can substitute offence for lesser offence – i.e. substitute a careless driving charge for a dangerous driving charge.
[40] S.I. No.4/2006 – E C (Compulsory Use of Safety Belts and Child Restraint Systems in Motor Vehicles) Regulations 2006.

certain exemptions which apply to seatbelt requirements. If a defendant wishes to rely on one of these exemptions, then they must demonstrate to the court that they come within those specified exemptions.

(3) Where a defendant wishes to raise a specific defence based on facts peculiarly within his/her own knowledge

For example, if a defendant wishes to rely on a defence that:

(a) their vehicle was no longer a "MPV" within the meaning of the Act as it had a defect which rendered it no longer capable of being mechanically-propelled or driven; or

(b) the defendant is no longer the registered owner of the vehicle having registered change of ownership with the Motor Taxation Office; or

(c) where a defendant, who is the registered owner of vehicle allegedly used seeks to rely on a defence that same vehicle was used without his/her consent and/or authority;

Then it is for the defendant to demonstrate that the defence raised applies.

Section 22 of the Road Traffic Act 2002[41] applies to most road traffic offences and states that at the hearing of such an offence, a defendant must produce his/her Driving Licence for inspection and copying by the Court Officer.

Again, practitioners should be aware of matters which have particular applicability to the prosecution of road traffic offences, including section 21 of the Road Traffic Act 2002 (as amended), section 35 of the Road Traffic Act 1994 and the Rules of the Road.

GENERAL COMMENT IN RESPECT OF ADVISING AND REPRESENTING DEFENDANTS

There are certain practical and procedural matters which should be considered any time you are representing a defendant in respect of a charge under Road Traffic Legislation.

CHARGES BEFORE COURT

The first step for practitioners is to establish precisely what charges are before court. Without knowing this, it is very difficult to give

---

[41] As substituted by s.21, Road Traffic Act 2004.

correct, accurate advice to your client. It is essential that your client provide you with all summons or charge sheets they have received.

Whilst this may seem very basic advice, it is not uncommon for clients to underplay the seriousness of charges or to give you only part of the required information. Clients may contact you looking for representation and advice you that they have a charge for failing to display a tax disc or NCT disc, omitting to tell you that they have also been charged with an offence of driving without insurance. You do not want to discover that there are additional charges you were unaware of half way through the Garda's evidence. It is essential that a client provide you with all of the summonses they have received, preferably in advance of court date and you should also clarify what summons/charges are with the prosecuting Garda before case is called on first date.

REQUIREMENT TO PRODUCE DOCUMENTATION

Again, whilst it may appear obvious that when a client is before the court in respect of charges of having no insurance, driving licence, tax cert or NCT cert, they should bring any relevant documentation with them to court, clients often do not bring same documentation with them unless explicitly advised. Where a client is before the court in respect of any road traffic offence, it is advisable that they bring their driving licence to court and indeed it is often preferable if they also bring their insurance policy. Currently there are a very limited number of offences in respect of which an individual is not required to bring their driving licence to court (see section 22 Road Traffic Act 2002, as amended by section 21 of the Road Traffic Act 2004 and also section 63 of the Road Traffic Act 2010,[42] which extend this responsibility to almost all offences under Road Traffic Acts 1961-2010); in practice, clients should always be advised to bring their licence to court with them.

Where a client advises you that they have a valid insurance policy/driving licence/tax disc/NCT cert, it is always advisable to ask to be furnished with a copy of same in advance of any hearing date. Again, it is not prudent to simply rely on a client's assertion that they have same documentation. Very frequently a client will advice they are insured and will arrive in court on a hearing date with either an insurance disc and not the required policy document, or with a

---

[42] See s.63 – Road Traffic Act 2010 – when same s. comes into operation.

document which doesn't name them as a 'named driver', cover the vehicle in question, and/or the date on which they were driving.

It is important to stress to clients that driving without valid Insurance and/or driving without a valid driving licence charges are interpreted very strictly by the courts; either the individual has a valid insurance policy and/or driving licence covering them for the date of the offence, or they do not. A client's mistaken belief that they were insured or had a valid licence is not an excuse, or a defence, no matter how genuinely held their belief may be. However, it may constitute an explanation by way of mitigation.

APPLICABLE PENALTIES

In advance of any plea/hearing date, a defendant must be advised very clearly and correctly of all the penalties that may potentially apply, particularly the applicable disqualification period,[43] if any. Where the offence is a penalty point offence, a defendant should also be advised of applicable penalty points.[44] In order to advise a defendant fully of the potential penalties, Practitioners need to know the relevant applicable penalties and also if the defendant has any previous convictions. If a defendant has previous convictions, particularly in respect of other road traffic offences then this may adversely impact on the penalties imposed.

A defendant is further at risk if they have previously been disqualified from driving or, worse still, they were disqualified at the time of the alleged offence. Where a defendant is convicted of a second offence in respect of any offence carrying a consequential disqualification order, they are at increased risk of a disqualification period in excess of minimum mandatory disqualification period, and/or at risk of a custodial sentence and the defendant must be advised of this fact.

As with all criminal cases, it is prudent to check a defendant's previous convictions with Prosecuting Garda in advance of plea/ hearing as a defendant may not always give an accurate account of their previous convictions and/or previous driving disqualifications.

APPEALS PROCESS/APPLICATION FOR RESTORATION OF LICENCE

A defendant must be correctly advised in respect of both the appeals process and if and how they can apply to have their licence restored.

---

[43] See Disqualification Table in this book: Chapter 12.
[44] See Chapter 12 in respect of Penalty Point offences.

This is of particular importance given that if a defendant fails to appeal within 14 days, no stay will be placed on any disqualification imposed.[45] For that reason, it is essential that the appeals process and consequences of failing to appeal within the specified time limit are spelt out to the defendant, preferably in writing, even before the matter is heard in court.

Practitioners should generally apply for recognisance to be set for an appeal after sentence is imposed, although if matter dealt with very leniently[46] then obviously recognisance will not be sought. As previously stated, if an individual wishes to have a stay placed upon any period of disqualification imposed by the District Court pending an appeal then this appeal must be lodged within 14 days of the imposition of District Court order. If a defendant is convicted and disqualified in their absence, consideration should be given as to whether a set-aside application should be brought instead of an appeal. The procedure for setting aside an order of the District Court is set out in section 22 of the Courts Act 1991. A defendant should also be advised in respect of the procedure for applying for the early restoration of a licence, where applicable.[47]

DISCLOSURE

Most cases will turn on their own particular facts, hence the importance of getting a Gary Doyle order,[48] and/or as full disclosure as possible in respect of any case proceeding to hearing. In cases involving very minor road traffic offences, there will be little, if any, disclosure, but for more serious offences such as drink driving or dangerous driving offences, there may be considerable disclosure including witness statements, certificates from Medical Bureau of Road Safety, engineer reports etc. Practitioners should also be alert to inconsistencies which may arise between a précis, statements provided and/or notes in a Garda notebook and actual evidence given in court. Evidence in chief given by the Gardai in court tends to be very standard and uniform – it is therefore important to tease out the full facts and circumstances of the incident under cross examination.

---

[45] See Chapter 2 – Driving Disqualifications and the Appeals Process.
[46] For example if s.1(1), Probation of Offenders Act 1907 is applied – where Judge finds facts proved but declines to impose a criminal conviction; or if matter is struck out on payment of a charitable donation.
[47] See Chapter 2 – Driving Disqualifications and the Appeals Process.
[48] *Director of Public Prosecutions v. Gary Doyle* [1994] 2 I.R. 286.

CHAPTER 2

Disqualifications and the Appeals Process

This chapter deals with:

(a) the various disqualification orders which can be imposed;
(b) applications for the early restoration of driving licences;
(c) Set-Aside Applications and Appeals.

For most defendants appearing before a court in respect of road traffic charges, their primary concern is whether they are at risk of being disqualified or receiving penalty points. A defendant is only at risk of a custodial sentence in circumstances where they have either committed a very serious road traffic offence or they have a number of previous convictions for road traffic offences. Defendants need to be advised if they are at risk of a driving disqualification and practitioners must be in a position to correctly advice them of what disqualification period, if any, applies.

Presently, an individual may be disqualified from holding a driving licence by virtue of one of the following court orders made pursuant to the Principal Act:

(a) Consequential [mandatory] Disqualification order;[1] or
(b) Ancillary Disqualification order;[2] or
(c) Special Disqualification order–[unfit/incompetent to drive].[3]

However, they may also be disqualified by virtue of an administrative (non-judicial) order:

(d) accumulation of 12 penalty points;[4] or

---

[1] S.26, Road Traffic Act 1961 (as amended).
[2] S.27, Road Traffic Act 1961 (as amended).
[3] S.28, Road Traffic Act 1961 (as amended).
[4] S.3, Road Traffic Act 2002 (as amended).

(e) disqualification pursuant to the European Convention on Driving Disqualifications.[5]

Practitioners should note that the there is now a mutual recognition and enforcement of disqualification orders imposed on a driver by the courts in Ireland, mainland UK and Northern Ireland under a mutual agreement between the Irish, Northern Irish and British governments which came into force on the 28 January 2010.

It is advisable for practitioners to familiarise themselves with the relevant provisions so that they can advise their clients of the potential risks of the court imposing a disqualification. It is important to note that whilst there are a limited number of offences which accrue a consequential (mandatory) disqualification,[6] it is open to the court to impose an ancillary disqualification in respect of any other charge, if the court rules that the facts of the case merit such a penalty. Therefore, clients must be advised that there is always a risk that a court may impose a disqualification, although if this happened in the case of a very minor offence, where a client has no previous convictions, same should be appealed on grounds of severity.

CONSEQUENTIAL DISQUALIFICATION ORDER – SECTION 26 ROAD TRAFFIC ACT 1961

Section 26, Road Traffic Act 1961[7] sets out the circumstances in which a court is obliged to impose a consequential (mandatory) disqualification. The offences which incur a consequential order are set out in the second schedule to the Act[8] and have been amended on a number of subsequent occasions. A table of Mandatory Disqualification Offences are set out in this book. A consequential disqualification order comes into effect 15 days after the date of the order (unless already appealed).

Although different minimum periods are prescribed by law,[9] no consequential disqualification order can be less than 12 months in

---

[5] S.9, Road Traffic Act 2002, as amended by s.5, Road Traffic Act 2004 – see also Sch.2 to Road Traffic Act 2002 and S.I. No.11/2010 – Road Traffic Act 2002 (S.9) (Commencement) Order 2010.
[6] See Disqualification Table at back of this book in Appendix A.
[7] As substituted by s.26, Road Traffic Act 1994, and further amended by s.5, Road Traffic Act 1995, s.6, Road Traffic Act 2006 and s.65, Road Traffic Act 2010 – when same comes into operation
[8] As amended: see n.7 above.
[9] See s.6, Road Traffic Act 2006, which came into operation on 5 March 2007 (S.I.

duration, unless an individual is convicted of a first offence of driving without insurance.[10] This section allows that, in circumstances where a 'special reason' can be offered to the court[11] an individual convicted of a first offence can be left without a disqualification, or a disqualification of less than 2 years. Practitioners should note that this provision was also available in respect of a first conviction of dangerous driving:[12] however, the Road Traffic Act 2006 has deleted this provision.[13]

What constitutes a 'special reason' is not defined in law. However, it is generally some mitigating factor which might go somewhat to explain, if not excuse, the offence. For example, in the case of a conviction for a first offence of driving without insurance,[14] an honest but mistaken belief that an individual was covered as a named driver on an insurance policy in place for the vehicle, or by another insurance policy in his/her own name (as oppose to having no policy of insurance at all), might convince a Judge not to impose the minimum mandatory disqualification.

Practitioners should note that section 29 of the Road Traffic Act 2010[15] also provides for circumstances where an individual charged with a drink driving offence may avoid a disqualification or have a disqualification period of less than 12 months imposed.[16]

Practitioners should also note that there are certain offences in respect of dangerous driving[17] and breach of duties at the scene of an accident[18] where a court shall, or may,[19] disqualify an individual for a specified period AND until a certificate of competency[20]

No.86/2007) for most recent disqualification periods and also s.65, Road Traffic Act 2010, when same section comes into operation.

[10] S.56, Road Traffic Act 1961 – practitioners should also note that s.29, Road Traffic Act 2010 will allow for disqualification periods of less than 12 months, when same section comes into operation.

[11] S.26(5)(b), Road Traffic Act 1961 (as substituted by s.26, Road Traffic Act 1994.

[12] S.53, Road Traffic Act 1961 (as amended).

[13] S.6(1)(d), Road Traffic Act 2006.

[14] S.56, Road Traffic Act 1961 – practitioners should also note that ss.29 & 69, Road Traffic Act 2010 will allow for disqualification periods of less than 12 months, when same sections comes into operation.

[15] When same ss come into operation.

[16] See Chapter on Drink Driving.

[17] S.53, Road Traffic Act 1961 (as amended).

[18] S.106, Road Traffic Act 1961 (as amended).

[19] Where the court has discretion not to impose an additional certificate condition on grounds of 'special reasons'.

[20] See s.33, Road Traffic Act 1961 (as amended s.21, Road Traffic Act 1968) and s.9, Road Traffic Act 2006.

and/or certificate of fitness[21] is produced. In the case of any other disqualification period, this extra condition is discretionary and can be imposed by a Judge where, on the facts of the case, a reasonable concern has arisen in respect of an individual's fitness or ability to drive.

Where a certificate of competency and/or fitness must be produced, the disqualification imposed is not lifted upon the expiration of a specified period alone as this is only the first condition. An individual must, upon the expiration of the specified period, or at such later date as possible, produce the required certificate before the licence can be restored.[22] This will also apply in the case where an application is made for the early restoration of a licence[23] if the above condition was imposed by court.

Any consequential disqualification order imposed can be appealed, but unless that appeal is made within 14 days of the date of the conviction, no stay will be placed upon the operation of any period of disqualification pending the determination of an appeal.[24] It is open to the appellate court to lift a consequential disqualification, but only where the conviction itself is overturned: where the conviction stands there is an obligation on the court to impose a prescribed minimum period of disqualification. Where a consequential disqualification is appealed on grounds of severity only, it is open to the court to affirm the order, or increase or decrease the period of disqualification to a period not less than the minimum period prescribed by law unless, special conditions will apply permitting the court to exercise its jurisdiction not to disqualify an individual.[25]

An individual disqualified by means of a consequential disqualification order can, in certain circumstances, apply for early restoration of his/her driving licence.[26]

---

[21] See s.34, Road Traffic Act 1961, as amended by s.29, Road Traffic Act 1994 and article 19, S.I. No.352/1999, Road Traffic (Licensing of Drivers) Regulations 1999. and s.10, Road Traffic Act 2006.

[22] S.26(3), Road Traffic Act 1961 (as amended).

[23] S.29, Road Traffic Act, as substituted by s.7, Road Traffic Act 2006 and amended by s.67, Road Traffic Act 2010, when same s. comes into operation.

[24] *Waldron v. DPP* [2004] IEHC 227.

[25] See s.56, Road Traffic Act 1961 (as amended) and Chapter 6 on Driving without Insurance.

[26] S.29, Road Traffic Act, as substituted by s.7, Road Traffic Act 2006 and amended by s.67, Road Traffic Act 2010, when same s. comes into operation.

Consequential Disqualification Order – Section 65 of the Road Traffic Act 2010

Practitioners should note that section 65 of the Road Traffic Act 2010[27] replaces section 26 of the Road Traffic Act 1994.[28] The new section addresses the disqualification periods that apply to the new dangerous driving and careless driving (tried on indictment) offences[29] and sets out the disqualification periods that would apply to the new drink driving offences.[30] Section 65 of the Road Traffic Act 2010 retains the existing judicial discretion not to impose a consequential disqualification for a first offence of driving without insurance and makes similar provision in respect of the new offence of careless driving (tried summarily).[31] Section 65 also sets out a substituted second schedule of offences carrying a consequential disqualification order.[32] A new consequential disqualification table is to be found at the end of this book.

Postponement of a Disqualification Order – Section 30 of the Road Traffic Act 1961

Section 30 of the Road Traffic Act, 1961[33] allows for the postponement of any disqualification order, either:

(a) pending an appeal (if appeal lodged within 14 days);[34] or
(b) where the court is satisfied there are special reasons such as to warrant a postponement of the disqualification.[35]

Where a postponement is made because of 'special reasons' proffered, same postponement can be for no longer than six months.[36] The most common 'special reason' for the postponement of a disqualification is that the individual needs a period of time to

---

[27] S.69, Road Traffic Act 2010, when same s. comes into operation and Chapter 8 on Dangerous Driving Offences.
[28] Which itself was substituted by the original s.26, Road Traffic Act 1961.
[29] See Pt.7 and s.65(1)(4)(a), Road Traffic Act 2010 and Chapter on Dangerous Driving.
[30] See Pt.3 and s.65(1)(4)(b), Road Traffic Act 2010 and Chapter 10 on Drink Driving Offences.
[31] See s.65(1)(5)(b), Road Traffic Act 2010.
[32] See s.65(2), Road Traffic Act 2010.
[33] As substituted by s.20, Road Traffic Act 1968.
[34] S.30(4), Road Traffic Act 1961 and *Waldron v. DPP* [2004] IEHC 227.
[35] S.30(3)(e), Road Traffic Act 1961.
[36] S.30(3)(d), Road Traffic Act 1961.

put alternative arrangements in place in respect of work/family commitments.

Postponement of a Disqualification Order – Section 64 of the Road Traffic Act 2010

Practitioners should note that section 64 of the Road Traffic Act 2010[37] amends section 30 of the Road Traffic Act 1961 extending the omissions in respect of disqualification orders to holders of:

(a) an Irish driving licence or driving permit held at date order made

(b) a foreign driving licence to which the EC (Recognition of Driving Licences of other Member States) Regulations 2008[38] would otherwise have applied

(c) any other recognised foreign driving licence[39] held at the date order made.

Ancillary Disqualification – Section 27 of the Road Traffic Act 1961

An ancillary disqualification order is an order which a Judge can, at his/her discretion, impose in addition to any other penalty imposed. An ancillary disqualification order comes into effect 15 days after the date of the order (unless already appealed). Under section 27 of the Principal Act, such an order can be imposed where an individual has been convicted of any offence under:

(a) Road Traffic Acts 1961–2006.[40]

(b) otherwise, in relation to a driving offence or offence involving a vehicle – like those set out under;

(i) Road Traffic Regulations; and

(ii) other offences such as Hijacking[41] or Endangering Traffic[42]

---

[37] When same s. comes into operation.
[38] See S.I. No.464/2008 – European Communities (Recognition of Driving Licences of Other Member States) Regulations 2008.
[39] See S.I. No.527/2007 – Road Traffic (Recognition of Foreign Driving Licences) Order 2007.
[40] Or Road Traffic Acts 1961–2010 – when same Act comes into operation.
[41] S.10, Criminal Law(Jurisdiction) Act 1976.
[42] S.14, Non-Fatal Offences against the Person Act 1997.

(c) other offences, where the vehicle used in commission of an offence: for example, a getaway vehicle used during a robbery.

There is virtually no Irish case law in respect of circumstances where an ancillary disqualification might be imposed, however, it is clear that there would have to be some correlation between the facts of the offence and the imposition of a disqualification; the court should not hand someone convicted of shoplifting clothes[43] a driving disqualification.

There is neither a minimum nor a maximum duration for such a disqualification, but given that this disqualification applies to offences where the legislature has not considered it necessary to require the imposition of a mandatory disqualification,[44] there would have to be very strong grounds for a court to impose an ancillary order greater than the minimum mandatory disqualification periods presently set out in law (ranging for one to six years).

Any ancillary disqualification order imposed can be appealed, even if the conviction, or the severity of any other penalty imposed is not appealed; but unless that appeal is made within 14 days of the date of the conviction, no stay will be placed upon the operation of any period of disqualification pending the determination of an appeal.[45] An individual disqualified by means of an ancillary disqualification order can in certain circumstances apply for an early restoration of his/her driving licence.[46]

SPECIAL DISQUALIFICATION – SECTION 28 OF THE ROAD TRAFFIC ACT 1961

Under the provisions of section 28 of the Road Traffic Act 1961,[47] a Special Disqualification Order can be made upon an application by a Garda or a licensing authority officer.[48] There is no requirement that the individual has been convicted of any offence under the Road Traffic Acts, as the reason a disqualification is sought is on the grounds that an individual is unfit or incompetent to drive.

---

[43] S.4, Criminal Justice (Theft and Fraud Offences) Act 2001.
[44] S.26, Road Traffic Act 1961 (as amended). See p. 19 infra.
[45] S.30(4), Road Traffic Act 1961 and *Waldron v. DPP* [2004] IEHC 227.
[46] S.29, Road Traffic Act, as substituted by s.7, Road Traffic Act 2006 and amended by s.67, Road Traffic Act 2010, when same s. comes into operation.
[47] As amended by s.49, Road Traffic Act 1994.
[48] S.28(1), Road Traffic Act 1961, as amended by s.49, Road Traffic Act 1994.

The grounds upon which such an application would be made are that the licence holder is by reason of:

(a) a disease; or

(b) a mental disability; or

(c) a physical disability,

either unfit or incompetent to drive.[49]

If granted, an order will remain in place until the disqualified person produces a valid certificate of fitness[50] and/or competency.[51] In such circumstances, there is no fixed duration for a special disqualification: it remains in place until the court is satisfied that the disqualified individual is now fit and competent to drive. It also follows that the procedure for seeking an early restoration of a driving licence[52] does not apply to a special disqualification order. Similarly, there is no provision under section 30 to allow for the postponement of a special disqualification order, other than where it is appealed.[53] Any special disqualification order imposed can be appealed to the Circuit Court and the imposition of the Special Disqualification Order can be suspended pending the outcome of the appeal.[54]

EARLY RESTORATION OF LICENCE – SECTION 29 OF THE ROAD TRAFFIC ACT 1961

Under Section 29 of the Road Traffic Act 1961,[55] only people who have been disqualified for the first time, within a ten-year period,[56] and for a period in excess of two years (i.e. at least two years and one day[57]), can apply to the court to have their licence restored. The applicant must have served half of their disqualification period before an

---

[49] S.28(1), Road Traffic Act 1961, as amended by s.49, Road Traffic Act 1994.

[50] See s.34, Road Traffic Act 1961 (as amended s.23, Road Traffic Act 1968) and s.10, Road Traffic Act 2006.

[51] See s.33, Road Traffic Act 1961 (as amended s.21, Road Traffic Act 1968) and s.9, Road Traffic Act 2006.

[52] S.29, Road Traffic Act, as substituted by s.7, Road Traffic Act 2006 and amended by s.67, Road Traffic Act 2010, when same section comes into operation.

[53] S.30(3)(d), Road Traffic Act 1961.

[54] S.30(2), Road Traffic Act 1961.

[55] As substituted by s.7, Road Traffic Act 2006; same provision came into operation on 5 March 2007 – See S.I. No.86/2007, Road Traffic Act 2006 (Commencement) Order 2007.

[56] S.29(1), Road Traffic Act 1961, as substituted by s.7, Road Traffic Act 2006.

[57] S.29(1), Road Traffic Act 1961, as substituted by s.7, Road Traffic Act 2006.

application is made,[58] and their licence (if their application is successful) can only be restored after two thirds of their period of disqualification has expired.[59] An application should be made to the court where the disqualification order is made[60] and on 14 days notice to the Garda Superintendent in that district.[61]

In considering this application, the court will have regard to a number of factors including:

(a) the nature of the offence;

(b) whether the defendant was convicted of other RTA offences arising out of same incident;

(c) whether the defendant has accrued any previous or subsequent convictions for other RTA offences;

(d) and whether the defendant has accrued any previous or subsequent criminal convictions and the views of Gardaí.[62]

If an applicant has already had their licence restored within the previous ten years, they are statute-barred from making a second restoration of licence application within that 10-year period.[63] If an application is refused, it can be renewed after three months and matter can also be appealed. If disqualification was imposed before the commencement of section 7 of the Road Traffic Act 2006 (i.e. 5 March 2007), the previous provisions of section 29 of the Road Traffic Act 1961 will apply to any restoration application.

EARLY RESTORATION OF LICENCE – SECTION 66 OF THE ROAD TRAFFIC ACT 2010

Practitioners should note that section 66 of the Road Traffic Act 2010[64] amends section 29 of the Road Traffic Act 1961,[65] so that a licence can be restored by the court only after two-thirds of the period of disqualification, or a period of two years, whichever is greater,[66] has expired. This will mean that whatever disqualification period is

---

[58] S.29(2), Road Traffic Act 1961, as substituted by s.7, Road Traffic Act 2006.
[59] S.29(4), Road Traffic Act 1961, as substituted by s.7, Road Traffic Act 2006.
[60] S.29(2), Road Traffic Act 1961, as substituted by s.7, Road Traffic Act 2006.
[61] S.29(5), Road Traffic Act 1961, as substituted by s.7, Road Traffic Act 2006.
[62] S.29(3), Road Traffic Act 1961, as substituted by s.7, Road Traffic Act 2006.
[63] S.29(1), Road Traffic Act 1961, as substituted by s.7, Road Traffic Act 2006.
[64] When same s. comes into operation.
[65] As substituted by s.7, Road Traffic Act 2006.
[66] S.29(4)(b), Road Traffic Act 1961 as substituted by s.66(1), Road Traffic Act 2010.

imposed by the court, an individual will not be able to have their driving licence restored until at least two years of the period of disqualification has expired, AND until two-thirds of the period of disqualification has expired, if disqualification imposed is greater than two years.

DISQUALIFICATION BY REASON OF PENALTY POINTS – SECTION 3 OF THE ROAD TRAFFIC ACT 2002

Section 3 of the Road Traffic Act 2002 sets out the administrative procedure whereby an individual who has 12 penalty points endorsed on their licence within a three-year period can be disqualified from driving for a period of 6 months.[67] Section 3 must be read in conjunction with sections 1–8 of the Road Traffic Act 2002 (as amended).[68] The appropriate date[69] for the commencement of this administrative disqualification is 28 days after the date of the notice to the individual of their disqualification under section 5 of Road Traffic Act 2002.[70]

MUTUAL RECOGNITION OF DRIVING DISQUALIFICATIONS IN IRELAND AND UK – DISQUALIFICATION PURSUANT TO THE EUROPEAN CONVENTION ON DRIVING DISQUALIFICATIONS – SECTION 9 OF THE ROAD TRAFFIC ACT 2002

Practitioners should note that as of the 28 January 2010, section 9 of the Road Traffic Act 2002[71] in relation to disqualifications pursuant to the European Convention on driving disqualifications came into effect.[72] There is now a mutual agreement[73] between Ireland and the UK,[74] allowing for driving disqualifications imposed

---

[67] S.3(2), Road Traffic Act 2002.
[68] See also ss.1–8, Road Traffic Act 2002 (as amended) and Chapter on Penalty Point Offences.
[69] See s.7, Road Traffic Act 2002 (as amended) by s.17, Road Traffic Act 2004.
[70] See Chapter 12 on Penalty Point Offences.
[71] S.9, Road Traffic Act 2002 will be amended by s.67, Road Traffic Act 2010 – when same s. comes into operation.
[72] See s.9, Road Traffic Act 2002; Sch.2 to the Road Traffic Act 2002; Convention 98/C 216/01 drawn up on the basis of Art.K.3 of the Treaty on European Union on Driving Disqualifications and S.I. No.11/2010 – Road Traffic Act 2002 (S.9) (Commencement) Order 2010.
[73] This mutual agreement came into force 90 days after a formal declaration to EU council in October 2009 pursuant to the 1998 EU Convention of Driving Disqualifications 98/C 216/01
[74] See also S.I. No.3010/2008 (UK) – The Mutual Recognition of Driving Disqualifications (Great Britain and Ireland) Regulations 2008.

in Ireland, Northern Ireland and Great Britain to be recognised and enforced throughout the United Kingdom, Northern Ireland and Ireland.

APPEALS TO THE CIRCUIT COURT

Section 18 of the Courts of Justice Act 1928 confers a general right of appeal to anyone convicted of an offence in the District Court. This will obviously also apply to individuals convicted of offences under the road traffic legislation. Practitioners should have regard to Order 101, District Court Rules 1997[75] and Order 41, Rules of the Circuit Court[76] in respect of how to make same appeal.[77]

An appeal can be made in relation to the conviction itself, or the severity of sentence.[78] Where the matter is listed for a full appeal, as opposed to an appeal only against the severity of the sentence, the appellant is entitled to a *de novo* hearing and either party can introduce new evidence. Even when an individual has pleaded guilty to matters in the District Court, it is open to them to plead not guilty at the hearing of his/her appeal, and it is also open to them to challenge the validity of the original summons.

SERVICE OF NOTICE OF APPEAL

An appeal is made by way of a Notice of Appeal and should be served on the other parties to the proceedings – (in these cases, the prosecutor and relevant District Court Clerk) within 14 days of the making of the decision appealed.[79]

The Notice of Appeal, along with a statutory declaration of service, should also be lodged with the appropriate Circuit Court Office, with this 14-day period.[80]

It is possible (on 48 hours' notice to the above parties) to seek an extension for the service and lodgment of a Notice of Appeal.[81]

---

[75] S.I. No.93/1997 – District Court Rules 1997 as amended by S.I. No.41/2008: District Court (Criminal Justice Act 2007) Rules 2008.
[76] S.I. No.510/2001 Circuit Court Rules 2001.
[77] For a comprehensive outline of Criminal Procedure of the Appeal Process see Chapter 22 of Criminal Procedure by Dermot Walsh.
[78] S.18(1), Courts of Justice Act 1928 as amended by s.16, Criminal Justice Act 1951.
[79] O.101, r.1 – S.I. No.93/1997, District Court Rules, 1997.
[80] *Ibid.*, O.101, r.2.
[81] *Ibid.*, O.101, r.3.

RECOGNISANCE

In cases where an individual has been convicted of a Road Traffic Act (RTA) offence, the recognisance should be fixed by the Judge. Where the recognisance is set, same should also be entered into within a 14-day limit.[82] Where the recognisance has not been set, an *ex parte* application can be made within 14 days of the decision to a District Judge to sets the terms of the recognisance.[83] A District Judge is not entitled to refuse to set the terms of a recognisance when requested to do so within 14 days. If the application is not made within 14 days for a recognisance to be fixed – the same application must be made on notice.[84]

Once the recognisance is entered into, and an appeal lodged, it places a stay on the execution of the District Court order.[85] Recognisance terms can differ from appellant to appellant, be they:

(a) a defendant's own bond (no cash lodgment); or

(b) own bond (cash lodgment or partial cash lodgment); or

(c) own bond and Independent Surety (Sureties) – where an Independent Surety is required – same must be approved by the court; or

(d) own bond and either an Independent Surety, or cash lodgment in lieu of an surety; or

(e) any of the above with additional conditions such as curfew or residence requirement;

Again, it is possible (on 48 hours' notice to above-mentioned parties) to seek an extension for the service and lodgment of a Notice of Appeal and/or for entry into a recognisance, however, practitioners should note that same extension of time will not put a stay on a disqualification order imposed by the District Court.

STAY ON PENALTIES IMPOSED BY THE DISTRICT COURT

If the appeal is lodged within a 14-day period, then there is a stay placed upon any penalties imposed by the District Court including

---

[82] *Ibid.*, O.101, r.6.
[83] *Ibid.*, O.101, r.4 (as amended by S.I. No.41/2008: District Court (Criminal Justice Act 2007) Rules 2008.
[84] *Ibid.*, O.101, r.3.
[85] *Ibid.*, O.101, r.6.

fines, disqualifications and any custodial sentence, provided that the appellant has complied with the terms of the recognisance.[86] If a court extends the time for entry of a recognisance, then this will also place a stay upon any custodial sentence or fines imposed by the court – however, it will not place a stay upon any period of disqualification imposed.[87]

SET-ASIDE APPLICATION

If an individual wishes to have a stay placed upon any period of disqualification pending an appeal, then this appeal must be lodged within 14 days of the imposition of District Court order.[88] This can present particular difficulties where an individual is convicted in his/her absence as they may not receive notification of the penalty imposed until after the 14-day period has expired. Where an individual has been convicted in his/her absence, a key question will be whether they received the summons or the notification of hearing date. If they did not, then an application can be made to the court to have the District Court decision set aside and remitted back to the original court for another hearing date. If an order is set aside, then any penalties imposed, including any period of disqualification, are set aside and cannot be enforced.

The procedure for setting aside an order of the District Court is set out in section 22 of the Courts Act 1991.[89] It is of particular relevance to convictions under the Road Traffic Acts for two reasons.

Firstly, these matters are primarily prosecuted under the summons procedure, and therefore an individual who does not receive his/her summons is generally unaware of his/her court date, and as most RTA offences are very minor in nature, same defendant can often be convicted in his/her absence.

Secondly, any disqualification period imposed, if not appealed within 14 days, cannot be postponed pending an appeal. If an individual is convicted in his/her absence, they are generally not notified of his/her conviction in time to lodge an appeal within 14 days: therefore it may be preferable for them, where possible, to make a set-aside application instead of an appeal.

---

[86] *Ibid.*, O.101, r.6.
[87] S.30(4), Road Traffic Act 1961 and *Waldron v. DPP* [2004] IEHC 227.
[88] See *Waldron v. DPP* [2004] IEHC 227.
[89] See also S.I. No.116/1992 – District Court (Service of Summonses) Rules 1992.

According to section 22(6) of the Courts Act 1991, where:

(a) the District Court has proceeded to convict an individual in his/her absence; and

(b) the person did not receive notice of the summons; or

(c) of the hearing date to which the summons relates.

That person can, within 21 days of becoming aware of the conviction or such other period as the District Court may allow, apply upon notice, and in accordance with prescribed rules, to have the proceedings set aside.

Complications can arise in cases where an individual receives the original summons, but matters are then adjourned (perhaps a number of times) before being heard and the defendant is not notified of the subsequent hearing date and is convicted in his/her absence. While there is generally a responsibility on an individual to attend court on each date they are summoned to appear, there are circumstances where this does not always happen. For example, where a prosecuting Garda is unable to proceed on first date, an application can be made (on notice to, but in absence of the defendant) to adjourn matters back, with the Garda undertaking to notify the defendant of adjourned date. In other circumstances, a defendant may appear in court on first date, but may be excused from attending court on a subsequent mentioned date. In these circumstances, whilst the defendant has received summons, they may not actually receive notification of the hearing date to which the summons relates.

The view adopted by some District Court Offices is that once an individual has received a summons to attend court, they will have been notified to attend court and cannot therefore make an application to have his/her conviction set aside. The set-aside application is only available to an individual who never received his/her court summons, and in all other circumstances, the appropriate application is to appeal the decision of the District Court instead. However, it is clear that not all cases are dealt with on the first date in court. Article 4 of the District Court (Service of Summonses) Rules 1992[90] states that:

'Where…the Court adjourns pursuant to section 22 (4) of the 1991 Act the hearing of a complaint or an accusation to which a particular summons relates and requires the person to whom the summons was

---

[90] S.I. No.116/1992, District Court (Service of Summonses) Rules 1992.

directed to be notified of the adjourned hearing, the Clerk shall, unless the Court otherwise directs, issue and serve upon the person a notice in the Form 1 in the schedule hereto.'

Practitioners should note that, notwithstanding the views expressed by some District Court Officers as to the limitations of set-aside applications, District Judges have set aside orders in circumstances where an individual had received the original summons but did not receive any notification of the adjourned hearing date. Furthermore, set-aside applications are made on notice to the prosecutor and it is therefore open to them to dispute any argument advanced by the applicant that did not receive notification of the adjourned hearing date.

The issue of how section 22 of the Courts Act 1991 should be interpreted, particularly when read in light in conjunction with District Court (Service of Summonses) Rules 1992, is in this author's view a matter which is solely for the court to decide. In the circumstances, any applicant who states that they did not receive notification of his/her hearing date should be allowed to make an application to a District Court Judge to have the decision set aside. The District Court Judge can then decide whether to allow or refuse the application upon full consideration of the particular facts of the case and submissions of the parties to the proceedings. This is, however, a matter which might yet form the subject of a case stated to the High Court.

APPEAL FROM THE DISTRICT COURT TO THE HIGH COURT BY WAY OF A CASE STATED

It is not proposed to discuss this application in any detail except to say that in any case before the District Court, the opinion of the High Court on a question of law, or whether a particular opinion is correct in law may be obtained by way of case stated. This can be done either by way of a 'case stated after decision', or a 'consultative case stated'. Where a case is stated following an application by a defendant (case stated after decision), the defendant should be advised that he/she will lose his/her right to appeal the decision: it is an alternative application to an appeal and the defendant cannot pursue both applications. A Judge can refuse to state a case if they feel same is frivolous by signing a certificate of refusal, except where application made by the AG, DPP, a Minister or the Revenue Commissioners.[91]

---

[91] For a comprehensive outline of criminal procedure in respect of case stated process see Chapter 22 of *Criminal Procedure* by Dermot Walsh.

APPEAL FROM THE CIRCUIT COURT TO THE
SUPREME COURT BY WAY OF A CASE STATED

Again, it is not proposed to discuss this application in any detail except to say that in any case before the Circuit Court, a Circuit Judge may, on an application by a party to the proceedings or of his/her own volition, and if they feel a question of law of sufficient importance has arisen, refer same to the Supreme Court by way of a case stated and may adjourn a decision pending the determination of same case stated.[92]

JUDICIAL REVIEW

It is open to an individual convicted before the District Court to make an application to the High Court to have a District Court decision judicially reviewed by way of an application made under Order 84 of the Rules of the Superior Court.[93] Generally, a judicial review is concerned not with the decision itself, but the manner in which decision was reached and the procedures followed. The grounds upon which a decision may be challenged, the procedure involved and the remedies available are set out in detail in many textbooks[94] and in a number of seminal cases[95] and it is not proposed to examine same here except to say that an application can be made for leave to judicially review any District Court decision[96] and leave will be granted by a High Court Judge if the court is satisfied that there is a stateable case.

---

[92] *Ibid.*
[93] S.I. No.15/1986 – Rules of the Superior Courts 1986.
[94] For example see *Judicial Review* - Mark De Blacam.
[95] *State (Keegan) v. Stardust Victims Compensation Tribunal* [1986] I.R. 642; *O'Keeffe v. An Bord Pleanala & Others* [1993] 1 I.R. 39.
[96] O.84, r.20 – S.I. No.15 (2nd edn, Bloomsbury Professional) 1986.

CHAPTER 3

Speeding Offences

This chapter covers the area relating to speeding offences. Speeding offences constitute some of the most common road traffic infringements to occur on our roads. There are a number of different speed limits operating on our national roads and an infringement of any valid speed limit will constitute an offence.

This chapter will deal with:

(a) the offence of speeding;

(b) the speed limits which apply under the Road Traffic Act 2004;

(c) the evidence required to be adduced in respect of prosecuting speeding offences;

(d) the exemptions which apply to the drivers of emergency vehicles;

(e) the offence of tailgating and the requirement that a vehicle be driven at a safe breaking speed;

(f) offences in respect of speed detectors.

SPEEDING –
SECTION 47 OF THE ROAD TRAFFIC ACT 1961

Section 47 of the Road Traffic Act 1961[1] sets out the offence of driving a vehicle at a speed in excess of the speed limit which:

(a) applies in respect of that vehicle, or

(b) applies to the road on which that vehicle is being driven, if that speed limit is lower than speed limit applying to vehicle;[2]

---

[1] As substituted by s.11, Road Traffic Act 2004.
[2] S.47(1), Road Traffic Act 1961, as substituted by s.11, Road Traffic Act 2004.

Speed limit means a speed limit which is:

(a) an ordinary speed limit;

(b) the built-up area speed limit;

(c) the regional and local roads speed limit;

(d) the national roads speed limit;

(e) the motorway speed limit;

(f) a special speed limit; or

(g) a road works speed limit.[3]

Penalties

In respect of offences under section 47(2), the penalties are as follows:

Fixed Charge Penalty: €80 (paid in 28 days),[4] €120 (paid in subsequent 28 days).[5]

Upon Conviction: General penalty under section 102, Road Traffic Act 1961[6] applies.

First Offence: Fine of up to €1,000.[7]

Second Offence: (under same section) – Fine of up to €2,000.[8]

Third/Subsequent Offence: (under same section within 12 consecutive months) – Fine of up to €2,000 and/or a term of imprisonment of up to three months.[9]

Penalty Points: Two (payment of fixed charge); four (upon conviction).[10] Under section 2(8) of the Road Traffic Act 2002 where

---

[3] See s.47(3), Road Traffic Act 1961, as substituted by s.11, Road Traffic Act 2004.
[4] See s.103(7)(b), Road Traffic Act 1961 as inserted by s.14(c), Road Traffic Act 2006 and see art.5(a)(ii) and Sch.1 Pt.1 of S.I. No.135/2006 – Road Traffic Acts 1961 to 2005 (Fixed Charge Offences) Regulations 2006.
[5] See s.103(7)(c), Road Traffic Act 1961 and art.5(a)(ii) and Sch.1 Pt.1 of S.I. No.135/2006 – Road Traffic Acts 1961 to 2005 (Fixed Charge Offences) Regulations 2006.
[6] See s.18(1), Road Traffic Act 2006.
[7] S.102(a), Road Traffic Act 1961, as amended by s.18(1) – Table – Pt.1 – Reference 20.
[8] S.102(b), Road Traffic Act 1961, as amended by s.18(1) – Table – Pt.1 – Reference 21.
[9] S.102(c), Road Traffic Act 1961, as amended by s.18(1) – Table – Pt.1 – Reference 22.
[10] See Reference 7 of Pt.1 of the First Schedule of Road Traffic Act 2002 and also S.I. No.491/2002 — Road Traffic Act 2002 (Commencement) Order 2002 – which came into effect on 31 October 2002.

an individual receives an ancillary disqualification (section 27, Road Traffic Act 1961), no penalty points will be imposed.

Disqualification:

Ancillary Disqualification: Whilst a conviction under section 47 does not carry a mandatory disqualification, it is open to the court to make an ancillary disqualification order (section 27, Road Traffic Act 1961) on the particular facts of the case.

Penalty Point Disqualification: If a defendant accrues 12 penalty points upon conviction for this offence, then they will be disqualified under the administrative procedure set out under section 3 of the Road Traffic Act 2002.

Given the amendments made to section 47 of the Road Traffic Act 1961 by the substituted section 11 of the Road Traffic Act 2004, it is important for practitioners seeking to defend someone to be aware of, and understand, the different speed limits which apply on Irish roads. The speed limits referred to in the substituted section 47 are set out in Part 2 of the Road Traffic Act 2004. Practitioners should be familiar with these provisions and the statutory basis on which a particular speed limit has been imposed as well as the proofs required to prosecute speeding offences.

Practitioners should note that section 76 of the Road Traffic Act 2010[11] adds and additional subsection 2A to section 47 which states:

"In any prosecution for an offence under this section, it is presumed, until the contrary is shown by the defendant, that the speed limit indicated on a traffic sign is the speed limit that has been applied under this Act to the road when the offence is alleged to have been committed."

This shifts the burden of proof to the defence by making it a rebuttable presumption that whatever speed limit was signposted at a particular location was the applicable speed limit."

ORDINARY SPEED LIMIT – SECTION 4 OF THE ROAD TRAFFIC ACT 2004

This section allows the Minister to prescribe by way of regulation:[12]

(a) an "ordinary speed limit" in respect of all public roads (with exceptions for any class of vehicle specified under regulations);[13]

---

[11] When same section comes into operation.
[12] See s.3, Road Traffic Act 2004.
[13] *Ibid.*, s.4(2).

(b) different speed limits (by regulations made under this section) for any class of vehicle and different categories of road;[14]

(c) that certain class(es) of vehicles may be exempt from speed limit set (if and as specified by regulations).[15]

Practitioners should also be cognisant of the provisions of the Road Traffic (Ordinary Speed Limits Buses, Heavy Goods Vehicles, Etc) Regulations 2008,[16] which set out that an ordinary speed limit of 80km per hour applies to:

(a) a non passenger carrier vehicle with a weight in excess of 3,500 kilos;[17]

(b) a combination of a vehicle drawing another vehicle.[18]

It also provides that where a double-decker or single-decker passenger carrier vehicle (accommodating more than 8 persons) – neither designed nor adapted for the carriage of standing passengers, the ordinary speed limit that applies:

(a) when driven on motorway is 100km per hour;[19]

(b) any other public road is 80km per hour.[20]

Where a double-decker or single-decker passenger carrier vehicle (accommodating more than 8 persons) – is designed and adapted for the carriage of standing passengers, the ordinary speed limit that applies on any public road is 65km per hour.[21]

BUILT-UP AREAS' SPEED LIMIT – SECTION 5 OF THE ROAD TRAFFIC ACT 2004

This section provides that in any built-up area (as specified under the Local Government Act 2001) a 'built-up speed limit' of 50 km per hour will apply.[22] Exceptions to this speed limit are motorways, or any road covered by a 'special speed limit' or a 'roadworks' speed limit'.[23]

---

[14] *Ibid.*, s.4(2).
[15] *Ibid.*, s.4(2).
[16] S.I. No.546/2008, Road Traffic (Ordinary Speed Limits Buses, Heavy Goods Vehicles, Etc) Regulations 2008 – which came into operation on 1 February 2009.
[17] Art.4(a), S.I. No.546/2008.
[18] *Ibid.*, art.4(b).
[19] *Ibid.*, art.3(a)(i).
[20] *Ibid.*, art.3(a)(ii).
[21] *Ibid.*, art.3(b)
[22] S.5(1), Road Traffic Act 2004.
[23] *Ibid.*, s.5(2).

Practitioners should note that as a result of recent High Court judicial review proceedings, which were settled by the State before hearing, District Judges are now striking out summonses relating to speeding offences under section 5 of the Road Traffic Act 2004 where the alleged offence took place on a road in 'townlands' outside a city, town or borough. This is because same locations cannot be considered a 'built-up area' within the meaning of the Local Government Act 2001, and therefore a 'built-up speed limit' under section 5 of the Road Traffic Act 2004 cannot apply at same location. It is not clear, at the time of writing, if the legislature will seek to amend section 5 of the Road Traffic Act 2004.

Non-Urban, Regional and Local Roads' Speed Limit – Section 6 of the Road Traffic Act 2004

This section provides that a 'Regional and Local Roads' speed limit' of 80km per hour will apply to all regional and local roads.[24] Exceptions to this speed limit are any roads in 'built-up areas', or any roads covered by a 'special speed limit' or a 'roadworks' speed limit'.[25]

National Speed Limit – Section 7 of the Road Traffic Act 2004

This section provides that a 'National Roads Speed Limit' of 100km per hour will apply to all national roads.[26] The exceptions to these speed limits are any roads covered by a 'special speed limit' or a 'roadworks' speed limit.'[27]

Motorway Speed Limit – Section 8 of the Road Traffic Act 2004

This section provides that a 'Motorway Speed Limit' of 120km per hour will apply to all motorways.[28] Exceptions to this speed limit are any motorway covered by a 'special speed limit' or a 'roadworks' speed limit'.[29]

---

[24] *Ibid.*, s.6(1).
[25] *Ibid.*, s.6(2).
[26] *Ibid.*, s.7(1).
[27] *Ibid.*, s.7(2).
[28] *Ibid.*, s.8(1).
[29] *Ibid.*, s.8(2).

SPECIAL SPEED LIMIT – SECTION 9 OF THE ROAD TRAFFIC ACT 2004

This section provides that a County Council or City Council may by means of a bye-law[30] specify a 'special speed limit' of:

30km[31] (built-up areas and in accordance with guidelines issued by Minister);[32]

50km (except in built-up areas);[33]

60km (except in built-up areas);[34]

80km (motorway/national Road/roads in built-up areas);[35]

100km (motorway/national Road/roads in built-up areas);[36] and

120km (motorway/national Road/roads in built-up areas).[37]

The bye-law must comply with all the provisions set out in the sub-sections (3)–(12), including all notice and publishing requirements,[38] the requirement of obtaining the advanced written consent of the National Roads Authority (NRA)[39] and the Ministerial guidelines for application of special speed limits,[40] (in this case the Ministerial Guidelines published 19th April 2005[41]). Practitioners seeking to defend such charges should familiarise themselves with these requirements. In the case of any prosecution of an individual for an alleged offence of speeding in a special speed limit area, the prosecution should be in a position to produce a certified copy of the bye-law, although there is a rebuttable presumption that a certified copy of same is evidence that bye-law was in force until contrary is shown.[42] A special speed limit of 30km per hour was passed by Dublin City Council[43] in respect of a limited area within Dublin City

---

[30] *Ibid.*, s.9(2).
[31] *Ibid.*, s.9(2)(a) .
[32] *Ibid.*, s.9(2)(a), Road Traffic Act 2004 is amended slightly by s.85, Road Traffic Act 2010 (when the section comes into operation) deleting the phrase 'other than a motorway'.
[33] *Ibid.*, s.9(2)(b).
[34] *Ibid.*, s.9(2)(c).
[35] *Ibid.*, s.9(2)(d).
[36] *Ibid.*, s.9(2)(e).
[37] *Ibid.*, s.9(2)(f).
[38] *Ibid.*, ss.9(3) and 9(4).
[39] *Ibid.*, s.9(7).
[40] *Ibid.*, s.9(2)(f).
[41] See http://www.transport.ie.
[42] S.9(12), Road Traffic Act 2004.
[43] The Dublin City Special Speed Bye Law 2010 was passed by Dublin City Council on 5 October 2009 and came into force on 31 January 2010.

Centre. However, to date no prosecutions have been brought fo the offence exceeding this 30km per hour special speed limit!

ROAD WORKS' SPEED LIMIT –
SECTION 10 OF THE ROAD TRAFFIC ACT 2004

This section provides that the manager of a County Council or City Council may by means of a 'road works' special limit order' specify a road works' speed limit of not less than 30km.[44] The same order stays in place for the duration of the road works, although no such order can be in effect for more than 12 months.[45] A road works order must comply with all the provisions set out in subsections (2)–(8), including all notice and publishing requirements,[46] and the requirement of obtaining the advanced written consent of the NRA.[47] Practitioners seeking to defend such charges should familiarise themselves with these requirements. In the case of a prosecution of an individual for an alleged offence of speeding in a special speed limit area, the prosecution should be in a position to produce a certified copy of the road works order.[48]

Practitioners should also be cognisant of the Road Traffic (Speed limit – Traffic Signs) Regulations 2005,[49] the Road Traffic (Traffic Signs – Periodic Special Speed Limits) Regulations 2005[50] and the Road Traffic (Signs) Regulations 2006[51] which set out the regulations for the signposting of speed limits. A client will often instruct that the road location was not signposted correctly and where raised, the prosecution should be able to demonstrate that the speed limit was properly signposted, in accordance with relevant regulations and bye-laws, at the location where the alleged offence occurred. There is no legal requirement to signpost the ordinary speed limit, however, if a short stretch of road has a number of speed limits in operation, an argument could be advanced that the ordinary speed limit should also have been signposted for the purpose of clarity.

---

[44] S.10)(1), Road Traffic Act 2004.
[45] *Ibid.*, s.10(2) .
[46] *Ibid.*, ss.10(4) and 10(6).
[47] *Ibid.*, s.10(3)
[48] *Ibid.*, s.10(8).
[49] S.I. No.10/2005.
[50] S.I. No.756/2005.
[51] S.I. No.637/2006.

In order to prosecute an individual for a speeding offence, certain proofs are required. These proofs may differ depending on the statutory provision under which the speed limit is imposed. However, in all cases the summons should indicate that the alleged offence took place on a public road (including a motorway), should give a specific location on same public road where the offence is alleged to have taken place, and should set out the speed limit that applied on that section of road and the type of speed limit in place. Evidence must be adduced in relation to the speed the vehicle was travelling at. This can be done by means of oral opinion evidence as to the speed (which is not very common given difficulties that can arise in corroborating same evidence), or by reliance on electronic or other equipment to measure the speed. Evidence required is set out in section 21 of the Road Traffic Act 2002.

Evidence in Respect of Speed – Section 21 of the Road Traffic Act 2002

The provisions of section 21 of the Road Traffic Act 2002[52] can be summarised as follows: prima facie proof of speed[53] may be established by tendering evidence obtained by means of:

(a) electronic or other apparatus (including a camera) capable of providing a permanent record;[54] or

(b) electronic or other apparatus (including a radar gun) not capable of producing a permanent record.[55]

There is no requirement to prove that the electronic or other apparatus was accurate or in good working order.[56]

---

[52] This replaced s.105, Road Traffic Act 1961 and was subsequently amended by s.15, Road Traffic 2004 and s.17, Road Traffic Act 2006. It is repealed and replaced by s.81, Road Traffic Act 2010 – when same section comes into operation.
[53] In fact s.21(1) (as amended) refers to prima facie evidence in respect of a constituent element of an offence (including speed and whether the accused was driving) and relates not just to an offence under this section (s.47) but also to offences contrary to ss.52, 53, 55, 91, 92, 93 and 94, Road Traffic Act 1961: offences brought in by way of regulation under s.35, Road Traffic Act 1994 and offences under s.138, Railway Safety Act 2005.
[54] S.21(1)(a), Road Traffic Act 2002.
[55] *Ibid.*, s.21(1)(b).
[56] *Ibid.*, s.21(1).

In proceedings for an offence under section 21(1):

(a) a document purporting to be a record, or copy of a record (other than a visual record) signed by a member of the Gardaí (or a person authorised under subsection (7)) and duly endorsed, shall be prima facie evidence of the indications and measurements therein contained without necessity to prove signature;[57]

(b) a copy of aforesaid document shall be furnished to the defendant person before commencement of trial of the offence.[58]

The electronic or other apparatus must:

(a) be capable or producing a record of measurements (or other indications) set out in subsection (1);[59]

(b) be of a type approved by,

(i) The Commissioner or a member of Gardaí not below rank of Chief Superintendent authorised on behalf of Commissioner,

(ii) the Chief Executive of National Roads Authority (NRA), or another officer of NRA duly authorised by Chief Executive of his/her behalf.

There is no requirement to prove the apparatus is of a type so approved.[60]

The uncorroborated evidence of one witness stating his/her opinion as to speed shall not be accepted as proof of that speed.[61]

It is presumed, until contrary is shown that:

(a) the apparatus used was provided and maintained by a member of Gardaí;

(b) the development, production and viewing of records produced was carried out by a member of Gardaí.[62]

'Radar Gun' means an apparatus which:

(a) can be used to measure the speed of vehicle by directing a signal at the vehicle and receiving a reflected signal from vehicle; and

---

[57] *Ibid.*, s.21(2)(a).
[58] *Ibid.*, s.21(2)(b).
[59] *Ibid.*, s.21(3)(a).
[60] *Ibid.*, s.21(3)(b).
[61] *Ibid.*, s.21(4).
[62] S.21(5), Road Traffic Act 2002.

(b) is capable of measuring and displaying the speed of vehicle on the apparatus 'Record' includes visual record which can be permanently stored on apparatus.[63]

The Minister for Justice may, by an agreement in writing, in adherence to terms and conditions of agreement and conditions set out in subsection (7)(a), provide for the authorisation of a person, (other than a Garda) to perform a function in respect of establishing prima facie proof of a speeding offence, including provision, maintenance and operation of an apparatus or the development, production and viewing of produced records.[64]

It is presumed, until the contrary is shown, that the electronic (or other) apparatus used for the tendering of evidence was provided and maintained by Garda (or authorised person),[65] and that the developed, production and viewing or records produced by such apparatus was carried out by Garda (or other authorised person).[66]

Where opinion evidence is given as to speed, evidence from at least two witnesses should generally be adduced, unless the evidence of one witness can be otherwise corroborated.[67] Both witnesses must give evidence of the defendant speeding at the same moment in time and on the exact same stretch of road. A careful note should be taken of any opinion evidence given in respect of a speeding offence because if the evidence of the second witness does not corroborate the evidence of the first witness, sufficient doubt may be raised to render evidence adduced insufficient to prove offence alleged. However, practitioners should note that the evidence of one witness may be sufficient, if it can be corroborated by some other means.

In reality, it is hard to see how opinion evidence, uncorroborated by some independent recording or documentary evidence establishing a defendant's speed could be considered sufficient to safely convict someone, unless the applicable speed limit was quite low and the opinion evidence given by more than one eye witness indicates a speed greatly in excess of the applicable speed limit.

Where admissible documentary evidence is produced in court indicating that an individual was travelling at a particular speed, that

---

[63] *Ibid.*, s.21(6).
[64] *Ibid.*, s.21(7).
[65] *Ibid.*, s.21(8)(a).
[66] *Ibid.*, s.21(8)(b).
[67] *Ibid.*, s.21.

individual cannot defend him/herself merely by denying that he was travelling at that speed. However, the prosecution is required to prove all essential elements of the offence including location, speed, speed limit in operation and signposting of the speed limit. It is therefore very important that practitioners familiarise themselves with the provisions set out above in respect of speeding offences so at they require the prosecution to provide court with all necessary proofs.

Practitioners should also be aware that where someone has been convicted of an offence of dangerous driving[68] where speed was an element of the driving offence, they should not be separately prosecuted for an offence of speeding as a defence of *autrefois convict* should apply, provided that it could be established that the dangerous driving conviction arose out of same incident. However, where someone has driven for some distance at speed (for example a high speed chase), a court may accept that a number of separate offences have arisen at different locations.

EVIDENCE IN RESPECT OF SPEED AND CERTAIN OTHER OFFENCES – SECTION 81 OF THE ROAD TRAFFIC ACT 2010

Practitioners should note that section 81 of the Road Traffic Bill 2010[69] repeals and replaces section 21 of the Road Traffic Act 2002. The provisions contained in the new section 81 are however broadly similar to the provisions set out above.

EXEMPTIONS FOR EMERGENCY VEHICLES – SECTION 27 OF THE ROAD TRAFFIC ACT 2004[70]

There is a general exemption for the drivers of emergency vehicles from the provisions of the Road Traffic Acts where they apply to speeding offences,[71] and provide that same provisions do not apply:

(a) to a driver of a fire brigade vehicle; or

(b) to a driver of an ambulance; or

---

[68] S.53, Road Traffic Act 1951 (as amended).

[69] When this section comes into operation.

[70] This section is repealed and replaced by s.87, Road Traffic Act 2010, when that section comes into operation. The offences exempted from the provisions of s.87 are the comparable drink driving and dangerous driving offences under the Road Traffic Act 2010.

[71] The exemption applies to all offences under the Road Traffic Acts 1961–2006 except for offences under ss.49, 50, 51A, 52 and 53, Road Traffic Act 1961, ss.12, 13, 14, 15, Road Traffic Act 1994, and s.138, Railway Safety Act 2005.

(c) the use by a member of the Gardaí of a vehicle in the perform-ance of his/her duties; or

(d) a person driving or using a vehicle under the direction of a member of the Gardaí.

However, such exemptions will not apply in circumstances where the safety of a road user was endangered.

EXEMPTIONS FOR EMERGENCY VEHICLES –
SECTION 87 OF THE ROAD TRAFFIC ACT 2010

Practitioners should note that section 87 of the Road Traffic Act 2010[72] repeals and replaces section 27 of the Road Traffic Act 2004. The provisions contained in the new section 87 are, however, broadly similar to the provisions set out above, and are the same in terms of their applicability to speeding offences.

SPEEDING IN ANY PUBLIC PLACE – ARTICLE 7 –
ROAD TRAFFIC (TRAFFIC & PARKING) REGULATIONS 1997[73]

Practitioners should note that whilst the above legislation applies to speed limits on a public road, there is also a general obligation regarding speeding in any public place set out in article 7 of the Road Traffic (Traffic & Parking) Regulations 1997.[74] Article 7 sets out the offence of driving a vehicle in a public place at a speed exceeding that which will enable its driver to bring it to a halt within the dis-tance which the driver can see to be clear of traffic, an offence more commonly known as tailgating.

This general speed restriction applies to driving any vehicle in a public place. A vehicle must be driven at a safe breaking distance behind any vehicle in front. Article 7 applies irrespective of what-ever maximum speed limit may apply.

Penalties

In respect of offence under article 7, the penalties are as follows:

Fixed Charge Penalty: €80 (paid in 28 days):[75] €120 (paid in subse-quent 28 days).[76]

---

[72] When the section comes into operation.
[73] S.I. No.182/1997 – Road Traffic (Traffic and Parking) Regulations 1997.
[74] Regulations made under s.35, Road Traffic Act 1994.
[75] Art.5(a)(ii) and Sch.1, 1 Pt.2 of S.I. No.135/2006.
[76] See s.103(7)(c), Road Traffic Act 1961 and art.5(a)(ii) and Sch.1, Pt.2 of S.I. No.135/2006.

Upon Conviction: General penalty under section 102 Road Traffic Act 1961.[77]

Penalty Points: Two (payment of fixed charge): Four (upon conviction).[78]

Section 2(8) of the Road Traffic Act 2002 applies if the court imposes an ancillary disqualification order under section 27 of the Road Traffic Act 1961 – in those circumstances, penalty points will not be endorsed on the licence record.

Disqualification:

Ancillary Disqualification: a conviction under article 7 does not carry a mandatory disqualification. However, it is open to the court to make an ancillary disqualification order under section 27 of the Road Traffic Act 1961 on the particular facts of the case.

Penalty Point Disqualification: if a defendant accrues 12 penalty points upon conviction for this offence, then they will be disqualified under the administrative procedure set out under section 3 of the Road Traffic Act 2002.

Speed Detectors – Section 9 of the Road Traffic Act 1968

It is illegal for any person to use or import, supply or fit any device which can indicate or frustrate the operation of an electronic or other apparatus being used to detect a vehicle's speed.

The Minister has the power to make regulations in relation to the importation, supply and fitting of vehicle parts.[79] A 'vehicle part' is defined as including any article made or adapted for use as part of the equipment of any device capable of indicating the existence of, or frustrating the operation of, electronic or other apparatus being used to detect a vehicle's speed.[80] The relevant regulations referred to in section 9(1) are the Road Traffic (Speed Meter Detectors) Regulations 1991.[81]

---

[77] First conviction: fine up to €1,000; second conviction: fine up to €2,000; third conviction: fine up to €1,000 and/or imprisonment for up to 3 months – see also s.18, Road Traffic Act 2006.

[78] See Reference 1 of Pt.4 of Sch.1, Road Traffic Act 2002 and also S.I. No.134/2006, Road Traffic Act 2002 (Commencement of Certain Provisions) Order 2006 – which came into effect on 3 April 2006.

[79] S.9(1), Road Traffic Act 1968.

[80] *Ibid.*, s.9(5).

[81] S.I. No.50/1991, Road Traffic (Speed Meter Detectors) Regulations 1991.

It is an offence for an individual to use in a public place of a vehicle fitted with a speed meter detector,[82] or it is an offence for an individual to import, supply, offer to supply, fit or offer to fit any such speed meter detector.[83]

Penalties

Articles 4 and 5 of the 1991 Regulations carried the general penalty provided for under section 102 of the Road Traffic Act 1961.[84]

First Offence – fine of up to €1,000.[85]

Second Offence (under same section) – fine of up to €2,000.[86]

Third/Subsequent Offence (under same section within 12 consecutive months) – fine of up to €2,000 and/or a term of imprisonment of up to three months.[87]

Disqualification:

Ancillary Disqualification: a conviction under articles 4 or 5 does not carry a mandatory disqualification: however, it is open to the court to make an ancillary disqualification order under section 27 of the Road Traffic Act 1961 on the particular facts of the case.

---

[82] Art.4, S.I. No.50/1991.

[83] *Ibid.*

[84] See s.18(1), Road Traffic Act 2006.

[85] S.102(a), Road Traffic Act 1961, as amended by s.18(1) – Table – Pt.1 – Reference 20.

[86] S.102(b), Road Traffic Act 1961, as amended by s.18(1) – Table – Pt.1 – Reference 21.

[87] S.102(c), Road Traffic Act 1961, as amended by s.18(1) – Table – Pt.1 – Reference 22.

CHAPTER 4

Driving Licences

This chapter covers the area of driving licences and in particular the obligation on all drivers of motor vehicles to have a valid driving licence.

Practitioners should note that in practical terms, whatever road traffic summonses are before the court, one of the court's primary concerns will be to know that the defendant had a valid driving licence and a valid policy of insurance. A defendant should always be advised to bring their original licence with them to court.

This chapter will deal with:

(a) the offence of driving without a valid driving licence;

(b) the offence of driving without a qualified driver whilst on a provisional licence/learning permit;

(c) the offence of applying for a driving licence whilst disqualified;

(d) the requirements to carry driving licence while driving;

(e) the requirements in respect of producing a driving licence to the Gardaí;

(f) the provisions allowing the Gardaí to seize driving licences;

(g) the requirement to produce a driving licence in court for inspection;

(h) provisions allowing the Gardaí to detain/remove or immobilise a vehicle;

(i) the obligation on individuals to give their current address to the Gardaí;

PROHIBITION ON DRIVING WITHOUT DRIVING LICENCE – SECTION 38 OF THE ROAD TRAFFIC ACT 1961

This section covers offences relating to driving a vehicle without a valid driving licence. Section 38 of the 1961 Act[1] sets out the following

---

[1] As amended by s.23, Road Traffic Act 2002 and s.12, Road Traffic Act 2006.

criminal offences:

'(1) Driving a vehicle in public place without a valid driving licence.[2]

(2) Driving a vehicle in a public place whilst disqualified.[3]

(3) Driving a vehicle in public place without having produced requisite valid certificate of competency or valid certificate of fitness to obtain licence.[4]

(4) Employing another individual to drive a vehicle you own in public place when said employee is without valid driving licence.[5]

(5) Employing another individual to drive a vehicle you own in public place when said employee has been disqualified from driving.[6]

(6) Employing another individual to drive a vehicle you own in public place without said employee having produced requisite valid certificate of competency or valid certificate of fitness to obtain licence.[7]'

Under section 38, any individual who wishes to drive a vehicle in a public place must have a valid driving licence.[8] Under section 38, there is a presumption, unless and until proved otherwise, that the individual charged did not have the requisite licence:[9] therefore any individual seeking to defend such a charge must be in a position to produce (to the Gardaí and the court), a valid driving licence covering the date of the alleged offence and covering the relevant category of motor vehicle.[10]

A valid Irish driving licence, provisional licence[11] (or learner permit) will generally be accepted once it covers the relevant date and category of motor vehicle. Furthermore, a valid driving licence from another EU Member State (or member of European Economic

---

[2] S.38(1), Road Traffic Act 1961.
[3] S.38(1), Road Traffic Act 1961
[4] *Ibid.*
[5] *Ibid.*, s.38(3).
[6] *Ibid.*, s.38(3)
[7] *Ibid.*, s.38(3).
[8] See also s.22(1), Road Traffic Act 1961 and also S.I. No.537/2006: Road Traffic (Licensing of Drivers) Regulations 2006.
[9] See s.38(2)(b) and s.38(4)(b), Road Traffic Act 1961.
[10] See also s.22(1), Road Traffic Act 1961 – S.I. No.537/2006, Road Traffic (Licensing of Drivers) Regulations 2006.
[11] See s.35, Road Traffic Act 1961 (as substituted by s.11, Road Traffic Act 2006).

Area EEA)[12] or a recognised foreign licence[13] will also be accepted.[14] However, in respect of either a provisional licence (or learner permit) if the individual was unaccompanied then they may face a charge of driving without a qualified driver.[15]

Practitioners should note that section 56 of the Road Traffic Act 2010[16] changes the definition of a driving licence under section 3 of the Road Traffic Act 1961 to read that a 'driving licence' means:

(a) an 'Irish driving licence;[17] or

(b) a 'foreign driving licence'

with a foreign driving licence meaning a licence or permit in respect of a category of vehicle referred to in the EC (Recognition of Driving Licences of other Member States) Regulations 2008, issued by a competent authority in another EU state or member of the EEA, but does not include a learning permit/provisional licence issued by another EU State and foreign licences recognised by an order made under section 23A of the Road Traffic Act 1961.[18]

Section 64 of the Road Traffic Act 2010[19] amends section 30 of the Road Traffic Act 1961 and section 3 of the Road Traffic Act 2006 to ensure that penalty points and disqualifications can be applied to the holders of non-national driver licences.

DRIVING WITHOUT A LICENSED DRIVER – SECTION 42 OF THE ROAD TRAFFIC ACT 1961[20]

From 30 October 2007, it became an offence for any learner driver, even a driver on a second provisional licence, to drive a vehicle in a

---

[12] S.I. No.464/2008: European Communities (Recognition of Driving Licences of Other Member States) Regulations 2008.

[13] S.I. No.527/2007: Road Traffic (Recognition of Foreign Driving Licences) Order 2007.

[14] See s.23A, Road Traffic Act 1961 (as inserted by s.8, Road Traffic Act 2006).

[15] See s.42, Road Traffic Act 1961 (as substituted by s.10, Road Traffic Act 2006 and amended by s.12(2), Roads Act 2007 – see also reg.2(b)(i) and S.I. No.719/200 7 – Road Traffic (Licensing of Learner Drivers) Regulations 2007; S.I. No.724/2007 – Road Traffic (Licensing of Learner Drivers) (No. 2) Regulations 2007.

[16] When same comes into operation.

[17] This includes provisional licence and learner permit – see s.22(1) and see s.23A, Road Traffic Act 1961 (as inserted by s.8, Road Traffic Act 2006).

[18] Namely – Australia, Gibraltar, Guernsey, Iceland, Isle of Man, Japan, Jersey, Liechtenstein, Norway, South Africa, South Korea and Switzerland See S.I. No.527/2007, Road Traffic (Recognition of Foreign Driving Licences) Order 2007.

[19] When same section comes into operation.

[20] As Substituted by s.10, Road Traffic Act 2006 – see also s.20(6)(b)(iv), Road Traffic

public place when not accompanied by a licensed/qualified driver.[21] A licensed/qualified driver is a driver who holds a full, valid driving licence for the class of vehicle being driven by the learner driver they are accompanying.

An offence contrary to section 42 carries a general penalty under section 102 of the Road Traffic Act 1961.[22]

First Offence – fine of up to €1,000.[23]

Second Offence (under same section) – fine of up to €2,000.[24]

Third/Subsequent Offence (under same section within 12 consecutive months) – fine of up to €2,000 and/or a term of imprisonment of up to three months.[25]

In respect of an offence contrary to section 38 of the Road Traffic Act 1961, a valid driving licence or permit from another EU State or EEA country should be accepted, provided that it covers the date and category of vehicle in question.[26] Similarly, a valid driving licence or permit, issued by a competent authority of a non EU/EEA State, should be accepted provided that the Minister has recognised the national licence in question.[27]

If an individual was disqualified from driving,[28] either generally, or in relation to the particular category/class of vehicle for which he/she was stopped on the date of the offence, any driving licence

---

(Licensing of Drivers) Regulations 1999–2008.

[21] See Regulation 2(b)(i) and (iii), S.I. No.719/2007 – Road Traffic (Licensing of Learner Drivers) Regulations 2007; S.I. No.724/2007 – Road Traffic (Licensing of Learner Drivers) (No.2) Regulations 2007.

[22] See s.18(1), Road Traffic Act 2006.

[23] S.102(a), Road Traffic Act 1961, as amended by s.18(1) – Table – Pt.1 – Reference 20.

[24] S.102(b), Road Traffic Act 1961, as amended by s.18(1) – Table – Pt.1 – Reference 21.

[25] S.102(c), Road Traffic Act 1961, as amended by s.18(1) – Table – Pt.1 – Reference 22.

[26] See S.I. No.537/2006, Road Traffic (Licensing of Drivers) Regulations 2006. See also S.I. No.464/2008, European Communities (Recognition of Driving Licences of Other Member States) Regulations 2008.

[27] See S.I. No.537/2006, Road Traffic (Licensing of Drivers) Regulations 2006. See also S.I. No.527/2007, Road Traffic (Recognition of Foreign Driving Licences) Order 2007.

[28] See ss.26, 27, and 28, Road Traffic Act 1961, s.3 and s.9, Road Traffic Act 2002; Sch.2 of the Road Traffic Act 2002; Convention 98/C 216/01 drawn up on the basis of art K.3 of the Treaty on European Union on Driving Disqualifications and S.I. No.11/2010 – Road Traffic Act 2002 (Section 9) (Commencement) Order 2010.

covering the date of the offence subsequently produced will be void. Similarly, if a driving licence was obtained on foot of a fraudulent, false or otherwise invalid certificate of competency or certificate of fitness, that licence will be void and of no effect.

It is obviously a defence for an individual to demonstrate that he/she was not driving the vehicle at the time of the alleged offence. In respect of employees, it is presumed that an employee stopped, driving his/her employer's vehicle, did not have the requisite licence.[29] Again, it is a good defence if the employee can produce a valid driving licence or permit (as set out above). It is also a defence if the employer can demonstrate that the employee was not using the vehicle in the course of his/her employment (unauthorised use) and/or was driving without consent of owner.

It may also be a defence if an employer can demonstrate that they had genuinely and reasonable believed that his/her employee had a valid driving licence, although this will depend on the circumstances of the case and the employer will have to demonstrate that they took reasonable steps to verify that his/her employee had a valid licence.

Section 38 does not apply to exempt categories of drivers – namely, Gardaí driving in the course of their duty,[30] persons undergoing a driving test,[31] or drivers of specified pedestrian-controlled vehicles.[32]

Penalties

In respect of offences under section 38, the penalties are as follows:

Drivers (who held a valid licence (other than learner permit) which expired less than 12 months before date of offence) – fine of up to €1,000.[33]

Drivers (who held a valid licence (other than learner permit) which expired more than 12 months before date of offence) – fine of up to €2,000.[34]

Disqualified Drivers/Drivers without licence/Drivers who failed to produce required certificate of competency/fitness to

---

[29] S.38(4), Road Traffic Act 1961.
[30] S.38(6), Road Traffic Act 1961.
[31] S.33(7), Road Traffic Act 1961 – they must however have a valid provisional licence/learner permit.
[32] S.38(7), Road Traffic Act 1961 and art.8, S.I. No.537/2006.
[33] S.38(2)(a)(i), Road Traffic Act 1961 as substituted by s.12(a), Road Traffic Act 2006.
[34] S.38(2)(a)(ii), Road Traffic Act 1961 as substituted by s.12(a), Road Traffic Act 2006.

obtain licence – fine of up to €5,000 and/or a term of imprisonment of up to 6 months.[35]

Disqualification:

Mandatory Disqualification: a conviction under section 38(5)(a) – driving a vehicle without a driving licence while disqualified carries a mandatory consequential disqualification period of one year.[36]

Ancillary Disqualification: in other circumstances, a conviction under section 38 does not carry a mandatory disqualification; however, it is open to the court to make an ancillary disqualification order under section 27, Road Traffic Act 1961 on the particular facts of the case.

PROHIBITION ON APPLYING FOR A DRIVING LICENCE WHILE DISQUALIFIED – SECTION 39 OF THE ROAD TRAFFIC ACT 1961

It is illegal for any individual to apply for a driving licence[38] in circumstances where they have been disqualified from driving. This includes applying for a licence for a category (or categories) of vehicle in respect of which they are disqualified. Generally, an individual who has been disqualified from driving is not permitted to drive any class of vehicle, but there are circumstances where the disqualification applies to only a particular category (or categories) of vehicle.

An individual may be disqualified from holding a licence (or particular class of licence) by virtue of a court order:

(a) Consequential [mandatory] Disqualification order;[39]

(b) Ancillary Disqualification order;[40]

(c) Special Disqualification order – [unfit/incompetent to drive].[41]

---

[35] S.38(5)(b)(ii), Road Traffic Act 1961 as substituted by s.12(b), Road Traffic Act 2006.

[36] See s.26, Road Traffic Act 1961 and Sch.2, 1961 Act, as substituted by s.26, Road Traffic Act 1995 and amended by s.6(2), Road Traffic Act 2006.

[37] As amended by s.23, Road Traffic Act 2002 and substituted by s.58, Road Traffic Act 2010, when same section comes into operation.

[38] Practitioners should also have regard to ss.21–23, Road Traffic Act 1961 (as amended) in respect of applying for driving licences.

[39] S.26, Road Traffic Act 1961 (as amended).

[40] *Ibid.*, s.27.

[41] *Ibid.*, s.28.

However, they may also be disqualified by virtue of an administrative (non judicial) order:

(d) accumulation penalty points;[42]

(e) under provisions of Section 9 – Road Traffic Act 2002[43] – Recognition of Foreign Disqualification Orders.

Penalties

In respect of offences under section 39, the penalties are as follows:

Summary Conviction: fine of up to €5,000 and/or a term of imprisonment of up to six months.[44]

Disqualification: whilst a conviction under section 39 does not carry a mandatory disqualification, a driver found guilty of an offence under section 39, is, by nature of the offence, already disqualified from driving so it is likely that a court would make a further ancillary disqualification order.

PROHIBITION ON APPLYING FOR A DRIVING LICENCE WHILE DISQUALIFIED – SECTION 58 OF THE ROAD TRAFFIC ACT 2010

Practitioners should note that section 58 of the Road Traffic Act 2010[45] will replace the current section 39 provision and prohibits a person applying for an Irish driving licence or permit if disqualified. The applicable penalty under section 39 and the new section 58 is the same – see above.

Practitioners should also note the provisions of section 57 of the Road Traffic Act 2010,[46] which substitutes and replaces by sections 21–23 of the Road Traffic Act 1961, and in particular the substituted section 22A which sets out that when an individual applies for an Irish driving licence or permit whilst disqualified, and obtains such a licence, this licence is void and of no effect. The substituted section 22B sets out the prohibition on applying for a duplicate driving licence or learner permit in respect of a licence or permit already held.

---

[42] S.3, Road Traffic Act 2002.
[43] Practitioners should note that from 28 January 2010, disqualification orders imposed in the mainland UK and Northern Ireland can be recognised and enforced by the Irish Authorities.
[44] S.39(2), Road Traffic Act 1961, as amended by s.18, Table One, Pt.1, Ref No. 5.
[45] When same section comes into operation.
[46] When same section comes into operation.

Requirement to Carry Driving Licence While Driving Vehicle – Section 40 of the Road Traffic Act 1961[47]

Section 40 of the 1961 Act sets out the following criminal offences:

'(1) Failing to produce a valid driving licence, there and then, having been lawfully requested, whilst driving a vehicle in a public place.[48]

(2) Failing to produce a valid driving licence, there and then, having been lawfully requested, whilst accompanying a learner driver, who is driving a vehicle in a public place.[49]

(3) Failing to produce a valid provisional driving licence or driving permit (if not the holder of valid driving licence), there and then, having been lawfully requested, whilst driving a vehicle in a public place.[50]

(4) Failing to produce a valid driving licence (including a provisional licence/driving permit where applicable), having been lawfully requested, within 10 days at a nominated Garda Station.[51]

(5) Having produced a valid driving licence, upon lawful request, failing to allow a Garda to read/examine produced licence.[52]

(6) Having produced a valid driving licence, upon lawful request and having failed to allow a Garda to read/examine produced licence, further failing to give a true name and address upon lawful request'.[53]

As there are a number of separate charges that may arise under section 40, it is important for a practitioners to have regard to the exact wording of the charge set out, i.e., the precise allegation being made and consideration should be given to whether the particular facts set out in the summons, précis and/or statements support the particular charge brought. In any prosecution for an offence of failing to

---

[47] As substituted by s.25, Road Traffic Act 1994 and amended by s.18, Road Traffic Act 2002 and s.13(a), Road Traffic Act 2006.

[48] S.40(1)(a) as substituted by s.25, Road Traffic Act 1994 and amended s.13(a), Road Traffic Act 2006.

[49] S.40(1)(A)(a), Road Traffic Act 1961.

[50] *Ibid.*

[51] S.40(1)(b) as substituted by s.25, Road Traffic Act 1994 and amended s.13(a), Road Traffic Act 2006.

[52] S.40(2), Road Traffic Act 1961.

[53] *Ibid.*, s.40(3).

produce a valid driving licence within 10 days, it is presumed, until the contrary is shown, that the defendant failed to produce the licence as required. Furthermore, any written certificate signed by the member in charge of the Garda station (at which the defendant nominated to produce his licence), indicating that they failed to produce his/her licence, as lawfully requested, shall be evidence of the facts contained therein, unless and until the contrary is shown.[54]

It is a key element of this offence that a lawful demand was made of the user to produce his/her driving licence within 10 days at a nominated Garda station, and positive evidence to that effect must be adduced by the prosecuting Garda in court. Where an individual fails/refuses to allow a Garda to read his/her licence upon production,[55] or where they fail/refuse to give a true name and address, or give a name which is false or misleading,[56] same individual may be arrested without warrant by the Garda who made the lawful request.[57]

It is a defence to a charge under section 40, if a defendant can demonstrate that he/she was not driving the vehicle at the time of the offence, or that they belonged to an exempt category of drivers: namely, Gardaí driving in the course of his/her duty,[58] persons undergoing a driving test,[59] or drivers of specified pedestrian-controlled vehicles.[60]

Given the charge before the court, even if your client's driving licence has already been produced to the prosecuting Garda, a practitioner should advise his/her client to bring their original licence to the court. While production of the licence in court is not, in itself, a defence to a charge under section 40 (as the defendant still failed to produce their licence within 10 days as required), it will at least satisfy the court that you do have a valid licence. Indeed, in most cases where a valid driving licence is produced in court, a charge under section 40 is struck out by the prosecution.

This will not be the case, however, if the charge before court is that the defendant failed/refused to allow a Garda to read their licence upon production[61], failed/refused to give a true name and address,

---

[54] *Ibid.,* s.40(1)(c).
[55] *Ibid.,* s.40(2).
[56] *Ibid.,* s.40(3).
[57] *Ibid.,* s.40(4).
[58] *Ibid.,* s.38(6).
[59] S.33(7), Road Traffic Act 1961 – they must, however, have valid provisional licence/learner permit.
[60] S.38(7), Road Traffic Act 1961 and art.8, S.I. No.537/2006.
[61] S.40(2), Road Traffic Act 1961.

or gave a name which is false or misleading.[62] In these circumstances, producing a valid driving licence in court will not generally constitute a sufficient defence to the charge brought.

Penalties

An offence contrary to section 40 carries a general penalty under section 102 of the Road Traffic Act 1961.[63]

First Offence – fine of up to €1,000.[64]

Second Offence (under same section) – fine of up to €2,000.[65]

Third/Subsequent Offence (under same section within 12 consecutive months) – fine of up to €2,000 and/or a term of imprisonment of up to three months.[66]

Disqualification:

Ancillary Disqualification: whilst a conviction under section 40 does not carry a mandatory disqualification, a driver found guilty of an offence under section 40 may also be guilty of an offence of driving without a valid driving licence,[67] and in those circumstances an ancillary disqualification order may be imposed. If, however, the defendant did have a valid driving licence at the time of the offence and simply failed to produce it, upon lawful request, or within 10 days at a nominated Garda station, it is highly unlikely that a court would deal with the matter by way of an ancillary disqualification order.

REQUIREMENT TO CARRY DRIVING LICENCE WHILE DRIVING VEHICLE – SECTION 59 OF THE ROAD TRAFFIC ACT 2010

Practitioners should note that section 59 of the Road Traffic Act 2010[68] replaces section 40 of the Principle Act.[69] The new section allows the

---

[62] *Ibid.*, s.40(3).
[63] See s.18(1), Road Traffic Act 2006.
[64] S.102(a), Road Traffic Act 1961, as amended by s.18(1) – Table – Pt.1 – Reference 20.
[65] S.102(b), Road Traffic Act 1961, as amended by s.18(1) – Table – Pt.1 – Reference 21.
[66] S.102(c), Road Traffic Act 1961, as amended by s.18(1) – Table – Pt.1 – Reference 22.
[67] See s.38, Road Traffic Act 1961.
[68] When same section comes into operation.
[69] As amended by s.25, Road Traffic Act 1004; s.18, Road Traffic Act 2002 and s.13, Road Traffic Act 2006.

Gardaí to demand of:

(a) an individual driving in a public place;[70]

(b) a passenger accompanying a learner driver (as a qualified driver) driving in a public place,[71]

to produce their licence there and then to Gardaí.[72] Failure to so do is a criminal offence.[73] The production of a learner permit is a defence to a charge under the substituted section 40(1) and 40(4),[74] however if driver is unaccompanied, they are still liable for driving whilst unaccompanied by a qualified driver.[75] If an individual cannot produce their driving licence, provisional licence or learner permit, there and then, a lawful demand can be made on them to produce it at a nominated Garda station within 10 days.[76] Failure to so produce is a criminal offence.[77] Any written certificate, signed by the member in charge of the Garda station (at which the defendant nominated to produce his licence), indicating that they failed to produce his/her licence, as lawfully requested, shall be evidence of the facts contained therein, unless and until the contrary is shown.[78]

Furthermore, under substituted section 40, where an individual fails/refuses to allow a produced driving licence, provisional licence or leaner permit to be read or examined, then they commit an offence[79] and a lawful demand can be made of them to give their name, address and date of birth.[80] If that individual fails/refuses to give a real name and/or address and/or upon lawful demand or they give a name and/or address and/or date of birth which a Garda has reasonable grounds for believing is false or misleading,[81] that Garda may arrest that individual without warrant.[82]

---

[70] S.40(1)(a) as substituted by s.57, Road Traffic Act 2010, when same section comes into operation.
[71] *Ibid.*
[72] S.40(1) as inserted by new s.57.
[73] S.40(1) as inserted by new s.57.
[74] S.40(2) as inserted by new s.57.
[75] See s.42 – Road Traffic Act 1961 (as amended).
[76] S.40(4)(a) as inserted by new s.57.
[77] S.40(4)(a) as inserted by new s.57.
[78] S.40(4)(b), Road Traffic Act 1961.
[79] S.40(5) as inserted by new s.57.
[80] S.40(6) as inserted by new s.57.
[81] S.40(6) as inserted by new s.57.
[82] S.40(7) as inserted by new s.57.

MEMBER OF GARDAI MAY SEIZE LICENCE IN CERTAIN CIRCUMSTANCES – SECTION 60 OF THE ROAD TRAFFIC ACT 2010

Practitioners should note that section 60 of the Road Traffic Act 2010[83] sets out that where an individual is asked to produce their driving licence within 10 days under section 40 of the Road Traffic Act 1961, a Garda may seize their licence (including permit/foreign licence) where the Garda has reasonable grounds for believing that:

(a) a holder of licence has been disqualified from holding driving licence;

(b) a driving licence produced has been fraudulently obtained, forged or altered.[84]

Gardaí can make a copy of the licence/permit, and, in the case of an Irish licence, return it to the relevant licensing authority. In the case of a foreign licence the Gardaí can send it to licensing authority where the holder is resident or another licensing authority as appropriate.[85] Where a licence has been so seized, a person shall not continue to drive in a public place, or accompany the holder or a permit, which has been seized, while such an individual is driving in a public place.[86] A seized foreign licence may also be retained (for a reasonable period) for purposes of having it translated into English/Irish or to have its validity confirmed.[87]

Penalties

In respect of offences under section 60(4), the penalties will be as follows:

Summary Conviction: – fine of up to €5,000 and/or a term of imprisonment of up to six months.[88]

INSPECTION OF DRIVING LICENCES OF PERSONS CHARGED WITH CERTAIN OFFENCES – SECTION 22 OF THE ROAD TRAFFIC ACT 2002

Section 22 of the Road Traffic Act 2002[89] states that where a defendant is before the court charged with any road traffic offence under

---

[83] When same section comes into operation.
[84] S.60(1), Road Traffic Act 2010.
[85] *Ibid.*, s.60(2).
[86] *Ibid.*, s.60(3).
[87] *Ibid.*, s.60(6).
[88] *Ibid.*, s.60(4).
[89] As substituted by s.21, Road Traffic Act 2004.

Road Traffic legislation, except for an offence under:

(a) section 84,[90] section 85[91] or section 101 of Road Traffic Act 1961, or

(b) section 35 of Road Traffic Act 1961 (as it relates to parking of vehicles) or section 36 of Road Traffic Act 1994.

the defendant shall, on the date they are first due to attend court, or at the discretion of the judge a later date, produce to the court their driving licence/permit AND furnish a copy of same licence/ permit to court. It further states that court will record whether both licence and copy of licence/permit have been produced.

Any individual who fails to comply with the provisions of this section is guilty of an offence.[92]

Penalties

In respect of offences under section 22, the penalties are as follows:

First Offence – fine of up to €1,000.[93]

Second Offence (under same section) – fine of up to €2,000.[94]

Third/Subsequent Offence (under same section within 12 consecutive months) – fine of up to €2,000 and/or a term of imprisonment of up to three months.[95]

Disqualification:

Ancillary Disqualification: whilst a conviction under section 22 does not carry a mandatory disqualification, it is open to the court to make an Ancillary Disqualification Order on the particular facts of the case.

PRODUCTION OF DRIVING LICENCE IN COURT – SECTION 63 OF THE ROAD TRAFFIC ACT 2010

Practitioners should note that section 63 of the Road Traffic Act 2010[96] amends section 22(1) of the Road Traffic Act 2002, so that

---

[90] Inserted by s.15, Road Traffic Act 2002.
[91] Inserted by s.16, Road Traffic Act 2002.
[92] S.22(2), Road Traffic Act 2002.
[93] S.102(a), Road Traffic Act 1961, as amended by s.18(1) – Table – Pt.1 – Reference 20.
[94] S.102(b), Road Traffic Act 1961, as amended by s.18(1) – Table – Pt.1 – Reference 21.
[95] S.102(c), Road Traffic Act 1961, as amended by s.18(1) – Table – Pt.1 – Reference 22.
[96] When same section comes into operation.

where a defendant is before the court charged with any road traffic offence under Road Traffic Acts 1961–2010, except for an offence under;

(c) section 84,[97] section 85[98] or section 101 of Road Traffic Act 1961; or

(d) section 35 of the Road Traffic Act 1961 (as it relates to parking of vehicles); section 36 or section 36A[99] of the Road Traffic Act 1994;

the defendant shall, on the date they are first due to attend court or at the discretion of the judge a later date, produce to the court their driving licence/or permit AND a copy of that licence/permit to be furnished to court. It further states that court will record whether both licence and copy of licence/permit have been produced.

Penalties

An offence contrary to section 63 carries a general penalty under section 102 of the Road Traffic Act 1961.[100]

First Offence – fine of up to €1,000.[101]

Second Offence (under same section) – fine of up to €2,000.[102]

Third/Subsequent Offence (under same section within 12 consecutive months) – fine of up to €2,000 and/or a term of imprisonment of up to three months.[103]

Disqualification:

Ancillary Disqualification: whilst a conviction under section 63 does not carry a mandatory disqualification, it is open to the court to make an ancillary disqualification order on the particular facts of the case.

---

[97] As inserted by s.15, Road Traffic Act 2002.
[98] As inserted by s.16, Road Traffic Act 2002.
[99] As inserted by s.16, Road Traffic Act 2002.
[100] See s.18(1), Road Traffic Act 2006.
[101] S.102(a), Road Traffic Act 1961, as amended by s.18(1) – Table – Pt.1 – Reference 20.
[102] S.102(b), Road Traffic Act 1961, as amended by s.18(1) – Table – Pt.1 – Reference 21.
[103] S.102(c), Road Traffic Act 1961, as amended by s.18(1) – Table – Pt.1 – Reference 22.

Detention/Removal or Immobilisation of Vehicles – Section 41 of the Road Traffic Act 1994

Section 41(1) of the Road Traffic Act 1994[104] states that where the Gardaí believe that an individual driving a vehicle in a public place is:

(a) too young to hold a valid driving licence;[105] or

(b) is driving vehicle without a valid insurance certificate or otherwise in contravention of section 56(1) of the Road Traffic Act 1961;[106] or

(c) is driving vehicle without a valid tax disc (or otherwise in contravention of section 1 of the Finance (Excise Duties)(Vehicles) Act 1952, for a period of 2 continuous months immediately prior to same use.[107]

(d) is driving vehicle without a valid NCT certificate or otherwise in contravention of section 18(1) of the Road Traffic Act 1961;[108]

(e) is driving vehicle without a valid DOE certificate or otherwise in contravention of regulation 19(1) of Statutory Instrument No. 771/2004 – European Communities (Vehicle Testing) Regulations 2004[109]; or

(f) is driving vehicle, registered in another member state without proof of passing roadworthiness test pursuant to Council Directive 96/96/EC[110];

same vehicle may be detained, removed or otherwise immobilised in accordance with the powers conferred upon a Garda under section 3 and section 41 of the Road Traffic Act 1994 and the Road Traffic Act 1994 (Section 41) Regulations 1995–1998.

Penalties

It is an offence to obstruct or otherwise impede a Garda from exercising his powers under section 41. The general penalties under

---

[104] As amended by s.19, Road Traffic Act 2006.
[105] S.41(1)(a), Road Traffic Act 1994.
[106] S.41(1)(b), Road Traffic Act 1994, as substituted by s.19(a), Road Traffic Act 2006.
[107] S.41(1)(c), Road Traffic Act 1994, as substituted by s.19(b), Road Traffic Act 2006.
[108] S.41(1)(d), Road Traffic Act 1994, as inserted by s.19(c), Road Traffic Act 2006.
[109] S.41(1)(e), Road Traffic Act 1994, as inserted by s.19(c), Road Traffic Act 2006.
[110] S.41(1)(f), Road Traffic Act 1994, as inserted by s.19(c), Road Traffic Act 2006.

section 102 of the Road Traffic Act 1961[111] are as follows:

First Offence – fine of up to €1,000.[112]

Second Offence (under same section) – fine of up to €2,000.[113]

Third/Subsequent Offence (under same section) – fine of up to €2,000 and/or a term of imprisonment of up to three months.[114]

Disqualification:

> **Ancillary Disqualification:** whilst a conviction under section 41 does not carry a mandatory disqualification, it is open to the court to make an ancillary disqualification order under section 27 of the Road Traffic Act 1961 on the particular facts of the case.

ROAD TRAFFIC ACT 1994 (SECTION 41) REGULATIONS 1995[115]

Where a Garda is of the opinion that an offence contrary to section 41(1) of the Road Traffic Act 1994:

(a) is being committed; or

(b) has been committed,

then the Garda, or any other person the Garda deems fit, may take such steps as required to detain, remove and store the vehicle.[116]

Article 5 sets out the monetary charges that will apply in respect of the detention/removal and storage of a vehicle where articles 6, 7, 8 and 9 do not apply.

Article 6 allows for the subsequent release of a vehicle (without charge) to the lawful owner, where a Garda was satisfied the vehicle was taken without the consent/authority of the owner.

Article 7 allows for the subsequent release of a vehicle (without charge) to the lawful owner, where a Garda was satisfied that a valid insurance certificate for the vehicle exists in accordance with section 56 of the Road Traffic Act 1961.

---

[111] See s.18(1), Road Traffic Act 2006.

[112] S.102(a), Road Traffic Act 1961, as amended by s.18(1) – Table – Pt.1 – Reference 20.

[113] S.102(b), Road Traffic Act 1961, as amended by s.18(1) – Table – Pt.1 – Reference 21.

[114] S.102(c), Road Traffic Act 1961, as amended by s.18(1) – Table – Pt.1 – Reference 22.

[115] S.I. No.89/1995, Road Traffic Act 1994 (S.41) Regulations 1995.

[116] Art.4, S.I. No.89/1995, Road Traffic Act 1994 (S.41) Regulations 1995.

Article 8 permits the subsequent release of a vehicle (without charge) to the lawful owner, where a Garda was satisfied that all excise duty (motor tax) in respect of the vehicle had been paid prior to detention of the vehicle.

Article 9 provides that where a vehicle was abandoned or illegally parked, monetary charges under article 5 shall not apply in addition to monetary charges set out by regulation under section 97 of the Road Traffic Act 1961.[117]

Articles 10 and 11 set out the circumstances in which a vehicle may be disposed of if the vehicle is not claimed by the owner or charges under article 5 are not paid.

DUTY TO PRODUCE DRIVING LICENCE WITHIN 10 DAYS – SECTION 33 OF THE ROAD TRAFFIC ACT 2004

Under section 33 of the Road Traffic Act 2004, if a Garda forms the opinion that:

(a) a vehicle was used in a public place;

(b) the use of vehicle may have involved the commission a road traffic offence;

(c) the actual user of vehicle was a particular person,

that Garda may, at any time subsequent, require of such person that they produce their driving licence at a Garda station or other specified place within 10 days of such lawful demand. If an individual refuses/fails to comply with a lawful demand under this section, they will be guilty of an offence.[118]

A Garda's powers to require a person to produce their driving licence are based upon the Garda having formed an opinion that a road traffic offence has been committed by the user. In such circumstances, evidence should be adduced by the Garda: firstly, that they had formed such an opinion and as to how and why the Garda formed this opinion. Evidence should also be adduced that the individual upon whom the demand was made was advised by the Garda of the opinion formed and the statutory basis upon which they was being asked to give produce their driving licence. The statutory basis on which the demand is made is an essential element

---

[117] As substituted by s.63, Road Traffic Act 1968 and subsequently amended by s.49, Road Traffic Act 1994.

[118] S.33(1), Road Traffic Act 2004.

of the offence, and if direct evidence such as to satisfy this requirement is not given, then a direction should be sought at the close of the prosecution case.

It is a key element of this offence that a lawful demand was made of the user to produce a their driving licence within 10 days at a nominated Garda Station, or other specified place and positive evidence to that effect must be adduced by the prosecuting Garda in court.

Penalties

An offence contrary to section 33(2) carries a general penalty under section 102 of the Road Traffic Act 1961.[119]

First Offence – fine of up to €1,000.[120]

Second Offence (under same section) – fine of up to €2,000.[121]

Third/Subsequent Offence (under same section within 12 consecutive months) – fine of up to €2,000 and/or a term of imprisonment of up to three months.[122]

Disqualification:

Ancillary Disqualification: a conviction under section 33 does not carry a mandatory consequential disqualification, however, as the offence is one which relates to the use of a motor vehicle, it is open to the court to make an ancillary disqualification order under section 27 of the Road Traffic Act 1961 on the particular facts of the case.

DUTY TO PRODUCE DRIVING LICENCE WITHIN 10 DAYS – SECTION 61 OF THE ROAD TRAFFIC ACT 2010

Practitioners should note that section 33 of the Road Traffic Act 2004 is repealed and replaced by section 61 of the Road Traffic Act 2010.[123] Under section 61, if a Garda forms the opinion that:

(a) a vehicle was used in a public place;

---

[119] See s.18(1), Road Traffic Act 2006.

[120] S.102(a), Road Traffic Act 1961, as amended by s.18(1) – Table – Pt.1 – Reference 20.

[121] S.102(b), Road Traffic Act 1961, as amended by s.18(1) – Table – Pt.1 – Reference 21.

[122] S.102(c), Road Traffic Act 1961, as amended by s.18(1) – Table – Pt.1 – Reference 22.

[123] When same section comes into operation.

(b) the use of vehicle may have involved the commission a road traffic offence;

(c) the actual user of vehicle was a particular person,

that Garda may, at any time subsequent, require of such person that they produce their driving licence/permit at a Garda station or other specified place within 10 days of such lawful demand. If an individual refuses/fails to comply with a lawful demand under this section, they will be guilty of an offence.[124]

If such an individual:

(a) fails/refuses to produce licence/permit;

(b) produces licence/permit but fails/refuses to allow Gardaí to read same.

Then the Garda may demand same individual to provide their name, address and date of birth – failing to provide same information, or providing false/misleading information is an offence.[125] Gardaí may arrest such an individual without warrant.[126]

Penalties

An offence contrary to section 61(2) carries a general penalty under section 102 of the Road Traffic Act 1961.[127]

First Offence – fine of up to €1,000.[128]

Second Offence (under same section) – fine of up to €2,000.[129]

Third/Subsequent Offence (under same section within 12 consecutive months) – fine of up to €2,000 and/or a term of imprisonment of up to three months.[130]

Disqualification:

Ancillary Disqualification: a conviction under section 61 does not carry a mandatory consequential disqualification,

---

[124] S.61(1), Road Traffic Act 2010.

[125] *Ibid.*, s.61(3).

[126] *Ibid.*, s.61(4).

[127] See s.18(1), Road Traffic Act 2006.

[128] S.102(a), Road Traffic Act 1961, as amended by s.18(1) – Table – Pt.1 – Reference 20.

[129] S.102(b), Road Traffic Act 1961, as amended by s.18(1) – Table – Pt.1 – Reference 21.

[130] S.102(c), Road Traffic Act 1961, as amended by s.18(1) – Table – Pt.1 – Reference 22.

however, as the offence is one which relates to the use of a motor vehicle, it is open to the court to make an ancillary disqualification order under section 27 of the Road Traffic Act 1961 on the particular facts of the case.

OBLIGATION TO GIVE CURRENT ADDRESS TO GARDAI – SECTION 62 OF THE ROAD TRAFFIC ACT 2010

Section 62 of the Road Traffic Act 2010[131] provides that where an individual produces their licence at a Garda station following a lawful demand, the Gardaí may inquire if the address on driving licence/permit produced is that individual's current address.[132] If it is not that individual's current address, the Gardaí may demand that the individual give their current address. Failure to comply with a lawful demand under section 62(1) is an offence.[133]

Penalties

In respect of an offence contrary to section 62 of the Road Traffic Act 2010, the following penalties apply:

Summary Conviction: general penalty under section 102 of the Road Traffic Act 1961 applies.[134]

First Offence – fine of up to €1,000.[135]

Second Offence (under same section) – fine of up to €2,000.[136]

Third/Subsequent Offence (under same section within 12 consecutive months) – fine of up to €2,000 and/or a term of imprisonment of up to three months.[137]

Disqualification:

Ancillary Disqualification: a conviction under section 62 does not carry a mandatory consequential disqualification,

---

[131] When same section comes into operation.
[132] S.62(1), Road Traffic Act 2010, when same section comes into operation.
[133] S.62(2), Road Traffic Act 2010, when same section comes into operation.
[134] See s.18(1), Road Traffic Act 2006.
[135] S.102(a), Road Traffic Act 1961, as amended by s.18(1) – Table – Pt.1 – Reference 20.
[136] S.102(b), Road Traffic Act 1961, as amended by s.18(1) – Table – Pt.1 – Reference 21.
[137] S.102(c), Road Traffic Act 1961, as amended by s.18(1) – Table – Pt.1 – Reference 22.

however, as the offence is one which relates to the use of a motor vehicle, it is open to the court to make an ancillary disqualification order under section 27 of the Road Traffic Act 1961 on the particular facts of the case.

CHAPTER 5

Motor Tax and Certificates of Road Worthiness

This chapter deals with offences in respect of Motor Tax and the NCT/DOE tests which vehicles are required to undergo to confirm that they are roadworthy.

This chapter sets out the offences of:

(a) using vehicle without road tax/licence – driver/owner – see section 13(1) of the Roads Act 1920[1] (as amended);

(b) making a false declaration in connection with or furnishing false particulars in respect of any application for tax disc/licence/vehicle registration – section 13(2) of the Roads Act 1920 (as amended);

(c) fraudulent use of a tax disc or forging/fraudulently altering licence/vehicle registration – section 13(4) of the Roads Act 1920[2] (as amended);

(d) using a vehicle in a public place without a valid tax disc/certificate – see section 71 of the Finance Act 1976 (as amended);

(e) parking a vehicle in a public place without a valid tax disc/certificate – see section 71 of the Finance Act 1976 (as amended);

(f) keeping a vehicle in a public place without a valid tax disc/certificate – see section 71 of the Finance Act 1976[3] (as amended);

---

[1] Penalty for an offence contrary to s.13(1), Roads Act 1920 (as amended) is an excise penalty not exceeding €1,269.74.

[2] Penalty for an offence contrary to s.13(2) or s.13(4), Roads Act 1920 (as amended) is an excise penalty not exceeding €1,269.74 and up to 6 months imprisonment.

[3] Penalty for an offence contrary to s.71, Finance Act 1976 is an excise penalty not exceeding €1,269.74.

(g)   incorrect rate of motor tax paid – section 2 of the Finance (Excise Duties)(Vehicles) Act 1952[4] and section 20(3) of the Finance Act 1968;

(h)   failure to display tax disc (section 73 of the Finance Act 1976[5] (as amended);

(i)   alteration/defacement tax disc: see article 5 of the Road Vehicles (Registration and Licensing) Regulations 1992[6] as amended;

(j)   failure to furnish details or giving false details in respect of unlicensed vehicle – section 67(1) of the Finance Act 1976[7] (as amended);

(k)   failure of former owner to notify authority of transfer of ownership within prescribed period or giving false details in respect of transfer of ownership – section 67(2) of the Finance Act 1976 (as amended).

This chapter will also deal with the following NCT/DOE certificate offences:

(l)   using a vehicle without a valid NCT certificate;

(m)   failing to produce a valid NCT certificate within 10 days of a lawful demand;

(n)   failing to display a valid NCT Disc;

(o)   using a vehicle without a valid DOE Road-Worthiness Certificate;

(p)   failing to produce a valid DOE Road-Worthiness Certificate within 10 days of lawful demand.

MOTOR TAX

Motor tax is dealt with primarily under the Roads Act 1920 and the Finances Acts, particularly the Finance Act 1976. All vehicles being driven, used, kept, parked or even left stationary in a public place

---

[4] Penalty for an offence contrary to s.2, Finance (Excise Duties)(Vehicles) Act 1952 – i.e. not paying sufficient rate of duty is an excise penalty not exceeding €1,269.74.
[5] Penalty for an offence contrary to s.73, Finance Act 1976 is an excise penalty not exceeding €1,269.74.
[6] S.I. No.385/1992, Road Vehicles (Registration and Licensing) (Amendment) Regulations 1992.
[7] Penalty for an offence contrary to s.67, Finance Act 1976 is an excise penalty not exceeding €1,269.74

are required to have, and display, a valid motor tax certificate/disc. Anyone who uses a vehicle in a public place for which motor tax is required to be paid without having paid the required motor tax, shall be guilty of an offence.[8] Furthermore, anyone who fails to display a valid motor tax disc on the windscreen of their vehicle is also guilty of an offence.[9] It is an offence to: alter or tamper with a motor tax disc;[10] to display a fraudulent motor tax disc;[11] to pay an incorrect rate of motor tax for your vehicle;[12] and also to give fraudulent information for the purposes of obtaining a tax disc.[13]

USING A VEHICLE WITHOUT VALID MOTOR TAXATION CERTIFICATE – SECTION 13 OF THE ROADS ACT 1920[14]

Under section 13 of the Roads Act 1920, it is an offence to use a vehicle without a valid motor tax.[15] This section also creates an offence of using or furnishing false or misleading information for the purposes of obtaining motor tax/licence/vehicle registration and would include circumstances where a person uses false insurance or a false NCT/DOE certificate for the purpose of obtaining/renewing their motor tax.[16]

It further creates the offences of forging/fraudulently altering any tax disc/licence/vehicle registration.[17] Practitioners should note that a charge under section 13 can be brought within 12 months of the date of the offence,[18] and not six months as applies to most summary road traffic offences.[19] Practitioners should also note that an individual can be charged with an offence contrary to section 13 of the Roads Act 1920, or section 71 of the Finance Act 1976: however, they cannot be charged with both offences arising out of the same incident.[20]

---

[8] See s.13, Roads Act 1920 and s.71, Finance Act 1976.
[9] S.71, Finance Act 1976.
[10] Art. 5, S.I. No.385/1992, Road Vehicles (Registration and Licensing) (Amendment) Regulations 1992.
[11] S.13(4), Roads Act 1920.
[12] S.2, Finance (Excise Duties)(Vehicles) Act 1952 and s.20(3), Finance Act 1968.
[13] S.13(2), Roads Act 1920.
[14] As amended by s.63, Finance Act 1993.
[15] S.13(1), Roads Act 1920.
[16] *Ibid.*, s.13(2),.
[17] *Ibid.*, s.13(2).
[18] *Ibid.*, s.13(1).
[19] See s.10(4), Petty Sessions (Ireland) Act 1851.
[20] S.71(3), Finance Act 1976.

Penalties

In respect of an offence under section 13(1), the penalties are as follows:
Summary Conviction – fine of up to €1,269.74.[21]

In respect of an offence under section 13(2), the penalties are as follows:
Summary Conviction – fine of up to €1,269.74 and a term of imprisonment of up to six months.[22]

In respect of an offence under section 13(4), the penalties are as follows;
Summary Conviction – fine of up to €1,269.74 and a term of imprisonment of up to six months.[23]

Disqualification:

Ancillary disqualification – a conviction under section 13 does not carry a mandatory disqualification, however, as the offence is one which relates to the use of a motor vehicle, it is open to the court to make an ancillary disqualification order under section 27 of the Road Traffic Act 1961 on the particular facts of the case.

The above section must to be read in conjunction with other relevant and statutory instruments including section 1(1) of the Finance (Excise Duties) (Vehicles) Act 1952[24] which states that:

'All vehicles used (including keeping or leaving a vehicle stationary) in a public place, will be required to pay excise duty (in this case motor tax) as may be prescribed by the Minister by way of regulation.'[25]

Also, relevant are sections 68–78 of the Finance Act 1976, in particular section 71.

Using and Keeping Vehicles on which Chargeable Vehicle Excise Duty is Unpaid – Section 71 of the Finance Act 1976

Section 71 of the Finance Act 1976 sets out the obligation that any vehicles[26] in respect of which there is a requirement to pay excise

---

[21] S.13(1), Roads Act 1920, penalty increased by s.63, Finance Act 1993 – Table – Reference 2.

[22] *Ibid.*, s.13(2), penalty increased by s.63, Finance Act 1993 – Table – Reference 3.

[23] *Ibid.*, s.13(4), Roads Act 1920, penalty increased by s.63, Finance Act 1993 – Table – Reference 4.

[24] As amended by s.78, Finance Act 1976.

[25] S.1(1), Finance Act 1952, as amended by s.78, Finance Act 1976.

[26] S.21(5), Finance Act 1992 sets out that this section shall not apply to any vehicle at any time during which a trade licence under s.21 is exhibited on vehicle.

duty cannot be used, parked or kept in a public place in circumstances where that excise duty is unpaid.

Section 71(1) sets out the offences of:

'(a) Using a vehicle in a public place without a valid tax disc/certificate.

(b) Parking a vehicle in a public place without a valid tax disc/certificate.

(c) Keeping a vehicle in a public place without a valid tax disc/certificate.'

It is a defence for the user of a vehicle to demonstrate that they were not the owner of the vehicle and were using the vehicle with the consent of and under the express order of the owner.[27] An individual can be charged with an offence contrary to section 71 of the Finance Act 1976 or section 13 of the Roads Act 1920: however, they cannot be charged with both offences arising out of the same incident.[28]

Penalties

In respect of an offence under section 71(1), the penalties are as follows:

Summary Conviction – fine of up to €1,269.74.[29]

Disqualification:

Ancillary Disqualification: a conviction under section 71(1) does not carry a mandatory disqualification, however, as the offence is one which relates to the use of a motor vehicle, it is open to the court to make an ancillary disqualification order under section 27 of the Road Traffic Act 1961 on the particular facts of the case.

The Finance Acts, as they relate to motor tax, have been amended on several occasions and there are also an extensive number of regulations – in particular the Road Vehicles (Registration and Licensing) Regulations 1992–2008. It is not proposed to examine this in detail here except to say that motor tax rates can change from year to year and will differ depending on the type of vehicle you

---

[27] S.71(2), Finance Act 1976.
[28] *Ibid.*, s.71(3).
[29] See s.76, Finance Act 1976 as amended by s.63, Finance Act 1993 – Table – Reference 6.

drive. It is important for practitioners to note that with the enactment of the Motor Vehicle (Duties and Licences)(No. 2) Act 2008, motor tax rates are now calculated on the basis of seven CO_2 emissions bands[30] and the most up-to-date rates can be obtained from the Motor Tax Office.

The onus is on the prosecution to prove that the alleged vehicle was a vehicle for which a liability to pay motor tax arose, that vehicle did not have valid motor tax and that the offence occurred in a public place.[31] Practitioners should note that this offence can occur, not just when a vehicle is being used on any public road, but if the vehicle is used, parked or kept in any place which is not private property; therefore an individual cannot leave their vehicle parked outside their own property, without a valid tax disc, unless the place where vehicle is parked is on private property.

Not all vehicles have a motor tax liability and exemptions will apply to:

(a) state-owned vehicles;[32]

(b) diplomatic vehicles;[33]

(c) ambulances, fire engines and road rollers;[34]

(d) vehicles covered by articles 8, 10 and 12 of the Disabled Drivers and Disabled Passengers (Tax Concessions) Regulations 1994;[35]

(e) vehicles (including mechanically-propelled cycles) with unladen weight of up to 400kg adapted and used for invalids;[36]

(f) vehicles used exclusively for transport of lifeboats or any equipment used by lifeboat and sea rescue services;[37]

(g) vehicles used exclusively for underwater search and recovery;[38]

---

[30] See in particular s.6, Pt.1, Sch. to Motor Vehicle (Duties and Licensees)(No.2) Act 2008.

[31] S.71(2), Finance Act 1976.

[32] Art.25(2)(b), S.I. No.385/1992, Road Vehicles (Registration and Licensing) (Amendment) Regulations 1992.

[33] *Ibid.*, art.25(2)(a).

[34] S.1(4)(b), Finance (Excise Duties)(Vehicles)Act 1952.

[35] Art.17, S.I. No.353/1994, Disabled Drivers and Disabled Passengers (Tax Concessions) Regulations 1994.

[36] S.1(4)(f), Finance (Excise Duties)(Vehicles)Act 1952 as inserted by s.75, Finance Act 1991 and amended by s.3, Motor Vehicle (Duties and Licences) Act 2001.

[37] S.1(4)(e), Finance (Excise Duties)(Vehicles)Act 1952.

[38] *Ibid.*, s.1(4)(h) as inserted by s.3, Motor Vehicle (Duties and Licences) Act 2001.

(h) local authority vehicles kept and used exclusively for use by the fire service;[39]

(i) vehicles used exclusively for mountain/cave rescues;[40]

(j) vehicles such as refuse cart and sweeping machines used exclusively for cleaning public streets;[41]

(k) vehicles used exclusively for the transport (whether by carriage or traction) of road construction machinery and machinery and equipment used for construction/repair or roads.[42]

There are limited defences available to an individual charged with having no motor tax. Where it is established that the offence occurred in a public place, the owner of the vehicle must demonstrate that:

He/she was not using vehicle at time of offence as:

(a) the vehicle was being driven without his/her consent or knowledge;

(b) the vehicle, before being taken (without his/her consent), was 'off the road' and had been kept in a stationary private place.

It is always a defence if the owner/user can demonstrate that the location of the alleged offence was not in fact a public place. However, the vehicle cannot be parked in any public place, including a public road, path or grass area outside the owner's dwelling. Any vehicle which requires motor tax can only be used without a valid disc on private property. It is never a defence to state that vehicle was simply parked in a public place without being driven, although in certain circumstances this may be advanced by way of mitigation, i.e. the owner held an honest but mistaken belief that the parked vehicle did not require motor tax.

It is a defence for the user of a vehicle if they can demonstrate that he/she was not the owner of the vehicle and were driving same vehicle under the express order of the owner.

As already stated, it is always a defence if the owner/user can demonstrate that a statutory exemption applied to the vehicle and no motor tax was required.

---

[39] *Ibid.*, s.1(4)(c).
[40] *Ibid.*, s.1(4)(g) as inserted by s.3, Motor Vehicle (Duties and Licences) Act 2001.
[41] *Ibid.*, s.1(4)(a).
[42] *Ibid.*, s.1(4)(d).

FAILURE BY A DRIVER TO HAVE A TAX DISC FIXED AND DISPLAYED ON THE WINDSCREEN OF A VEHICLE – SECTION 73 OF THE FINANCE ACT 1976

Section 73(1) provides that it is an offence:

> 'To fail to display a tax disc on any vehicle which is being used, parked or kept in any public place, if same vehicle is one for which motor tax must be paid and displayed.'

The onus is on the prosecution to prove that it was a vehicle which required a tax disc:[44] that a valid tax disc was not displayed and that offence occurred in a public place.

Again, there are limited defences available to a charge of failing to display a valid tax disc. The most obvious one is if the owner/user can demonstrate that a statutory exemption applied to vehicle and no road tax was required. It is also a defence if the owner/user can demonstrate that the location of the alleged offence was not a public place. Again, it is a defence if an owner can demonstrate that vehicle was being stored on private property, but was taken and used in a public place without their consent, or that the user of the vehicle can demonstrate that they were not the owner of the vehicle and were driving same vehicle under the express order of the owner. An individual can be charged with an offence contrary to section 73 of the Finance Act 1976 or section 12(4) of the Roads Act 1920: however, they cannot be charged with both.[45]

Penalties

Fixed Charge Penalty: €60 (paid in 28 days),[46] €90 (paid in subsequent 28 days).[47]

Penalty (on conviction): fine of up to €1,269.74.[48]

Disqualification:

Ancillary Disqualification: a conviction under section 73 does not carry a mandatory disqualification, however, as the

---

[43] See s.75(3), Finance Act 1976.
[44] I.e. – not an exempt vehicle, however, in reality, it is hard to see circumstances where a prosecution would be brought in respect of a vehicle which was clearly exempt from motor tax.
[45] S.73(2), Finance Act 1976.
[46] See art.5(b)(iii), S.I. No.135/2006.
[47] See s.103(7)(c), Road Traffic Act 1961 and art.5(b)(iii), S.I. No.135/2006.
[48] See s.76, Finance Act 1976 as amended by s.63, Finance Act 1993 – Table – Reference 6.

offence is one which relates to the use of a motor vehicle, it is open to the court to make an ancillary disqualification order under section 27 of the Road Traffic Act 1961 on the particular facts of the case.

PARTICULARS RELATING TO AND TRANSFERS OF CERTAIN VEHICLES TO BE FURNISHED TO LICENSING AUTHORITIES – SECTION 67 OF THE FINANCE ACT 1976

Section 67(1) provides that where a person:

(a) keeps for any period a vehicle in respect of which vehicle excise duty is chargeable, and

(b) a licence referred to in section 1 of the Act of 1952 has not been issued in respect of the vehicle;

that person shall, within 7 days, furnish to the relevant licensing authority the particulars prescribed.[49]

It is an offence to fail to notify a licensing authority in respect of unlicensed vehicle or to give false/misleading information in respect of an unlicensed vehicle.[50] It is also an offence for the former owner of a vehicle to either fail to notify an authority of transfer of ownership within the prescribed period or to give false/misleading details in respect of transfer of ownership.[51]

Penalties

In respect of an offence under section 67, the penalties are as follows:

Summary Conviction: fine of up to €1,269.74.[52]

Disqualification:

    Ancillary Disqualification: a conviction under section 67 does not carry a mandatory disqualification, however, as the offence is one which relates to the use of a motor vehicle, it is open to the court to make an ancillary disqualification order under section 27 of the Road Traffic Act 1961 on the particular facts of the case.

---

[49] S.67(1), Finance Act 1976.
[50] *Ibid.*, ss.67(1) and 67(5).
[51] *Ibid.*, ss.67(2) and 67(5).
[52] *Ibid.*, s.76, Finance Act 1976 as amended by s.63, Finance Act 1993 – Table – Reference 6.

Using a Vehicle without a Test Certificate –
Section 18 of the Road Traffic Act 1961

Section 18 of the Road Traffic Act 1961,[53] provides that it is an offence:

> 'For any class of vehicle to which section 18 applies to be used in a public place without a valid test certificate.'[54]

Both the user and the owner of vehicle are liable to prosecution under this section.[55] It is a defence if the owner can demonstrate that the vehicle was used without their consent.[56] It is also a defence if the user can demonstrate that they were using vehicle in obedience to the express orders of the owner.[57] In a prosecution for an offence contrary to section 18, it is presumed, until the contrary is shown, that the vehicle was used in contravention of section 18.[58]

Under section 19 of the Road Traffic Act 1961,[59] a Garda, who has reasonable grounds for believing that a vehicle they have observed being used in a public place requires a test certificate, can, within one month of so observing, make a lawful demand of the user and/or owner of the vehicle to produce a National Car Test Certificate (NCT), or any other applicable certificate of roadworthiness, there and then, or within 10 days at a nominated Garda station.[60]

It is a criminal offence if an individual:

(a) being the user of vehicle, fails to produce a valid test certificate, having been lawfully requested, within 10 days at a nominated Garda station;[61]

(b) being the owner of vehicle, fails to produce a valid test certificate, having been lawfully requested, within 10 days at a nominated Garda station;[62]

(c) having produced a valid test certificate of roadworthiness, upon lawful request, fails to allow a Garda to read/examine the produced licence;[63]

---

[53] As amended by s.8, Road Traffic Act 1968 and s.23, Road Traffic Act 2002.
[54] S.18(1), Road Traffic Act 1961 as amended by s.8, Road Traffic Act 1968.
[55] *Ibid.*, s.18(2) as amended by s.23, Road Traffic Act 2002.
[56] *Ibid.*, s.18(4).
[57] *Ibid.*, s.18(4).
[58] *Ibid.*, s.18(3). See also s.19, Road Traffic Act 1961.
[59] As amended by s.8, Road Traffic Act 1968.
[60] S.19(1), Road Traffic Act 1961, as amended by s.8, Road Traffic Act 1968.
[61] *Ibid.*, s.19(1) as amended by s.8, Road Traffic Act 1968.
[62] *Ibid.*, s.19(2)(a) as amended by s.8, Road Traffic Act 1968.
[63] *Ibid.*, s.19(3).

(d) having produced a valid test certificate of roadworthiness, upon lawful request and having failed to allow a Garda to read/examine the produced licence, further fails to give a true name and address upon lawful request.[64]

It is presumed, until the contrary is shown' that the vehicle was used without a valid certificate once there is evidence that a lawful demand was made for the certificate to be produced.[65]

An individual who fails to allow the Gardaí to read a produced certificate, or who gives the Gardaí a false/misleading name and address, can be arrested without charge.[66] It is a good defence to a charge under section 19 for the owner of the vehicle to demonstrate that they were not driving the vehicle and that vehicle was being driven without their consent.[67]

Penalties

In respect of an offence under section 19 of the Road Traffic Act 1961, the penalties are as follows:

Summary Conviction: general penalty under section 102 of the Road Traffic Act 1961 applies.[68]

First Offence – fine of up to €1,000.[69]

Second Offence (under same section) – fine of up to €2,000.[70]

Third/Subsequent Offence (under same section within 12 consecutive months) – fine of up to €2,000 and/or a term of imprisonment of up to three months.[71]

Disqualification:

Ancillary Disqualification: a conviction under section 19 does not carry a mandatory consequential disqualification, however, as the offence is one which relates to the use of a motor vehicle, it is open to the court to make an ancillary

---

[64] *Ibid.*, s.19(4) .
[65] *Ibid.*, s.19(2)(b).
[66] *Ibid.*, s.19(5).
[67] *Ibid.*, s.19(2)(c).
[68] See s.18(1), Road Traffic Act 2006.
[69] S.102(a) as amended by s.18(1) – Table – Pt.1 – Reference 20.
[70] *Ibid.*, s.102(b) as amended by s.18(1) – Table – Pt.1 – Reference 21.
[71] *Ibid.*, s.102(c) as amended by s.18(1) – Table – Pt.1 – Reference 22.

disqualification order under section 27 of the Road Traffic Act 1961 on the particular facts of the case.

In practical terms, the test which has most applicability to individuals who might find themselves before the court on a charge contrary to section 18 of the Road Traffic Act 1961 is the National Car Test or NCT. The NCT is a compulsory car test brought in to give effect to Council Directive 96/96/EC. The applicable regulations are set out in the Road Traffic (National Car Test) Regulations 2009[72] and the Road Traffic (Display of Test Disc) Regulations 2009.[73]

All cars which are four years (and older)[74] must be tested every two years[75] in respect of areas such as wheels and tyres, transmission, interior and fuel systems, brakes, exhaust emission, lights, steering and suspension, chassis and underbody, electrical systems and glass and mirrors. The relevant date for calculation of NCT test is the date of vehicle's first registration in Ireland (or in the jurisdiction of origin if different from Ireland).

The NCT applies to all cars imported to Ireland once they are four years or older, regardless of whether they have passed similar tests in other jurisdictions. Exemptions apply to vehicles which are 30 years or older, as they are classified as vintage cars and also vehicles permanently based on one of the offshore islands, provided they are not connected to the Irish mainland by a road bridge.[76]

The NCT also does not apply to commercial vehicles[77] which must instead get a Department of Environment Certificate of Roadworthiness (DOE Cert) every year.[78] It may be a defence to a charge of not having a valid NCT certificate to demonstrate that you applied for an NCT test before the expiration of a previous NCT certificate or due date for the first NCT and through an administrative delay are still awaiting your test date:[79] however, a defendant should be able to produce documentary evidence to that effect.

---

[72] S.I. No.567/2009, Road Traffic (National Car Test) Regulations 2009.
[73] S.I. No.548/2009, Road Traffic (Display of Test Disc) Regulations 2009.
[74] Art.3(1), S.I. No.567/2009, Road Traffic (National Car Test) Regulations 2009.
[75] *Ibid.*, art.3(2).
[76] *Ibid.*, art.3(5).
[77] Art.3, S.I. No.771/2004 European Communities (Vehicle Testing) Regulations 2004.
[78] *Ibid.*, art.4.
[79] This defence will not apply in circumstances where you have failed your NCT and continued driving for a period of time while awaiting a new NCT.

Penalties

In respect of offences under section 18(1), the penalties are as follows;

Summary Conviction – fine of up to €2,000 and/or a term of imprisonment of up to three months.[80]

Penalty Points: Five (upon conviction)[81] – this offence does not carry an option of paying a fixed penalty notice. Section 2(8) of the Road Traffic Act 2002 applies if the court imposes an ancillary disqualification order under section 27 of the Road Traffic Act 1961. In those circumstances, penalty points will also be endorsed on the licence record.

Disqualification:

Ancillary Disqualification: a first conviction under section 18 does not carry a mandatory disqualification. However, it is open to the court to make an ancillary disqualification order on the particular facts of the case.

Mandatory Disqualification: if a defendant is convicted of a second or subsequent conviction under this section within a three year period, a consequential disqualification period of not less than one year will apply.[82]

Penalty Point Disqualification: if a defendant accrues 12 penalty points upon a conviction for this offence, then they will be disqualified under the administrative procedure set out under section 3 of the Road Traffic Act 2002.

Penalties

In respect of an offence under section 18(12), the penalties are as follows:

Summary Conviction: general penalty under section 102 of the Road Traffic Act 1961.

First Offence: fine of up to €1,000.

---

[80] S.18(2), Road Traffic Act 1961 as amended by s.18, Road Traffic Act 2006 – Table – Pt.1, Reference 3.

[81] See Reference 2 of Pt.1 of Sch.1 of Road Traffic Act 2002 and also S.I. No.149/2009 – Road Traffic Act 2002 (Commencement of Certain Provisions) (Penalty Points) Order 2009 – which came into effect on 1 May 2009.

[82] S.26, Road Traffic Act 1961, as substituted by s.26, Road Traffic Act 1994 and amended by s.6(1)(e), Road Traffic Act 2006.

Second Offence: (under same section) – fine of up to €2,000.

Third/Subsequent Offence: (under same section within 12 consecutive months) – fine of up to €2,000 and/or a term of imprisonment of up to three months.

Disqualification:

Ancillary Disqualification: a first conviction under section 18(12) does not carry a mandatory disqualification: however, it is open to the court to make an ancillary disqualification order on the particular facts of the case.

Penalties

In respect of an offence under section 19, the penalties are as follows:

Summary Conviction: general penalty under section 102 of the Road Traffic Act 1961.

First Offence: fine of up to €1,000.

Second Offence: (under same section) – fine of up to €2,000.

Third/Subsequent Offence: (under same section within 12 consecutive months) – fine of up to €2,000 and/or a term of imprisonment of up to three months.

Disqualification:

Ancillary Disqualification: a first conviction under section 19 does not carry a mandatory disqualification: however, it is open to the court to make an ancillary disqualification order on particular facts of case.

DISPLAY OF NCT DISC REQUIREMENT – ARTICLE 3 OF THE ROAD TRAFFIC (DISPLAY OF TEST DISC) REGUALTIONS 2009

Article 3 of the Road Traffic (Display of Test Disc) Regulations 2009[83] also sets out a requirement to the effect that a NCT disc must be displayed on the front windscreen of relevant vehicle, although this does not appear to be a penal offence. These regulations should be read in conjunction with the Road Traffic (National Car Test) Regulations 2009,[84] and practitioners should note that the 2009 regulations

---

[83] S.I. No.548/2009, Road Traffic (Display of Test Disc) Regulations 2009.
[84] S.I. No.567/2009, Road Traffic (National Car Test) Regulations 2009.

repeal and replace the Road Traffic (National Car Test) Regulations 2003 (as amended).[85]

Practitioners should also note that section 92 of the Road Traffic Act 2010[86] amends section 33 of the Road Traffic Act 1961 so that a test for a certificate of competency can not be carried out in a vehicle which does not display a valid NCT disc on its front windscreen.

USING A VEHICLE WITHOUT A CERTIFICATE OF ROAD WORTHINESS – ARTICLE 19 OF THE EUROPEAN COMMUNITIES (VEHICLE TESTING) REGULATIONS 2004

Private vehicles which are four years old are required to complete the NCT every two years to ensure that they comply with all safety regulations. Commercial and public service vehicles[87] like goods vehicles, including HGVs, buses, trucks, large trailers, ambulances, and cars designed to carry more than eight passengers are required to undergo a Commercial Vehicle Test (more commonly known as a Department of the Environment Certificate of Road Worthiness (DOE cert), to ensure that the vehicle is roadworthy. All qualifying commercial vehicles must be tested when they are one year old and every year thereafter.[88]

Although there is presently no requirement to display a DOE cert on a commercial/public service vehicle, all commercial vehicles are required to undergo the examination and obtain his/her certificate of roadworthiness.

Article 19 of the European Communities (Vehicle Testing) Regulations 2004[89] clearly sets out that it is a criminal offence:

> 'To drive or otherwise cause to be used (in a public place) a vehicle to which these Regulations apply unless there is in force in respect of the vehicle a Certificate of Roadworthiness.'

Both the user and the owner of vehicle are liable to prosecution under this regulation.[90] It is a defence if the owner can demonstrate that the vehicle was used without his/her consent.[91] In a prosecution for an

---

[85] Art.6, S.I. No.405/2003 required that a NCT disc be displayed on a vehicle but it was not a penal offence.
[86] When same section comes into operation.
[87] Art.3, S.I. No.771/2004, European Communities (Vehicle Testing) Regulations 2004.
[88] Ibid., art.4.
[89] Ibid.
[90] Ibid., art.19(2).
[91] Ibid., art.19(3).

offence contrary to regulation 19, it is presumed until the contrary is shown that vehicle was used in contravention of regulation 19.[92]

Under article 20, a Garda who has reasonable grounds for believing that a vehicle they have observed being used in a public place requires a certificate of roadworthiness, can within one month of so observing, make a lawful demand of the user and/or owner of the vehicle to produce a certificate of roadworthiness there and then, or within 10 days at a nominated Garda station. It is a criminal offence if an individual:[93] fails to produce a valid Certificate of Roadworthiness, having been lawfully requested, within 10 days at a nominated Garda station,[94] or having produced a valid Certificate of Roadworthiness, upon lawful request, fails to allow a Garda to read/examine produced licence,[95] or having produced a valid Certificate of Roadworthiness, upon lawful request and having failed to allow a Garda to read/examine produced licence, further fails to give a true name and address upon lawful request.[96]

It is presumed, until the contrary is shown, that the vehicle was used without a valid certificate once there is evidence that a lawful demand was made for the certificate to be produced.[97] Both the owner and the user of the vehicle can be guilty of an offence under regulations 19 and 20. It is a good defence for the owner of the vehicle to demonstrate that they were not driving the vehicle and that the vehicle was being driven without his/her consent.[98]

Only an offence contrary to regulation 19 incurs penalty points (five) upon conviction,[99] but given that there is no requirement to display a DOE disk, it is likely that an individual will only be charged with an offence contrary to regulation 19 if they fail to produce their certificate within 10 days. An individual who fails to allow the Gardaí to read a produced certificate, or who gives a Garda a false/misleading name and address can be arrested without charge.[100]

---

[92] *Ibid.*, art.19(4).
[93] *Ibid.*, art.20(1).
[94] *Ibid.*, art.20(2).
[95] *Ibid.*, art.20(3).
[96] *Ibid.*, art.20(4).
[97] *Ibid.*, art.19(4).
[98] *Ibid.*, art.19(3).
[99] See Reference 1 of Pt.8 of Sch.1, of Road Traffic Act 2002 as inserted by s.16, Road Traffic Act 2006 and also S.I. No.149/2009 – Road Traffic Act 2002 (Commencement of Certain Provisions) (Penalty Points) Order 2009 – which came into effect on 1 May 2009.
[100] Art.20(5), S.I. 771/2004 European Communities (Vehicle Testing) Regulations 2004.

Gardaí also have a power under regulation 21 to inspect a vehicle for the purposes of forming an opinion as to its roadworthiness.

Penalties

In respect of offence under these regulations, the penalties are as follows:

Summary Offence: fine of up to €3,000 and/or a term of imprisonment of up to three months.[101]

Penalty Points: Five (upon conviction for breach of regulation 19).[102] The offence doesn't carry option of paying fixed penalty notice. Section 2(8) of the Road Traffic Act 2002 applies if court imposes an ancillary disqualification order under section 27 of the Road Traffic Act 1961. In those circumstances, penalty points will not be endorsed on the licence record.

Disqualification:

Ancillary Disqualification: a first conviction under regulation 19 does not carry a mandatory disqualification. However, it is open to the court to make an ancillary disqualification order on the particular facts of the case.

Mandatory Disqualification: if a defendant is convicted of a second or subsequent conviction under this section within a three year period, a consequential disqualification period of not less than one year will apply.[103]

Penalty Point Disqualification: if a defendant accrues 12 penalty points upon conviction for this offence, then they will be disqualified under the administrative procedure set out under section 3 of the Road Traffic Act 2002.

---

[101] *Ibid.*, art.22.

[102] See Reference 1 of Pt.8 of Sch.1 of Road Traffic Act 2002 as inserted by s.16, Road Traffic Act 2006 and also S.I. No.149/2009 — Road Traffic Act 2002 (Commencement of Certain Provisions) (Penalty Points) Order 2009 – which came into effect on 1 May 2009.

[103] S.26, Road Traffic Act 1961, as substituted by s.26, Road Traffic Act 1994 and amended by s.6(1)(e), Road Traffic Act 2006.

CHAPTER 6

Motor Vehicle Insurance

This chapter relates to motor insurance offences. Practitioners should note that in practical terms, whatever road traffic summonses are before the court, one of the court's primary concerns will be to know that the defendant had a valid policy of insurance at the time of the alleged offence and it is often a question a Judge may ask a defendant directly. Irrespective of what charges are before the court, a defendant should always be advised to bring their original insurance certificate with them to court.

The offence of driving without a valid policy of insurance is strictly interpreted by the court. Generally speaking, unless a defendant has a valid insurance policy which specifically covers them to drive the vehicle in question at the time and date of the offence, they will be guilty of an offence, irrespective of any honest but mistaken belief they may have held that they were insured. Furthermore, if a defendant is disqualified from driving at the date of the offence, or if they have obtained a policy of insurance through fraud or misrepresentation, that policy will be void and of no effect. The prosecution will always be afforded the opportunity to make inquiries with the insurance provider to verify that a valid insurance policy was in effect and a defendant must be so advised.

This chapter will deal with:

(a) the offence of driving without a valid insurance policy (or guarantee);

(b) the offence of obtaining a Certificate of Insurance through fraud;

(c) the requirements in respect of producing an Insurance Certificate to Gardaí;

(f) the obligation to deliver up an Insurance Certificate;

(g) the requirement to display a valid insurance disc on the vehicle.

Obligation to be Insured or Guaranteed – Section 56 of the Road Traffic Act 1961

Section 56 of the Road Traffic Act 1961[1] provides that a user shall not use a MPV (mechanically-propelled vehicle) in a public place unless either:

(a) an approved vehicle insurer, or an exempted person (usually a state sponsored body),[2] would be liable for injury caused by negligent use of vehicle by user;[3] or

(b) there is a valid approved policy of insurance in place covering either the user for any liability for injury caused to any person (exclusive of excepted persons[4]) by negligent use of vehicle.[5]

The issue of what constitutes a valid insurance policy and or valid guarantee against liability for loss/injury can be very complicated.[6] However, generally speaking, an individual must be able to demonstrate to the court that they themselves were insured to drive the specific vehicle under a valid insurance policy[7] which covers the time and date of the offence, or that they were using the vehicle as a servant/agent of the owner and with the express consent of the owner.[8] Generally, a valid third-party motor insurance policy provides the minimum motor insurance policy require by law and will be sufficient for the purposes of section 56 of the Road Traffic Act 1961.

---

[1] As substituted by s.34, Road Traffic Act 2004. Practitioners should read s.34, Road Traffic Act 2004 which sets out substituted s.56 and not the original act: also note art.2, S.I. No.248/2008 European Communities (Road Traffic) Compulsory Insurance) Regulations 2008.

[2] See s.60, Road Traffic Act 1961 as substituted by ss.54 and 55, Road Traffic Act 1968 and relevant statutory instruments.

[3] S.56(1)(a), Road Traffic Act 1961 as substituted by s.34, Road Traffic Act 2004.

[4] S.65(1), Road Traffic Act 1961 (as amended by art.7, S.I. No.347/1992, European Communities (Road Traffic) (Compulsory Insurance) (Amendment) Regulations 1992. See *Delargy v.The Minister for the Environment and Local Government* [2005] IEHC 94.

[5] S.56(1)(b), Road Traffic Act 1961 as substituted by s.34, Road Traffic Act 2004.

[6] See *Delargy v.The Minister for the Environment and Local Government* [2005] IEHC 94 and *Farrell v. Whitty & Others* [2008] IEHC 124; *Smith v. Meade & Ors* [2009] IEHC 99.

[7] Which complies with the requirements of s.56(2), Road Traffic Act 1961 – generally speaking any third party motor insurance policy issued will comply with provisions of s.56(2).

[8] See s.56(7), Road Traffic Act 1961 as substituted by s.34, Road Traffic Act 2004.

There is a presumption under this section that unless and until otherwise shown, the vehicle was used in contravention of section 56,[9] although there must have been a lawful demand made of an individual to produce insurance within 10 days.[10] Depending on the facts of the case, both the user and/or owner of the vehicle can be prosecuted for offences under this section.[11]

The most obvious defence to this charge, apart from a defence that the defendant was not driving the vehicle at the time of the offence, is that the defendant either had a valid certificate of insurance, or comes under a lawful exemption. It is a defence for the owner of the vehicle to demonstrate that the vehicle was being used without his/her consent or authority, and that they had taken all reasonable precautions to prevent its use.[12]

It is also a defence for a user of a vehicle (like an employee) to demonstrate that he/she was using the vehicle as an agent/servant of the owner[13] and under the express order of the owner, unless the user goes beyond the terms of consent given by owner.[14] Where a vehicle is being used with the express consent of the owner, the legal obligation is on the owner to demonstrate to the court that they had a valid policy of insurance for the vehicle in question. If the owner's insurance policy did not cover the particular user to drive the vehicle, but the user was driving with the owner's express consent, then it is the owner who is liable under section 56.

It is a key element of this offence that a lawful demand was made of the user or owner to produce a certificate of insurance within 10 days at a nominated Garda station,[15] and that the defendant failed to so produce: positive evidence to that effect must be adduced by the prosecuting Garda in court.[16] There is a legal presumption that an individual who has been lawfully asked to produce a certificate of insurance at a nominated station within 10 days, failed to so produce, unless and until the defence shows otherwise,[17] although, it is

---

[9] *Ibid.*, s.56(5).
[10] *Ibid.*, s.56(5) and s.69, Road Traffic Act 1961 (as amended).
[11] *Ibid.*, ss.56(4) as substituted by s.34, Road Traffic Act 2004.
[12] *Ibid.*, s.56(6).
[13] S.56(7), Road Traffic Act 1961. In respect of what constitutes a servant under meaning of this Act – see the Supreme Court decision in *Buckley v. Musgrave Brook Bond Ltd* [1969] I.R. 440 also s.118, Road Traffic Act 1961.
[14] *Ibid.*, s.56(7) (as amended).
[15] *Ibid.*, s.56(5) and s.69 (as amended).
[16] See *Stokes v. O'Donnell* [1999] 3 I.R. 218.
[17] See also the provisions of s.69, Road Traffic Act 1961.

a defence to a charge under section 56, if the owner/user of the vehicle was not given ten days to produce a certificate of insurance.[18] It is also a defence if the user can demonstrate that he/she was not driving in a public place.[19]

Section 79 of the Road Traffic Act 1961 exempts pedestrian-controlled vehicles, specified by ministerial regulations, from these insurance provisions. Therefore it is a defence to a charge under section 56 to show that you were using an exempted pedestrian-controlled vehicle.

It is very important for an individual charged under this section to consider the particular contractual terms which may be contained in his/her insurance policy as it may not be sufficient to simply produce an insurance certificate in court (or at a designated Garda station). Gardaí can investigate the validity of the certificate produced with the insurer. If a defendant was disqualified from driving at the date of the offence,[20] or had obtained a certificate of insurance through fraud or misrepresentation,[21] then the policy will be either *void ab initio* or voidable, and the vehicle insurer can indicate to the Gardaí and/or Court that the insurance policy has been voided for breach of contract.

Where an individual believes that the insurance provider has wrongly voided his/her policy, it is open to them to challenge the purported breach of contract in the civil courts (or through arbitration). Practitioners should be aware of provisions of section 64 of the Road Traffic Act 1961 which sets out that it is a criminal offence to obtain a certificate of insurance by fraudulent means.

It is not a defence that an individual genuinely, though mistakenly, believed he/she was insured. However, it might be a mitigating factor (particularly for the purposes of considering whether to impose a disqualification for a first offence[22]), if a defendant can show that (for example):

(a) the vehicle itself was covered by a valid insurance certificate, and they had, honestly, but mistakenly believed, they had the

---

[18] See State *(McDonagh) v. Sheerin* [1981] I.L.R.M. 149.
[19] Under s.56(1), Road Traffic Act 1961, it is clear that vehicle must be being used in a public place for an offence to arise.
[20] Under ss.26, 27 or 28, Road Traffic Act 1961 or s.3 or s.9, Road Traffic Act 2002.
[21] S.64, Road Traffic Act 1961.
[22] There is a discretion not to impose a disqualification or impose a disqualification of less than 2 years for a first offence: see s.26(5)(b), Road Traffic Act 1961 as substituted by s.26, Road Traffic Act 1994 and amended by s.6, Road Traffic Act 2006.

express consent of the owner to drive, or were a named driver on the insurance policy;

(b) that the defendant had a valid motor insurance policy for a different vehicle and had, honestly but mistakenly, believed it covered them to drive other motor vehicles; or

(c) that a valid insurance certificate had lapsed very proximately to the date of the offence without being renewed due to an honest oversight.

Penalties

In respect of offences under section 56(4),[23] the penalties are as follows:

Summary Conviction: fine of up to €5,000[24] and/or a term of imprisonment of up to 6 months.

There is also a provision under section 6(4), Criminal Justice Act 1993 to make a compensation order in respect of any loss or injury determined to have been caused as a result of a breach of section 56(3).

Penalty Points: five (upon conviction).[25]

There is no option to pay a fixed penalty notice. In most cases, a consequential disqualification order is imposed instead of penalty points. Practitioners should note that section 2(8), Road Traffic Act 2002 does not apply to section 56 offences as any disqualification imposed is consequential.

Disqualification:

Consequential Disqualification:

First Offence – two years.[26]

In the circumstances where it is a first offence under section 56, a court may decline to make a consequential disqualification order, or make a disqualification

---

[23] See s.56(4), Road Traffic Act as substituted by s.34, Road Traffic Act 1994 and s.18, Road Traffic Act 2006.

[24] See s.18, Table, Pt.1 – Reference 17, Road Traffic Act 2006.

[25] See Reference 12 of Pt.1 of Sch.1 of Road Traffic Act 2002 and also S.I. No.214/2003 — Road Traffic Act 2002 (Commencement) Order 2003 – which came into effect on 1 June 2003.

[26] See s.26(5)(a), Road Traffic Act 1961 as substituted by s.26, Road Traffic Act 1994 and amended by s.6, Road Traffic Act 2006.

order of less than two years,[27] but only where a special reason has been provided to the court to justify not applying the consequential disqualification order. If a disqualification order is not imposed of a first offence, than penalty points are imposed instead.

Second or Subsequent Offence (within three years) not less than four years.[28] Obviously, it is open to the court to impose a longer disqualification period on the particular facts of the case.

Penalty Point Disqualification: if a defendant accrues 12 penalty points upon conviction for this offence, then they will be disqualified under the administrative procedure set out under section 3 of the Road Traffic Act 2002.

Where an individual charged with a section 56 offence, they almost invariably find themselves also charged with an offence contrary to section 69 of the Road Traffic Act 1961. If a Garda believes that a vehicle is being used in contravention of this section, they are authorised to detain or remove the vehicle – see section 41 of the Road Traffic Act 1994.

FINE IN LIEU OF DAMAGES AND IMPRISONMENT ADDITION TO DAMAGES – SECTION 57 OF THE ROAD TRAFFIC ACT 1961

Practitioners should be aware that following the Supreme Court decision in *Cullen v. AG*,[29] subsections (1) and (2) of section 57 of the Road Traffic Act 1961 were held to be unconstitutional and void.

However, section 57(3) is still in force and provides that where damages are awarded in a civil action against a person convicted of an offence under section 56 in respect of loss/injury to a person or property, and if same damages are not paid within 14 days (or such longer period as the court may determine), the court which made the order can imprison the convicted person until these damages paid for up to six months (whichever is shorter).

---

[27] *Ibid.*, s.26(5)(b) as substituted by s.26, Road Traffic Act 1994 and amended by s.6, Road Traffic Act 2006.
[28] *Ibid.*, s.26(5)(a) as substituted by s.26, Road Traffic Act 1994 and amended by s.6, Road Traffic Act 2006.
[29] *Cullen v. AG* [1979] I.R. 394.

Obtaining a Certificate of Insurance Through Fraud – Section 64 of the Road Traffic Act 1961

Section 64(1) sets out the following offence of obtaining a certificate of insurance through:

(a) committing any fraud; or

(b) making any false or misleading representation (orally, in writing, or by conduct).

It is an offence[30] for an insurance provider to fail/refuse to comply with a legal written request by the Gardaí to provide any document relating to application for insurance[31] within three months of a lawful request.[32]

This section covers offences which arise where an individual has taken deliberate steps to fraudulently obtain a certificate of insurance. The fraud or misrepresentation must be in respect of a material fact which would influence a prudent insurer's judgement as to whether to offer a policy of insurance, or the premium to fix on such a policy of insurance.

It is a matter for the prosecution to prove, by way of expert evidence, that the false or misleading representation was a material fact.[33] It is presumed that any document (like a proposal/application form) relating to an application for an insurance certificate signed by an individual, is so signed, unless and until otherwise shown.[34] An individual will be guilty of an offence under this section if they apply for an insurance certificate using an alternative name or alias, unless they also disclosure his/her legal name to insurance provider at time of the application.[35]

The time limits for the prosecution of this offence are set out in section 48 of the Road Traffic Act 1994 and extend beyond the six-month time period provided for under section 10 of the Petty Session Act 1851. However, there is a maximum time limit of three years after the date of offence to institute summary proceedings.[36]

---

[30] S.64(4)(b), Road Traffic Act 1961 as substituted by s.49, Road Traffic Act 1994.
[31] Documents relating to application for insurance – See s.64(3), Road Traffic Act 1961.
[32] S.64(4)(a), Road Traffic Act 1961 as substituted by s.49, Road Traffic Act 1994.
[33] See *Chariot Inns Limited v. Assicurazioni Generali* [1981] I.R. 199; *Keenan v. Shield Insurance Co. Ltd* [1987] I.R. 113.
[34] S.64(3)(b), Road Traffic Act 1961.
[35] See *Clark v. Chalmers* (1961) S.L.T. 325.
[36] S.48(3), Road Traffic Act 1994.

Penalties

In respect of offences under section 64,[37] the penalties are as follows:

Summary Conviction:

Subsection (1) – fine of up to €5,000 and/or a term of imprisonment of up to six months.[38]

Subsection (4)

> **First Offence** – fine of up to €1,000.[39]
>
> **Second Offence** (under same section) – fine of up to €2,000.[40]
>
> **Third/Subsequent Offence** (under same section within 12 consecutive months) – fine of up to €2,000 and/or a term of imprisonment of up to three months.[41]

Disqualification:

> **Ancillary Disqualification:** whilst a conviction under section 64 does not carry a mandatory consequential disqualification, it is open to the court to make an ancillary disqualification order (section 27 of the Road Traffic Act 1961) on particular facts of case.

PRODUCTION OF AN INSURANCE CERTIFICATE ON DEMAND – SECTION 69 OF THE ROAD TRAFFIC ACT 1961

This section covers offences relating to failing to produce a certificate of insurance upon lawful demand. Section 69 of the Road Traffic Act 1961[42] sets out the following criminal offences:

(a) upon lawful demand of user of vehicle (within 1 month of date of use of vehicle); failing to produce a certificate of Insurance (or exemption), within 10 days, at nominated Garda station.[43]

---

[37] S.64(2) and s.18, Road Traffic Act 2006.

[38] S.64(2) and s.18, Table, Pt.1, Reference 18, Road Traffic Act 2006.

[39] S.102(a), Road Traffic Act 1961, as amended by s.18(1) – Table – Pt.1 – Reference 20.

[40] *Ibid.*, s.102(b), Road Traffic Act 1961, as amended by s.18(1) – Table – Pt.1 – Reference 21.

[41] *Ibid.*, s.102(c), Road Traffic Act 1961, as amended by s.18(1) – Table – Pt.1 – Reference 22.

[42] As amended by art.6, S.I. No.178/1975, European Communities (Road Traffic) (Compulsory Insurance) Regulations, 1975, s.49, Road Traffic Act 1994, s.23, Road Traffic Act 2002 and s.22, Road Traffic Act 2006.

[43] S.69(1)(a), Road Traffic Act 1961.

(b) upon lawful demand of owner of vehicle (within 3 months of date of use of vehicle); failing to produce a certificate of Insurance (or exemption), within 10 days, at nominated Garda station.[44]

(c) upon producing a Certificate of Insurance, failing/refusing to allow member of Gardaí to read or examine certificate.[45]

(d) having produced a Certificate of Insurance, but having failed/refused to allow the Gardaí to examine the certificate, further failing/refusing to give real name and address upon lawful request from the Gardaí.[46]

(e) upon lawful demand of user of vehicle entering State with vehicle not ordinarily used in the Irish State (or certain designated territories),[47] failing to produce a Certificate of Insurance or other evidence that use of vehicle entering Irish State is covered by Insurance policy – (see section 69A(2)).[48]

If a Garda has formed the opinion that an individual has committed an offence of:

(a) failing/refusing to allow a produced certificate of insurance to be read or examined;[49] or

(b) failing to give a real name and address upon lawful demand; or

(c) giving a name and address which a Garda has reasonable grounds for believing is false or misleading[50]

he may arrest that individual without warrant.[51]

As there are a number of separate charges that may arise under section 69, it is important for a practitioner to have regard to the exact wording of the charge set out – i.e., the precise allegation being made. Consideration should be given to whether the particular facts

---

[44] *Ibid.*, s.69(2)(a) as amended by s.49, Road Traffic Act 1994.
[45] *Ibid.*, s.69(3), Road Traffic Act 1961.
[46] *Ibid.*, s.69(4).
[47] The designated territories set out on s.69A mean the Member States of European Communities, Croatia, Iceland, Norway and Switzerland.
[48] Inserted by art.6 of S.I. No.178/1975 – EC(Road Traffic) (Compulsory Insurance) Regulations 1975; s.69 further amended by S.I. No.463/2001 – European Communities (Road Traffic) Compulsory Insurance) (Amended) Regulations 2001.
[49] *Ibid.*, s.69(3), Road Traffic Act 1961.
[50] *Ibid.*, s.69(4).
[51] *Ibid.*, s.69(5).

set out in the charge sheet/summons, précis and/or statements support the particular charge brought. The most obvious defence to this charge is that the individual did produce a valid certificate of insurance or certificate of exemption within 10 days at his/her nominated Garda station, which they allowed Gardaí to examine.

There is a legal presumption that an individual who has been lawfully asked to produce a certificate of insurance at a nominated station within 10 days, failed to so produce, unless and until the contrary is shown.[52] However, where an individual instructs that they did produce a certificate of insurance within 10 days, and the prosecuting Garda advised that he has no record of certificate being produced, production of the valid certificate of insurance in court is usually sufficient to satisfy the Judge.

Strictly speaking, as this offence relates to failing to produce certificate within 10 days, a defendant does not rebut the presumption under section 69 (that they did not produce certificate within 10 days) by subsequently producing it in court: however, the court's main concern is to ensure that the user/owner was properly insured at the time of the alleged offence, and if satisfactory evidence of same is adduced in court the charge is generally struck out.

This is not the case, however, if the charge before court is that the defendant failed/refused to allow the Gardaí to examine the certificate produced,[53] gave a false or misleading name and address,[54] or refused to comply with a direction to remove a vehicle to a directed place.[55] In these circumstances, producing a valid certificate in court will not generally constitute a sufficient defence to the charge brought.

It is a key element of this offence that a lawful demand was made of the user or owner to produce a certificate of insurance within 10 days at a nominated Garda station, and positive evidence to that effect must be adduced by the prosecuting Garda in court.[56] It is a defence if the owner/user of vehicle was not given 10 days to produce a certificate of insurance;[57] and a complaint cannot be made under section 69 until the expiration of this 10-day period as the

---

[52] *Ibid.*, s.69(2)(b) (as amended).
[53] *Ibid.*, s.69(3).
[54] *Ibid.*, s.69(4).
[55] See s.69(A)(2), Road Traffic Act 1961 as inserted by art.6, S.I. No.178/1975 – EC (Road Traffic) (Compulsory Insurance) Regulations 1975.
[56] See *Stokes v. O'Donnell* [1999] 3 I.R. 218.
[57] See *State (McDonagh) v. Sheerin* [1981] I.L.R.M. 149.

offence is not complete, although as this offence is predominantly prosecuted by summons procedure, it is hard to see how such a defence would routinely arise in practice.

It is a defence if the user can demonstrate that the vehicle was not used by him at all, or not in a public place, or that it he was an agent/servant of the owner and was using vehicle on the express order of owner.[58] It is also a defence if the owner can demonstrate that the vehicle was not used at all, or not in a public place,[59] or that it was not used by him and was used by some other party without his consent, in circumstances where, he had taken all reasonable steps to prevent such use.[60]

Furthermore, section 79 exempts from the insurance provisions pedestrian controlled vehicles specified by ministerial regulations. Therefore it is a defence to a charge under section 69 to show that you were using an exempt pedestrian controlled vehicle.

Penalties

In respect of offences under section 69, the penalties are as follows:

Summary Conviction:

> **First offence** – fine of up to €1,000.[61]

> **Second Offence** (under same section) – fine of up to €2,000.[62]

> **Third/Subsequent Offence** (under same section within 12 consecutive months) – fine of up to €2,000 and/or a term of imprisonment of up to three months.[63]

Section 69A(5) penalties are as follows:

Summary Conviction: – fine of up to €5,000.[64]

Disqualification:

> **Ancillary Disqualification:** whilst a conviction under section 69 does not carry a mandatory consequential disqualification, it is open to the court to make an ancillary disqualification

---

[58] See s.69(1)(c), Road Traffic Act 1961.
[59] Under s.56(1), Road Traffic Act 1961, it is clear that vehicle must be being used in a public place for an offence to arise.
[60] See s.69(2)(c), Road Traffic Act 1961.
[61] *Ibid.*, s.102(a) as amended by s.18(1) – Table – Pt.1 – Reference 20.
[62] *Ibid.*, s.102(b) as amended by s.18(1) – Table – Pt.1 – Reference 21.
[63] *Ibid.*, s.102(c) as amended by s.18(1) – Table – Pt.1 – Reference 22.
[64] *Ibid.*, s.69(A)(5), Road Traffic Act 1961 as inserted by art.6, S.I. No.178/1975 – EC (Road Traffic) (Compulsory Insurance) Regulations 1975.

order (section 27 of the Road Traffic Act 1961) on the particular facts of the case.

PRODUCTION OF INSURANCE OR GUARANTEE – SECTION 73 OF THE ROAD TRAFFIC ACT 2010

Practitioners should note that section 73 of the Road Traffic Act 2010[65] replaces subsections 3–5 of section 69 of the Principal Act in respect of production of insurance certificate. Under substituted section, where an individual:

(a) fails/refuses to allow a produced certificate of insurance to be read or examined they commit an offence and can be lawful demand can be made of them to give their name, address and date of birth;[66] and

(b) fails/refuses to give a real name and/or address and/or date of both upon lawful demand; or

(c) giving a name and/or address and/or date of birth which a Garda has reasonable grounds for believing is false or misleading;[67]

he may arrest that individual without warrant.[68]

OBLIGATION TO DELIVER UP CERTIFICATE – SECTION 70 OF THE ROAD TRAFFIC ACT 1961

Under section 70(1), where a certificate of insurance is terminated or suspended by an insurance provider before its expiration date:

'It is an offence to fail to deliver up the latest certificate of insurance to the insurer within 7 days of termination/suspension of policy.'

Penalties

In respect of offences under section 70, the penalties are as follows:

Summary Conviction: general penalty under section 102 of the Road Traffic Act 1961 applies:

First Offence – fine of up to €1,000.[69]

---

[65] When that section comes into operation.
[66] See s.73(3), Road Traffic Act 2010.
[67] *Ibid.*, s.73(4).
[68] *Ibid.*, s.73(5).
[69] S.102(a), Road Traffic Act 1961 as amended by s.18(1) – Table – Pt.1 – Reference 20.

Second Offence (under same section) – fine of up to €2,000.[70]

Third/Subsequent Offence (under same section within 12 months) – fine of up to €2,000 and/or a term of imprisonment of up to three months.[71]

Disqualification:

Ancillary Disqualification: whilst a conviction under section 70 does not carry a mandatory consequential disqualification, it is open to the court to make an ancillary disqualification order (section 27 of the Road Traffic Act 1961) on the particular facts of the case.

OBLIGATION TO DISPLAY INSURANCE DISC – ARTICLE 5 OF THE ROAD TRAFFIC (INSURANCE DISC) REGULATIONS 1984[72]

Article 5 (as substituted by article 4 of the Road Traffic (Insurance Disc) (Amendment) Regulations 1986[73]) and made under section 11 of the Road Traffic Act 1961) sets out the offence of using a vehicle without displaying a valid insurance disc. Article 5 states that (after 10 days from the authentication of insurance certificate), an individual shall not use a vehicle in a public place without displaying a valid insurance disc on the windscreen, or, in the absence of same, on a conspicuous place near side vehicle.

It is a defence to a charge under article 5, that if the owner of a vehicle can demonstrate that they were not using the vehicle at time of the offence, and that vehicle was being used without their authority or consent.[74]

Article 6 further provides that:

'(1) No one shall, either by writing, drawing or in any other matter alter, deface, mutilate or add anything to any insurance disc for any vehicle, and/or

(2) No one shall exhibit upon any vehicle any insurance disc which has been altered, defaced, mutilated or added to.'

---

[70] *Ibid.*, s.102(b) as amended by s.18(1) – Table – Pt.1 – Reference 21.

[71] *Ibid.*, s.102(c) as amended by s.18(1) – Table – Pt.1 – Reference 22.

[72] S.I. No.355/1984 – RT (Insurance Disc) Regulations 1984 – made under s.11, Road Traffic Act 1961.

[73] S.I. No.227/1986 – RT (Insurance Disc) (Amendment) Regulations 1986 made under s.11, Road Traffic Act 1961.

[74] Art.5(4), S.I. No.355/1984 as substituted by art.4, S.I. No.227/1986.

Penalties

In respect of offences under article 5, the penalties are as follows:

Fixed Charge Penalty: €60 (paid in 28 days),[75] €90 (paid in subsequent 28 days).[76]

Penalty (on conviction) – general penalty under section 102 of the Road Traffic Act 1961 applies.

First Offence – fine of up to €1,000.[77]

Second Offence (under same section) – fine of up to €2,000.[78]

Third/Subsequent Offence (under same section within 12 consecutive months) – fine of up to €2,000 and/or a term of imprisonment of up to three months.[79]

Ancillary Disqualification: a conviction under article 5 does not carry a mandatory disqualification. However, the court may impose an ancillary disqualification order under section 27 of the Road Traffic Act 1961 on the particular facts of the case.

---

[75] Art.5(b)(i) and Sch.2, Pt.1, S.I. No.135/2006.
[76] See s.103(7)(c), Road Traffic Act 1961 and art.5(b)(i) and Sch.2, Pt.1, S.I. No.135/2006.
[77] *Ibid.*, s.102(a) as amended by s.18(1) – Table – Pt.1 – Reference 20.
[78] *Ibid.*, s.102(b) as amended by s.18(1) – Table – Pt.1 – Reference 21.
[79] *Ibid.*, s.102(c) as amended by s.18(1) – Table – Pt.1 – Reference 22.

CHAPTER 7

Duties and Obligations at the Scene of an Accident

This chapter covers a motorist's duties and obligations at the scene of an accident. The principle purpose of these legislative provisions is to address situations where people are involved in 'hit and run' offences, i.e. they have been involved in an accident but have fled the scene before the Gardaí arrive. For obvious reasons, the courts tend to take a dim view of an individual who has been involved in an accident, particularly where someone has suffered a serious injury and leaves the scene of an accident before emergency services arrive.

In making a determination in respect of such offences, the court will examine the defendant's intentions and consider if there was a deliberate attempt to avoid criminal responsibility for other offences under the Road Traffic Acts 1961–2010. Unsurprisingly, individuals charged with offences in respect of leaving the scene of an accident are often charged with other offences like dangerous/careless driving, drink driving, driving without a valid licence or insurance or joyriding. Practitioners need to be cognisant that there is often a reason why the defendant has left the scene without waiting for the Gardaí to arrive.

This chapter will deal with:

(a) the duties at the scene of an accident;

(b) the distinct offences which can arise from a breach of duty at the scene of an accident;

(c) the disqualification orders than can be made;

(d) the power to arrest an individual without a warrant;

(e) the power to enter a place to affect an arrest;

(f) the obligation to provide a breath specimen when vehicle involved in accident;

(g) the obligation on the insured to give notice of an accident;

(h) the obligation on the vehicle user to give notice of an accident;

(i) the obligation to give notice of an accident involving vehicle temporarily in the State;

(j) the obligation to give information as to insurance;

(k) the duty to give information upon a lawful demand.

BREACH OF DUTIES AT THE SCENE OF AN ACCIDENT – SECTION 106 OF THE ROAD TRAFFIC ACT 1961

Section 106 of the Road Traffic Act 1961[1] sets out the general duties and obligations which apply to the driver/person in charge of a vehicle at the scene of an accident (in a public place) which causes injury to any member of the public or damage to any property. These duties apply to the driver of any vehicle involved in an accident, irrespective of whether his/her vehicle caused an accident and/or injury or damage.

Any driver/other person in charge (if the driver is dead/incapacitated)[2] of the vehicle involved in an accident where an injury occurs to any person or property must:

(a) stop his/her vehicle after the accident;[3]

(b) keep his/her vehicle at or near the accident scene for such time as is reasonable in all the circumstances;[4]

(c) give on demand all appropriate information (subsection (4)) to the Gardaí, or other authorised person (subsection (5));[5]

(d) if an injury is caused to property, other than the driver's own property, or to any person other than driver – and information is not given to a Garda (or authorised person) at the scene of accident, report same information to a member of the Gardaí as soon as possible, even if the driver/other person in charge has to attend his/her nearest convenient Garda station to so report.[6]

---

[1] As amended by s.6, Road Traffic Act 1968 and s.45, Road Traffic Act 1994.
[2] S.106(1), Road Traffic Act 1961.
[3] *Ibid.*, s.106(1)(a).
[4] *Ibid.*, s.106(1)(b).
[5] *Ibid.*, s.106(1)(c).
[6] *Ibid.*, s.106(1)(d) as substituted by s.6, Road Traffic Act 1968.

The above duties must be complied with where, as a result of an accident/occurrence on a public road, any person is injured or any property is damaged, regardless of whether a vehicle involved was an MPV or any other kind of vehicle.[7]

There are a number of distinct offences created under this section, and a driver/person in charge can be charged with more than one offence under section 106(1). Indeed, an individual could find themselves facing separate charges of failing to stop *and* leaving the scene of an accident *and* failing to give the requisite information to a Garda, either at the scene or as soon as possible, all arising out of the same incident.

It is important for practitioners to have regard to the exact wording of the charge set out and to consider whether the particular facts set out by the prosecution support the charge(s) brought: as with all RTA offences, where more than one offence is created by a particular section, the summons has to specify the particular offence or offences alleged rather than simply state that an offence contrary to section 106 had occurred.

One of the key elements of the offence is that injury must have occurred to a person or property, and the prosecution must be able to demonstrate that the injury/damage caused was as a result of accident involving the defendant's vehicle, though the prosecution does not have to show that any person charged under this section had any responsibility or culpability for injury/damage caused.[8] If the accident did not involve the defendant's vehicle, there is no obligation under section 106 to stop and remain at the scene.

A possible defence to a charge under this section may arise if an individual can demonstrate that they were unaware that an accident involving their vehicle had occurred at all.[9] Although if a defendant can successfully demonstrate that they were unaware there had been in an accident, notwithstanding positive evidence before the court that same accident had resulted in injury to another person or property, then it is very likely that as a result of raising such a defence, they might instead face charges of dangerous driving,[10] careless

---

[7] *Ibid.*, s.106(1) as substituted by s.6, Road Traffic Act 1968.
[8] *Ibid.*, s.106(1) as substituted by s.6, Road Traffic Act 1968.
[9] See *Hampson v. Powell* [1970] 1 All E.R. 929, where it was held that the knowledge of the driver was a necessary ingredient of the offence.
[10] *Ibid.*, s.53; see also s.69, Road Traffic Act 2010 – when same section comes into operation.

driving,[11] or at the very least driving without due care or attention.[12] If the hearing takes place some time after the alleged incident, further summary charges may be statute-barred (the complaint not been made within the statutory time limit) but this would not preclude a charge of dangerous driving.

Certainly, if a defendant accepts that an accident occurred involving his/her vehicle, it will not be a defence to say that they believed no injury or damage occurred in the circumstances where they failed to stop and wait at the scene of the accident Although arguably such a defence may be advanced if an individual stopped their vehicle and having taken all reasonable steps to investigate situation, left the scene honestly believing that no injury or damage had occurred.

In a case where an individual is charged with failing to report the accident/give information as soon as possible after the accident, the onus is on the defendant to demonstrate where and when they reported the accident, and that the report was made with all reasonable expediency, as this is information peculiarly within the defendant's own knowledge. It is not a defence to state that no lawful demand was made of the defendant to provide information, that no one at the scene sought information,[13] or that there was no one else present. The driver's duty to advise a member of the Gardaí that an accident has taken place can only be satisfied by actually advising a member of the Gardaí (or other authorised person) of such an occurrence.

Where a Garda reasonably believes that a vehicle was involved in an accident causing injury to a person or property, and the Garda is unaware of where same vehicle is being kept, a lawful demand can be made of the vehicle's owner to provide such knowledge,[14] and it will be an offence for any such owner to fail to provide the requested information.[15] A Garda can arrest someone without warrant who, in their opinion, is committing/has committed an offence under subsection (3).[16]

---

[11] *Ibid.*, s.52; see also s.69, Road Traffic Act 2010 – when same section comes into operation.

[12] *Ibid.*, s.51, Road Traffic Act 1961; see also s.69, Road Traffic Act 2010 – when same section comes into operation.

[13] See *Peek v. Towle* [1945] 2 All E.R. 611.

[14] S.106(2), Road Traffic Act 1961.

[15] *Ibid.*, s.106(3).

[16] *Ibid.*, s.106(3)(A) as inserted by s.45, Road Traffic Act 1994.

Subsection (4) sets out the details of the 'appropriate information' required as:

(a) name and address of driver/other person in charge of vehicle;

(b) name and address of owner (if different);

(c) licence number;

(d) particulars of insurance.

A 'person authorised to demand information' is:

(a) any injured person, or if the injured person is dead or incapacitated, the other person in charge of injured person;[17]

(b) any owner of damaged property, or if the owner is dead or incapacitated, the other person in charge of property;[18]

(c) where there is no person authorised under (a) or (b) above present, any other person present when the injury/damage occurred who is not an employer/employee of the person required to give such information.[19]

Penalties

In respect of an offence under section 106, the penalties are as follows:

Summary Conviction:

Where injury caused to a person – fine of up to €2,000 and/or a term of imprisonment of up to six months.[20]

Where no injury is caused to a person – fine of up to €1,000 and/ or a term of imprisonment of up to three months.[21]

Penalty Points: five (upon conviction).[22]

The offence does not carry the option of paying a fixed penalty notice. Section 2(8) of the Road Traffic Act 2002 applies if the court imposes an Ancillary Disqualification

---

[17] *Ibid.,* s.106(5)(a).
[18] *Ibid.,* s.106(5)(b).
[19] *Ibid.,* s.106(5)(c).
[20] *Ibid.,* s.103(3)(a) as amended by s.18, Road Traffic Act 2006.
[21] *Ibid.,* s.103(3)(a) as amended by s.18, Road Traffic Act 2006.
[22] See Reference 14 of Pt.1 of Sch.4, Road Traffic Act 2002 and also S.I. No.134/2006 – Road Traffic Act 2002 (Commencement of Certain Provisions) Order 2006 – which came into effect on 3 June 2006.

Order under section 27 of the Road Traffic Act 1961. In those circumstances, penalty points will not be endorsed on licence record.

Disqualification:

Consequential Disqualification will be made in circumstances where:

(a) the defendant failed to stop (subsection (1)(a), or remain at the scene of the accident (subsection (1)(b); **and**

(b) injury was caused to another person; **and**

(c) an MPV was involved in the occurrence of same injury; **and**

(d) the convicted defendant was driving the vehicle which caused the injury.

First Offence: minimum four years' disqualification.

Second/Subsequent Offence (same section): minimum six years' disqualification.[23]

Where a consequential disqualification is imposed under the above criteria, the court shall, or may (where the court has the discretion not to impose an additional certificate condition on the grounds of 'special reasons') disqualify an individual for a specified period set above **and** until a certificate of competency[24] and/or fitness[25] is produced.[26] In those circumstances, disqualification is not lifted upon the expiration of a specified period , this is only the first condition. An individual must, upon the expiration of the specified period, or at such later date as is possible, produce the required certificate before the licence can be restored.

Ancillary Disqualification: where an offence under this section does not carry a mandatory disqualification, it is open to the court to make an Ancillary Disqualification Order on the particular facts of the case.

Penalty Point Disqualification: if a defendant accrues 12 penalty points upon conviction for this offence, then they will be

---

[23] *Ibid.*, s.26(4) as substituted by s.26, Road Traffic Act 1994 and amended by s.6, Road Traffic Act 2006.

[24] *Ibid.*, s.33 as amended by s.10, Road Traffic Act 2006.

[25] *Ibid.*, s.34 as amended by s.10, Road Traffic Act 2006.

[26] *Ibid.*, s.26(3) as substituted by s.26, Road Traffic Act 1994 and amended by s.6, Road Traffic Act 2006.

disqualified under the administrative procedure set out under section 3 of the Road Traffic Act 2002.

POWER TO ARREST WITHOUT WARRANT – SECTION 45 OF THE ROAD TRAFFIC ACT 1994

Subsection (3A)[27] states that where, in the opinion of a member of the Gardaí, a person is committing, or has committed and offence under subsection (1) in circumstances where:

(a) an individual failed to stop,[28] or failed to remain at the scene of an accident;[29] AND

(b) injury was caused to another person; AND

(c) an MPV was involved in occurrence of same injury; AND

(d) an individual was driving the vehicle which caused injury,

the Garda has the power to arrest that person without a warrant.

POWER TO ENTER A PLACE TO AFFECT ARREST – SECTION 39 OF THE ROAD TRAFFIC ACT 1994

Under section 39 of the Road Traffic Act 1994, a member of the Gardaí can, for the purposes of affecting an arrest under subsection (3A) above:

(a) enter, without a warrant, and with reasonable force necessary;

(b) any place (including a dwelling);

(c) where a person is or where a Garda has reasonable cause to suspect a person is;

(d) however, where the place is a dwelling, the Garda must have observed the person to have entered same dwelling.[30]

OBLIGATION TO PROVIDE A PRELIMINARY BREATH SPECIMEN WHEN A VEHICLE IS IN AN ACCIDENT – SECTION 12 OF THE ROAD TRAFFIC ACT 1994

Under section 12 of the Road Traffic Act 1994,[31] if a Garda forms the opinion that an individual is or has, been involved in a collision with

---

[27] As inserted by s.45, Road Traffic Act 1994.
[28] S.106(1)(a), Road Traffic Act 1961.
[29] *Ibid.*
[30] S.39(1), Road Traffic Act 1994.
[31] As substituted by s.3, Road Traffic Act 2003.

driving a vehicle,[32] that Garda may require that the individual:

'(i) provides a breath-test sample there,[33] or in the vicinity of the public place concerned,[34] or

(ii) if he does not have apparatus to conduct breath test, remain at the place in presence of a member of the Gardaí (for a period of no more than 1 hour) until apparatus becomes available,[35]'

If an individual refuses/fails to comply immediately with a lawful requirement under this section, or a lawful requirement indicated by Garda, they will be guilty of an offence[36] and may be arrested without a warrant.[37]

Again, the Garda's powers to require a person to provide a breath test sample are based upon the Garda having formed an opinion that the individual is either intoxicated, has committed a road traffic offence or has been involved in a road traffic accident. If an individual is to be breathalysed on the basis of a Garda's opinion, positive evidence should be adduced as to how and why the Garda formed this opinion.[38]

Penalties

In respect of an offence contrary to section 12 of the Road Traffic Act 1994, the following penalties apply:

Summary Conviction: fine of up to €5,000 and/or a term of imprisonment of up to six months.[39]

OBLIGATION TO PROVIDE A PRELIMINARY BREATH SPECIMEN WHEN A VEHICLE IS IN AN ACCIDENT – SECTION 9 OF THE ROAD TRAFFIC ACT 2010

Section 12 of the Road Traffic Act 1994 is repealed by section 33 of the Road Traffic Act 2010 and replaced by section 9 of the Road Traffic Act.[40] This provision sets out that if a Garda forms the opinion that

---

[32] S.12(1)(b), Road Traffic Act 1994 as substituted by s.3, Road Traffic Act 2003.
[33] *Ibid.*, s.12(2)(a) as substituted by s.3, Road Traffic Act 2003.
[34] *Ibid.*, s.12(2)(b) as substituted by s.3, Road Traffic Act 2003.
[35] *Ibid.*, s.12(2)(c) as substituted by s.3, Road Traffic Act 2003.
[36] *Ibid.*, s.12(3) as substituted by s.3, Road Traffic Act 2003.
[37] *Ibid.*, s.12(4) as substituted by s.3, Road Traffic Act 2003.
[38] See Chapter 10 on Drink Driving.
[39] S.12(3), Road Traffic Act 1994 as substituted by s.3, Road Traffic Act 2003 and amended by s.18, Table, Pt.4, Road Traffic Act 2006.
[40] When ss.9 and 33 come into operation.

a person in charge of a vehicle in a public place:

(a) has consumed intoxicating liquor;

(b) has committed a road traffic offence (other than drink driving offence) or;

(c) has been involved in a road traffic collision;[41]

or attends at an accident (in public place) resulting in injury to any person and involving the defendant's vehicle,[42] that Garda may require that the person in charge of the vehicle provides a breath-test sample, either there[43] or at a place in the vicinity of the public place concerned,[44] or if he does not have apparatus to conduct breath test, remain at the place in presence of a member of Garda (for a period of no more than 1 hour) until such an apparatus becomes available.[45]

If a defendant refuses/fails to comply immediately with a lawful requirement under this section, or a lawful requirement indicated by Garda, they will be guilty of an offence[46] and may be arrested without warrant.[47] A Garda shall not make a lawful request of any person to provide a preliminary specimen if Garda is of opinion that such person is, as a result of an accident, incapable of complying with such a request.[48]

Penalties

In respect of an offence contrary to section 9 of the Road Traffic Act 2010 the following penalties apply;

Summary Conviction: fine of up to €5,000 and/or term of imprisonment of up to 6 months.[49]

Disqualification: whilst a conviction does not carry a mandatory disqualification, theoretically, it would open to the court to make an ancillary disqualification order under section 27 of the Road Traffic Act 1961 on the particular facts of case. However, someone who fails to provide a specimen under this section

---

[41] S.9(1)(a), Road Traffic Act 2010, when same section comes into operation.
[42] Ibid., s.9(1)(b) when same section comes into operation.
[43] Ibid., s.9(i) when same section comes into operation.
[44] Ibid., s.9(ii) when same section comes into operation.
[45] Ibid., s.9(iii) when same section comes into operation.
[46] Ibid., s.9(3) when same section comes into operation.
[47] Ibid., s.9(4) when same section comes into operation.
[48] Ibid., s.9(2) when same section comes into operation.
[49] Ibid., s.9(3) when same section comes into operation.

will be arrested and brought to a Garda station where section 10 of the Road Traffic Act 2010 would be invoked.[50]

OBLIGATION ON INSURED OR PRINCIPLE DEBTOR TO GIVE NOTICE OF AN ACCIDENT – SECTION 71 OF THE ROAD TRAFFIC ACT 1961

Section 71 of the Road Traffic Act 1961 sets out that:

'Where an accident occurs, the insured party (or principle debtor) must give the insurer notice of same accident in writing either;

(a) as soon as practicable after the accident occurs; or

(b) within 48 hours of be coming aware the accident occurred (if not present)

unless the approved policy of insurance contains a provision relieving the insured person of an obligation to give the notice set out in this section.[51]'

Penalties

In respect of offences under section 71, the penalties are as follows:

Summary Conviction:

First Offence – fine of up to €1,000.[52]

Second Offence (under same section) – fine of up to €2,000.[53]

Third/Subsequent Offence (under same section within 12 months) – fine of up to €2,000 and/or a term of imprisonment of up to three months.[54]

Disqualification: whilst a conviction under section 71 does not carry a mandatory consequential disqualification, it is open to the court to make an ancillary disqualification order (section 27 of the Road Traffic Act 1961) on the particular facts of the case.

OBLIGATION ON THE VEHICLE USER TO GIVE NOTICE OF THE ACCIDENT – SECTION 72 OF THE ROAD TRAFFIC ACT 1961

Section 72(1) sets out that:

'Where an accident occurs the user must given the insured party notice of same accident, as soon as practicable after the accident occurs, unless accident occurs in the presence of the insured person.'

---

[50] See also Chapter 10.
[51] S.71, Road Traffic Act 1961.
[52] S.102(a), Road Traffic Act 1961, as amended by s.18(1) – Table – Pt.1 – Reference 20.
[53] *Ibid.*, s.102(b) as amended by s.18(1) – Table – Pt.1 – Reference 21.
[54] *Ibid.*, s.102(c) as amended by s.18(1) – Table – Pt.1 – Reference 22.

The user is also obligated, upon demand, to give the insured person such full particulars in respect of the accident as might be reasonably within his/her knowledge, and might be reasonably required by the insured person.

NOTICE OF AN ACCIDENT INVOLVING A VEHICLE TEMPORARILY IN THE STATE – SECTION 72A OF THE ROAD TRAFFIC ACT 1961

Under section 72A,[55] there is an obligation on users of foreign-registered vehicles (from one of designated territories) involved in an accident to provide the Motor Insurers' Bureau of Ireland with full particulars of the accident, and full particulars in respect of the territory in which the vehicle normally based along with the registration and insurance details of the motor vehicle.[56]

Penalties

In respect of offences under section 72, the penalties are as follows:

Summary Conviction:

First Offence – fine of up to €1,000.[57]

Second Offence (under same section) – fine of up to €2,000.[58]

Third/Subsequent Offence (under same section within 12 consecutive months) – fine of up to €2,000 and/or a term of imprisonment of up to three months.[59]

Disqualification:

Ancillary Disqualification: whilst a conviction under section 72 does not carry a mandatory consequential disqualification, it is open to the court to make an ancillary disqualification order (section 27 of the Road Traffic Act 1961) on the particular facts of the case.

---

[55] As inserted by S.I. No.178/1975, European Communities (Road Traffic) (Compulsory Insurance) Regulations 1975 as amended by S.I. No.347/1992 European Communities (Road Traffic) (Compulsory Insurance) (Amendment) Regulations 1992.

[56] Practitioners should note that non-compliance with s.72A is not a criminal offence and does not carry any criminal penalty.

[57] S.102(a), Road Traffic Act 1961, as amended by s.18(1) – Table – Pt.1 – Reference 20.

[58] *Ibid.*, s.102(b) as amended by s.18(1) – Table – Pt.1 – Reference 21.

[59] *Ibid.*, s.102(c) as amended by s.18(1) – Table – Pt.1 – Reference 22.

OBLIGATION TO GIVE INFORMATION AS TO INSURANCE – SECTION 73 OF THE ROAD TRAFFIC ACT 1961

Section 73(1) sets out that:

'Where an accident has occurred and a party is seeking to make a claim against the insured person, that insured person shall, upon written demand by or on behalf of injured party;

(a) if liability is covered by insurance policy, provide the name and address of insurance provider along with details of particular insurance policy (i.e. policy number etc)

(b) if liability not covered by an insurance policy because same policy was avoided or otherwise cancelled, informer claimant of this fact and provide the name and address of insurance provider

(c) if liability not covered because the party against who claim made was vehicle insurer or exempt party, inform claimant of this fact and provide the details set out in certificate exemption

(d) if liability not covered because party against which claim is made is not covered by one of proceeding set of circumstances, inform claimant of that fact.'

Penalties

In respect of offences under section 73, the penalties are as follows:

First Offence – fine of up to €1,000.[60]

Second Offence (under same section) – fine of up to €2,000.[61]

Third/Subsequent Offence (under same section within 12 consecutive months) – fine of up to €2,000 and/or a term of imprisonment of up to three months.[62]

Disqualification:

Ancillary Disqualification: a conviction under section 73 does not carry a mandatory consequential disqualification. However, it is open to the court to make an ancillary disqualification order (section 27 of the Road Traffic Act 1961) on the particular facts of the case.

---

[60] *Ibid.*, s.102(a) as amended by s.18(1) – Table – Pt.1 – Reference 20.
[61] *Ibid.*, s.102(b) as amended by s.18(1) – Table – Pt.1 – Reference 21.
[62] *Ibid.*, s.102(c) as amended by s.18(1) – Table – Pt.1 – Reference 22.

DUTY TO GIVE INFORMATION ON DEMAND –
SECTION 107 OF THE ROAD TRAFFIC ACT 1961

Under section 107 of the Road Traffic Act 1961,[63] if a Garda forms the opinion that an individual driving a vehicle has committed a road traffic offence:

'That Garda may demand of such person that they provide his/her name and address.

Where a lawful demand is made of an individual under subsection (1), it is an offence for that individual to;

(a) refuse/fail to give his/her name and address; or

(b) give a false or misleading name and address;

If an individual refuses/fails to comply with a lawful demand under this section, or a Garda has reasonable grounds for believing they have given a false name and address, they will be guilty of an offence and may be arrested without warrant.'[64]

Where a Garda has reasonable grounds for believing that:

(a) an offence under the Road Traffic Acts has taken place; and

(b) that a vehicle involved in this offence does not carry its correct registration plate (or identification mark),

the Garda can arrest without warrant any person they have reasonable grounds for believing was using the vehicle when offence was being committed.[65]

Where a Garda has reasonable grounds for believing that an offence under the Road Traffic Acts has taken place, they may require the owner of the vehicle to:

'(a) state whether or not he/she was using the vehicle in question at time of the offence[66]

(b) if he/she was not using vehicle, to give any such information as might be required to identify the user of the vehicle[67]

(c) furthermore, any person, other than the owner of the vehicle can be required to give any such information (in his/her power to give) as might be required to identify the user of the vehicle.[68']

---

[63] As amended by ss.46 and 49, Road Traffic Act 1994.
[64] S.107(1), Road Traffic Act 1961 as amended by s.49, Road Traffic Act 1994.
[65] *Ibid.*, s.107(2) 1 as amended by s.49, Road Traffic Act 1994.
[66] *Ibid.*, s.107(4)(a) as amended by s.49, Road Traffic Act 1994
[67] *Ibid.*, s.107(4)(b) as amended by s.49, Road Traffic Act 1994.
[68] *Ibid.*, s.107(4)(c) as amended by s.49, Road Traffic Act 1994.

Any individual who fails to comply with a lawful request for information shall be guilty of an offence,[69] unless they can demonstrate to the satisfaction of the court that, after taking all reasonable steps to identify the user of the vehicle (or to obtain any information that would identify the user), they did not know identity of the user.[70]

A request for information under subsection (4) can now be made in person or by a written notice served personally or by registered post. An individual has 14 days from date of the personal service or the sending of written notice to comply with request before they can be charged with an offence.[71]

A Garda's powers to require a person to provide his/her name and address, or information so as to identify the user of the vehicle at the time of the offence, is based upon the Garda having formed an opinion that a road traffic offence has been committed. In such circumstances, positive evidence should be adduced by the Garda: firstly, that they had formed such an opinion and secondly, as to how and why they formed this opinion. Positive evidence should also be adduced that the individual upon whom the demand was made was advised by the Garda of the opinion formed and of the statutory basis upon which they were being asked to give the information requested; at the very least where a defendant is failing/refusing to comply with the request, they must be advised that it is a criminal offence to fail/refuse to provide information sought and of the penalties which may apply.[72] If direct evidence such as to satisfy this requirement is not given, then a direction should be sought at the close of the prosecution case.

As stated, it is a defence if the owner of the vehicle can demonstrate that the vehicle was being used without their consent at the time of the offence and that, despite taking all reasonable steps to ascertain the identity of the user, they were unable to furnish information requested because they genuinely did not know who was using the vehicle.[73]

---

[69] *Ibid.*, s.107(3).

[70] *Ibid.*, s.107(4)(b) as amended by s.49, Road Traffic Act 1994.

[71] See s.4A inserted by s.46, Road Traffic Act 1994.

[72] See *DPP v. Shane Canavan* [2007] IEHC 46, unreported, Birmingham J., 1 August 2007 – this is a drink driving case, however, it is presumed that the principles expressed – i.e. that an accused must be advised, if failing to comply with the lawful demand, that it is an offence to fail/refuse to comply and of the applicable penalties under this section.

[73] S.107(4)(b), Road Traffic Act 1961 as amended by s.49, Road Traffic Act 1994.

Penalties

In respect of an offence contrary to section 107 of the Road Traffic Act 1961, the following penalties apply:

Summary Conviction: fine of up to €2,000 and/or a term of imprisonment of up to three months.[74]

Disqualification:

Ancillary Disqualification: a conviction under section 107 does not carry a mandatory consequential disqualification. However, as the offence is one which relates to the use of a motor vehicle, it is open to the court to make an ancillary disqualification order under section 27 of the Road Traffic Act 1961 on the particular facts of the case.

---

[74] *Ibid.*, s.107(5) as amended by s.49, Road Traffic Act 1994.

CHAPTER 8

Dangerous Driving

This chapter covers dangerous driving and related offences. Dangerous driving constitutes one of the most serious road traffic offences as evidenced by the fact that, where an allegation is made in respect of an incident which allegedly results in death or serious injury to another person, the offence will be dealt with on indictment. This text constitutes only a brief overview of the relevant legislation, categories of offences and penalties provided for under the law.

Practitioners should note that the Road Traffic Act 2010 makes significant amendments to this area of law, creating distinct offences of careless driving *simpliciter*, and careless driving causing death or serious harm.

This chapter will deal with the offences of:

(a) driving whilst unfit;

(b) driving without reasonable consideration;

(c) careless driving;

(d) dangerous driving;

(e) driving a dangerously defective vehicle;

(f) parking a vehicle in a dangerous position.

Driving Whilst Unfit – Section 48 of the Road Traffic Act 1961

Section 48 of the Road Traffic Act 1961[1] covers offences relating to driving a vehicle whilst unfit and states that it is a criminal offence

---

[1] As amended by s.3, Road Traffic (Amendment) Act 1984, s.23, Road Traffic Act 2002 and s.18, Road Traffic Act 2006.

for an individual to:

(a) drive a vehicle in a public place when, to his/her knowledge, he/she is suffering from a disease which would be likely to cause his/her driving to be a danger to the public;[2]

(b) drive a vehicle in a public place when, to his/her knowledge, he/she is suffering from a mental or physical disability which would be likely to cause his/her driving to be a danger to the public;[3]

(c) attempt to drive a vehicle in a public place when, to his/her knowledge, he/she is suffering from a disease which would be likely to cause his/her driving to be a danger to the public;[4]

(d) attempt to drive a vehicle in a public place when, to his/her knowledge, he/she is suffering from a mental or physical disability which would be likely to cause his/her driving to be a danger to the public.[5]

There is no definitive or exhaustive list of diseases or disabilities which would render an individual unfit to drive. The key issue is whether the effect of the disease or disability is such as to render the defendant's driving/attempt to drive a danger to the public. The prosecution must be able to demonstrate, by medical evidence or otherwise, the likelihood that members of the public would be endangered by the defendant's driving. Another element of the offence is that the individual must have some knowledge that they were unfit to drive – in the case of certain mental illnesses this may be a considerably difficult element of the offence to prove. In cases where a defendant is judged as mentally incapable of forming the requisite mens rea, then they cannot be guilty of an offence under section 48 and the more appropriate application might be to seek a Special Disqualification Order under section 28 of the Road Traffic Act 1961.

Penalties

In respect of offences under section 48, the penalties are as follows:

First Offence: fine of up to €1,000 and/or a term of imprisonment of up to one month.[6]

---

[2] S.48(1), Road Traffic Act 1961.
[3] *Ibid.*, s.48(1).
[4] *Ibid.*, s.48(1).
[5] *Ibid.*, s.48(1).
[6] *Ibid.*, s.48(2) as substituted by s.3, Road Traffic (Amendment) Act 1984 – penalties

Second/Subsequent Offence: (under same section) – fine of up to €2,000 and/or a term of imprisonment of up to three months.[7]

Penalty Points: three (upon conviction[8])

This offence does not carry the option of paying a fixed penalty notice. Section 2(8) of the Road Traffic Act 2002 applies if the court imposes an ancillary disqualification order under section 27 of the Road Traffic Act 1961. In those circumstances, penalty points will not be endorsed on the licence record.

Disqualification:

Ancillary Disqualification: a first conviction under section 48 does not carry a mandatory disqualification. It is open to the court to make an ancillary disqualification order on the particular facts of the case.

Mandatory Disqualification: if a defendant is convicted of a second or subsequent conviction under this section within a three year period, a consequential disqualification period of not less than one year will apply.

Penalty Point Disqualification: if a defendant accrues 12 penalty points upon conviction for this offence, then they will be disqualified under the administrative procedure set out under section 3 of the Road Traffic Act 2002.

Special Disqualification Order: this can be made by the District Court under section 28 of the Road Traffic Act 1961 upon an application by Garda. Grounds upon which such an application would be made are that the licence holder is by reason of a disease, or a mental or physical disability, either unfit or incompetent to drive. If granted, the order will remain in place until the disqualified person produces a valid certificate of fitness[10] and/or competency.[11]

---

increased by s.18, Table, Pt.1, Reference 6, Road Traffic Act 2006.

[7] *Ibid.*, s.48(2) as substituted by s.3, Road Traffic (Amendment) Act 1984 – penalties increased by s.18, Table, Pt.1, Reference 6, Road Traffic Act 2006.

[8] See Reference 8, Pt.1, Sch.4, Road Traffic Act 2002 – and S.I. No.134/2006, Road Traffic Act 2002 (Commencement of Certain Provisions) Order 2006 – which came into effect on 3 April 2006.

[9] S.26(7), Road Traffic Act 1961, as substituted by s.26, Road Traffic Act 1994 and amended s.6(1)(e), Road Traffic Act 2006 see also s.3, Sch.2, Road Traffic Act (as amended).

[10] *Ibid.*, s.34.

[11] *Ibid.*, s.33.

DRIVING WITHOUT REASONABLE CONSIDERATION – SECTION 51A OF THE ROAD TRAFFIC ACT 1961

This section, which was inserted by section 49 of the Road Traffic Act 1968, deals with the offence of driving a vehicle in a public place without exercising reasonable consideration for other road users.

This offence is more minor in nature than careless driving.[12] There is very little by way of Irish case law in respect of this offence, however, it appears from case law in the UK that there is some necessity for the prosecution to show that the defendant lacked consideration for other road users and that, as a result, another road user (which can include those inside same vehicle) was inconvenienced or nuisanced.[13] This section applies to all drivers in a public place and there is no exemption for members of the Gardaí or emergency vehicles.[14]

Penalties

In respect of offences under section 51A, the penalties are as follows:

Fixed Charge Penalty: €80 (paid in 28 days):[15] €120 (paid in subsequent 28 days).[16]

Upon Conviction:

First Offence – fine of up to €1,000.[17]

Second Offence (under same section) – fine of up to €2,000.[18]

Third/Subsequent Offence (under same section within 12 months) – fine of up to €2,000 and/or a term of imprisonment of up to three months.[19]

Penalty Points: two (payment of fixed charge): four (upon conviction).[20]

Section 2(8) of the Road Traffic Act 2002 applies if the court

---

[12] *Ibid.*, s.52 (as amended), this s. is replaced by s.69, Road Traffic Act 2010, when same s. comes into effect.

[13] See *Pawley v. Whardell* [1965] 2 All E.R. 757; *R v. Griffith* [1998] EWCA Crim. 191; and *Dilkes v. Bowman Shaw* (1981) R.T.R. 4.

[14] See s.27, Road Traffic Act 2004 in respect of exemptions for emergency vehicles – the provisions of s.27 only applies where the driving does not endanger the safety of road users.

[15] Art.5(a)(i) and Pt.1, Sch.1, S.I. No.135/2006.

[16] See s.103(7)(c), Road Traffic Act 1961 and art.5(a)(i) and Sch.1, Pt.1 of S.I. No.135/2006.

[17] *Ibid.*, s.102(a) as amended by s.18(1) – Table – Pt.1 – Reference 20.

[18] *Ibid.*, s.102(b) as amended by s.18(1) – Table – Pt.1 – Reference 21.

[19] *Ibid.*, s.102(c) as amended by s.18(1) – Table – Pt.1 – Reference 22.

[20] See Reference 17 of Pt.1, Sch.1, Road Traffic Act 2002 as inserted by s.22, Road

imposes an ancillary disqualification order under section 27 of the Road Traffic Act 1961 – in those circumstances, penalty points will not be endorsed on licence record.

Disqualification:

Ancillary Disqualification: a conviction under section 51(A) does not carry a mandatory disqualification. However, it is open to the court to make an ancillary disqualification order under section 27 of the Road Traffic Act 1961 on the particular facts of the case.

Penalty Point Disqualification: if a defendant accrues 12 penalty points upon conviction for this offence, then they will be disqualified under the administrative procedure set out under section 3 of the Road Traffic Act 2002.

DRIVING WITHOUT REASONABLE CONSIDERATION – SECTION 69 OF THE ROAD TRAFFIC ACT 2010

Practitioners should note that section 51A of the Road Traffic Act 1961[21] is replaced by a new section 51A as inserted by section 69 of the Road Traffic Act 2010.[22] The new offence is identical in substance to section 51A, namely driving a vehicle in a public place without reasonable consideration for other road users.

Penalties

In respect of offences under section 51A (as substituted by section 69 of the Road Traffic Act 2010, the penalties are as follows:

Fixed Charge Penalty: €80 (paid in 28 days):[23] €120 (paid in subsequent 28 days).[24]

Upon Conviction:

First offence – fine of up to €1,000.[25]

Second Offence (under same section) – fine of up to €2,000.[26]

Traffic Act 2004 and also S.I. No.134/2006, Road Traffic Act 2002 (Commencement of Certain Provisions) Order 2006 – which came into effect on 3 April 2006.

[21] As inserted by s.49, Road Traffic Act 1968.

[22] When same section comes into operation.

[23] Art.5(a)(i) and Sch.1, Pt.1, S.I. No.135/2006.

[24] See s.103(7)(c), Road Traffic Act 1961 and art.5(a)(i) and Sch.1, Pt.1, S.I. No.135/2006.

[25] S.102(a), Road Traffic Act 1961, as amended by s.18(1) – Table – Pt.1 – Reference 20.

[26] Ibid., s.102(b) as amended by s.18(1) – Table – Pt.1 – Reference 21.

Third/Subsequent Offence (under same section within 12 consecutive months) – fine of up to €2,000 and/or a term of imprisonment of up to three months.[27]

Penalty Points: two (payment of fixed charge): four (upon conviction).[28]
Section 2(8) of the Road Traffic Act 2002 applies if the court imposes an ancillary disqualification order under section 27 of the Road Traffic Act 1961 – in those circumstances, penalty points will not be endorsed on licence record.

Disqualification:

Ancillary Disqualification: a conviction under section 51A does not carry a mandatory disqualification; however, it is open to the court to make an ancillary disqualification order on the particular facts of the case.

Penalty Point Disqualification: if a defendant accrues 12 penalty points upon conviction for this offence, then they will be disqualified under the administrative procedure set out under section 3 of the Road Traffic Act 2002.

CARELESS DRIVING – SECTION 52 OF THE ROAD TRAFFIC ACT 1961

This section deals with the offence of driving a vehicle in a public place without exercising due care and attention.

The distinction between careless driving as covered by this section and dangerous driving *simpliciter*[29] is not always clear and the charge brought will depend upon the particular facts of the case. Generally speaking, this section covers driving which is bad, incompetent, unskilled or inept as opposed to inherently dangerous. This section applies to all drivers in a public place and there is no exemption for members of the Gardaí or emergency vehicles.[30] Furthermore, a charge under this section can be brought against a learner driver[31] and/or the qualified driver who has failed to properly supervise them.

---

[27] *Ibid.*, s.102(c) as amended by s.18(1) – Table – Pt.1 – Reference 22.
[28] See Reference 17, of Pt.1, Sch.1, Road Traffic Act 2002 as inserted by s.22, Road Traffic Act 2004 and also S.I. No.134/2006 — Road Traffic Act 2002 (Commencement of Certain Provisions) Order 2006 – which came into effect on 3 April 2006.
[29] S.53, Road Traffic Act 1961, will be substituted by s.69, Road Traffic Act 2010, when same section comes into operation.
[30] See s.27, Road Traffic Act 2004 in respect of exemptions for emergency vehicles – practitioners should note that the provisions of s.27 only ever applies where the driving does not endanger the safety of other road users.
[31] *McCrone v. Riding* [1938] 1 All E.R. 137.

The question the court must address is whether the defendant has exercised the requisite standard of care and skill which a reasonably prudent and competent driver would have exercised in the same particular set of circumstances. To secure a conviction under this section, it is not necessary to prove that the defendant was deliberately or recklessly careless in how they drove, it is sufficient simply to prove that they did not exercise due care and attention.[32] If, objectively speaking, the defendant did not exercise proper care and attention, it will not be a defence to argue that they genuinely believed such driving to be appropriate.

It is a defence to a charge of careless driving if an individual can demonstrate they were not driving the vehicle at the time of the alleged offence. It is possible to defend a charge of careless driving on the grounds of automatism[33] (provided that it amounts to a total loss of voluntary control,[34] was not reasonably foreseeable[35] or self-induced): sudden emergency[36] (like perhaps evasive action taken to avoid a collision): unexpected/unforeseen event (sudden engine failure/ lightening strike), or in exceptional circumstances, necessity or duress.[37] However, in all of these cases, it will be a matter for the defence to prove that the particular defence pleaded applies to the facts of the case.[38] Practitioners should be aware that the notice requirement under section 104 of the Road Traffic Act 1961 has been repealed.

Penalties

In respect of offences under section 52, the penalties are as follows:

Summary Conviction – fine of up to €2,000 and/or a term of imprisonment of up to three months.[39]

Penalty Points: five (upon conviction).[40]

---

[32] *Hampson v. Powell* [1970] 1 All E.R. 929.

[33] *R v. Quick* [1973] 3 All E.R. 347 and *O'Brien v. Parker* [1997] 2 I.L.R.M. 170.

[34] *O'Brien v. Parker* [1997] 2 I.L.R.M. 170, where it was held that there are strict limits to be maintained in order for a successful defence to be established. There must be a total destruction of voluntary control on the defendant's part. Impaired, reduced or partial control is not sufficient to maintain the defence.

[35] *Ibid.*

[36] *Simpson v. Peat* [1952] 2 Q.B. 24.

[37] *R v. Miller* [1987] RTR 22 and *R v. Conway* [1989] R.T.R. 35.

[38] *O'Brien v. Parker* [1997] 2 I.L.R.M. 170.

[39] S.52(2), Road Traffic Act 1961 as amended by s.18, Table, Pt.1, Reference 11, Road Traffic Act 2006.

[40] See Reference 8, Pt.1, Sch.1, Road Traffic Act 2002 and also S.I. No.248/2004 – Road Traffic Act 2002 (Commencement of Certain Provisions) Order 2004 – which

The offence does not carry the option of paying a fixed penalty notice. Section 2(8) of the Road Traffic Act 2002 applies if the court imposes an Ancillary Disqualification Order under section 27 of the Road Traffic Act 1961. In those circumstances, penalty points will not be endorsed on licence record.

Disqualification:

Ancillary Disqualification: a first conviction under section 52 does not carry a mandatory disqualification. It is open to the court to make an Ancillary Disqualification Order on the particular facts of the case.

Mandatory Disqualification: if a defendant is convicted of a third or subsequent conviction under this section within a three year period, a consequential disqualification period of not less than one year will apply.[41]

Penalty Point Disqualification: if a defendant accrues 12 penalty points upon conviction for this offence, then they will be disqualified under the administrative procedure set out under section 3 of the Road Traffic Act 2002.

CARELESS DRIVING – SECTION 69(1) OF THE ROAD TRAFFIC ACT 2010

Practitioners should note that section 52 of the Road Traffic Act 1961 is replaced by a new section 52 as inserted by section 69(1) of the Road Traffic Act 2010.[42] This new section creates two separate offences of careless driving:

(a) careless driving which causes death or serious bodily harm;[43]

(b) careless driving *simpliciter.*[44]

The manner of prosecution and penalties which applies depend upon how serious the particular facts are:

(a) careless driving which causes death or serious bodily harm can be tried on indictment or summarily;

---

came into effect on 4 June 2004.

[41] S.26(7), Road Traffic Act 1961, as substituted by s.26, Road Traffic Act 1994 and amended s.6(1)(e), Road Traffic Act 2006 see also s.7, Sch.2, Road Traffic Act (as amended).

[42] When same section comes into operation.

[43] S.52(2)(a), Road Traffic Act 1961, as inserted by s.69(1), Road Traffic Act 2010, when same section comes into operation.

[44] *Ibid.*, s.52(2)(b) as inserted by s.69(1), Road Traffic Act 2010, when same section comes into operation.

It will be a matter for the prosecution to elect the mode of prosecution by way of DPP directions and defendant will have no right of election. The DPP will also be able to direct that charge be dealt with in the District Court on a guilty plea only (section 13 of the Criminal Procedure Act 1967)

(b) any other case of careless driving will be tried summarily.

Again, it will not be a defence to a charge of careless driving to prove that you were driving under the relevant speed limit for your class of vehicle,[45] the issue is whether the speed was appropriate in all the particular circumstances of the case. If a Garda has formed the opinion that an individual has committed a careless driving offence which has resulted in death or serious harm to another person, they may arrest a defendant person without a warrant.[46]

Penalties

In respect of offences under section 52 (as substituted by section 69 of the Road Traffic Act 2010), the penalties are as follows:

Summary Conviction – fine of up to €5,000.[47]

Penalty Points: three (upon summary conviction)[48] – offence does not carry the option of paying a fixed penalty notice.

Indictable Conviction – fine of up to €10,000 and/or a term of imprisonment of up to 2 years.[49]

Disqualification:

Mandatory Disqualification: a conviction under section 52 also carries a mandatory consequential disqualification period of two years for a first offence and not less than four years for a second or subsequent offence within three

---

[45] *Ibid.*, s.52(3) as inserted by s.69(1), Road Traffic Act 2010, when same section comes into operation.

[46] *Ibid.*, s.52(3) as inserted by s.69(1), Road Traffic Act 2010, when same section comes into operation.

[47] *Ibid.*, s.52(2)(b) as inserted by s.69(1), Road Traffic Act 2010, when same section comes into operation.

[48] S.54(a), Road Traffic Act 2010 (when same section comes into operation) substitutes the Careless Driving offence at Reference 9 of Pt.1, Sch.1, Road Traffic Act 2002 for the new Careless Driving (tried summarily) offence contained at s.69, Road Traffic Act 2010 – with new penalty point offence carrying only three and not five penalty points.

[49] S.52(2)(a), Road Traffic Act 1961, as inserted by s.69(1), Road Traffic Act 2010, when same section comes into operation.

years,[50] although it is obviously open to the court to impose a longer disqualification period on the particular facts of the case.

In the case of a conviction for careless driving tried on indictment, there is a mandatory disqualification period of four years for a first offence and six years for a second/subsequent offence AND the court shall, disqualify an individual for a specified period set above AND until a certificate of competency and/or fitness is produced.[51] In those circumstances, the disqualification is not lifted upon the expiration of a specified period alone, this is only the first condition: an individual must, upon the expiration of the specified period, or at such later date as possible produce the required certificate before the licence can be restored.

Practitioners should note that section 65(5)(b) of the Road Traffic Act 2010[52] allows for a judicial discretion, similar to what currently operates in respect of a first conviction for driving without insurance.[53] In the circumstances where it is a first offence of careless driving, tried summarily, a court may decline to make a consequential disqualification order, or make a disqualification order of less than 2 years, but only where a special reason has been provided to the court to justify not applying the consequential disqualification order. If a consequential disqualification order is not imposed for a first offence, than penalty points are imposed instead.

DANGEROUS DRIVING – SECTION 53 OF THE ROAD TRAFFIC ACT 1961

This section sets out the offence of driving a vehicle in a public place at a speed, or in a manner which, having regard to all the circumstances of the case (including the nature, condition and use of the place and the amount of traffic) is dangerous to the public.[54]
A further distinction can be drawn between:

(a) dangerous driving which causes death or serious bodily harm;[55]

---

[50] *Ibid.*, s.26 as substituted by s.65, Road Traffic Act 2010 (when same section comes into operation). The relevant subsection is s.65(4)(a).
[51] *Ibid.*, s.26 as substituted by s.65, Road Traffic Act 2010 (when same section comes into operation). Relevant subsection is s.65(3)(a).
[52] When same section comes into operation.
[53] S.56, Road Traffic Act 1961 (as amended).
[54] *Ibid.*, s.53(1) as amended by s.51, Road Traffic Act 1968.
[55] *Ibid.*, s.53(2)(a).

(b) dangerous driving *simpliciter*.[56]

The manner of prosecution and penalties which apply depend upon how serious the particular facts are:

(a) dangerous driving which causes death or serious bodily harm; This is the most serious offence under section 53 and can be tried on indictment or summarily. It is a matter for the prosecution to elect the mode of prosecution by means of DPP directions and defendant has no right of election. The DPP can also direct that charge be dealt with in the District Court on a guilty plea only (section 13 of the Criminal Procedure Act 1967). Practitioners should be aware that the notice requirement under section 104 of the Principal Act has been repealed

(b) dangerous driving *simpliciter* is a summary offence.

This section applies to all drivers in a public place and there is no exemption for members of the Gardaí or emergency vehicles.[57] What constitutes dangerous driving in any particular case will depend on the particular facts of the case, including the alleged location, condition of vehicle and whether driver under influence of intoxicant, as well as the particular weather and traffic conditions.[58]

It is not a defence to a charge of dangerous driving to prove that you were driving under the relevant speed limit for your class of vehicle,[59] the issue is whether the speed was appropriate in all the particular circumstances of the case. If a Garda has formed the opinion that an individual has committed an offence under section 53, they may arrest a defendant person without a warrant.[60]

The degree of negligence may also vary considerably from case to case: however, generally speaking, the manner of driving must have been such as to have constituted a direct and serious risk of harm to the public and the defendant must be shown to have been somehow at fault in failing to have driven with the standard of care and skill

---

[56] *Ibid.*, s.53(2)(b).

[57] See s.27, Road Traffic Act 2004 in respect of exemptions for emergency vehicles – practitioners should note that the provisions of s.27 only ever applies where the driving does not endanger the safety of other road users.

[58] See *AG v. Fitzgerald* [1964] I.R. 458; *DPP v. Patrick Quinlan* unreported, High Court, Budd J., July 17, 1962; *DPP v. Keith Kirwan* (No. 2), (unreported, High Court, October 28, 2005.

[59] S.53(3), Road Traffic Act 1961 as substituted by s.13, Road Traffic Act 2004.

[60] *Ibid.*, s.53(6) as amended by s.51, Road Traffic Act 1968.

of a competent and prudent driver.[61] Where a judge (or jury in the case of a prosecution on indictment), is of the view that a defendant is not guilty of an offence under dangerous driving,[62] but is guilty of a lesser offence of careless driving,[63] it is open to them to find a defendant guilty of an offence of careless driving instead.[64]

In respect of a charge of dangerous driving causing death or serious bodily harm, practitioners should be cognisant of the fact that the question of causation will be central to any prosecution, particularly in circumstances where no time limit applies as to when death should occur.[65] It is not necessary to show that the dangerous driving was the sole cause of the death/serious bodily injury, it is sufficient to prove that it is one of the causes.[66]

It is a defence to a charge of dangerous driving if an individual can demonstrate they were not driving the vehicle at the time of the alleged offence. Again, it is possible to defend a charge of careless driving on the grounds of: automatism[67] (provided that it amounts to a total loss of voluntary control,[68] was not reasonably foreseeable[69] or self induced); sudden emergency[70] (like perhaps evasive action taken to avoid a collision); unexpected/unforeseen event (sudden engine failure/lightening strike); or in exceptional circumstances, necessity or duress.[71] However, in all of these cases, it will be a matter for the defence to prove that the particular defence pleaded applies to the facts of the case.[72]

Penalties

In respect of offences under section 53, the penalties are as follows:

Summary Conviction – fine of up to €5,000 and/or a term of

---

[61] See *R v. Gosney* [1971] 3 W.L.R. 343.

[62] S.53, Road Traffic Act 1961 (as amended).

[63] *Ibid.*, s.52.

[64] See s.53(4), Road Traffic Act 1961 and also *DPP v. Peter O'Dwyer* [2005] IE CCA 94 and *DPP v. Bridie Shinnors* [2007] IECCA 50.

[65] See also s.38, Criminal Justice Act 1999.

[66] *The People (AG) v. Mathew Gallagher* [1972] I.R. 365.

[67] *R v. Quick* [1973] 3 All E.R. 347 and *O'Brien v. Parker* [1997] 2 I.L.R.M. 170.

[68] *O'Brien v. Parker* [1997] 2 I.L.R.M. 170, where it was held that there are strict limits to be maintained in order for a successful defence to be established. There must be a total destruction of voluntary control on the defendant's part. Impaired, reduced or partial control is not sufficient to maintain the defence.

[69] *O'Brien v. Parker* [1997] 2 I.L.R.M. 170.

[70] *Simpson v. Peat* [1952] 2 Q.B. 24.

[71] *R v. Miller* [1987] RTR 22 and *R v. Conway* [1989] R.T.R. 35.

[72] *O'Brien v. Parker* [1997] 2 I.L.R.M. 170.

imprisonment of up to six months.[73]

Indictable Conviction – fine of up to €20,000 and/or a term of imprisonment of up to 10 years.[74]

Mandatory Disqualification:

Summary Conviction: carries a mandatory consequential disqualification period of two years for a first offence and not less than four years for a second or subsequent offence within three years: although it is obviously open to the court to impose a longer disqualification period on the particular facts of the case.[75]

Conviction on Indictment: carries a mandatory disqualification period of four years for a first offence and six years for a second/subsequent offence.[76] Where a consequential disqualification is imposed upon a conviction for dangerous driving tried on indictment, the court shall, or may (where court has discretion not to impose an additional certificate condition on grounds of 'special reasons') disqualify an individual for a specified period set above AND until a certificate of competency and/or fitness is produced.[77] In those circumstances, the disqualification is not lifted upon the expiration of a specified period alone, this is only the first condition: an individual must, upon the expiration of the specified period, or at such later date as possible produce the required certificate before the licence can be restored.

Practitioners should note that the judicial discretion not to impose a consequential disqualification order of less than two years in the circumstances where it is a first offence under section 53 (tried summarily) has been abolished.[78]

---

[73] S.53(2)(b), Road Traffic Act 1961 as amended by s.18, Table, Pt.1, Reference 13, Road Traffic Act 2006.

[74] *Ibid.*, s.53(2)(a) as amended by s.49, Road Traffic Act 1994 and s.18, Table, Pt.1, Reference 12, Road Traffic Act 2006.

[75] *Ibid.*, s.26(5)(a)(i) as substituted by s.26, Road Traffic Act 1994 and amended by s.6(1)(c), Road Traffic Act 2006.

[76] *Ibid.*, s.26(4)(a)(iii) as substituted by s.26, Road Traffic Act 1994 and amended by s.6(1)(a)(iii), Road Traffic Act 2006.

[77] *Ibid.*, s.26(3)(a).

[78] *Ibid.*, s.26(5)(b) as substituted by s.26, Road Traffic Act 1994 and amended by s.6(1)(d), Road Traffic Act 2006.

Dangerous Driving – Section 69 of the Road Traffic Act 2010

Practitioners should note that section 53 of the Road Traffic Act 1961 is replaced by a new section 53 as inserted by section 69(1) of the Road Traffic Act 2010.[79] This section sets out the offence of driving a vehicle in a public place at a speed, or in a manner which, having regard to all the circumstances of the case (including the nature, condition and use of the place and the amount of traffic) is dangerous to the public.

Penalties

In respect of offences under section 53 (as substituted by section 69(1) of the Road Traffic Act 2010), the penalties are as follows:

Summary Conviction – fine of up to €5,000 and/or a term of imprisonment for up to 6 months.

Indictable Conviction – fine of up to €20,000 and/or a term of imprisonment of up to 10 years.

Disqualification:

Mandatory Disqualification:

Summary conviction: carries a mandatory consequential disqualification period of two years for a first offence and not less than four years for a second or subsequent offence within three years: although it is obviously open to the court to impose a longer disqualification period on the particular facts of the case.[82]

Conviction on Indictment: carries a mandatory disqualification period of four years for a first offence and six years for a second/subsequent offence.[83] Where a consequential disqualification is imposed upon a conviction for dangerous driving tried on indictment, the court shall, or may (where court has discretion not to impose an additional certificate

---

[79] When same section comes into operation.
[80] S.53(2)(b), Road Traffic Act 1961 as substituted by s.69(1), Road Traffic Act 2010, when same section comes into operation.
[81] *Ibid.*, s.53(2)(a) as substituted by s.69(1), Road Traffic Act 2010, when same section comes into operation.
[82] *Ibid.*, s.26(5)(a)(i) as substituted by s.26, Road Traffic Act 1994 and amended by s.6(1)(c), Road Traffic Act 2006.
[83] *Ibid.*, s.26(4)(a)(iii) as substituted by s.26, Road Traffic Act 1994 and amended by s.6(1)(a)(iii), Road Traffic Act 2006.

condition on grounds of 'special reasons') disqualify an individual for a specified period set above and until a certificate of competency and/or fitness is produced.[84] In those circumstances, the disqualification is not lifted upon the expiration of a specified period alone, this is only the first condition: an individual must, upon the expiration of the specified period, or at such later date as possible produce the required certificate before the licence can be restored.

DRIVING OF A DANGEROUSLY DEFECTIVE VEHICLE – SECTION 54 OF THE ROAD TRAFFIC ACT 1961

Section 54 of the Road Traffic Act 1961[85] deals with the offence of driving a dangerously defective vehicle in a public place. It a criminal offence for any individual to drive a mechanically-propelled vehicle in a public place while there is a defect affecting the vehicle which the owner of the vehicle either:

(a) knows; or

(b) ought to have discovered through the exercise of ordinary care, and same defect is such that the vehicle, when driven, is a danger to the public.[86]

This section deals specifically with an owner's liability in respect of dangerously defective vehicles and it is the owner of the vehicle, irrespective of who was actually driving the vehicle that commits the offence under section 54. Consequentially, and logically, it is a good defence to a charge under section 54 if the owner of the can demonstrate, to the satisfaction of the court, that they car was being driven by another person without their authority or consent at the time of the offence.[87]

This section does not specifically refer to the registered owner and is understood to include those who ordinarily own and keep the vehicle, if different from the registered owner, including those who hire vehicle under hire purchase scheme. The prosecution must demonstrate that the alleged defect was so serious in nature as to

---

[84] *Ibid.*, s.26(3)(a).
[85] As amended by s.6, Road Traffic Act 1968.
[86] S.54(2), Road Traffic Act 1961.
[87] *Ibid.*, s.54(3).

render the vehicle dangerous to other road users and members of the public, if driven and/or in motion.

Penalties

In respect of offences under section 54, the penalties are as follows:

Summary Conviction – fine of up to €2,000 and/or a term of imprisonment of up to three months.[88]

Penalty Points: five (upon conviction).[89]
This offence does not carry the option of paying a fixed penalty notice. Section 2(8) of the Road Traffic Act 2002 applies if the court imposes an ancillary disqualification order under section 27 of the Road Traffic Act 1961. In those circumstances, penalty points will not be endorsed on licence record.

Disqualification:

Ancillary Disqualification: a first conviction under section 54 does not carry a mandatory disqualification. It is open to the court to make an ancillary disqualification order on the particular facts of the case.

Mandatory Disqualification: if a defendant is convicted of a second or subsequent conviction under this section within three years, a consequential disqualification period of not less than one year will apply.[90]

Penalty Point Disqualification: if a defendant accrues 12 penalty points upon conviction for this offence, then they will be disqualified under the administrative procedure set out under section 3 of the Road Traffic Act 2002.

DRIVING OF A DANGEROUSLY DEFECTIVE VEHICLE – SECTION 69 OF THE ROAD TRAFFIC ACT 2010

Practitioners should note that section 54 of the Road Traffic Act 1961 is replaced by a new section 54 as inserted by section 69 of the Road

---

[88] *Ibid.*, s.54(4) as amended by s.6, Road Traffic Act 1968 and s.18, Table, Pt.1, Reference 14, Road Traffic Act 2006.
[89] See Reference 11 of Pt.1, Sch.1, Road Traffic Act 2002 and also S.I. No.149/2009 — Road Traffic Act 2002 (Commencement of Certain Provisions) (Penalty Points) Order 2009 – which came into effect on 1 May 2009.
[90] S.26(7), Road Traffic Act 1961, as substituted by s.26, Road Traffic Act 1994 and amended s.6(1)(e), Road Traffic Act 2006 see also s.3, Sch.3, Road Traffic Act (as amended).

Traffic Act 2010.[91] This section deals with the offence of driving a dangerously defective vehicle in a public place. It a criminal offence for any individual to drive a mechanically-propelled vehicle in a public place while there is a defect affecting the vehicle which the driver and the owner of the vehicle, either:

(a) knows; or

(b) ought to have discovered through the exercise of ordinary care, and same defect is such that the vehicle, when driven, is a danger to the public.[92]

This section changes the original section 54, as it creates two separate offences in respect of both the driver and the owner of such a vehicle. It states that, where the driver is different from the owner, each is guilty of an offence.[93]

Consequentially, and logically, it is a good defence to a charge under section 54 if the owner of the can demonstrate, to the satisfaction of the court, that they car was being driven by another person without their authority or consent at the time of the offence.[94] It is also a defence to a charge under section 54 if the user can demonstrate that they were an employee of the owner and driving the vehicle under the owner's express order.[95]

Penalties

In respect of offences under section 54 (as substituted by section 69 of the Road Traffic Act 2010), the penalties are as follows:

Summary Conviction – fine of up to €5,000 and/or a term of imprisonment of up to three months.[96]

Penalty Points: five (upon conviction).[97]

---

[91] When same section comes into operation.

[92] S.54(1), Road Traffic Act 1961 as substituted by s.69(1), Road Traffic Act 2010, when same section comes into operation.

[93] *Ibid.*, s.54(1) as substituted by s.69(1), Road Traffic Act 2010, when same section comes into operation.

[94] *Ibid.*, s.54(2) as substituted by s.69(1), Road Traffic Act 2010, when same section comes into operation.

[95] *Ibid.*, s.54(4) as substituted by s.69(1), Road Traffic Act 2010, when same section comes into operation.

[96] *Ibid.*, s.54(3) as substituted by s.69(1), Road Traffic Act 2010, when same section comes into operation.

[97] See Reference 11, Pt.1, Sch.1, Road Traffic Act 2002 and also S.I. No.149/2009 – Road Traffic Act 2002 (Commencement of Certain Provisions) (Penalty Points) O. 2009 – which came into effect on 1 May 2009.

This offence does not carry the option of paying a fixed penalty notice. Section 2(8) of the Road Traffic Act 2002 applies if the court imposes an ancillary disqualification order under section 27 of the Road Traffic Act 1961. In those circumstances, penalty points will not be endorsed on licence record.

Disqualification:

Ancillary Disqualification: a first conviction under section 54 does not carry a mandatory disqualification. It is open to the court to make an ancillary disqualification order on the particular facts of the case.

Mandatory Disqualification: if a defendant is convicted of a second or subsequent conviction under this section within three years, a consequential disqualification period of not less than one year will apply.[98]

Penalty Point Disqualification: if a defendant accrues 12 penalty points upon conviction for this offence, then they will be disqualified under the administrative procedure set out under section 3 of the Road Traffic Act 2002.

PARKING A VEHICLE IN A DANGEROUS POSITION – SECTION 55 OF THE ROAD TRAFFIC ACT 1961

Section 55 of the Road Traffic Act 1961[99] covers offences of relating to parking a vehicle in a dangerous position and provides that it is a criminal offence for an individual to park a vehicle in a public place if the vehicle, as parked, would be likely to cause danger to other persons using that place.[100]

A further distinction is drawn between regular dangerous parking offences and offences which occur when any part of the contravention occurs during a period within lighting-up hours and the dangerously parked vehicle did not fulfil all legal requirements in respect of lighting and/or reflectors.[101]

The above offence, which is closely related to that of obstructing traffic,[102] deals with offences where vehicles are parked in a public

---

[98] S.26(7), Road Traffic Act 1961, as substituted by s.26, Road Traffic Act 1994 and amended s.6(1)(e), Road Traffic Act 2006 see also s.3, Second Schedule to Road Traffic Act (as amended).

[99] As amended by s.52, Road Traffic Act 1968.

[100] S.55(1), Road Traffic Act 1961 as substituted by s.52, Road Traffic Act 1968.

[101] S.55(2)(a), Road Traffic Act 1961.

[102] *Ibid.*, s.98.

place in a manner which is likely to endanger other road users and the general public, particularly if vehicle is parked unlit at night. A parked vehicle, which was lawfully and safely parked during daylight, may become dangerous by virtue of remaining parked in same place unlit at night. It is important for practitioners to be cognisant of the fact that the 'offender' under section 55 is the person who has parked the vehicle dangerously.

Consequentially, and logically, it is a good defence to a charge under section 55 if the owner of the can demonstrate that they car was being driven by another person at the time of the offence. There is no requirement that same use be unauthorised. If a Garda forms an opinion that someone is committing, or has committed and offence under section 55, they can arrest same person without warrant.[103]

Where the registered owner of the vehicle wishes to defend a charge under section 55, they should disclose to the court what information they have about who might have been driving the car. However, if the owner was not present during the act of parking, then it can be reasonably argued that they cannot say who has committed the offence, merely who may have been given the use of their vehicle. It is not a defence to plead that the vehicle had broken-down as there is an obligation under parking regulations for owner (or driver) to remove broken down vehicle from public place if contravening regulations.[104]

Penalties

In respect of offences under section 55, the penalties are as follows:

Summary Conviction:

First Offence – where any part of offence occurred during lighting-up hours and contravened legal lighting requirements – a fine of up to €2,000 and/or a term of imprisonment of up to three months:[105] in all other cases a fine of up to €1,000 and/or a term of imprisonment of up to one month.[106]

---

[103] *Ibid.*, s.55(4) as substituted by s.52, Road Traffic Act 1968.

[104] See art.37(g), S.I. No.182/1997, Road Traffic (Traffic and Parking) Regulations 1997 as inserted by art.3(g), S.I. No.274/1998, Road Traffic (Traffic and Parking) (Amendment) Regulations 1998.

[105] S.55(2)(a), Road Traffic Act 1961 as amended by s.18, Table, Pt.1, Reference 15, Road Traffic Act 2006.

[106] *Ibid.*, s.55(2)(a), Road Traffic Act 1961 as amended by s.18, Table, Pt.1, Reference 16, Road Traffic Act 2006.

Second/Subsequent Offence – fine of up to €2,000 and/or a term of imprisonment of up to three months.[107]

Penalty Points: five (upon conviction).[108]
This offence does not carry the option of paying a fixed penalty notice. Section 2(8) of the Road Traffic Act 2002 applies if the court imposes an ancillary disqualification order under section 27 of the Road Traffic Act 1961. In those circumstances, penalty points will not be endorsed on licence record.

Disqualification:

Ancillary Disqualification: a first conviction under section 55 does not carry a mandatory disqualification. However, it is open to the court to make an ancillary disqualification order (section 27 of the Road Traffic Act 1961) on the particular facts of the case.

Mandatory Disqualification: if a defendant is convicted of a second or subsequent offence (where any part of second offence occurred during lighting-up hours and contravened legal lighting/reflector requirements under this section) within a three year period, a consequential disqualification period of not less than one year will apply.[109]

Penalty Point Disqualification: if a defendant accrues 12 penalty points upon conviction for this offence, then they will be disqualified under the administrative procedure set out under section 3 of the Road Traffic Act 2002.

PARKING A VEHICLE IN A DANGEROUS POSITION – SECTION 69 OF THE ROAD TRAFFIC ACT 2010

Practitioners should note that section 55 of the Road Traffic Act 1961 is replaced by a new section 55 as inserted by section 69 of the Road Traffic Act 2001.[110] The section is identical to the original section and

---

[107] *Ibid.*, s.55(2)(a) as amended by s.18, Table, Pt.1, Reference 15, Road Traffic Act 2006.
[108] See Reference 11, Pt.1, Sch.1, Road Traffic Act 2002 and also S.I. No.134/2006 – Road Traffic Act 2002 (Commencement of Certain Provisions) Order 2006 – which came into effect on 3 June 2006.
[109] S.26(7), Road Traffic Act 1961, as substituted by s.26, Road Traffic Act 1994 and amended s.6(1)(e), Road Traffic Act 2006 see also s.3, Sch.2, Road Traffic Act (as amended).
[110] When same section comes into operation.

states that it is an offence to; Park a vehicle in a public place if the vehicle, as parked, would be likely to cause danger to other persons using that place.[111] A further distinction is drawn between regular dangerous parking offences and offences which occur when: Any part of the contravention occurs during a period within lighting-up hours (section 11 of the Road Traffic Act 1961 and declared regulations) and the dangerously parked vehicle did not fulfil all legal requirements in respect of lighting and/or reflectors.[112]

Penalties

In respect of offences under section 55 as substituted by section 69 of the Road Traffic Act 2010, the penalties are as follows:

Summary Conviction:

> **First Offence** – where any part of offence occurred during lighting-up hours and contravened legal lighting requirements– a fine of up to €3,000[113] and/or a term of imprisonment of up to one month: in all other cases – a fine of up to €2,000 and/or a term of imprisonment of up to one month.[114]

> **Second/Subsequent Offence** – fine of up to €3,000 and/or a term of imprisonment of up to one month.[115]

> **Penalty Points:** five (upon conviction).[116]
> This offence does not carry the option of paying a fixed penalty notice. Section 2(8) of the Road Traffic Act 2002 applies if the court imposes an ancillary disqualification order under section 27 of the Road Traffic Act 1961. In those circumstances, penalty points will not be endorsed on licence record.

---

[111] *Ibid.*, s.55(1) as substituted by s.69, Road Traffic Act 2010, when same section comes into operation.

[112] *Ibid.*, s.55(2)(a) as substituted by s.69, Road Traffic Act 2010, when same section comes into operation.

[113] *Ibid.*, s.55(2)(b) as substituted by s.69, Road Traffic Act 2010, when same section comes into operation.

[114] *Ibid.*, s.55(2)(a) as substituted by s.69, Road Traffic Act 2010, when same section comes into operation.

[115] *Ibid.*, s.55(2)(a), Road Traffic Act 1961 as substituted by s.69, Road Traffic Act 2010, when same section comes into operation.

[116] See Reference 11, Pt.1, Sch.1, Road Traffic Act 2002 and also S.I. No.134/2006 – Road Traffic Act 2002 (Commencement of Certain Provisions) Order 2006 – which came into effect on 3 June 2006.

Disqualification:

Ancillary Disqualification: a first conviction under section 55 does not carry a mandatory disqualification. However, it is open to the court to make an ancillary disqualification order (section 27 of the Road Traffic Act 1961) on the particular facts of the case.

Mandatory Disqualification: if a defendant is convicted of a second or subsequent offence (where any part of second offence occurred during lighting-up hours and contravened legal lighting/reflector requirements under this section) within a three year period, a consequential disqualification period of not less than one year will apply.[117]

Penalty Point Disqualification: if a defendant accrues 12 penalty points upon conviction for this offence, then they will be disqualified under the administrative procedure set out under section 3 of the Road Traffic Act 2002.

---

[117] S.26(7), Road Traffic Act 1961, as substituted by s.26, Road Traffic Act 1994 and amended s.6(1)(e), Road Traffic Act 2006 see also s.3, Second Schedule to Road Traffic Act (as amended).

CHAPTER 9

Unauthorised Taking of a Vehicle

This chapter deals with the offences of stealing cars: joyriding; hijacking; unlawfully entering stationary vehicles; and interfering with the mechanisms of vehicles. It focuses on offences where there are often additional allegations of theft and/or criminal damage which are usually dealt with by way of a charge sheet procedure. Many of the offences dealt with in the chapter often involve defendants who are juvenile and/or unlicensed drivers, so it is important for practitioners to be cognisant of the provisions relating to the prosecution of offences in the Children's Court.[1]

This chapter will deal with the offences of:

(a) unauthorised taking of a vehicle;

(b) knowingly allowing oneself to be carried in a vehicle taken without authority;

(c) unauthorised taking of a bicycle;

(d) interfering/attempting to interfere with the mechanism of a vehicle;

(e) getting on to or into (or attempting to) a stationary vehicle;

(f) hijacking/unlawfully seizing a vehicle;

(g) possessing an article with the intention of committing an offence under section 112 of the Road Traffic Act 1961;

(h) supplying a mechanically-propelledvehicle to a minor;

and also Garda powers to detain/remove or immobilise a vehicle.

---

[1] See in particular the provisions of the Children's Act 2001 (as amended).

Taking a Vehicle without Authority – Section 112 of the Road Traffic Act 1961

Section 112 of the Road Traffic Act 1961[2] covers the offences of taking and using a vehicle without authority: more commonly described as 'joyriding' and sets out the following criminal offences:

(a) taking or using a vehicle without the consent or authority of the owner;[3]

(b) knowingly allowing oneself to be carried in a vehicle which has been taken without lawful authority;[4]

(c) taking or using a pedal cycle without lawful authority.[5]

The offences set out above can be dealt with summarily in the District Court, or on indictment. Section 112 is one of the few offences under the Road Traffic Acts 1961–2010 where prosecutions are generally initiated by way of a charge sheet. This is because the offences arising relate to either the stealing of a car or an offence of allowing oneself to be carried in a stolen car. As a result, a defendant has usually been arrested and taken to a Garda Station where they have been charged, cautioned and either released on station bail or brought before a District Court in custody.[6] There is no requirement under this section that the offence take place in a public place.

It is a good defence to any charge under section 112 if a defendant can demonstrate that they owned the car or believed, and had reasonable grounds to believe, that they had lawful authority to take, use or be carried in the vehicle.[7] Where such a defence is pleaded, the key issue for the court will be the reasonableness of the defendant's belief.

Where a Garda has reasonable grounds for believing that a person is committing, or has committed an offence under this section, they may arrest that person without a warrant.[8] Practitioners should also be aware that the Gardaí have the power to search a vehicle and or

---

[2] As amended by s.65, Road Traffic Act 1968, s.3, Road Traffic (Amendment) Act 1984.

[3] S.112(1)(a), Road Traffic Act 1961 as substituted by s.65, Road Traffic Act 1968.

[4] *Ibid.*, s.112(1)(b) as substituted by s.65, Road Traffic Act 1968.

[5] *Ibid.*, s.112(3).

[6] See Chapter 1 – Prosecution of Offences.

[7] S.112(5), Road Traffic Act 1961.

[8] *Ibid.*, s.112(6) as substituted by s.65, Road Traffic Act 1968.

persons in vehicle where they believe an offence has taken place under this section.[9]

As there are a number of separate charges that may arise under section 112, it is important for a practitioner to have regard to the exact wording of the charge set out, i.e., the precise allegation made and consideration should be given to whether the particular facts set out in the précis and/or statements support the particular charge brought. However, where an individual is charged with stealing a car, and a Judge (or Jury if the matter is prosecuted on indictment believes they are not guilty of that offence) but are guilty of another offence under this section, then a defendant may be found guilty of that offence instead.[10] Offences relating to taking, using or knowingly being carried in stolen vehicle can be dealt with summarily or on indictment.[11] A defendant does not have a right of election.

Given the nature of joyriding offences, it is not unusual for a person charged with an offence under section 112 to be under 18 and/or not in possession of a valid driving licence or valid insurance policy. Practitioners must bear in mind that notwithstanding the penalties set out above, special considerations will apply to prosecution of minors charged with an offence under section 112 and cognisance should be taken of Part 9 of the Children's Act 2001 and in particular section 96 of the Children's Act 2001.

As a practitioner, it is also important to bear in mind that where an individual finds themselves before the court charged with an offence contrary to section 112 of the Road Traffic Act 1961, they may also find themselves charged with a number of other offences arising out of the same incident. It is not uncommon for a defendant to also find themselves facing charges of other driving offences such as: careless driving;[12] dangerous driving;[13] driving whilst under the influence of drink/drugs;[14] driving without a valid driving licence[15] or driving without a valid insurance certificate.[16]

---

[9] S.8, Criminal Law Act 1976 (as amended by s.6, Illegal Immigrants (Trafficking) Act 2000.
[10] S.112(7), Road Traffic Act 1961; see also *The State (McCarthy) v. Governor of Mountjoy Prison* [1965] WJSC-SC 1516.
[11] *Ibid.*, s.112(2).
[12] *Ibid.*, s.52.
[13] *Ibid.*, s.53.
[14] *Ibid.*, ss.49 and 50.
[15] *Ibid.*, s.38.
[16] *Ibid.*, s.56.

Penalties

In respect of offences under section 112, the penalties are as follows:

Summary Conviction – fine of up to €5,000 and/or a term of imprisonment of up to 12 months.[17]

Indictable Conviction – fine of up to €20,000 and/or a term of imprisonment of up to 5 years.[18]

Disqualification:

Mandatory Disqualification: a conviction for an offence under subsection (1) carries a mandatory consequential disqualification period of not less than one year,[19] although the court may impose a longer disqualification period on the particular facts of the case. The court may also require that a defendant remain disqualified until a certificate of competency[20] and/or fitness[21] is produced. In those circumstances, disqualification is not lifted upon the expiration of a specified period; this is only the first condition. An individual must, upon the expiration of the specified period, or at such later date as is possible, produce the required certificate before the licence can be restored.

Penalties

In respect of offences in relation to taking or using a stolen bicycle, these are summary offences only and the general penalty under section 102 of the Road Traffic Act applies:

First Offence – fine of up to €1,000.[22]

Second Offence (under same section) – fine of up to €2,000.[23]

Third/Subsequent Offence (under same section within 12 consecutive months) – fine of up to €2,000 and/or a term of imprisonment of up to three months.[24]

---

[17] *Ibid.*, s.112(2)(a) as amended by s.18, Table, Pt.1, Reference 26, Road Traffic Act 2006.

[18] *Ibid.*, s.112(2)(b) as amended by s.18, Table, Pt.1, Reference 27, Road Traffic Act 2006.

[19] *Ibid.*, s.26(7) as substituted by s.26, Road Traffic Act 1994 and amended by s.6(1)(e), Road Traffic Act 2006 and Reference 11, Sch.2.

[20] *Ibid.*, s.33 as amended by s.10, Road Traffic Act 2006.

[21] *Ibid.*, s.34 as amended by s.10, Road Traffic Act 2006.

[22] *Ibid.*, s.102(a) as amended by s.18(1) – Table – Pt.1 – Reference 20.

[23] *Ibid.*, s.102(b) as amended by s.18(1) – Table – Pt.1 – Reference 21.

[24] *Ibid.*, s.102(c) as amended by s.18(1) – Table – Pt.1 – Reference 22.

Unauthorised Interference with the Mechanism of a Vehicle – Section 113 of the Road Traffic Act 1961

Section 113 of the Road Traffic Act 1961[25] sets out the following criminal offences:

(a) interfering with the mechanism of a stationary vehicle;[26]

(b) attempting to interfere with the mechanism of a stationary vehicle;[27]

(c) get on or into a stationary vehicle;[28]

(d) attempting to get on or into a stationary vehicle.[29]

Where a Garda has reasonable grounds for believing that a person is committing, or has committed an offence under this section, they may arrest that person without a warrant.[30] There is no requirement under this section that offence take place in a public place.[31]

Again, a number of separate charges may arise under section 113, so it is important for a practitioner to have regard to the exact wording of the charge set out and to consider whether the particular facts set out by the prosecution support the charge brought. Another difference between section 113 and section 112 is that there is no power for a Judge to substitute one charge for another charge under section 113. Therefore, if a defendant is charged with interfering, or attempting to interfere with, the mechanism of a vehicle, but the subsequent evidence adduced only supports an offence of getting into a stationary vehicle without lawful authority (or reasonable cause) then they cannot be found guilty of the former offence.

There is a defence of reasonable cause and section 113 does not apply to a person who has only taken such reasonable steps as were necessary to move (by human propulsion) a vehicle obstructing their lawful passage.[32] More generally, it is a good defence to any charge under section 113 if a defendant can demonstrate that they believed, and had reasonable grounds to believe, that they had lawful

---

[25] As amended by s.6, Road Traffic Act 1968, s.3, Road Traffic (Amendment) Act 1984, and s.23, Road Traffic Act 2002.
[26] S.113(1) as amended by s.3, Road Traffic (Amendment) Act 1984.
[27] *Ibid.*, s.113(1) as amended by s.3, Road Traffic (Amendment) Act 1984.
[28] *Ibid.*, s.113(1) as amended by s.3, Road Traffic (Amendment) Act 1984.
[29] *Ibid.*, s.113(1) as amended by s.3, Road Traffic (Amendment) Act 1984.
[30] *Ibid.*, s.113(3) as amended by s.6, Road Traffic Act 1968.
[31] Same requirement was removed by s.3, Road Traffic (Amendment) Act 1984.
[32] S.113(4), Road Traffic Act 1961.

authority for doing act in question[33], i.e., they owned vehicle, or believed they had consent of lawful owner. Again, where such a defence is pleaded, the key issue for the court will be the reasonableness of the defendant's belief.

Penalties

In respect of offences under section 113, the penalties are as follows:

Summary Conviction – fine of up to €2,000 and/or a term of imprisonment of up to three months.[34]

Disqualification:

Ancillary Disqualification: whilst a conviction under section 113 does not carry a mandatory disqualification, it is open to the court to make an ancillary disqualification order under section 27 of the Road Traffic Act 1961 on the particular facts of the case.

UNLAWFUL SEIZURE OF A VEHICLE –
SECTION 10 OF THE CRIMINAL LAW (JURISDICTION) ACT 1976

The related offence of hijacking or unlawful seizure of a vehicle is set out in section 10 of the Criminal Law (Jurisdiction) Act 1976 which states that it is an offence for:

'any vehicle, including but not limited to MPVs and trains, ship (including boats) or hovercraft to be unlawfully seized, controlled, or have its control interfered with, either by force, threat or any other intimidation, by any individual, or:

for that individual to compel or induce another person to so seize or use vehicle for unlawful purpose.[35']

This is very obviously a more serious offence than merely unlawfully taking a vehicle and involves the actual use of force, a threat of force or harm, or some other form of intimidation. This is an indictable offence, and can only be dealt with in the District Court on a guilty plea and with the express consent of the DPP.[36]

---

[33] *Ibid.*, s.113(5).
[34] *Ibid.*, s.113(2) as substituted by s.3, Road Traffic (Amendment) Act 1984 and amended by s.18, Table, Pt.1, Reference 28, Road Traffic Act 2006.
[35] S.10(1), Criminal Law (Jurisdiction) Act 1976.
[36] S.13, Criminal Procedure Act 1967.

Penalties

In respect of offences under section 10, the penalties are as follows:

Indictable Offence: a term of imprisonment of up to 15 years.[37]

Summary Conviction (Guilty Plea): fine not exceeding €1270(or €5,000)[38] and/or a term of imprisonment of up to 12 months.[39]

Disqualification:

Ancillary Disqualification: where a conviction under section 10 involves hijacking/unlawful use of a mechanically-propelled vehicle it is not only open to the Court, but very probable that a judge would imposed an ancillary disqualification order under section 27 of the Road Traffic Act 1961 on the particular facts of the case.

POSSESION OF CERTAIN ARTICLES WITH THE INTENTION OF COMMITTING CERTAIN OFFENCES – SECTION 15 OF THE CRIMINAL JUSTICE (THEFT AND FRAUD OFFENCES) ACT 2001

Section 15 of the Criminal Justice (Theft and Fraud Offences) Act 2001 states that it is an offence for:

'a person who is not at their place of residence to have in their possession any article with the intention that it be used in the course of, or in connection with an offence under section 112 of the Road Traffic Act 1961.[40]'

It is a defence to a charge under section 15 if a defendant can, by means of a reasonable alternative explanation, demonstrate that the article was not in their possession for the purposes of committing an offence.[41] Upon conviction for an offence contrary to section 15, the article in question can be forfeited and destroyed or otherwise disposed of by direction of the court.[42]

This is an indictable offence, which can be tried summarily if the District Judge is satisfied that offence is minor in nature and DPP

---

[37] S.10(1), Criminal Law (Jurisdiction) Act 1976.
[38] S.13(3)(a), Criminal Procedure Act 1967 which set the fine at £1,000. Practitioners should note that same fine is increased to €5,000 by s.3 and s.10(2), Fines Act 2010, when same subsection comes into operation.
[39] *Ibid.*, s.13(3)(a).
[40] See s.15(1)(d), Criminal Justice (Theft and Fraud Offences) Act 2001.
[41] *Ibid.*, s.15(2) as amended by s.47, Criminal Justice Act 2007.
[42] *Ibid.*, s.15(3).

consents to summary disposal.[43] Furthermore, the defendant has a right of election and can elect for a summary trial or a trial in the Circuit Court by a jury of their peers (obviously issue of election only applies where the DPP directs summary disposal and Jurisdiction accepted by the District Judge[44]).

Penalties

In respect of offences under section 15, the penalties are as follows:

Indictable Offence: a fine and/or a term of imprisonment of up to five years.

Summary Conviction (Guilty Plea): fine not exceeding €1,904.10 (or €5,000)[45] and/or a term of imprisonment of up to 12 months.[46]

DETENTION, REMOVAL OR IMMOBILISATION OF VEHICLES – SECTION 41 OF THE ROAD TRAFFIC ACT 1994

Where the Gardaí believe that an individual driving a vehicle in a public place is:

(a) too young to hold a valid driving licence;[47] or

(b) driving a vehicle without a valid insurance certificate or otherwise in contravention of section 56(1) of the Road Traffic Act 1961;[48] or

(c) driving a vehicle without a valid tax disc (or otherwise in contravention of section 1 of the Finance (Excise Duties)(Vehicles) Act 1952, for a period of 2 continuous months immediately prior to same use;[49]

(d) driving a vehicle without a valid NCT certificate or otherwise in contravention of section 18(1) of the Road Traffic Act 1961;[50]

(e) driving a vehicle without a valid DOE certificate or otherwise

---

[43] See ss.53(1)(a) and 53(1)(c), Criminal Justice (Theft and Fraud Offences) Act 2001.
[44] *Ibid.*, s.53(1)(b).
[45] See s.53(2), Criminal Justice (Theft and Fraud Offences) Act 2001 which sets fine at £1,500. Practitioners should note that same fine is increased to €5,000 by s.3 and s.10(3), Fines Act 2010, when same subsection comes into operation.
[46] *Ibid.*, s.53(2).
[47] S.41(1)(a), Road Traffic Act 1994.
[48] *Ibid.*, s.41(1)(b) as substituted by s.19(a), Road Traffic Act 2006.
[49] *Ibid.*, s.41(1)(c) as substituted by s.19(b), Road Traffic Act 2006.
[50] *Ibid.*, s.41(1)(d) as inserted by s.19(c), Road Traffic Act 2006.

in contravention of regulation 19(1) of S.I. No.771/2004 – European Communities (Vehicle Testing) Regulations 2004;[51] or

(f) driving a vehicle, registered in another Member State without proof of passing roadworthiness test pursuant to Council Directive 96/96/EC,[52]

same vehicle may be detained, removed or otherwise immobilised in accordance with the powers conferred upon a Garda under section 3 and section 41 of the Road Traffic Act 1994 and the Road Traffic Act 1994 (Section 41) Regulations 1995 – 1998.[53] It is an offence to obstruct or otherwise impede a Garda from exercising his powers under section 41.[54]

Penalties

The general penalty under section 102 of the Road Traffic Act 1961[55] applies:

First Offence – fine of up to €1,000.[56]

Second Offence (under same section) – fine of up to €2,000.[57]

Third/Subsequent Offence (under same section within 12 consecutive months) – fine of up to €2,000 and/or a term of imprisonment of up to three months.[58]

Disqualification:

Ancillary Disqualification: whilst a conviction under section 41 does not carry a mandatory disqualification, it is open to the court to make an ancillary disqualification order under section 27 of the Road Traffic Act 1961 on the particular facts of the case.

---

[51] *Ibid.*, s.41(1)(e) as inserted by s.19(c), Road Traffic Act 2006.
[52] *Ibid.*, s.41(1)(f) as inserted by s.19(c), Road Traffic Act 2006.
[53] See also Chapter 4 – in respect of driving licences.
[54] S.41(4), Road Traffic Act 1994.
[55] As amended by s.2, Road Traffic (Amendment) Act 1984, s.23, Road Traffic Act 2002 and s.18, Road Traffic Act 2006 – see also S.I. No.86/2007, Road Traffic Act 2006 (Commencement) Order 2007, which came into operation on the 5 March 2007.
[56] S.102(a), Road Traffic Act 1961, as amended by s.18(1) – Table – Pt.1 – Reference 20.
[57] *Ibid.*, s.102(b) as amended by s.18(1) – Table – Pt.1 – Reference 21.
[58] *Ibid.*, s.102(c) as amended by s.18(1) – Table – Pt.1 – Reference 22.

This Garda power does not directly relate to the above offences, except that offences under section 112 and section 113 (in particular) can often involve juvenile drivers who are too young to hold a driving licence. When a Garda comes upon such a driver, they have the power to detain, remove or immobilise the vehicle they are driving in addition to any powers of arrest they can exercise under section 112 or section 113.[59]

SUPPLY OF MECHANICALLY-PROPELLED VEHICLES TO MINORS – SECTION 30 OF THE ROAD TRAFFIC ACT 2004

Section 30 of the Road Traffic Act 2004 states that it is an offence for any person to supply a mechanically-propelled vehicle:

(a) to a person who is under the age of 16 years;[60] or

(b) other than a mechanically-propelled vehicle in respect of which a person who has attained the age of 16 years is entitled to hold a driving licence to drive, to a person who is under the age of 17 years.[61]

'To supply' includes sale, hire, loan, gift, or other means of making the vehicle available to a person.[62]

Penalties

The general penalty under section 30 of the Road Traffic Act 2004[63] which applies is:

Summary Conviction – fine of up to €3,000 and/or imprisonment for up to 6 months.[64]

Disqualification:

Ancillary Disqualification: whilst a conviction under section 30 does not carry a mandatory disqualification, it is open to the court to make an ancillary disqualification order under section 27 of the Road Traffic Act 1961 on the particular facts of the case.

---

[59] For further information on the power to detain/remove/immobilise vehicles, see Chapter 4 on Driving Licences.
[60] S.30(1)(a), Road Traffic Act 2004.
[61] *Ibid.*, s.30(1)(b).
[62] *Ibid.*, s.30(3).
[63] *Ibid.*, s.30(2).
[64] *Ibid.*, s.30(2).

SUPPLY OF MECHANICALLY-PROPELLED VEHICLES TO MINORS – SECTION 88 OF THE ROAD TRAFFIC ACT 2010

Section 30(2) of the Road Traffic Act 2004 is amended by section 88 of the Road Traffic Act 2010 to increase the penalty for an offence under section 30.

Penalties

The general penalty under section 88 of the Road Traffic Act 2010 which applies is:

Summary Conviction – fine of up to €5,000 and/or imprisonment for up to 6 months.

Disqualification:

Ancillary Disqualification: whilst a conviction under this section does not carry a mandatory disqualification, it is open to the court to make an ancillary disqualification order under section 27 of the Road Traffic Act 1961 on the particular facts of the case.

---

[65] When same section comes into operation.
[66] S.30(2), Road Traffic Act 2004 as substituted by s.88, Road Traffic Act 2010, when same section comes into operation.

CHAPTER 10

Drink Driving

This chapter covers the area of driving whilst under the influence of an intoxicant and related offences. Drink driving is one of the most litigated areas of road traffic law and what is contained below is only a brief overview of the relevant legislation, categories of offences and penalties provided for under the law.

This chapter will deal with:

(a) driving/attempting to drive whilst intoxicated;

(b) being in charge of a vehicle with the intention of driving/ attempting to drive whilst intoxicated;

(c) driving/attempting to drive an animal-drawn vehicle or pedal cycle whilst intoxicated;

(d) the obligation to provide a preliminary breath specimen;

(e) the obligation to provide a mandatory breath specimen;

(f) the obligation to provide a specimen following arrest;

(g) the statutory defence to refusal to permit the taking of a specimen;

(h) the obligation to accompany a Garda to the Garda Station to provide a specimen;

(i) the obligation to provide a blood or urine specimen while in hospital;

(j) the Garda power of entry to any place to affect an arrest in respect of certain offences;

(k) taking alcohol with a view to frustrating a prosecution;

(l) costs of prosecutions;

(m) fixed charge and disqualification for certain drink driving offences;

(n)   early restoration of licence applications;

(o)   provisions of Road Traffic Act 2010.

Most defendants who are before the court in charged with a drink/ drug driving offence are charged under section 49[1] or section 50[2] of the Road Traffic Act 1961 or section 13 of the Road Traffic Act 1994.[3] This area of Road Traffic law is complex, frequently litigated and has given rise to a large amount of case law. There are several excellent textbooks and recent articles dealing in detail with the procedural issues, available defences and relevant case law,[4] and practitioners are referred to same for a more detailed analysis.

Before setting out the relevant statutory provisions, some general comment should be made about representing clients in respect of drink driving cases. There are certain practical matters which should be considered in all cases.

APPLICABLE PENALTIES

In advance of any plea/hearing date, a defendant must be advised very clearly and correctly of the applicable penalties, particularly the applicable minimum mandatory disqualification period. In order to advise a defendant correctly, practitioners must inform themselves of the relevant applicable penalties (same are set out below) and also consider if the defendant has any previous convictions. A defendant will generally have little to lose by contesting a drink/drug driving charge when it's a first offence (other than perhaps receiving a larger fine), as the minimum mandatory disqualification periods set out in law will apply whether the defendant pleads guilty or is found guilty following a full hearing.

The situation is very different, however, if they have previous convictions, particularly in respect of other drink driving offences or convictions for other serious offences under the Road Traffic

---

[1] S.49, Road Traffic Act 1961 – what is commonly known as drink driving.

[2] *Ibid.*, s.50, i.e. 'in charge of vehicle with intention to drive whilst intoxicated'.

[3] *Ibid.*, s.13 – failure/refusal to give a specimen upon lawful demand.

[4] For further reading see: Mark De Blacam, *Drink Driving*; James Woods, *Road Traffic Offences* and Robert Pierse *Road Traffic Law in Ireland*. Practitioners are also referred to recent Bar Council CPD papers on Drink Driving Law, 'Driving under the Influence', 20 May 2009, Martin Dully BL and David Staunton BL; 'Drink Driving Offences', Ronan Munro BL, 30 January 2008 and also the Recent *Law Society Gazette* Article, 'Road to Nowhere', Vincent Deane, April 2009.

Acts 1961–2010, like driving without insurance,[5] or dangerous driving.[6] A defendant is further at risk if they have previously been disqualified from driving or worse still, were disqualified at the time of the alleged offence. Where a defendant is at risk of incurring a disqualification period in excess of minimum mandatory disqualification period, and/or is at risk of a custodial sentence, any decision to contest the charge must be made on the basis of a consideration of the possible adverse consequences for the defendant if they are subsequently found guilty.

It is always prudent to check a defendant's previous convictions with the prosecuting Garda in advance, as a defendant may not always give an accurate account of their previous convictions or any previous driving disqualifications. The defendant should further be advised of their right to ask the court to postpone any disqualification period imposed for up to six months.[7]

APPEALS PROCESS/APPLICATION FOR EARLY RESTORATION OF LICENCE

A defendant must be correctly advised in respect of both the appeals process[8] and if, and how, they can apply to have their licence restored. If an individual wishes to have a stay placed upon any period of disqualification pending an appeal, then this appeal must be lodged within 14 days of the imposition of District Court order:[9] it is therefore essential that any defendant is advised correctly in this respect, as any appeal made outside of this 14-day period will not put a stay on any period of disqualification imposed.

If a defendant is convicted and disqualified in their absence, consideration should be given as to whether a set-aside application can be brought instead of an appeal.[10] The procedure in respect of applying for the early restoration of a licence is set out in this chapter.

Most cases will turn on their own particular facts, hence the importance of getting a full disclosure/Gary Doyle order[11] in respect of

---

[5] S.56, Road Traffic Act 1961 – see also Chapter 6 on Driving without Insurance Offences.
[6] Robert Pierse, *op. cit.*, p.53 – see also Chapter 8 on Dangerous Driving Offences.
[7] See s.30(3)(d), Road Traffic Act 1961 as substituted by s.20, Road Traffic Act 1968 (as amended).
[8] See Chapter 2 in respect of the Appeal Process.
[9] *Waldron v. DPP* [2004] IEHC 227.
[10] See Chapter 2 in respect of the Set-Aside Procedure.
[11] See *Director of Public Prosecutions v. Gary Doyle* [1994] 2 I.R. 286.

any case proceeding to hearing. However, practitioners seeking to defend drink driving charges should always give consideration to circumstances in which the defendant is stopped and asked to provide a specimen:

(a) evidence given by a Garda as to opinion formed and basis on which they formed their opinion;

(b) circumstances surrounding the defendant's arrest;

(c) what occurred at the Garda Station and what is recorded in custody record;

(d) the circumstances in which breath/blood/urine specimen obtained and whether there has been proper compliance with statutory provisions.

Practitioners should also be alert to inconsistencies which may arise between a précis, statements provided and/or notes in a Garda's notebook and actual evidence given in court.

Practitioners should also note that Part Two of the Road Traffic Act 2010 makes a number of significant changes to drink driving legislation, including reducing the blood alcohol level, introducing a preliminary impairment test in respect of alleged drug driving offences. If further legislates for some drink driving offences to be dealt with by way of a fixed charge penalty notice. Part Two is not yet in operation, and indeed it is unlikely to come into effect until mid late 2011[12] at the earliest.

Driving Whilst Under the Influence of an Intoxicating Liquor or Drug – Section 49 of the Road Traffic Act 1961

Section 49 of the Road Traffic Act 1961[13] sets out the offence of driving whilst under the influence of an intoxicant and creates the following four distinct offences:

1. driving or attempting to drive a mechanically-propelled vehicle in a public place whilst under the influence of an intoxicant

---

[12] This delay is as a result of the fact that evidential breath-testing machines used in Garda stations to measure the alcohol in a driver's breath cannot be recalibrated to the 20 mg limit proposed for 'specified persons'. The Medical Bureau of Road Safety has advised that it will be the middle of 2011 at the earliest before new replacement breath-testing machines can be purchased, tested and installed in Garda stations.

[13] As amended by s.10, Road Traffic Act 1994 and ss.6 and 18, Road Traffic Act 2006.

to such an extent as being incapable of having proper control of the vehicle;[14]

2. driving or attempting to drive a mechanically-propelled vehicle in a public place whilst there is present in your body a quantity of alcohol, such that within three hours of driving, the concentration of alcohol in your blood exceeds 80mg/100ml;[15]

3. driving or attempting to drive a mechanically-propelled vehicle in a public place whilst there is present in your body a quantity of alcohol, such that within three hours of driving, the concentration of alcohol in your urine exceeds 107mg/100ml;[16]

4. driving or attempting to drive a mechanically-propelled vehicle in a public place whilst there is present in your body a quantity of alcohol, such that within three hours of driving, the concentration of alcohol in your breath exceeds 35mg/100ml.[17]

Although section 49 offences are commonly known as 'Drink driving' offences, this section also covers offences where a defendant is under the influence of some other intoxicant, or combination of intoxicants, primarily drugs (illegal or prescription)[18] which impair their ability to drive to such an extent as to render the defendant incapable of properly controlling a vehicle.

Whilst a defendant cannot be found guilty of an offence under more than one subsection of section 49 arising out of the same incident,[19] they can be found guilty of separate offences contrary to section 49 and section 50 of the Road Traffic Act 1961: namely an offence of being in charge of mechanically-propelled vehicle while under influence of intoxicating liquor or drug.

Furthermore, a defendant can be charged with an offence contrary to section 49, but following a consideration of the facts adduced actually found guilty of an offence contrary to section 50 (or vice versa).[20] However, practitioners should note that as a power of arrest can arise under both sections 49[21] and 50,[22] where an issue subsequently arises

---

[14] S.49(1), Road Traffic Act 1961 – as substituted by s.10, Road Traffic Act 1994.
[15] Ibid., s.49(2) as substituted by s.10, Road Traffic Act 1994.
[16] Ibid., s.49(3)as substituted by s.10, Road Traffic Act 1994.
[17] Ibid., s.49(4) as substituted by s.10, Road Traffic Act 1994.
[18] Ibid., s.49(1)(b) as substituted by s.10, Road Traffic Act 1994.
[19] Ibid., s.49(6)(a) as substituted by s.10, Road Traffic Act 1994.
[20] Ibid., s.49(6)(b) as substituted by s.10, Road Traffic Act 1994.
[21] Ibid., s.49(8) as substituted by s.10, Road Traffic Act 1994.
[22] Ibid., s.50(10) as substituted by s.11, Road Traffic Act 1994.

as to under which section the Garda formed his opinion that an arrestable offence had taken place, the court will have to consider the factual evidence given by the Garda. High Court case law has clearly stated that any power of arrest invoked must be properly exercised for the arrest to be deemed lawful.[23]

The Gardaí's powers to breathalyse drivers have increased significantly with recent legislation. Before the Road Traffic Act of 2006, the Gardaí had the power to breath-test a driver under section 12 of the Road Traffic Act 1994,[24] only in circumstances where the Garda had formed the opinion that they the defendant had:

(a) committed a road traffic offence (other than drink driving offence):[25] or

(b) been involved in a road traffic accident;[26] or

(c) if Garda had formed the opinion that a driver had consumed alcohol (or some other intoxicant).[27]

Now, under section 4 of the Road Traffic Act 2006, the Gardaí can set up mandatory breath-testing checkpoints and test any driver, without the requirement of forming an opinion under section 12 of the Road Traffic Act 1994.

Most drink driving charges now brought are for offences contrary to section 49(2), section 49(3), section 49(4) – i.e. driving with a blood alcohol reading above 80mg/100ml (blood),[28] 107mg/100ml (urine)[29] or 35mg/100ml (breath).[30] There are obvious reasons why most prosecutions for drink driving offences now proceed under the above sections. Unlike section 49(1), which requires evidence to be adduced that a defendant was under the influence of an intoxicant to such an extent as to be incapable of having proper control of the vehicle, in prosecuting offences under sections 49(2), 49(3) and 49(4), once the prosecution can demonstrate that a defendant was driving/or attempting to drive whilst over the prescribed Blood Alcohol Count (BAC) limit, they will be guilty of an offence.

---

[23] See *DPP v. Moloney* (unreported, Finnegan J., 20 December 2001); *DPP v. Haslam* (unreported, O'Caoimh J, 27 January 2003); *DPP v. Edward Byrne* [2002] 2 I.L.R.M. 268, [2002] I.R. 397; *DPP v. O'Neill* (unreported, Edwards J., 15 February 2008).
[24] S.12, Road Traffic Act 1994 as substituted by s.10, Road Traffic Act 2002.
[25] *Ibid.*, s.12(1)(a) as substituted by s.10, Road Traffic Act 2002.
[26] *Ibid.*, s.12(1)(b) as substituted by s.10, Road Traffic Act 2002.
[27] *Ibid.*, s.12(1)(b) as substituted by s.10, Road Traffic Act 2002.
[28] S.49(2), Road Traffic Act 1961 as substituted by s.10, Road Traffic Act 1994.
[29] *Ibid.*, s.49(3) as substituted by s.10, Road Traffic Act 1994.
[30] *Ibid.*, s.49(4) as substituted by s.10, Road Traffic Act 1994.

However, in respect of drug driving offences, the charge must be brought under section 49(1). Practitioners should therefore bear in mind that when their client has been accused of driving whilst under the influence of a drug/drugs, it is not sufficient for the prosecution to provide a certificate from the Medical Bureau of Road Safety which demonstrates that a particular drug was in a defendant's system at the time of the offence. The prosecution must be able to demonstrate that at the time of the offence, the defendant was under the influence of this drug, and they were under the influence of this drug/intoxicant to such and extent that they were incapable of having proper control of a vehicle.

As previously stated, the Road Traffic Act 2006 now allows the Gardaí to set up mandatory breath testing checkpoints.[31] It is therefore essential for practitioners to establish not only the particular charge brought but the circumstances under which their client was asked to provide a specimen. In respect of mandatory testing checkpoint operated under section 4 of the Road Traffic 2006 Act, a Garda's powers can only be exercised on foot of a valid written authorisation given by a Garda not below the rank of Inspector.[32] The original/copy authorisation should be produced during prosecution of the offence,[33] and practitioners should carefully examine the authorisation to ensure that all the details (location, date, time, signature of authorised person etc.) contained in same are correct and sufficiently detailed and specific to grant the Gardaí the powers exercised. In this respect, practitioners should have regard to the provisions set out in section 4 of the Road Traffic Act 2006.

Where a defendant is asked to provide a breath specimen on the grounds that a Garda has formed an opinion the defendant is intoxicated, has committed a road traffic offence or been involved in a road traffic accident,[34] then in any subsequent prosecution, positive evidence must be adduced as to the power exercised by the Garda and the statutory authority invoked.

Where a defendant is breathalysed on the basis of a Garda's opinion, positive evidence should be adduced as to the particular opinion formed and how and why the Garda formed this opinion.[35] Very

---

[31] S.4, Road Traffic Act 2006.
[32] Ibid., s.4(2).
[33] *Weir v. DPP* [2008] IEHC 268.
[34] S.12(1), Road Traffic Act 1994 as substituted by s.10, Road Traffic Act 2002.
[35] See *DPP v. O'Connor* [1985] I.L.R.M. 333; *DPP v. Lynch* [1991] 1 I.R. 43; *DPP v. Ó Súilleabháin* [1995] 2 I.L.R.M. 617; *DPP v. Tyndall* [2005] 1 I.R. 593.

careful attention should be given to the evidence a Garda gives in respect of the factors which led them to forming their opinion. Similarly attention should be given to the procedure under which the defendant was arrested, for instance, was the Defendant properly cautioned and advised in plain ordinary language of the offence for which they have been arrested.[36]

Anyone who refuses to provide a preliminary breath specimen is guilty of offence contrary to section 12 of the Road Traffic Act 1994 and may be arrested without a warrant.[37] Anyone who refuses to provide a specimen at a Garda Station following arrest is also guilty of an offence contrary to section 13(2) of the Road Traffic Act 1994.

POWERS OF ENTRY – SECTION 39 OF THE ROAD TRAFFIC ACT 1994

Practitioners should also be aware of the provisions of section 39 of the Road Traffic Act 1994, which confers a power of entry without a warrant to a member of the Gardaí to enter, without a warrant, and with reasonable force necessary any place (including curtilage of dwelling but not the dwelling itself) where the individual is, or the Garda has reasonable cause to suspect him to be for the purposes of making an arrest under section 49(8) or section 50(10) of the Road Traffic Act 1961.[38]

Section 39 also sets out the powers of entry in respect of breaches of duties at the scene of an accident[39] and the obligation to provide a specimen while in hospital.[40] Practitioners should note that section 7 of the Road Traffic Act 2010[41] gives the Gardaí additional powers of entry in respect of offences under the Part II of the Road Traffic Act 2010.

In prosecuting any offence of driving whilst under influence of an intoxicant contrary to section 49(1) of the Road Traffic Act 1961, proof should be adduced of all the main elements of the offence, namely:

(a) that the defendant was either driving/attempting to drive a mechanically-propelled vehicle, in a public place; and

---

[36] See *DPP v. Mooney* [1992] 1 I.R. 548; *DPP v. Connell* [1998] 3 I.R. 62; *DPP v. McCormack* [2000] 1 I.L.R.M.
[37] S.12(4), Road Traffic Act 1994.
[38] *Ibid.*, s.39(2).
[39] *Ibid.*, s.39(1) and s.106(3A), Road Traffic Act 1961.
[40] *Ibid.*, s.39(3) and s.15(1), Road Traffic Act 1994.
[41] When same section comes into operation.

(b) that the defendant was under influence of an intoxicant (alcohol and/or drugs) to such a degree that they could not properly control vehicle.

The prosecuting Garda should give evidence of observations that led to them forming their opinion that the defendant was firstly, under the influence of an intoxicant (observations such as smell of alcohol on breath or slurred speech): and secondly, intoxicated to such an extent that they could not properly control the vehicle (like an observation, perhaps, that a defendant was unfit to perform a simple coordination test voluntarily undertaken).

Evidence might also be adduced from other witnesses such as doctors who examined the defendant, or individuals who may have witnessed the defendant consuming drink/drugs immediately prior to attempting to drive.

In respect of offences of driving over the prescribed concentration of alcohol limits, evidence of the defendant's breathalyser test result a section 17 certificate (or certified copy) must be produced. In respect of prosecutions relying on evidence of a blood/urine test, a section 18 certificate (or certified copy) must be produced. Doctor's forms are also regarded as essential proof.

PROCEDURE FOLLOWING PROVISION OF BREATH SPECIMEN UNDER SECTION 13 – SECTION 17 OF THE ROAD TRAFFIC ACT 1994

Section 17 of the Road Traffic Act 1994 sets out the following procedures in respect of the provision of a breath specimen:

(a) where pursuant to lawful requirement made under section 13, a person provides two specimens of his breath; and the concentration of alcohol in each specimen is determined, the specimen with the lower concentration of alcohol (except where both specimens contain same concentration) shall be taken into account for the purposes of sections 49 (4) and 50 (4) of the Principal Act and the other specimen shall be disregarded;[42]

(b) a defendant shall be supplied forthwith by the Garda with two identical statements, automatically produced in the prescribed form and duly completed by the member in the prescribed manner, stating the concentration of alcohol in the said specimen;[43]

---

[42] S.17(1), Road Traffic Act 1994.
[43] Ibid., s.17(2).

(c) a defendant shall, upon Garda request, sign each statement and return either statement to the Gardaí.[44]

Practitioners should pay particular attention to the procedures followed in the intoxiliser room. They should also familiarise themselves with the manner in which the intoxiliser machine is operated, including recommended temperature and humidity parameters.[45] The legal requirement is that the defendant provide two specimens of breath,[46] this is a strict requirement and any divergence from same procedure may prove fatal.[47]

Similarly, the order in which the statements are signed is clearly set out:[48] the Garda should sign the statements before presenting them to the defendant and any divergence from same procedure shall prove fatal.[49] However, case law suggests that some technical breaches of procedures under section 17 will not be sufficient as to defeat prosecution, particularly where there is an absence of evidence that technical breach resulted in any prejudice to the defendant or exposed him to any risk of injustice.[50]

PROCEDURE REGARDING TAKING OF SPECIMENS OF BLOOD AND PROVISION OF SPECIMENS OF URINE – SECTION 18 OF THE ROAD TRAFFIC ACT 1994

Section 18 of the Road Traffic Act 1994 sets out the following procedures in respect of the provision of a blood or urine specimen:

(a) where a designated doctor has taken a specimen of blood from a person or has been provided by the person with a specimen of his urine, the doctor shall divide the specimen into two

---

[44] *Ibid.*, s.17(3).

[45] The right of the defence to inspect intoxiliser apparatus used is not absolute but a pre-trial application can be made to inspect same. See *David Whelan v. Judge Kirby & DPP* [2004] IESC 16.

[46] The legality of this process was unsuccessfully challenged in the cases of *Ashley McGonnell, Oliver Quinlan & John Purcell v. Attorney General and DPP* [2006] IESC 64.

[47] See *DPP v. Frank McDonagh* (unreported, Denham J., 16 October 2008) – in this case, the defendant was requested to provide two specimens of their breath, notwithstanding the provision by that person of one incomplete breath specimen within a previous incomplete test result.

[48] S.17(2), Road Traffic Act 1994.

[49] See *DPP v. Thomas Keogh* (unreported, Murphy J., 9 February 2004); *DPP v. Lloyd Freeman* [2010] IEHC 179; and *Smith v. Judge NiChonduin* [2007] IEHC 270.

[50] *DPP (O'Reilly) v. Barnes* [2005] 4 I.R. 176; *Ruttledge v. District Judge Clyne & DPP* (unreported, High Court, Dunne J., 7April 2006).

parts, place each part in a container which he shall forthwith seal and complete the form prescribed for the purposes of this section;[51]

(b) where a specimen of blood or urine of a person has been divided into 2 parts, Garda shall offer to the person one of the sealed containers together with a statement in writing indicating that he may retain either of the containers;[52]

(c) as soon as practicable after subsection (b) complied with, a member of Garda shall cause to be forwarded to the Bureau the completed form referred to in subsection (a), together with the relevant sealed container or, where the person has declined to retain one of the sealed containers, both relevant sealed containers.[53]

The prosecution must be able to satisfy the court that the specimen(s) were obtained in a manner which fully complied with all legal requirements and proper procedures,[54] including offering the defendant a statement in writing indicating that he may retain either of the containers.[55]

Again, case law suggests that some technical breaches of procedures under section 18 will not be sufficient to defeat prosecution, particularly where there is an absence of evidence that technical breach resulted in any prejudice to the defendant or exposed him to any risk of injustice.[56] The Garda must forward the specimen to the Medical Bureau of Road Safety as soon as practicable; another member of Gardaí may forward specimen to Medical Bureau on their behalf,[57] however, the Gardaí must be able to prove continuity in the chain of possession of specimen taken.

In cases involving the provision of a specimen, particularly cases involving the provision of a blood/urine sample, consideration should be given as to whether any undue delay arises in terms of contacting a doctor and the doctor's arrival and taking of the

---

[51] S.18(1), Road Traffic Act 1994.
[52] *Ibid.*, s.18(2), Road Traffic Act 1994.
[53] *Ibid.*, s.18(3), Road Traffic Act 1994.
[54] *DPP v. Croom-Carroll* [1999] 4 I.R. 126; *DPP v. Bernard Egan* [2010] IEHC 233.
[55] *McCarron v. Groake & DPP* (unreported; Kelly J., 4 April 2000); *DPP v. Reville* (unreported, O'Caoimh J., 21 December 2000).
[56] See *DPP v. David Hopkins* [2009] IEHC 337; *DPP v. Gerard Kennedy* [2009] IEHC 361.
[57] S.18(3), Road Traffic Act 1994.

specimen.[58] Practitioners should note that the onus is on the prosecution to explain any delay as being both reasonable and necessary. However, not every delay will require an explanation: the court has held that a delay of one hour from the time at which a doctor was first called to attend a Garda Station and that Doctor's subsequent arrival is not a delay which requires an explanation.[59]

A defendant must be formally advised of their obligation to give a specimen and advised of the consequences of failing/refusing to give a specimen upon a lawful request. There is very considerable case law in respect of the statutory procedure involved in obtaining alcohol specimens and practitioners seeking to effectively defend a defendant should familiarise themselves with it.

Penalties

In respect of offences under section 49, a range of penalties exist:

Summary Conviction: fine of up to €5,000 and/or a term of imprisonment of up six months.[60]

Section 1(1) of the Probation of Offenders Act 1907 shall not apply to this offence.[61]

Disqualification:

Mandatory Disqualification: a conviction under section 49 carries a minimum mandatory consequential disqualification.

Section 49(1): – i.e. under the influence of an intoxicant to such an extent as being incapable of having proper control of the vehicle is as follows:

First Offence – minimum four year consequential disqualification.

Second/Subsequent Offence (drink driving offence): minimum six years' disqualification.[62]

---

[58] There have been a number of recent court decisions in respect of the 20 minute observation rule and the issue of delay in taking a specimen – See *DPP v. Michael Finn* [2002] I.L.R.M. 32; *DPP v. Damien McNiece* [2003] 2 I.R. 614; *DPP v. Tim O'Connor* [2005] IEHC 442; *DPP v. David O'Neill* [2007] IEHC 83; *DPP v. Robin Fox* [2008] 4 I.R. 811; *DPP v. Garett Foley* [2006] IEHC 11; *DPP v. Brendan Walsh* [2005] IEHC 77.
[59] *DPP v David O'Neill* [2007] IEHC 83.
[60] S.49(6), Road Traffic Act 1961 as substituted by s.10, Road Traffic Act 1994 and amended by s.18, Road Traffic Act 2006.
[61] *Ibid.*, s.49(1) as substituted by s.10, Road Traffic Act 1994.
[62] *Ibid.*, s.26(4)(a) as substituted by s.26, Road Traffic Act 1994 and further substituted by s.6(1)(a), Road Traffic Act 2006.

Lowest category – concentration of alcohol not exceeding: 100mg/ 100ml (blood): 135mg/100ml (urine): 44mg/100ml (breath).

First Offence – one-year consequential disqualification.

Second Offence – two-year consequential disqualification.[63]

Middle category – concentration of alcohol between: 100–150mg/ 100ml (blood): 135–200mg/100ml (urine): 44–66mg/100ml (breath)

First Offence – two-year consequential disqualification.

Second Offence – four-year consequential disqualification.[64]

Highest category – concentration of alcohol exceeding: 150mg/ 100ml (blood): 200mg/100ml (urine): 66mg/100ml (breath).

First Offence – three-year consequential disqualification.

Second Offence – six-year consequential disqualification.[65]

These are minimum periods of disqualification and it is open to a Judge to impose a greater penalty than set out above, particularly in the case of a second or subsequent conviction, a conviction which occurs whilst a driver is disqualified and/or uninsured, or if there are other exacerbating factors like concurrent charges for careless/dangerous driving or unauthorised taking of a vehicle.

Where an individual is found guilty of an offence contrary to section 49 and wishes to appeal their conviction, they should do so within 14 days of the conviction. After this time period has expired, it is still open to them to seek an extension of time by which to appeal, however same leave to appeal will not place a stay on any disqualification period imposed by the court.[66] In circumstances where an individual has been convicted under section 49 in their absence, and where they did not received court summons and/or notification of court appearance, it is open to them to apply to have the order set aside instead.[67] If the order is set aside and remitted

---

[63] *Ibid.*, s.26(4)(b) as substituted by s.26, Road Traffic Act 1994, further substituted by s.2, Road Traffic Act 1995 and substituted by table inserted by s.6(1)(b), Road Traffic Act 2006.

[64] *Ibid.*, s.26(4)(b) as substituted by s.6(1)(b), Road Traffic Act 2006.

[65] *Ibid.*, s.26(4)(b) as substituted by s.6(1)(b), Road Traffic Act 2006.

[66] See *Waldron v. DPP* [2004] IEHC 227.

[67] See Chapter 2 in respect of Appeal and Set-Aside Procedures.

back for a new hearing date, any disqualification imposed will also be set aside.

FIXED CHARGES AND DISQUALIFICATION FOR CERTAIN DRINK DRIVING OFFENCES – SECTION 5 OF THE ROAD TRAFFIC ACT 2006

Practitioners should note that the provisions of section 5 of the Road Traffic Act 2006 which provides for a fixed charge notice in respect of certain drink driving offences. Section 5 of the Road Traffic Act 2006 sets out that a driver arrested under section 49 or section 50 of the Road Traffic Act 1961, for a first offence (or who has not been convicted of a similar offence[68] within the previous five years),[69] in the lowest category of alcohol concentration would avoid a court appearance by admitting their guilt and accepting a fixed charge notice fine.[70] Fixed Charge Fine payable would be €300,[71] and a six-month fixed disqualification notice.[72] If an individual was ineligible to avail of the fixed charge disqualification,[73] and knows or ought to have known same, they are guilty of an offence.[74]

Summary Conviction: fine of up to €5,000 and/or imprisonment of up to six months.[75]

Section 5 has not been brought into law as of the date of this publication and is due to be repealed and replaced by section 29 of the Road Traffic Act 2010.[76] However, practitioners should also be aware of the transitional provisions of section 32 of the Road Traffic Act 2010, should section 5 of the Road Traffic Act 2006 come into operation before it is repealed by section 29 of the Road Traffic Act 2010.

PROHIBITION ON DRIVING MECHANICALLY-PROPELLED VEHICLE WHILE UNDER THE INFLUENCE OF AN INTOXICANT OR IF EXCEEDING ALCOHOL LIMITS – SECTION 4 OF THE ROAD TRAFFIC ACT 2010

Practitioners should note that section 49 of the Road Traffic Act 1961 is repealed by section 33 of the Road Traffic Act 2010 and replaced by

---

[68] Ss.49 or 50, Road Traffic Act 1961 or ss.13, 14, 15 Road Traffic Act 1994.
[69] *Ibid.*, s.5(2).
[70] *Ibid.*, s.5(2).
[71] *Ibid.*, s.5(4).
[72] *Ibid.*, s.5(5).
[73] *Ibid.*, s.5(2) and 5(3).
[74] *Ibid.*, s.5(8).
[75] *Ibid.*, s.5(8).
[76] When same section comes into operation.

section 4 of the Road Traffic Act 2010.[77] This provision in similar to existing section 49, but reduces the Blood Alcohol Count (BAC) from 80mg/100ml to 50mg/100ml, prescribing a further reduced limit of 20mg/100ml in the case of 'specified persons'.

Section 4 creates the following four distinct offences:

(a) driving or attempting to drive a mechanically-propelled vehicle in public place whilst under the influence of an intoxicant to such an extent as being incapable of having proper control of the vehicle;[78]

(b) driving or attempting to drive a mechanically-propelled vehicle in public place whilst there is present in your body a quantity of alcohol, such that within 3 hours of driving, the concentration of alcohol in your blood exceeds 50mg/100ml– (20mg/100ml for specified persons);[79]

(c) driving or attempting to drive a mechanically-propelled vehicle in public place whilst there is present in your body a quantity of alcohol, such that within 3 hours of driving, the concentration of alcohol in your urine exceeds 67mg/100ml (27mg/100ml for specified persons);[80]

(d) driving or attempting to drive a mechanically-propelled vehicle in public place whilst there is present in your body a quantity of alcohol, such that within 3 hours of driving, the concentration of alcohol in your breath exceeds 22mg/100ml (9mg/100ml for specified persons).[81]

A person charged with an offence under section 4 of the Road Traffic Act 2010 may alternatively be found guilty of an offence under section 5 of the Road Traffic Act 2010 (in charge of vehicle with intent to drive/attempt to drive).[82] Again, a power or arrest without warrant arises under both section 4[83] and section 5;[84] and where an issue subsequently arises as to under which section the Garda has formed his opinion that an arrestable offence had taken place, the court will have to consider the factual evidence given by the Garda. High Court

---

[77] When ss.4 and 33, Road Traffic Act 2010 come into operation.
[78] S.4(1), Road Traffic Act 2010.
[79] *Ibid.*, s.4(2).
[80] *Ibid.*, s.4(3).
[81] *Ibid.*, s.4(1).
[82] *Ibid.*, s.4(6).
[83] *Ibid.*, s.4(8).
[84] *Ibid.*, s.5(10).

case law has clearly stated that any power of arrest invoked must be properly exercised for the arrest to be deemed lawful.[85]

SPECIFIED PERSON – SECTION 3 OF THE ROAD TRAFFIC ACT 2010

Specified persons are defined under section 3 as:

(a) holders of driving permits;

(b) people who hold a first full licence for less than two years;

(c) people with a full licence for and driving (attempting to drive or being in charge of) vehicles in categories:
D (passenger vehicle – more 8 people); D1 (passenger vehicle – between 8 – 16 people); EB (vehicle – up to 8 passengers & trailer); EC (Goods vehicles over 3,500kg with a trailer); EC1 (Goods vehicles between 3,500kg – 7,500kg & trailer [combined max weight 12,000kg]); ED (Passenger vehicles in category D & trailer); ED1 (Passenger vehicles in category D1 & trailer – combined max weight less than 12,000kg) and W (Work vehicles with or without a trailer);

(d) holder of SPSV (small public service vehicle) licence – (taxi, hackney, limousine);

(e) persons who have no licence for category of vehicle being driven – either at the time of offence – or at any time in the five years preceding the offence.

There is a presumption in law, until the contrary is shown, that a person under subsection (c) or (d) is a 'specified person' for the purposes of Part II of the Road Traffic Act 2010.[86] Where a Garda forms the opinion that a person has committed and offence contrary to section 4, they may arrest that person without warrant.[87]

PROCEDURE IN RELATION TO PERSON REQUIRED TO UNDERGO BREATH TEST WHO CANNOT PRODUCE THEIR DRIVING LICENCE – SECTION 8 OF THE ROAD TRAFFIC ACT 2010

Under section 8 of the Road Traffic Act 2010,[88] where a person is required to produce a breath specimen either on the basis of a Garda

---

[85] See *DPP v. Moloney* (unreported, Finnegan J., 20 December 2001); *DPP v. Haslam* (unreported, O'Caoimh J., 27 January 2003); *DPP v. Edward Byrne* [2002] 2 I.L.R.M. 268, [2002] I.R. 397; *DPP v. O'Neill* (unreported, Edwards J., 15 February 2008).
[86] S.3, Road Traffic Act 2010 – when same section comes into operation.
[87] *Ibid.*, s.4(8).
[88] When same section comes into operation.

opinion,[89] or under mandatory testing provision,[90] and that person cannot produce a full driving licence there and then upon lawful demand,[91] they will be presumed to be a 'specified person' until they produce and present their licence (or evidence that they hold a licence), within 10 days of lawful demand at a nominated Garda station.[92] At the prosecution of an offence under section 4 or section 5 of the Road Traffic Act 2010, a defendant who cannot demonstrate in court that they produced and presented their driving licence at a nominated Garda Station shall be tried as a 'specified person,'[93] notwithstanding the fact that they may be in a position to produce a licence at the trial of the offence.

Preliminary Impairment Testing – Section 11 of the Road Traffic Act 2010

Where someone is charged with an offence of driving under the influence of an intoxicant,[94] practitioners should have special regard to the provisions of section 11 of the Road Traffic Act 2010,[95] which sets out the procedure in respect of preliminary impairment testing. Under this provision, a Garda may, for the purposes of assisting them to form an opinion that a person is under the influence of an intoxicant to such an extent as to impair their ability to drive, require that person to perform (in the presence of at least one other Garda)[96] such impairment tests[97] as may prescribed by the Minister under regulation.[98] Any person who fails to comply with provisions of section 11 will be guilty of an offence and may be arrested without warrant.[99] Failure to comply with a lawful request to perform a preliminary impairment test is an offence.[100]

---

[89] S.9, Road Traffic Act 2010.
[90] *Ibid.*, s.10.
[91] S.40, Road Traffic Act 1961.
[92] S.8(2), Road Traffic Act 2010.
[93] *Ibid.*, s.8(4)(b).
[94] *Ibid.*, s.4(1) or indeed s.5(1) in respect of an offence of being in charge with the intent to drive/attempt to drive whilst under influence of an intoxicant.
[95] When same section comes into operation.
[96] S.11(2), Road Traffic Act 2010.
[97] *Ibid.*, s.11(2).
[98] *Ibid.*, s.11(3).
[99] *Ibid.*, s.11(5).
[100] *Ibid.*, s.11(4).

Penalties

In respect of offences under section 11, a range of penalties exist:

Summary Conviction: fine of up to €5,000 and/or a term of imprisonment of up six months.[101]
Section 1(1) of the Probation of Offenders Act 1907 shall not apply to this offence.[102]

Disqualification:

Ancillary Disqualification: whilst a conviction under section 11 does not carry a mandatory disqualification, theoretically, it is open to the court to make an ancillary disqualification order under section 27 of the Road Traffic Act 1961 on the particular facts of the case.

However, someone who fails to provide a specimen under this section will be arrested and brought to a Garda Station where section 12 of the Road Traffic Act 2010[103] is invoked. Prosecutions under section 4, section 5 or section 12 will all carry mandatory disqualifications in their own right.[104]

Penalties

In respect of offences under section 4 of the Road Traffic Act 2010, a range of penalties will exist:

Summary Conviction: fine of up to €5,000 and/or a term of imprisonment of up six months.[105]
Section 1(1) of the Probation of Offenders Act 1907 shall not apply to this offence.[106]

Section 4(1): – i.e. under the influence of an intoxicant to such an extent as being incapable of having proper control of the vehicle is as follows:

First Offence – minimum four-year consequential disqualification.

Second/Subsequent Offence (drink driving offence): minimum six years' disqualification.[107]

---

[101] *Ibid.,* s.11(4).
[102] *Ibid.,* s.11(6).
[103] When same section comes into operation.
[104] *Ibid.,* s.65(4), when same section comes into operation.
[105] *Ibid.,* s.4(5).
[106] *Ibid.,* s.4(7).
[107] *Ibid.,* s.65(4)(a).

The periods of disqualification for a conviction for drink driving under subsections (2)–(4) will be as follows:

Section 4(2), 4(3) and 4(4) – driving with BAC over 50mg/100ml: (New lowest category) Concentration of alcohol not exceeding; 80mg/100ml (blood); 107mg/100ml (urine); 35mg/100ml (breath).

There is an option to pay a fixed penalty notice without going to court.[108] In this case, where the fixed penalty charge is paid within the appropriate time, a fine and penalty points will be imposed without a prosecution being initiated against the defendant.[109] This option is only open to defendant for a first offence in respect of this category who has no drink driving conviction within the previous three years. A defendant who does not hold a valid driving licence or is disqualified from driving cannot avail of this option.[110]

A defendant is not eligible to be served with a second fixed penalty notice within a three-year period[111] and any second offence under sections 49 or 50 of the Road Traffic Act 1961, section 13 of the Road Traffic Act 1994, sections 4, 5 or 12 of the Road Traffic Act 2010 will involve a court prosecution. If a defendant is eligible to avail of, and does avail of, this option they will incur;

Penalty points: three penalty points[112] – no mandatory disqualification.

Fine: €200.[113]

Upon conviction in Court:

First Offence – six months' consequential disqualification

Second Offence – one year consequential disqualification[114]

Fine: up to €5,000 and/or term of imprisonment of up to six months.[115]
Section 1(1) of the Probation of Offenders Act 1907 shall not apply to this offence.[116]

---

[108] *Ibid.*, s.29.
[109] *Ibid.*, s.29(1).
[110] *Ibid.*, s.29(4).
[111] *Ibid.*, s.29(5).
[112] *Ibid.*, s.29(11)(e).
[113] *Ibid.*, s.29(7).
[114] *Ibid.*, s.65(4)(b).
[115] *Ibid.*, s.4(5).
[116] *Ibid.*, s.4(7).

It is also open to a 'specified person' for whom the 20mg/100ml BAC applies to avail of option of dealing with matter by way of paying the fixed penalty charge. If a defendant is eligible (see above) to avail of, and does avail of, this option they will incur:

First Offence – three months' consequential disqualification.[117]

Fine: €200.[118]

Upon conviction in Court:

> **First Offence** – six months' consequential disqualification.

> **Second Offence** – one year consequential disqualification.[119]

> **Fine:** up to €5,000 and/or term of imprisonment of up to six months.[120]
> Section 1(1) of the Probation of Offenders Act 1907 shall not apply to this offence.[121]

Section 4(2), 4(3), 4(4): Concentration of alcohol between: 80–100mg/100ml (blood); 107–135mg/100ml (urine); 35–44mg/100ml (breath)

There is an option to pay a fixed penalty notice without going to court.[122] In this case, where the fixed penalty charge is paid within the appropriate time, a fine and disqualification will be imposed without a prosecution being initiated against the defendant.[123] This option is only open to defendant for a first offence in respect of this category who has no previous drink driving conviction within the previous three years. A defendant who does not hold a valid driving licence or is disqualified from driving cannot avail of this option.[124]

A defendant is not eligible to be served with a second fixed penalty notice within a three-year period[125] and any second offence under sections 49 or 50 of the Road Traffic Act 1961, section 13 of the Road Traffic Act 1994 and sections 4, 5 or 1 of the Road Traffic Act 2010 will involve a court prosecution. If a defendant is eligible to avail of, and

---

[117] *Ibid.*, s.29(8)(b).
[118] *Ibid.*, s.29(7)(a).
[119] *Ibid.*, s.65(4)(b).
[120] *Ibid.*, s.4(5).
[121] *Ibid.*, s.4(7).
[122] *Ibid.*, s.29.
[123] *Ibid.*, s.29(1).
[124] *Ibid.*, s.29(4).
[125] *Ibid.*, s.29(5).

does avail of, this option they will incur:

First Offence – six months' consequential disqualification.[126]

Fine: €400.[127]

Upon conviction in Court:

First Offence – one year consequential disqualification.

Second Offence – two years' consequential disqualification.[128]

Fine: Up to €5,000 and/or term of imprisonment of up to six months.[129]

Section 1(1) of the Probation of Offenders Act 1907 shall not apply to this offence.[130]

Section 4(2), 4(3), 4(4): Concentration of alcohol between: 100–150mg/100ml (blood); 135–200mg/100ml (urine); 44–66mg/100ml (breath)

Upon Conviction:

First Offence – two years' consequential disqualification.

Second Offence – four years' consequential disqualification.[131]

Fine: up to €5,000 and/or term of imprisonment of up to six months.[132]

Section 1(1) of the Probation of Offenders Act 1907 shall not apply to this offence.[133]

Section 4(2), 4(3), 4(4): Concentration of alcohol exceeding: 150mg/100ml (blood); 200mg/100ml (urine); 66mg/100ml (breath)

First Offence – three years' consequential disqualification.

Second Offence – six years' consequential disqualification.[134]

Fine: up to €5,000 and/or term of imprisonment of up to six months.[135]

---

[126] *Ibid.*, s 29(8)(ii).
[127] *Ibid.*, s.29(7)(b).
[128] *Ibid.*, s.65(4)(b).
[129] *Ibid.*, s.4(5).
[130] *Ibid.*, s.4(7).
[131] *Ibid.*, s.65(4)(b).
[132] *Ibid.*, s.4(5).
[133] *Ibid.*, s.4(7).
[134] *Ibid.*, s.65(4)(b).
[135] *Ibid.*, s.4(5).

Section 1(1) of the Probation of Offenders Act 1907 shall not apply to this offence.[136]

EARLY RESTORATION OF LICENCE – REMOVAL OF DISQUALIFICATION – SECTION 29 OF THE ROAD TRAFFIC ACT 1961

Under section 29 of the Road Traffic Act 1961 as substituted by section 7 of the Road Traffic Act 2006, only people who have been disqualified for the first time and for a period in excess of two years[137] (i.e. at least two years and one day), can apply to the court to have their licence restored. The applicant must have served half of their disqualification period before an application is made,[138] and their licence (if the application is successful) can only be restored after they have served two thirds of their period of disqualification.[139] An application should be made to the court where a disqualification order is made (or a court in same district/circuit, if disqualification order was altered on appeal or the matter was tried on indictment).[140]

In considering this application, the court will have regard to a number of factors including the nature of the offence, whether the defendant was convicted of other road traffic offences arising out of same incident, whether the defendant has accrued any previous or subsequent convictions for other road traffic offences, whether the defendant has accrued any previous or subsequent criminal convictions and the views of the Gardaí.[141]

As stated above, if the court is agreeable to reducing a defendant's period of disqualification, they can only reduce the overall period of disqualification to two thirds the period of the disqualification order. Furthermore, if an applicant has already had their licence restored within the previous ten years, they are statute-barred from making a second restoration of licence application within that 10-year period.[142] If an application is refused, it can be renewed after three months and matter can also be appealed. If disqualification was imposed before the commencement of section 7 of the Road Traffic Act 2006 (i.e. 5 March 2007[143]), the previous provisions of

---

[136] *Ibid.*, s.4(7).
[137] S.29(1), Road Traffic Act 1961 as substituted by s.7, Road Traffic Act 2006.
[138] *Ibid.*, s.29(2) as substituted by s.7, Road Traffic Act 2006.
[139] *Ibid.*, s.29(4) as substituted by s.7, Road Traffic Act 2006.
[140] *Ibid.*, s.29(2) as substituted by s.7, Road Traffic Act 2006.
[141] *Ibid.*, s.29(3) as substituted by s.7, Road Traffic Act 2006.
[142] *Ibid.*, s.29(1) as substituted by s.7, Road Traffic Act 2006.
[143] S.I. No.86/2007, Road Traffic Act 2006 (Commencement) Order 2007.

section 29 of the Road Traffic Act 1961 apply to the restoration application.

Early Restoration of Licence – Section 67 of the Road Traffic Act 2010

Practitioners should note that section 67 of the Road Traffic Act 2010[144] amends section 29 of the Principle Act (as substituted by section 7 of the Road Traffic Act 2006), so that a licence can be restored by the court only after two thirds of the period of disqualification, or a period of two years, whichever is greater,[145] has expired. This will mean that whatever disqualification period is imposed by the court, an individual will not be able to have their driving licence restored until at least two years of the period of disqualification has expired, and until two thirds of the period of disqualification has expired if disqualification imposed is greater than two years.

Being in Charge of a Mechanically-Propelled Vehicle While Under the Influence of an Intoxicating Liquor or Drug – Section 50 of the Road Traffic Act 1961

Section 50 of the Road Traffic Act 1961[146] sets out the following offences:

(a) being in charge of a mechanically-propelled vehicle, with the intent to drive or attempt to drive, (but not driving/attempting to drive) whilst under the influence of an intoxicant to such an extent as being incapable of having proper control of the vehicle;[147]

(b) being in charge of a mechanically-propelled vehicle, with the intent to drive or attempt to drive, (but not driving/attempting to drive) whilst there is present in your body a quantity of alcohol, such that within three hours of being in charge, the concentration of alcohol in your blood exceeds 80mg/100ml;[148]

(c) being in charge of a mechanically-propelled vehicle, with the intent to drive or attempt to drive, (but not driving/attempt-

---

[144] When same section comes into operation.
[145] S.29(4)(b), Road Traffic Act 1961 as substituted by s.66(1), Road Traffic Act 2010.
[146] As substituted by s.11, Road Traffic Act 1994, amended by s.23, Road Traffic Act 2002 and amended by s.18, Road Traffic Act 2006.
[147] S.50(1), Road Traffic Act 1961 as substituted by s.11, Road Traffic Act 1994.
[148] *Ibid.*, s.50(2) as substituted by s.11, Road Traffic Act 1994.

ing to drive) whilst there is present in your body a quantity of
alcohol, such that within three hours of being in charge, the
concentration of alcohol in your urine exceeds 107mg/100ml;[149]

(d) being in charge of a mechanically-propelled vehicle, with the
intent to drive or attempt to drive, (but not driving/attempt-
ing to drive) whilst there is present in your body a quantity of
alcohol, such that within three hours of being in charge, the
concentration of alcohol in your breath exceeds 35mg/100ml.[150]

There is a rebuttable presumption under section 50 that the defendant, if found in charge of a vehicle in a state of intoxication which
would render him unfit to drive, that he intended to drive, or attempt
to drive.[151] The key issue in this case is whether the defendant
intended to drive.[152] However, an essential element of the offence is
that the Garda can give evidence of having formed an opinion that
the defendant was in charge of the vehicle with the intention to drive.
Positive evidence should be adduced to that effect.

The prosecuting Garda should give evidence of observations that
led to them forming their opinion that the defendant was firstly,
under the influence of an intoxicant (observations such as smell of
alcohol on breath or slurred speech) and secondly, intoxicated to
such an extent that they could not properly control vehicle, like perhaps an observation that a defendant was unfit to perform a simple
co-ordination test voluntarily undertaken.

Evidence might also be adduced from other witnesses such as doctors who examined the defendant, or individuals who may have
witnessed the defendant consuming drink/drugs immediately prior
to attempting to drive.

In respect of offences of driving over the prescribed concentration of alcohol limits, evidence of the defendant's breathalyser test
result, a section 17 certificate (or a certified copy) must be produced.[153] In respect of prosecutions relying on the evidence of a
blood/urine test – a section 18 certificate (or a certified copy) must

---

[149] *Ibid.*, s.50(3) as substituted by s.11, Road Traffic Act 1994.
[150] *Ibid.*, s.50(1) as substituted by s.11, Road Traffic Act 1994.
[151] *Ibid.*, s.50(8) as substituted by s.11, Road Traffic Act 1994.
[152] *DPP v. Edward Byrne* [2002] 2 I.L.R.M. 268, [2002] 2 I.R. 397 – where Supreme
Court held that the intentions of the defendant (who was found asleep behind
wheel) before he fell asleep could be considered for purposes of s.50. However,
also see *DPP v. Gerard O'Neill* [2008] IEHC 457.
[153] See page 157 above.

be produced. Doctors' forms have also been held to be essential proof.[154]

Penalties

In respect of offences contrary to section 50, a range of penalties exist:

Summary Conviction: fine of up to €5,000 and/or a term of imprisonment of up to six months.[155]
Section 1(1) of the Probation of Offenders Act 1907 shall not apply to this offence.[156]

Disqualification: a conviction under section 50 carries a mandatory consequential disqualification.

Section 50(1) – i.e. under the influence of an intoxicant to such an extent as being incapable of having proper control of the vehicle is as follows:

First Offence – minimum four years' consequential disqualification.

Second/Subsequent Offence (drink driving offence) – minimum six years' consequential disqualification.[157]

The periods of disqualification for a conviction for drink driving under subsections (2)–(4) are as follows:

Lowest category – concentration of alcohol not exceeding: 100mg/100ml (blood): 135mg/100ml (urine): 44mg/100ml (breath)

First Offence – one year's consequential disqualification.

Second Offence – two years' consequential disqualification.[158]

Middle category – concentration of alcohol between: 100–150mg/100ml (blood): 135–200mg/100ml (urine): 44–66mg/100ml (breath).

First Offence – two years' consequential disqualification.

---

[154] See page 157 above.
[155] S.50(6)(a), Road Traffic Act 1961 as substituted by s.11, Road Traffic Act 1994 and amended by s.18, Road Traffic Act 2006.
[156] S.50(7), Road Traffic Act 1961 as substituted by s.11, Road Traffic Act 1994.
[157] See s.26(4)(a) as substituted by s.26, Road Traffic Act 1994 and further substituted by s.6(1)(a), Road Traffic Act 2006.
[158] See s.26(4)(b), Road Traffic Act 1961, as substituted by s.26, Road Traffic Act 1994 and further substituted by s.2, Road Traffic Act 1995 and substituted by table inserted by s. 6(1)(b), Road Traffic Act 2006.

Second Offence – four years' consequential disqualification.[159]

Highest category – concentration of alcohol exceeding: 150mg/ 100ml (blood): 200mg/100ml (urine): 66mg/100ml (breath).

First Offence – three years' consequential disqualification.

Second Offence – six year's consequential disqualification.[160]

BEING IN CHARGE OF A MECHANICALLY-PROPELLED VEHICLE – SECTION 5 OF THE ROAD TRAFFIC ACT 2010

Practitioners should note that section 50 of the Road Traffic Act 1961 is repealed by section 33 of the Road Traffic Act 2010 and replaced by section 5 of the Road Traffic Act 2010.[161] This provision in similar to the existing section 50, but reduces the BAC from 80mg/100ml to 50mg/100ml, prescribing a further reduced limit of 20mg/100ml in the case of 'specified persons'.

Section 5 creates the following four distinct offences:

(a) being in charge of a mechanically-propelled vehicle, with the intent to drive or attempt to drive, (but not driving/attempting to drive) whilst under the influence of an intoxicant to such an extent as being incapable of having proper control of the vehicle;[162]

(b) being in charge of a mechanically-propelled vehicle, with the intent to drive or attempt to drive, (but not driving/attempting to drive) whilst there is present in your body a quantity of alcohol, such that within 3 hours of being in charge, the concentration of alcohol in your blood exceeds 50mg/100ml- (20mg/100ml for specified persons);[163]

(c) being in charge of a mechanically-propelled vehicle, with the intent to drive or attempt to drive, (but not driving/attempting to drive) whilst there is present in your body a quantity of alcohol, such that within 3 hours of being in charge, the concentration of alcohol in your urine exceeds 67mg/100ml (27mg/100ml for specified persons);[164]

---

[159] See s.6(1)(a), Road Traffic Act 2006.
[160] *Ibid.*, s.6(1)(a).
[161] When ss.5 and 33, Road Traffic Act 2010 come into operation.
[162] S.5(1), Road Traffic Act 2010.
[163] *Ibid.*, s.5(2).
[164] *Ibid.*, s.5(3), Road Traffic Act 2010.

(d) being in charge of a mechanically-propelled vehicle, with the intent to drive or attempt to drive, (but not driving/attempting to drive) whilst there is present in your body a quantity of alcohol, such that within three hours of being in charge, the concentration of alcohol in your breath exceeds 22mg/100ml (9mg/100ml for specified persons).[165]

There is a rebuttable presumption that a defendant intended to drive/attempt to drive until the contrary is shown.[166] A person charged with an offence under section 5 may be found guilty of an offence of driving/attempting to drive whilst intoxicated[167] instead.[168] Again, a power of- arrest will arise under both section 4(8) and section 5(10) (like section 49(8) and section 50(10) of the original act) and where an issue subsequently arises as to under which section the Garda has formed his opinion that an arrestable offence had taken place, the court will have to consider the factual evidence given by the Garda. High Court case law has clearly stated that any power of arrest invoked must be properly exercised for the arrest to be deemed lawful.[169]

A defendant will not be able to be charged under section 5 and also under section 12 of the Licensing Act 1872 arising out of the same incident.[170] Where a Garda forms the opinion that a person has committed and offence contrary to section 5, they may arrest that person without warrant.[171]

Penalties

Section 5(1), Road Traffic Act 2010

Summary Conviction: fine of up to €5,000 and/or a term of imprisonment of up to six months.[172]

Section 1(1) Probation of Offenders Act 1907 shall not apply to this offence.[173]

---

[165] *Ibid.*, s.5(4).
[166] *Ibid.*, s.5(8).
[167] *Ibid.*, s.4.
[168] *Ibid.*, s.5(6).
[169] See *DPP v. Moloney* (unreported, Finnegan J., 20 December 2001); *DPP v. Haslam* (unreported, Ó Caoimh J., 27 January 2003); *DPP v. Edward Byrne* [2002] 2 I.L.R.M. 268, [2002] I.R. 397; *DPP v. O'Neill* (unreported, Edwards J., 15 February 2008).
[170] S.5(9), Road Traffic Act 2010.
[171] *Ibid.*, s.5(10).
[172] *Ibid.*, s.5(5).
[173] *Ibid.*, s.5(7).

Disqualification: a conviction under section 5(1) carries a minimum mandatory consequential disqualification.

First Offence – four years' consequential disqualification.

Second Offence – six years' consequential disqualification.[174]

The periods of disqualification for a conviction for drink driving under subsections (2)–(4) will be as follows:

Section 5(2), 5(3) and 5(4) – driving with BAC over 50mg/100ml: (New lowest category) Concentration of alcohol not exceeding;80mg/100ml (blood); 107mg/100ml (urine); 35mg/100ml (breath).

There is an option to pay a fixed penalty notice without going to court.[175] In this case, where the fixed penalty charge is paid within the appropriate time, a fine and penalty points will be imposed without a prosecution being initiated against the defendant.[176] This option is only open to defendant for a first offence in respect of this category who has no drink driving conviction within the previous three years. A defendant who does not hold a valid driving licence or is disqualified from driving cannot avail of this option.[177]

A defendant is not eligible to be served with a second fixed penalty notice within a three-year period[178] and any second offence under sections 49 and 50 of the Road Traffic Act 1961, section 13 of the Road Traffic Act 1994 or sections 4 and 5 of the Road Traffic Act 2010 will involve a court prosecution. If a defendant is eligible to avail of, and does avail of, this option they will incur:

Penalty points: three penalty points[179] – No mandatory disqualification.

Fine: €200.[180]

Upon conviction in Court:

First Offence – six months' consequential disqualification.

Second Offence – one year consequential disqualification.[181]

---

174 *Ibid.*, s.65(4)(a).
175 *Ibid.*, s.29.
176 *Ibid.*, s.29(1).
177 *Ibid.*, s.29(4).
178 *Ibid.*, s.29(5).
179 *Ibid.*, s.29(11)(e).
180 *Ibid.*, s.29(7).
181 *Ibid.*, s.65(4)(b).

Fine: Up to €5,000 and/or term of imprisonment of up to six months.[182]

Section 1(1) of the Probation of Offenders Act 1907 shall not apply to this offence.[183]

It is also open to a 'specified person' for whom the 20mg/100ml BAC applies to avail of option of dealing with matter by way of paying fixed penalty charge. If a defendant is eligible (see above) to avail of, and does avail of, this option they will incur;

First Offence – three months consequential disqualification.[184]

Fine: €200.[185]

Upon conviction in Court:

First Offence – six months' consequential disqualification.

Second Offence – one year consequential disqualification.[186]

Fine: up to €5,000 and/or term of imprisonment of up to six months.[187]

Section 1(1) of the Probation of Offenders Act 1907 shall not apply to this offence.[188]

Section 5(2), 5(3), 5(4): Concentration of alcohol between: 80–100mg/100ml (blood); 107–135mg/100ml (urine); 35–44mg/100ml (breath)

There is an option to pay a fixed penalty notice without going to court.[189] In this case, where the fixed penalty charge is paid within the appropriate time, a fine and disqualification will be imposed without a prosecution being initiated against the defendant.[190] This option is only open to defendant for a first offence in respect of this category who has no previous drink driving conviction within previous three years. A defendant who does not hold a valid driving licence or is disqualified from driving cannot avail of this option.[191]

---

[182] *Ibid.*, s.5(5).
[183] *Ibid.*, s.5(7).
[184] *Ibid.*, s.29(8)(b).
[185] *Ibid.*, s.29(7)(a).
[186] *Ibid.*, s.65(4)(b).
[187] *Ibid.*, s.5(5).
[188] *Ibid.*, s.5(7).
[189] *Ibid.*, s.29.
[190] *Ibid.*, s.29(1).
[191] *Ibid.*, s.29(4).

A defendant is not eligible to be served with a second fixed penalty notice within a three-year period[192] and any second offence under sections 49 and 50 of the Road Traffic Act 1961, section 13 of the Road Traffic Act 1994, sections 4 and 5 of the Road Traffic Act 2010 will involve a court prosecution. If a defendant is eligible to avail of, and does avail of, this option they will incur:

First Offence – six months' consequential disqualification.[193]

Fine: €400.[194]

Upon conviction in Court:

First Offence – one year's consequential disqualification.

Second Offence – two years' consequential disqualification.[195]

Fine: up to €5,000 and/or term of imprisonment of up to six months.[196] Section 1(1) of the Probation of Offenders Act 1907 shall not apply to this offence.[197]

Section 5(2), 5(3), 5(4): Concentration of alcohol between: 100–150mg/100ml (blood); 135–200mg/100ml (urine); 44–66mg/100ml (breath)

Upon Conviction:

First Offence – two years' consequential disqualification.

Second Offence – four years' consequential disqualification.[198]

Fine: up to €5,000 and/or term of imprisonment of up to six months.[199] Section 1(1) of the Probation of Offenders Act 1907 shall not apply to this offence.[200]

Section 5(2), 5(3), 5(4): Concentration of alcohol exceeding: 150mg/100ml (blood); 200mg/ 100ml (urine); 66mg/100ml (breath)

First Offence – three years' consequential disqualification.

---

[192] *Ibid.*, s.29(5).
[193] *Ibid.*, s.29(8)(ii).
[194] *Ibid.*, s.29(7)(b).
[195] *Ibid.*, s.65(4)(b).
[196] *Ibid.*, s.5(5).
[197] *Ibid.*, s.5(7).
[198] *Ibid.*, s.65(4)(b).
[199] *Ibid.*, s.5(5).
[200] *Ibid.*, s.5(7).

Second Offence – six years' consequential disqualification.[201]

Fine: up to €5,000 and/or term of imprisonment of up to six months.[202] Section 1(1) of the Probation of Offenders Act 1907 shall not apply to this offence.[203]

DRIVING OR ATTEMPTING TO DRIVE AN ANIMAL-DRAWN VEHICLE OR A PEDAL CYCLE WHILE UNDER INFLUENCE OF AN INTOXICATING LIQUOR OR DRUG – SECTION 51 OF THE ROAD TRAFFIC ACT 1961

A less commonly known and indeed less frequently prosecuted series of offences are set out under section 51:[204]

(a) driving or attempting to drive an animal drawn-vehicle,[205] or

(b) cycling or attempting to cycle in a public place,[206]

whilst under the influence of an intoxicant to such an extent as being incapable of having proper control of an animal-drawn vehicle or cycle.

Prosecutions in respect of offences involving animal-drawn vehicles are obviously extremely rare in the 21st century. In respect of pedal cycle offences, prosecutions would also be uncommon. In many cases, where a Garda stops an individual attempting to cycle whilst drunk, they are more likely to be dealt with under section 4 of the Criminal Justice (Public Order) Act 1994,[207] or to be charged with endangerment of traffic[208] than under drink driving provisions. A defendant cannot be charged under section 51 and also under section 12 of the Licensing Act 1872 arising out of the same incident.[209]

Penalties

In respect of offences contrary to section 51(2),[210] the penalties are as

---

[201] *Ibid.*, s.65(4)(b).

[202] *Ibid.*, s.5(5).

[203] *Ibid.*, s.5(7).

[204] As amended by s.3, Road Traffic (Amendment) Act 1984, s.23, Road Traffic Act 2002 and s.18, Road Traffic Act 2006.

[205] S.51(1)(a), Road Traffic Act 1961.

[206] *Ibid.*, s.51(1)(b).

[207] Intoxicated in a public place.

[208] S.14, Non Fatal Offences against the Person Act 1997.

[209] S.51(3), Road Traffic Act 1961.

[210] As amended by s.3, Road Traffic (Amendment) Act 1984, s.23, Road Traffic Act 2002 and s.18, Road Traffic Act 2006.

follows:

Animal-Drawn Vehicle – Summary Conviction:

First Offence – fine of up to €1000 and/or a term of imprisonment of up to one month.[211]

Second/subsequent Offence – fine of up to €2000 and/or a term of imprisonment of up to three months.[212]

Pedal Cycle – Summary Conviction:
Fine of up to €1000 and/or a term of imprisonment of up to three months.[213]

Disqualification:

Ancillary Disqualification: whilst a conviction under section 51 does not carry a mandatory disqualification, it is open to the court to make an ancillary disqualification order under section 27 of the Road Traffic Act 1961 on the particular facts of the case.

DRIVING OR ATTEMPTING TO DRIVE AN ANIMAL-DRAWN VEHICLE OR A PEDAL CYCLE WHILE UNDER INFLUENCE OF AN INTOXICATING LIQUOR OR DRUG – SECTION 6 OF THE ROAD TRAFFIC ACT 2010

Practitioners should note that section 51 of the Road Traffic Act 1961 is repealed by section 33 of the Road Traffic Act 2010 and replaced by section 6 of the Road Traffic Act 2010.[214] It creates similar offences to those existing under the current section 51, namely:

(a) driving or attempting to drive an animal-drawn vehicle,[215] or

(b) cycling or attempting to cycle in a public place,[216]

whilst under the influence of an intoxicant to such an extent as being incapable of having proper control of an animal-drawn vehicle or cycle.

A defendant will not be able to be charged under section 6 and also under section 12 of the Licensing Act 1872 arising out of the same incident.[217]

---

[211] S.51(2)(a), Road Traffic Act 1961 – see also s.18, Road Traffic Act 2006.
[212] *Ibid.*
[213] *Ibid.*
[214] When ss.6 and 33, Road Traffic Act 2010 come into operation.
[215] S.6(1)(a), Road Traffic Act 2010.
[216] *Ibid.*, s.6(1)(b).
[217] *Ibid.*, s.6(3).

Penalties

In respect of offences contrary to section 6(2), the penalties are as follows:

Animal Drawn Vehicle – Summary Conviction:

First Offence – fine of up to €3000 and/or a term of imprisonment of up to one month.[218]

Second/subsequent Offence – fine of up to €5000 and/or a term of imprisonment of up to three months.[219]

Pedal Cycle – Summary Conviction: fine of up to €2000.[220]

Disqualification:

Ancillary Disqualification: whilst a conviction under section 6 does not carry a mandatory disqualification, it is open to the court to make an ancillary disqualification order under section 27 of the Road Traffic Act 1961 on the particular facts of the case.

OBLIGATION TO PROVIDE A PRELIMINARY BREATH SPECIMEN – SECTION 12 OF THE ROAD TRAFFIC ACT 1994

Under section 12 of the Road Traffic Act 1994,[221] if a Garda forms the opinion that an individual:

(a) is intoxicated, or has consumed intoxicating liquor;[222]

(b) has committed a road traffic offence (other than drink driving offence);[223] or

(c) has been involved in a road traffic accident;[224]

then the Garda may require that the defendant provide a breath-test sample in the vicinity of the public place concerned, or if he does not have apparatus to conduct breath test, remain at the place in presence of a member of the Gardaí (for a period of no more than one hour) until such apparatus becomes available.[225]

---

[218] *Ibid.*, s.6(2)(a).
[219] *Ibid.*, s.6(2)(a).
[220] *Ibid.*, s.6(2)(b).
[221] As substituted by s.3, Road Traffic Act 2003 and amended by s.18, Road Traffic Act 2006.
[222] S.12(1)(a), Road traffic Act 1994 as substituted by s.3, Road Traffic Act 2003.
[223] *Ibid.*, s.12(1)(b) as substituted by s.3, Road Traffic Act 2003.
[224] *Ibid.*, s.12(1)(c) as substituted by s.3, Road Traffic Act 2003.
[225] *Ibid.*, s.12(2) as substituted by s.3, Road Traffic Act 2003.

If a defendant refuses/fails to comply immediately with a lawful requirement under this section, or a lawful requirement indicated by a Garda, they will be guilty of an offence[226] and may be arrested without a warrant.[227]

The Garda's powers to require a person to provide a breath specimen are based upon the Garda having formed an opinion that the defendant is either intoxicated, has committed a road traffic offence or been involved in a road traffic accident. If a defendant is to be breathalysed on the basis of the Garda's opinion, positive evidence should be adduced as to how and why Garda formed this opinion. The Garda's opinion should be an honest and reasonably held opinion with regard to factual circumstances of case: such a reasonably and honestly held belief will not be defeated merely because it is later shown to be factually inaccurate. However, an opinion which is irrational or contrived will render any subsequent arrest unlawful.[228]

The prosecuting Garda should give evidence of observations that led to them forming their opinion that the defendant was firstly, under the influence of an intoxicant (observations such as smell of alcohol on breath or slurred speech); and secondly, intoxicated to such an extent that they could not properly control vehicle (like an observation, perhaps, that a defendant was unfit to perform a simple coordination test voluntarily undertaken).

OBLIGATION TO PROVIDE A MANDATORY BREATH SPECIMEN – SECTION 4(6) OF THE ROAD TRAFFIC ACT 2006

Practitioners should also note that in the case of Mandatory Breath Testing Checkpoints, an obligation to provide a required specimen is set out in section 4 of the Road Traffic Act 2006. In these cases, the statutory authority for the request is the written authorisation[229] signed by a Garda not below the rank of Inspector.[230] The original/ copy authorisation should be produced during prosecution of the

---

[226] *Ibid.*, s.12(3) as substituted by s.3, Road Traffic Act 2003.
[227] *Ibid.*, s.12(4) as substituted by s.3, Road Traffic Act 2003.
[228] *Hobbs v. Hurley* (unreported; High Court; Costello J., 10 June 1980); *DPP v. Breheny* (unreported, Supreme Court, 2 March 1993); *DPP v. Bernard Joyce* (unreported, High Court, Quirke J., 15 July, 2004; *DPP v. Penny* [2006] 3 I.R. 553; *DPP v. Jonathan Finnegan* [2008] IEHC 347.
[229] S.4(3), Road Traffic Act 2006.
[230] S.4(2), Road Traffic Act 2006.

offence[231] and practitioners should carefully examine the authorisation to ensure that all the details (location, date, time, signature of authorised person etc) contained in same are correct and sufficiently detailed and specific to grant the Gardaí the powers exercised.

In this respect, practitioners should have regard to the provisions set out in section 4 of the Road Traffic Act 2006. If a defendant refuses/fails to comply immediately with a lawful requirement under section 4 of the Road Traffic Act 2006, they will be guilty of an offence[232] and may be arrested without a warrant.[233]

A Garda may require that the person in charge of the vehicle[234] provides a breath-test sample, either there,[235] or at a place in the vicinity of the public place concerned,[236] and/or leave or move their vehicle as directed and keep or leave vehicle until they have complied with lawful demand to provide preliminary breath specimen.[237]

In cases under both section 12 of the Road Traffic Act 1994 and section 4 of the Road Traffic Act 2006, the Garda should give evidence of having made a lawful request for a specimen. Furthermore, the Garda should advise the defendant, there and then, of the statutory authority being exercised and the consequences for the defendant of refusing/failing to comply with the requirement. However, practitioners should note that where a defendant complies with the lawful request made by a Garda to provide a breath sample, the court is unlikely to draw any adverse inference from Garda failing to give evidence of having advised defendant that it was a criminal offence to refuse to give specimen and of the penalties that apply. Where a defendant is failing/refusing to comply with the request, however, they must be advised that it is a criminal offence to fail/refuse to provide breath sample and of the penalties which may apply.[238] There is a rebuttable presumption as to the legality of the apparatus used.[239] Practitioners should also be cognisant of the provisions of section 23 of the Road Traffic Act 1994 (defence to refusal to give a specimen).

---

[231] *Weir v. DPP* [2008] IEHC 268.

[232] S.4(6), Road Traffic Act 2006.

[233] *Ibid.*, s.4(7), Road Traffic Act 2006.

[234] *Ibid.*, s.4(4), Road Traffic Act 2006.

[235] *Ibid.*, s.4(4)(a)(i), Road Traffic Act 2006.

[236] *Ibid.*, s.4(4)(a)(ii), Road Traffic Act 2006.

[237] *Ibid.*, s.4(4)(b), Road Traffic Act 2006.

[238] See *DPP v. Shane Canavan* [2007] IEHC 46 (unreported, Birmingham J., 1 August 2007).

[239] See s.12(5), Road Traffic Act 1994 and s.4(8), Road Traffic Act 2006.

Penalties

In respect of an offence contrary to section 12(3) of the Road Traffic Act 1994 or section 4(6) of the Road Traffic Act 2006, the following penalties apply:

Summary Conviction: fine of up to €5,000,[240] and/or a term of imprisonment of up to six months.[241]

Disqualification:

Ancillary Disqualification: whilst a conviction under section 12(5) or section 4(6) does not carry a mandatory disqualification, theoretically it is open to the court to make an ancillary disqualification order under section 27 of the Road Traffic Act 1961 on the particular facts of the case.

However, someone who fails to provide a specimen under these sections will be arrested and brought to a Garda Station where section 13 of the Road Traffic Act 1994 will be invoked. Prosecutions under section 49, section 50 or section 13 (failure/refusal to give sample) all carry mandatory disqualifications in their own right.

OBLIGATION TO PROVIDE A PRELIMINARY BREATH SPECIMEN – SECTION 9 OF THE ROAD TRAFFIC ACT 2010

Practitioners should note that section 12 of the Road Traffic Act 1994 is repealed by section 33 of the Road Traffic Act 2010 and replaced by section 9 of the Road Traffic Act 2010.[242] This provision is similar to existing section 12 and sets out that if a Garda:

(1) forms the opinion that a person in charge of a vehicle in a public place;

(a) has consumed intoxicating liquor;[243]

(b) has committed a road traffic offence (other than drink driving offence);[244] or

(c) has been involved in a road traffic collision;[245] or

---

[240] See s.12(3)(b) as amended by s.18, Table, Pt.4, Reference 1, Road Traffic Act 2006.
[241] S.12(3)(b), Road Traffic Act 1994 and s.4(6)(b), Road Traffic Act 2006.
[242] When ss.9 and 33, Road Traffic Act 2010 come into operation.
[243] S.9(1)(a)(i), Road Traffic Act 2010.
[244] *Ibid.*, s.9(1)(a)(ii).
[245] *Ibid.*, s.9(1)(a)(iii).

(2) attends at an accident (in public place) resulting in injury to any person, such as to require that person to medical assistance and same accident involved the defendant's vehicle.[246]

then that Garda may require that the person in charge of the vehicle:

(i)   provides a breath-test sample, either there;[247] or

(ii)   at a place in the vicinity of the public place concerned;[248] or

(iii)   if he does not have apparatus to conduct breath test, that that person remain at that place, in presence of a member of Garda, for a period of no more than one hour) until apparatus becomes available and then provide breath-test sample.[249]

If a defendant refuses/fails to comply immediately with a lawful requirement under this section, or a lawful requirement indicated by Garda, they will be guilty of an offence[250] and may be arrested without warrant.[251] A Garda shall not make a lawful request of any person to provide a preliminary specimen if the Garda is of the opinion that such person is, as a result of an accident, is incapable of complying with such a request.[252]

Again, the Garda's powers to require a defendant to provide a preliminary breath-test sample are based upon either:

(a) the Garda having formed an opinion that the defendant is either intoxicated, has committed a road traffic offence or been involved in a road traffic accident; or

(b) the Garda having attended an accident involving the defendant's vehicle where injury was caused to any person.

If a defendant is to be breathalysed on the basis of a Garda's opinion, positive evidence should be adduced as to how and why a Garda formed this opinion. Prosecuting Gardaí should give evidence of observations that led to them forming their opinion that the defendant was firstly, under the influence of an intoxicant (observations such as smell of alcohol on breath or slurred speech); and secondly,

---

[246] *Ibid.*, s.9(1)(b).
[247] *Ibid.*, s.9(1)(i).
[248] *Ibid.*, s.9(1)(ii).
[249] *Ibid.*, s.9(1)(iii), Road Traffic Act 2010.
[250] *Ibid.*, s.9(3).
[251] *Ibid.*, s.9(4).
[252] *Ibid.*, s.9(2).

intoxicated to such an extent that they could not properly control vehicle (like an observation, perhaps, that a defendant was unfit to perform a simple coordination test voluntarily undertaken). There is a rebuttable presumption as to the legality of the apparatus used.[253]

Penalties

In respect of an offence contrary to section 9(3), the following penalties apply:

Summary Conviction: fine of up to €5,000 and/or term of imprisonment of up to 6 months.[254]
Section 1(1) of the Probation of Offenders Act 1907 does not apply.[255]

Disqualification: whilst a conviction does not carry a mandatory disqualification, theoretically it would open to the court to make an ancillary disqualification order under section 27 of the Road Traffic Act 1961 on the particular facts of the case. However, someone who fails to provide a specimen under this section will be arrested and brought to a Garda Station where section 12 of the Road Traffic Act 2010 would be invoked.

OBLIGATION TO PROVIDE A MANDATORY BREATH SPECIMEN – SECTION 10 OF THE ROAD TRAFFIC ACT 2010

Practitioners should note that section 4 of the Road Traffic Act 2006 is repealed by section 33 of the Road Traffic Act 2010 and replaced by section 10 of the Road Traffic Act 2010.[256] This provision is almost identical to the existing section 4 and sets out sets out the obligation to provide a required specimen at Mandatory Breath Testing Checkpoints. In these cases, the statutory authority for the request is the written authorisation[257] signed by a Garda not below rank of Inspector.[258] The original/copy authorisation should be produced during prosecution of the offence[259] and practitioners should carefully -

---

[253] *Ibid.*, s.9(5).
[254] *Ibid.*, s.9(3).
[255] *Ibid.*, s.9(6).
[256] When ss.9 and 33, Road Traffic Act 2010 come into operation.
[257] S.10(3), Road Traffic Act 2010.
[258] *Ibid.*, s.10(2).
[259] *Weir v. DPP* [2008] IEHC 268.

examine the authorisation to ensure that all the details (location, date, time, signature of authorised person etc) contained in same are correct and sufficiently detailed and specific to grant the Gardaí the powers exercised.

In this respect, practitioners should have regard to the provisions set out in section 10 of the Road Traffic Act 2010. If a defendant refuses/fails to comply immediately with a lawful requirement under section 10, they will be guilty of an offence[260] and may be arrested without a warrant.[261] There is a rebuttable presumption as to the legality of the apparatus used.[262]

Under this section, a Garda may require that the person in charge of the vehicle:

(i)   provides a breath-test sample, either there;[263]

(ii)   or at a place in the vicinity of the public place concerned,[264] and/or;

(iii) leave or move their vehicle as directed and keep or leave vehicle until they have complied with a lawful demand to provide a preliminary breath specimen.[265]

Penalties

In respect of an offence contrary to section 10 of the Road Traffic Act 2010, the following penalties apply:

Summary Conviction: fine of up to €5,000 and/or term of imprisonment of up to 6 months.[266]

Disqualification: whilst a conviction does not carry a mandatory disqualification, theoretically it would open to the court to make an ancillary disqualification order under section 27 of the Road Traffic Act 1961 on the particular facts of the case. However, someone who fails to provide a specimen under this section will be arrested and brought to a Garda Station where section 12 of the Road Traffic Act 2010 would be invoked.

---

[260] S.10(6), Road Traffic Act 2010.
[261] *Ibid.*, s.10(7).
[262] *Ibid.*, s.10(8).
[263] *Ibid.*, s.10(4)(a)(i).
[264] *Ibid.*, s.10(4)(a)(ii).
[265] *Ibid.*, s.10(4)(b).
[266] *Ibid.*, s.10(6).

OBLIGATION TO PROVIDE A SPECIMEN FOLLOWING ARREST – SECTION 13 OF THE ROAD TRAFFIC ACT 1994

Under section 13 of the Road Traffic Act 1994[267] where an individual is arrested for:

(a) driving whilst intoxicated;[268] or

(b) being in charge on vehicle (with intent to drive) whilst intoxicated;[269] or

(c) refusing/failing to provide preliminary breath sample;[270] or

(d) refusing/failing to provide mandatory breath sample;[271] or

(e) dangerous driving;[272] or:

(f) refusing/failing to comply with duties at scene of accident causing injury;[273]

(g) unauthorised taking of a vehicle,[274]

there is an obligation on that individual to provide a sample at a Garda Station upon lawful demand.[275]

Failing to provide a specimen is a strict liability offence and there is no onus on the State to prove beyond reasonable doubt that the defendant was actually driving the vehicle before a lawful demand can be made under section 13.[276] In the case of arrests made in respect of dangerous driving, breach of duties at scene of accident or unauthorised taking of vehicle offences, the Garda should have formed the opinion that the defendant has consumed an intoxicant.

At the Garda Station, a member of the Gardaí may require the defendant to:

(a) provides a breath-test sample,[277] and/or

---

[267] As amended by s.23, Road Traffic Act 2002, s.3, Road Traffic Act 2003, s.1(b) and s.1(1)(b)(ii), Road Traffic and Transport Act 2006 and s.18, Road Traffic Act 2006.

[268] S.49(8), Road Traffic Act 1961.

[269] *Ibid.*, s.50(10).

[270] S.12(4), Road Traffic Act 1994.

[271] S.4(6), Road Traffic Act 2006.

[272] S.53(6), Road Traffic Act 1961.

[273] *Ibid.*, s.106(3)(a).

[274] *Ibid.*, s.112(6).

[275] *Ibid.*, s.13(1) as substituted by s.1(b), Road Traffic and Transport Act 2006.

[276] See *DPP v. Patricia Behan* [2003] WJSC-HC 2930; *DPP v. Bernard Joyce* [2004] IEHC 132; *DPP v. Jonathan Finnegan* [2008] IEHC 347; and *DPP v. Regina Breheny* [1993] WJSC-SC 255.

[277] S.13(1)(a), Road Traffic Act 1961.

(b) provide either a blood[278] or urine sample.[279]

There is a clear distinction between offences under sections 12 and 13 of the Road Traffic Act 1994. Practitioners should have particular regard to the wording of the charge sheet or summons as a section 13 offence can only be committed at a Garda Station following an individual's arrest. Again, the statutory authority under which the defendant has arrested is a matter which must be established.

The Garda must give evidence of having made a lawful request for a specimen. Furthermore, the Garda is required to advise the defendant at the Garda station of the statutory authority upon which they are requiring that a breath specimen and/or a blood/urine specimen to be provided and the consequences for the defendant of refusing/failing to comply with the requirement, including advising them that, if convicted of an offence of failing/refusing to provide a required sample, a mandatory consequential disqualification will be imposed:[280] simply known as section 13 requirement.[281]

However, practitioners should note that where a defendant complies with the lawful request made by a Garda to provide a specimen, the court is unlikely to draw any adverse inference from a Garda failing to give evidence of having advised defendant that it was a criminal offence to refuse to give specimen and of the penalties that apply. Where a defendant is failing/refusing to comply with the request, however, they must be advised that it is a criminal offence to fail/refuse to provide breath sample and of the penalties which may apply.[282]

The procedure followed by the Garda at the Garda Station is extremely important. Practitioners should note that a charge contrary to section 13 may be dismissed if the court isn't satisfied that the defendant was afforded due process, including: a reasonable opportunity to speak to their solicitor,[283] reasonable access to an interpreter

---

[278] *Ibid.*, s.13(1)(b)(i).
[279] *Ibid.*, s.13(1)(b)(ii).
[280] Recent case law sets out the extent to which the Gardaí are obliged to advice a defendant of legal consequences of failing to provide a specimen – See *DPP v. Redmond Cabot* [2004] IEHC 79; *DPP v. Shane Canavan* [2007] IEHC 46 (unreported Birmingham J., 1 August 2007).
[281] *DPP v. Bridget Moorehouse* [2006] 1 I.L.R.M. 103; *DPP v. Tallon* [2006] IEHC 232; and *John Davitt v. Judge Deary & DPP* [2006] IEHC 84.
[282] See *DPP v. Shane Canavan* [2007] IEHC 46 (unreported, Birmingham J., 1 August 2007).
[283] *DPP v. Paul McCrea* [2010] IEHC 39 (under appeal to Supreme Court).

where an issue might arise as to the defendant's ability to understand the lawful request being made and the possible consequences of a refusal to comply with same, or reasonable access to a doctor where concerns may exist about the defendant's ability to comply with any lawful request.

There is a very limited defence[284] to a charge of refusing to provide a specimen of blood or two specimens of breath under section 23 of the Road Traffic Act 1994, namely:

(a) there were special and substantial reasons for defendant's refusal or failure to comply; and

(b) as soon as practicable after refusal/failure to comply concerned, the defendant complied, or offered, but was not called upon, to comply.[285]

A defendant can be given an option of providing a urine sample instead of a blood sample, but if they opt to provide a urine sample and subsequently cannot provide a specimen of urine, then the defendant's obligation to consent to a specimen of blood being taken revives.[286] However, the defendant should be charged with a refusal to allow a blood specimen be taken and not a refusal to provide a urine specimen. There is a rebuttable presumption as to the legality of the apparatus used.[287]

Penalties

In respect of an offence contrary to section 13(2) and 13(3) the following penalties apply:

Summary Conviction: fine of up to €5,000 and/or a term of imprisonment of up to six months.[288]
Section 1(1) of the Probation of Offenders Act 1907 shall not apply to this offence.[289]

Disqualification:

Mandatory Disqualification: a conviction under section 13 carries

---

[284] Ss.13(2) and 13(3), Road Traffic Act 1994.
[285] *Ibid.*, s.23(1).
[286] *Ibid.*, s.13(1)(b) – see also the decision of Kearns J. in the Supreme Court case of *DPP v. Peadar Malone* [2006] IESC 38.
[287] *Ibid.*, s.13(4).
[288] *Ibid.*, ss.13(2) and 13(3) as amended by s.18, Table, Pt.4, References 2 and 3, Road Traffic Act 2006.
[289] *Ibid.*, s.13(5).

a mandatory consequential disqualification as follows:

First Offence – minimum four years' disqualification.

Second/Subsequent Offence (drink driving offence): minimum six years' disqualification.[290]

OBLIGATION TO PROVIDE A SPECIMEN FOLLOWING ARREST – SECTION 12 OF THE ROAD TRAFFIC ACT 2010

Practitioners should note that section 13 of the Road Traffic Act 1994 is repealed by section 33 of the Road Traffic Act 2010 and replaced by section 12 of the Road Traffic Act 2010.[291] This provision is similar to the present section 13 and sets out that where an individual is arrested for:

(a) driving/attempting to drive whilst intoxicated;[292] or

(b) being in charge on vehicle (with intent to drive/attempt to drive) whilst intoxicated;[293] or

(c) driving/being in charge or animal-drawn vehicle or cycle whilst intoxicated;[294] or

(d) refusal/failure to provide preliminary breath sample;[295] or

(e) refusal/failure to provide mandatory breath sample;[296] or

(f) refusal/failure to perform impairment test;[297] or

(g) careless driving;[298] or

(h) dangerous driving;[299] or

(i) refusal/failure to comply with duties at scene of accident causing injury;[300]

(j) unauthorised taking of a vehicle,[301]

---

[290] *Ibid.*, s.26(4)(a) as substituted by s.26, Road Traffic Act 1994 and substituted by s.6(1)(a), Road Traffic Act 2006.
[291] When ss.12 and 33, Road Traffic Act 2010 come into operation.
[292] S.4(8), Road Traffic Act 2010.
[293] *Ibid.*, s.5(10).
[294] *Ibid.*, s.6(4).
[295] *Ibid.*, s.9(4).
[296] *Ibid.*, s.10(7).
[297] *Ibid.*, s.11(5).
[298] S.52(3), Road Traffic Act 1961 – same substituted by s.68, Road Traffic Act 2010 when same section commences.
[299] *Ibid.*, s.53(5) – same substituted by s.68, Road Traffic Act 2010 when same section commences.
[300] *Ibid.*, s.106(3)(a).
[301] *Ibid.*, s.112.

then a member of the Gardaí may require at a Garda station that the defendant:

(a) provides a breath-test sample;[302] and/or

(b) provide either a blood[303] or urine sample.[304]

There is a very limited defence to a charge of refusing to provide a specimen of blood or two specimens of breath under section 22 of the Road Traffic Act 2010,[305] namely:

(1) there were special and substantial reasons for defendant's refusal or failure to comply; and

(2) as soon as practicable after refusal/failure to comply concerned, the defendant complied, or offered, but not called upon, to comply.[306]

A defendant can be given an option of providing a urine sample instead of a blood sample, but if they opt to provide a urine sample and subsequently cannot provide same specimen, then the defendant's obligation to consent to a specimen of blood being taken revives;[307] however, the defendant should be charged with a refusal to allow a blood specimen be taken and not a refusal to provide a urine specimen.[308] If an individual chooses to give a urine specimen, and a designated doctor or nurse states in writing that they are unwilling to take a specimen on medical grounds,[309] or states in writing that the individual in unable or unwilling to provide specimen,[310] then a Garda may require than to provide a blood specimen instead.[311] There is a rebuttable presumption as to the legality of the apparatus used.[312]

---

[302] S.12(1)(a), Road Traffic Act 2010.
[303] *Ibid.*, s.12(1)(b)(i).
[304] *Ibid.*, s.12(1)(b)(ii).
[305] *Ibid.*, s.22 will replace s.23, Road Traffic act 1994, when same section comes into operation.
[306] *Ibid.*, s.22(1), Road Traffic Act 2010.
[307] See s.12(1)(b), Road Traffic Act 2010 and also the decision of Kearns J. in the Supreme Court case of *DPP v. Peadar Malone* [2006] IESC 38.
[308] See *DPP (Coughlan) v. Swan* [1994] I.L.R.M. 314.
[309] S.12(2)(a), Road Traffic Act 2010.
[310] *Ibid.*, s.12(2)(b), Road Traffic Act 2010.
[311] *Ibid.*, s.12(2).
[312] *Ibid.*, s.12(6).

Penalties

In respect of an offence contrary to section 12(3) and 12(4), the following penalties would apply:

Summary Conviction: fine of up to €5,000 and/or term of imprisonment of up to six months.[313]
Section 1(1) of the Probation of Offenders Act 1907 shall not apply to this offence.[314]

Disqualification: a conviction under section 12 carries a mandatory consequential disqualification as follows;

First Offence – minimum four years' disqualification.

Second/Subsequent Offence (drink driving offence): minimum six years' disqualification.[315]

PROCEDURE FOLLOWING PROVISION OF BREATH SPECIMEN UNDER SECTION 12 – SECTION 13 OF THE ROAD TRAFFIC ACT 2010

Practitioners should note that section 17 of the Road Traffic Act 1994 is repealed by section 33 of the Road Traffic Act 2010 and replaced by section 13 of the Road Traffic Act 2010,[316] which sets out the following procedures in respect of the provision of a breath specimen:

(a) where pursuant to lawful requirement made under section 12, a person provides two specimens of his breath; and the concentration of alcohol in each specimen is determined, the specimen with the lower concentration of alcohol (except where both specimens contain same concentration) shall be taken into account for the purposes of sections 4 (4) and 5 (4) of the Road Traffic Act 2010 and the other specimen shall be disregarded;[317]

(b) a defendant shall be supplied forthwith by the Garda with two identical statements, automatically produced in the prescribed form and duly completed by the member in the prescribed manner, stating the concentration of alcohol in the said specimen;[318]

---

[313] *Ibid.*, s.12(5).
[314] *Ibid.*, s.12(6).
[315] *Ibid.*, s.65(4)(a)(v).
[316] When ss.13 and 33 come into operation.
[317] S.13(1), Road Traffic Act 2010.
[318] *Ibid.*, s.13(2).

(c) a defendant shall, upon a Garda's request, immediately sign each statement and return either statement to a Garda.[319]

It is an offence to fail/refuse to comply with a request to sign both statements and return one statement to Garda.[320]

Penalties

In respect of an offence contrary to section 13(4) the following penalties would apply;

Summary Conviction: fine of up to €5,000 and/or term of imprisonment of up to three months.[321]

Procedure Regarding Taking of Specimens of Blood and Provision of Specimens of Urine – Section 15 of the Road Traffic Act 2010

Practitioners should note that section 18 of the Road Traffic Act 1994 is repealed by section 33 of the Road Traffic Act 2010 and replaced by section 15 of the Road Traffic Act 2010.[322] Section 15 of the Road Traffic Act 1994 sets out the following procedures in respect of the provision of a blood or urine specimen:

(a) where a designated doctor has taken a specimen of blood from a person or has been provided by the person with a specimen of his urine, the doctor shall divide the specimen into two parts, place each part in a container which he shall forthwith seal and complete the form prescribed for the purposes of this section;[323]

(b) where a specimen of blood or urine of a person has been divided into two parts, Garda shall offer to the person one of the sealed containers together with a statement in writing indicating that he may retain either of the containers;[324]

(c) as soon as practicable after subsection (2) is complied with, a member of the Gardaí shall cause to be forwarded to the Bureau the completed form referred to in subsection (1), together with the relevant sealed container or, where the person has declined

---

[319] *Ibid.*, s.13(3).
[320] *Ibid.*, s.13(4).
[321] *Ibid.*, s.14(5).
[322] When ss.15 and 33 come into operation.
[323] S.15(1), Road Traffic Act 2010.
[324] *Ibid.*, s.15(2).

to retain one of the sealed containers, both relevant sealed containers.[325]

Practitioners should also note that under section 15 of the Road Traffic Act 2010,[326] there is a rebuttable legal presumption that the procedure set out in section 15 has been complied with.[327]

OBLIGATION TO ACCOMPANY A GARDA TO THE GARDA STATION, NOT UNDER ARREST, TO PROVIDE A BLOOD OR URINE SPECIMEN – SECTION 14 OF THE ROAD TRAFFIC ACT 1994

Under section 14 of the Road Traffic Act 1994,[328] if a Garda forms the opinion that a person in charge of a vehicle in a public place is intoxicated to such an extent as to be incapable of having proper control of the vehicle, then that a Garda may require that the individual accompany him to a Garda Station.[329] If a defendant refuses/fails to comply immediately with a lawful requirement to accompany a Garda to a Garda Station they will be guilty of an offence[330] and may be arrested without a warrant.[331]

Where an individual is at a Garda Station, either because they have accompanied a Garda,[332] or have refused to accompany the Garda and have been arrested,[333] a member at the station may require the person to provide either:

(a) a blood specimen;[334] or

(b) a urine specimen,[335]

in accordance with statutory provisions and procedures.

If a designated doctor states in writing that he is unwilling, on medical grounds, to take the specimen required, the Garda may require the individual to provide a specimen other than the specimen first required.[336] If a defendant refuses/fails to comply with a

---

[325] *Ibid.*, s.15(3).
[326] When same section comes into operation.
[327] *Ibid.*, s.15(4).
[328] As amended by s.1, Road Traffic and Transport Act 2006.
[329] S.14(1), Road Traffic Act 1994.
[330] *Ibid.*, s.14(2) as amended by s.18, Road Traffic Act 2006.
[331] *Ibid.*, s.14(3).
[332] *Ibid.*, s.14(1).
[333] *Ibid.*, s.14(3).
[334] *Ibid.*, s.14(4)(a) as amended by s.1, Road Traffic and Transport Act 2006.
[335] *Ibid.*, s.14(4)(b) as amended by s.1, Road Traffic and Transport Act 2006.
[336] *Ibid.*, s.14(4).

lawful requirement to provide a specimen they will be guilty of an offence.[337]

Again, the statutory authority requiring an individual to accompany a Garda to a designated Garda Station is the opinion formed by the Garda that the individual was under influence of an intoxicant (alcohol and/or drugs), to such a degree, that they could not properly control the vehicle. In the circumstances, the prosecuting Garda should give evidence of the observations that led to them forming their opinion that the defendant was firstly, under the influence of an intoxicant (observations such as smell of alcohol on breath or slurred speech); and secondly, was intoxicated to such an extent that they could not properly control vehicle (like an observation that the defendant was unfit to perform a simple coordination test voluntarily undertaken).

Penalties

In respect of an offence contrary to section 14(2) and 14(4), the following penalties apply:

Summary Conviction: fine of up to €5,000 and/or a term of imprisonment of up to six months.[338]
Section 1(1) of the Probation of Offenders Act 1907 shall not apply to this offence.[339]

Disqualification:

Mandatory Disqualification: a conviction under section 14 carries a mandatory consequential disqualification as follows:

First Offence: minimum four years' disqualification.

Second/Subsequent Offence (drink driving offence): minimum six years' disqualification.[340]

Practitioners should note that section 33[341] of the Road Traffic Act 2010 repeals section 14 of the Road Traffic Act 1994.

---

[337] *Ibid.*, s.14(5) as amended by s.18, Road Traffic Act 2006.
[338] *Ibid.*, s.14(2) & 14(5), as amended by s.18, Table, Pt.4, References 4 and 5, Road Traffic Act 2006.
[339] *Ibid.*, s.14(6).
[340] *Ibid.*, s.26(4)(a) as substituted by s.26, Road Traffic Act 1994 and substituted by s.6(1)(a), Road Traffic Act 2006.
[341] When same section comes into operation.

OBLIGATION TO PROVIDE A BLOOD OR URINE SPECIMEN WHILE IN HOSPITAL – SECTION 15 OF THE ROAD TRAFFIC ACT 1994

Under section 15 of the Road Traffic Act 1994,[342] if an accident involving a vehicle occurs in a public place, in consequence of which a person was injured and attends and/or is admitted to hospital, and a member of the Gardaí is of the opinion that at the time of the accident the individual was:

(a) driving/attempting to drive the vehicle; or

(b) in charge of with the intent to drive, but not driving/attempting to drive;[343] and

(c) had consumed an intoxicant,[344]

the Garda may then require the person, in the hospital, to provide either:

(a) a blood specimen;[345] or

(b) an urine specimen,[346]

in accordance with statutory provisions and procedures.

If a doctor states in writing that he is unwilling, on medical grounds, to take the specimen required, the Garda may require the individual to provide a specimen other than specimen first required.[347] If an individual refuses or fails to comply with any requirement made lawfully under this section,[348] they shall be guilty of an offence,[349] unless the individual comes under the care of a doctor, following his attendance or admission, who refuses, on medical grounds, to permit the taking or provision of the specimen required.[350]

The statutory basis upon which a Garda can require that a specimen be taken or provided by an individual, while in hospital, is the opinion formed by the Garda that the individual has consumed an intoxicant. Therefore, the prosecuting Garda should give evidence

---

[342] As amended by Pt.1, Table, Road Traffic Act 2006.
[343] S.15(1)(a), Road Traffic Act 1994.
[344] *Ibid.*, s.15(1)(b).
[345] *Ibid.*, s.15(1)(i).
[346] *Ibid.*, s.15(1)(ii).
[347] *Ibid.*, s.15(1).
[348] Subject to the provisions of s.23, Road Traffic Act 1994.
[349] S.15(2), Road Traffic Act 1994 as amended by s.18, Road Traffic Act 2006.
[350] *Ibid.*, s.15(3).

of observations that led to them forming their opinion that the defendant had firstly consumed an intoxicant (observations such as smell of alcohol on breath or slurred speech); and secondly was intoxicated to such an extent that they could not properly control vehicle (like an observation that the vehicle was being driven erratically).

Practitioners should also be aware of the provisions of section 39 of the Road Traffic Act 1994, which confers a power of entry without a warrant to:

(a) a member of the Gardaí to enter, without a warrant, any hospital where the individual is, or the Garda has reasonable cause to suspect him to be for the purposes of making a requirement to provide a specimen under section 15(1) of the Road Traffic Act 1994;[351]

(b) a designated Doctor to enter any hospital where the individual is, or where the Doctor is informed by the Gardaí the individual is, for the purposes of making a taking a specimen in compliance with a requirement made lawfully under section 15(1) of the Road Traffic Act 1994.[352]

Penalties

In respect of an offence contrary to section 15(2), the following penalties apply:

Summary Conviction: fine of up to €5,000 and/or a term of imprisonment of up to six months.[353]
Section 1(1) of the Probation of Offenders Act 1907 shall not apply to this offence.[354]

Disqualification: a conviction under section 15 carries a mandatory consequential disqualification as follows:

First Offence – minimum four years' disqualification.

Second/Subsequent Offence (drink driving offence): minimum six years' disqualification.[355]

---

[351] *Ibid.*, s.39(3).
[352] *Ibid.*, s.39(4).
[353] *Ibid.*, s.15(2) as amended by s.18, Table, Pt.4, Reference 6 , Road Traffic Act 2006.
[354] *Ibid.*, s.15(4).
[355] S.26(4)(a), Road Traffic Act 1961, as substituted by s.26, Road Traffic Act 1994 and substituted by s.6(1)(a), Road Traffic Act 2006.

OBLIGATION TO PROVIDE A BLOOD OR URINE SPECIMEN WHILE IN HOSPITAL – SECTION 14 OF THE ROAD TRAFFIC ACT 2010

Practitioners should note that section 15 of the Road Traffic Act 1994 is repealed by section 33 of the Road Traffic Act 2010 and replaced by section 14 of the Road Traffic Act 2010,[356] which sets out that, if an accident involving a vehicle occurs in a public place, in consequence of which a person was injured and attends and/or is admitted to hospital, and a member of the Gardaí is of the opinion that at the time of the accident the individual[357] was:

(a) driving/attempting to drive the vehicle; or

(b) in charge of with the intent to drive, but not driving/attempting to drive,[358]

the Garda may, in the hospital, if such a requirement would not be prejudicial to the health of that individual, require same individual to provide either:[359]

(a) a blood specimen;[360] or

(b) an urine specimen;[361] or

(c) undergo a medical examination by designated doctor or nurse for the purposes of establishing if same individual was under the influence of intoxicant as to be incapable of having proper control of vehicle.[362]

If a designated doctor or nurse states in writing that he is unwilling, on medical grounds, to take the specimen required,[363] or states in writing that the individual is unable, or unlikely to provide same specimen,[364] the Garda may require the individual to provide a specimen other than specimen first required.[365] If an individual refuses or

---

[356] When ss.14 and 33 come into operation.
[357] Not a driver of a Fire Brigade engine, an ambulance or a Garda car, driving same vehicle in the performance of their duties, and in a manner which does not endanger the safety of other road users – see s.27, Road Traffic Act 2004.
[358] S.14(1), Road Traffic Act 2010.
[359] *Ibid.*, s.14(1).
[360] *Ibid.*, s.14(1)(a)(i).
[361] *Ibid.*, s.14(1)(a)(ii).
[362] *Ibid.*, s.14(1)(b).
[363] *Ibid.*, s.14(2)(a).
[364] *Ibid.*, s.14(2)(a).
[365] *Ibid.*, s.14(2).

fails to comply with any requirement made lawfully under this section, they shall be guilty of an offence,[366] unless the individual comes under the care of a designated doctor or nurse, following his attendance or admission, who refuses, on medical grounds, to permit the taking or provision of the specimen required.[367]

The statutory basis upon which a Garda can require that a specimen be taken or provided by an individual, while in hospital, is the opinion formed by the Garda that the individual has consumed an intoxicant. Therefore, the prosecuting Garda should give evidence of observations that led to them forming their opinion that the defendant had firstly consumed an intoxicant (observations such as smell of alcohol on breath or slurred speech) and secondly was intoxicated to such an extent that they could not properly control vehicle (like an observation that the vehicle was being driven erratically).

Practitioners should also be aware that:

(a) a member of the Gardaí may enter, without a warrant, any hospital where the individual is, or the Garda has reasonable cause to suspect him to be for the purposes of making a requirement to provide a specimen under section 14(1) of the Road Traffic Act 2010;[368]

(b) a designated Doctor may enter any hospital where the individual is, or where the Doctor is informed by the Gardaí the individual is, for the purposes of making a taking a specimen in compliance with a requirement made lawfully under section 14(1) of the Road Traffic Act 1994.[369]

Penalties

In respect of an offence contrary to section 14(3), the following penalties would apply:

Summary Conviction: fine of up to €5,000 and/or a term of imprisonment of up to six months.[370]

Section 1(1) of the Probation of Offenders Act 1907 shall not apply to this offence.[371]

---

[366] *Ibid.*, s.14(3).
[367] *Ibid.*, s.14(4).
[368] *Ibid.*, s.14(5).
[369] *Ibid.*, s.14(6).
[370] *Ibid.*, s.14(3).
[371] *Ibid.*, s.14(7).

Disqualification: a conviction under section 15 carries a mandatory consequential disqualification as follows:

First Offence – minimum four years' disqualification.

Second/Subsequent Offence (drink driving offence): minimum six years' disqualification.[372]

DEFENCE TO REFUSAL TO PERMIT TAKING OF SPECIMEN – SECTION 23 OF THE ROAD TRAFFIC ACT 1994

Section 23 of the Road Traffic Act 1994 sets out that:

(a) in the prosecution of an offence of refusing/failing to provide two specimens of breath upon lawful request at a Garda station following an individual's arrest,[373] it shall be a defence for an individual to satisfy the court that there was a special and substantial reason for their failure/refusal, and that as soon as practicable afterwards, they complied with, or offered to comply with but was not called upon to so do, a requirement in respect of providing a specimen of blood or urine.[374]

(b) in a prosecution for an offence under sections 13, 14 and 15 of the Road Traffic Act 1994, for failing/refusing to permit/comply with request to provide specimen of blood to designated doctor/nurse, it shall be a defence to satisfy the court that there was a special and substantial reason for the refusal/failure and that as soon as practicable afterwards, they complied with, or offered to comply with but was not called upon to so do, a requirement in respect of providing a specimen urine;[375]

(c) notwithstanding the defences available in this section, evidence may be given at the hearing of any offence[376] for drink driving,[377] of bring in charge of vehicle with intention to drive[378] that a defendant failed to comply with request to provide two specimen of breath,[379] or to comply with a request to provide a specimen of blood.[380]

---

[372] *Ibid.*, s.65(4)(a)(v).
[373] S.13, Road Traffic Act 1994.
[374] *Ibid.*, s.23(1).
[375] *Ibid.*, s.23(2) as amended by s.1(1)(g)(i), Road Traffic and Transport Act 2006.
[376] *Ibid.*, s.23(3) as amended by s.1(1)(g)(ii), Road Traffic and Transport Act 2006.
[377] S.49, Road Traffic Act 1961.
[378] *Ibid.*, s.50.
[379] S.13(1)(a), Road Traffic Act 1994.
[380] *Ibid.*, s.13(1)(b)(i).

DEFENCE TO REFUSAL TO PERMIT TAKING OF SPECIMEN –
SECTION 22 OF THE ROAD TRAFFIC ACT 2010

Practitioners should note that section 23 of the Road Traffic Act 1994 is repealed by section 33 of the Road Traffic Act 2010 and replaced by section 22 of the Road Traffic Act 2010.[381] Section 22 of the Road Traffic Act 2010 sets out that:

(a) in the prosecution of an offence of refusing/failing to provide two specimens of breath upon lawful request at a Garda station following an individual's arrest,[382] it shall be a defence for an individual to satisfy the court that there was a special and substantial reason for their failure/refusal, and that as soon as practicable afterwards, they complied with, or offered to comply with but was not called upon to so do, a requirement in respect of providing a specimen of blood or urine;[383]

(b) in a prosecution for an offence under sections 12 or 14 of the Road Traffic Act 2010, for failing/refusing to permit/comply with request to provide specimen of blood to designated doctor/nurse, it shall be a defence to satisfy the court that there was a special and substantial reason for the refusal/failure and that as soon as practicable afterwards, they complied with, or offered to comply with but was not called upon to so do, a requirement in respect of providing a specimen urine;[384]

(c) notwithstanding the defences available in this section, evidence may be given at the hearing of any offence[385] for drink driving,[386] of bring in charge of vehicle with intention to drive[387] that a defendant failed to comply with request to provide two specimen of breath,[388] or to comply with a request to provide a specimen of blood;[389]

(d) in a prosecution for failure to perform a preliminary impairment test,[390] it shall be a defence to satisfy the court that there

---

[381] When ss.22 and 33 come into operation.
[382] S.12(4), Road Traffic Act 2010.
[383] *Ibid.*, s.22(1).
[384] *Ibid.*, s.22(2).
[385] *Ibid.*, s.23(3).
[386] *Ibid.*, s.4(8).
[387] *Ibid.*, s.5(10).
[388] *Ibid.*, s.12(1)(a).
[389] *Ibid.*, s.12(1)(b)(i).
[390] *Ibid.*, s.11(4).

was a special and substantial reason for the refusal/failure to perform the test and that as soon as practicable afterwards, they complied with, or offered to comply with but was not called upon to so do, the requirement to perform a preliminary impairment test;

(e) notwithstanding the defence available in this section, evidence may be given at the hearing of any offence[391] for drink driving,[392] of bring in charge of vehicle with intention to drive[393] that a defendant failed to comply with request to perform a preliminary impairment test.

Taking Alcohol with a View to Frustrating a Prosecution – Section 20 of the Road Traffic Act 1994

Commonly known, not only in this jurisdiction, as the 'hip flask' defence, section 20 of the Road Traffic Act 1994 addresses the situation where a defendant may take a drink, perhaps post accident, to steady their nerves or to address the onset of shock, and subsequently seeks to rely on a defence of post-incident drinking when charged with a drink driving offence.

According to section 20 of the Road Traffic Act 1994, at the hearing of any offence under section 49/section 50 of the Road Traffic Act 1961, it shall not be necessary for the prosecution to show that the intoxicating liquor consumed was not consumed by the defendant after the time of the alleged offence but before the taking of any specimen required under section 13, 14 and 15 of this Act.[394]

If such a defence is advanced, the court shall disregard such evidence unless it is satisfied that, but for the post-incident alcohol consumption, the concentration of alcohol in the defendant's breath[395]/blood[396] or urine sample[397] would not have exceeded the legal limit.[398]

However, a further caveat is set out that a defendant shall not take any action (including but not limited to consuming alcohol post

---

[391] *Ibid.*, s.23(3).
[392] *Ibid.*, s.4(8).
[393] *Ibid.*, s.5(10).
[394] S.20(1), Road Traffic Act 1994.
[395] *Ibid.*, s.20(2)(c).
[396] *Ibid.*, s.20(2)(a).
[397] *Ibid.*, s.20(2)(b).
[398] *Ibid.*, s.20(2).

incident) with the intention of frustrating a prosecution under section 49 or section 50 of the Principal Act.[399] This does exclude a refusal/failure to give a specimen as same covered elsewhere.[400] Where, at a hearing, the court is satisfied that any action taken by the defendant, excluding refusing/failing to provide specimen, was taken with the intention of frustrating a prosecution, the court may find him guilty of an offence.[401]

It is presumed that a defence of post-incident drinking could only be advanced in circumstances where the defendant's consumption of alcohol was not following being stopped on suspicion of a drink driving offence but instead was perhaps after their involvement in an accident which was not immediately attended by the Gardaí and the defendant had thereafter taken a drink out of shock. However, given the drink driving laws in this country, if a defendant had not been drinking prior to their involvement in a road traffic accident, it would not be logical or advisable to take a drink immediately after the accident and before talking to a member of the Gardaí, given the real risk that they might be subsequently breathalysed by the Gardaí.

Penalties

In respect of an offence contrary to section 20(3)(b), the following penalties apply:

Summary Conviction: fine of up to €5,000 and/or a term of imprisonment of up to six months.[402]

Disqualification:

Ancillary Disqualification: whilst a conviction under section 20 does not carry a mandatory disqualification, it is open to the court to make an ancillary disqualification order (section 27 of the Road Traffic Act 1961) on the particular facts of the case. However, given that section 20 of the Road Traffic Act 1994 is not a stand alone offence and only relates to prosecutions of an offence contrary to either section 49 or section 50 of the Road Traffic Act 1961, it is clear that a mandatory disqualification would apply to a conviction in respect of either of those charges in any event.

---

[399] *Ibid.*, s.20(3).
[400] *Ibid.*, ss.13, 14, 15 and 23.
[401] *Ibid.*, s.20(4).
[402] *Ibid.*, s.20(3)(b) as amended by s.18, Table, Pt.4, Reference 8, Road Traffic Act 2006.

TAKING ALCOHOL WITH A VIEW TO FRUSTRATING A PROSECUTION – SECTION 18 OF THE ROAD TRAFFIC ACT 2010

Practitioners should note that section 20 of the Road Traffic Act 1994 is repealed by section 33 of the Road Traffic Act 2010 and replaced by section 18 of the Road Traffic Act 2010.[403]

Section 18 of the Road Traffic Act 2010 sets out that at the hearing of any offence under section 4/section 5 of the Road Traffic Act 2010, it shall not be necessary for the prosecution to show that the intoxicating liquor consumed was not consumed by the defendant after the time of the alleged offence but before the taking of any specimen required under section 12 of this Act.[404]

If such a defence is advanced, the court shall disregard such evidence unless it is satisfied that, but for the post-incident alcohol consumption, the concentration of alcohol in the defendant's breath[405]/blood[406] or urine sample[407] would not have exceeded the legal limit.[408]

However, a defendant shall not take any action (including but not limited to consuming alcohol post incident) with the intention of frustrating a prosecution under section 4 or section 5 of the Road Traffic Act 2010.[409] This does exclude a refusal/failure to give a specimen as same covered elsewhere.[410] Where, at a hearing, the court is satisfied that any action taken by the defendant, excluding refusing/failing to provide specimen, was taken with the intention of frustrating a prosecution, the court may find him guilty of an offence.[411]

Penalties

In respect of an offence contrary to section 18(3)(b), the following penalties apply:

Summary Conviction: fine of up to €5,000 and/or a term of imprisonment of up to six months.[412]

---

[403] When ss.18 and 33 come into operation.
[404] S.18(1), Road Traffic Act 2010.
[405] *Ibid.*, s.18(2)(c).
[406] *Ibid.*, s.18(2)(a).
[407] *Ibid.*, s.18(2)(b).
[408] *Ibid.*, s.18(2).
[409] *Ibid.*, s.18(3).
[410] See ss.13, 14, 15 and 23, Road Traffic Act 1994.
[411] S.18(4), Road Traffic Act 2010.
[412] S.20(3)(b), Road Traffic Act 1994 as amended by s.18, Table, Pt.4, Reference 8, Road Traffic Act 2006.

Disqualification:

Ancillary Disqualification: whilst a conviction under section 18 does not carry a mandatory disqualification, it is open to the court to make an ancillary disqualification order (section 27 of the Road Traffic Act 1961) on the particular facts of the case. However, given that section 18 of the Road Traffic Act 2010 is not a stand-alone offence and only relates to prosecutions of an offence contrary to either section 4 or section 5 of the Road Traffic Act 2010, it is clear that a mandatory disqualification would apply to a conviction in respect of either of those charges in any event.

COSTS OF DRINK/DRUG DRIVING PROSECUTIONS – SECTION 22 OF THE ROAD TRAFFIC ACT 1994

Where a person is convicted of an offence of:

(a) driving/attempting to drive whilst intoxicated;[413]

(b) being in charge of a vehicle with the intention of driving/ attempting to drive whilst intoxicated;[414]

(c) failing/refusing to provide a specimen following arrest;[415]

(d) failing/refusing to accompany a Garda to a Garda Station, not under arrest, to provide a specimen;[416]

(e) failing/refusing to provide a specimen whilst in hospital;[417]

the court shall, unless satisfied that there are 'special and substantial reasons' for not doing so, order the defendant to pay a contribution[418] towards the costs and expenses incurred by the Medical Bureau of Road Safety.

Practitioners should also note that in prosecutions where a defendant wishes to call a member of the Medical Bureau of Road Safety to court to give evidence,[419] that defendant will incur the costs of calling same witness, even if they succeed in their defence.

---

[413] S.49, Road Traffic Act 1961.
[414] *Ibid.*, s.50.
[415] S.13, Road Traffic Act 1994.
[416] *Ibid.*, s.14.
[417] *Ibid.*, s.15.
[418] Art.5(1), S.I. No.351/1994, Road Traffic Act, 1994 (Part III) Regulations 1994 prescribed this contribution to be £75 (€95.23).
[419] Perhaps in light of the recent High Court decision in *Thompkins v. DPP* [2010] IEHC 58.

COSTS OF DRINK/DRUG DRIVING PROSECUTIONS – SECTION 21 OF THE ROAD TRAFFIC ACT 2010

Practitioners should note that section 22 of the Road Traffic Act 1994 is repealed by section 33 of the Road Traffic Act 2010 and replaced by section 21 of the Road Traffic Act 2010,[420] which states that where a person is convicted of an offence of:

(a) driving/attempting to drive whilst intoxicated;[421]

(b) being in charge of a vehicle with the intention of driving/attempting to drive whilst intoxicated;[422]

(c) failing/Refusing to provide a specimen following arrest;[423]

(d) failing/Refusing to provide a specimen whilst in hospital;[424]

the court shall, unless satisfied that there are 'special and substantial reasons' for not doing so, order the defendant to pay a contribution[425] towards the costs and expenses incurred by the Medical Bureau of Road Safety.

Practitioners should also note that in prosecutions where a defendant wishes to call a member of the Medical Bureau of Road Safety to court to give evidence,[426] that defendant will incur the costs of calling same witness, even if they succeed in their defence.

FIXED PENALTY NOTICE – DRINK DRIVING – SECTION 26 OF THE ROAD TRAFFIC ACT 2010

Practitioners should note that section 6 of the Road Traffic Act 2006 is repealed and replaced by section 29 of the Road Traffic Act 2010.[427] Section 29 of the Road Traffic Act 2010 sets out the procedure in respect of the issuing of a fixed penalty notice for certain drink driving offences.

---

[420] When ss.18 and 33 come into operation.
[421] S.4, Road Traffic Act 2010.
[422] *Ibid.*, s.5.
[423] *Ibid.*, s.1.
[424] S.15, Road Traffic Act 1994.
[425] At present the relevant prescribed amount is set out in art.5(1), S.I. No.351/1994 Road Traffic Act, 1994 (Part III) Regulations, 1994 prescribed this contribution to be £75 (€95.23).
[426] Perhaps in light of the recent High Court decision in *Thompkins v. DPP* [2010] IEHC 58.
[427] When s.29 come into operation – see also s.32, Road Traffic Act 2010.

Provisions states that where a person has allegedly committed the offence of drink driving,[428] being in charge of a vehicle with the intention to drive whilst intoxicated,[429] and falls within the lowest category of BAC,[430] between 50mg and 80mg alcohol/100ml of blood[431] (or 20mg – 80mg alcohol/100ml blood – in case of 'specified person),[432] or within the category of BAC- between 80mg and 100mg alcohol/100ml of blood,[433] there is an option to pay a fixed penalty notice without going to court.[434]

In this case, where the fixed penalty charge is paid within the appropriate time, a fine and penalty points will be imposed without a prosecution being initiated against the defendant.[435] A defendant who does not hold a valid driving licence or is disqualified from driving cannot avail of this option.[436]

This option is only open to defendant for a first offence in respect of this category who has no drink driving conviction within the previous three years. A defendant is not eligible to be served with a second fixed penalty notice within a three-year period[437] and any second offence under sections 49 and 50 of the Road Traffic Act 1961, section 13 of the Road Traffic Act 1994, or sections 4, 5 or 12 of the Road Traffic Act 2010 will involve a court prosecution.

A fixed penalty notice may be served on an individual by means of personal service,[438] by delivering it to the person, or leaving it at the address:

(a) where the individual ordinarily resides;[439]

(b) the individual gave to the Gardaí at the time of the alleged offence;[440]

(c) of the registered owner of the vehicle.[441]

---

[428] S.4(8), Road Traffic Act 2010.
[429] S.5(10), Road Traffic Act 2010.
[430] Blood Alcohol Concentration.
[431] S.29(1)(a), Road Traffic Act 2010.
[432] *Ibid.*, s.29(2).
[433] *Ibid.*, s.29(1)(b).
[434] *Ibid.*, s.29.
[435] *Ibid.*, s.29(1).
[436] *Ibid.*, s.29(4).
[437] *Ibid.*, s.29(5).
[438] *Ibid.*, s.29(3)(a).
[439] *Ibid.*, s.29(3)(a)(I).
[440] *Ibid.*, s.29(3)(a)(II).
[441] *Ibid.*, s.29(3)(a)(III).

Or by postal service,[442] posting it to the address:

(a) where the individual ordinarily resides;[443]

(b) the individual gave to the Gardaí at the time of the alleged offence;[444]

(c) of the registered owner of the vehicle.[445]

A fixed penalty notice shall contain a statement containing/referring to the following information:[446]

(a) the individual has committed the specified offence;[447]

(b) the BAC is as stated or certified;[448]

(c) the circumstances in which an individual would be ineligible to be dealt with by way of fixed penalty notice;[449]

(d) how to pay fixed penalty notice (FPN) within 28 days;[450]

(e) the penalty points (where applicable) that will be endorsed on their licence;[451]

(f) that a prosecution will not be initiated, if the FPN is paid, unless individual was ineligible to be dealt with by way of FPN.[452]

Any person who is ineligible to be dealt with under the FPN provisions, and knows, or reasonably should have known they were ineligible, and who pays, or attempts to pay the FPN shall be guilty of an offence.[453] Summary conviction for an offence contrary to section 29(12) is as follows; fine of up to €5,000 and/or imprisonment for up to one month.[454]

Penalties

If a defendant is eligible to avail of the FPN provisions of section 29 and does avail of this option and where the BAC is between;

---

[442] *Ibid.*, s.29(3)(b).
[443] *Ibid.*, s.29(3) b)(I).
[444] *Ibid.*, s.29(3)(b)(II).
[445] *Ibid.*, s.3(b)(III).
[446] *Ibid.*, s.29(11).
[447] *Ibid.*, s.29(11)(a).
[448] *Ibid.*, s.29(11)(b).
[449] *Ibid.*, s.29(11)(c).
[450] *Ibid.*, s.29(11)(d).
[451] *Ibid.*, s.29(11)(e).
[452] *Ibid.*, s.29(11)(f).
[453] *Ibid.*, s.29(12).
[454] *Ibid.*, s.29(12).

50–800mg/100ml (blood); 67–107mg/100ml (urine); 22–35mg/100ml (breath), they will incur:

Penalty points: three penalty points[455] – no mandatory disqualification.

Fine: €200.[456]

It is also open to a 'specified person' for whom the 20mg/100ml BAC applies to avail of option of dealing with matter by way of paying FPN. If a defendant is eligible (see above) to avail of, and does avail of, this option they will incur;

First Offence – three months' consequential disqualification.[457]

Fine: €200.[458]

Where the BAC is between 80–100mg/100ml (blood); 107–135mg/100ml (urine); 35–44mg/100ml (breath), there is an option to pay a fixed penalty notice without going to court.[459] If a defendant is eligible to avail of, and does avail of, this option they will incur:

First Offence – six months' consequential disqualification.[460]

Fine: €400.[461]

---

[455] *Ibid.*, s.29(11)(e).
[456] *Ibid.*, s.29(7).
[457] *Ibid.*, s.29(8)(b).
[458] *Ibid.*, s.29(7)(a).
[459] *Ibid.*, s.29.
[460] *Ibid.*, s.29(8)(ii).
[461] *Ibid.*, s.29(7)(b).

CHAPTER 11

Fixed Charge Offences

There are presently 60 fixed charge offences in operation in Ireland: of these 60 fixed charge offences 32 are also Penalty Point offences. This chapter deal only with fixed charge offences which are not penalty point offences – as same are already set out below in chapter 12 on the penalty point offences. This chapter deals with fixed charge offences and the provision in respect of same.

There are presently 28 fixed charge offences which do not carry penalty points, namely:

(1) illegally parking a vehicle in a disabled parking bay;

(2) failure to have a tax disc fixed and displayed on the windscreen;

(3) failure by a driver to have an insurance disc fixed and displayed on the windscreen;

(4) illegally parking a vehicle in a taxi rank;

(5) taxis illegally standing for hire in places other than a taxi rank;

(6) illegally parking/using vehicle in a local authority car park;

(7) illegally parking where a time restriction applies;

(8) illegally parking where a local authority 'pay parking' applies;

(9) illegally parking vehicle in a bus lane or bus only street;

(10) illegally parking/stopping a vehicle at school entrances;

(11) illegally parking a vehicle in a loading bay;

(12) illegally parking a HGV/bus in area where weight restriction applies;

(13) illegally parking in a pedestrianised street;

(14) illegally parking a vehicle at a bus stop;

(15) illegally parking a bus outside an area allocated for buses at bus stop/stand;

(16) failure to remove a vehicle parked on a cycle track;

(17) parking a vehicle where prohibited;

(18) stopping/parking a vehicle in a clearway;

(19) illegally stopping/parking a vehicle on any part of a motorway;

(20) failure to obey traffic directions given by the Gardaí;

(21) failure by a passenger (17 or over) to comply with seatbelt requirements;

(22) illegally entering a road with HGV or a bus where weight restriction applies;

(23) failure by a driver to give appropriate signals;

(24) wholly or partly entering a yellow box unless z driver can clear the area;

(25) driving a prohibited vehicle in a bus lane;

(26) making a U-Turn on a dual carriageway where No U-turn sign is displayed;

(27) driving a vehicle (other than a light rail vehicle) on a tram line;

(28) stopping/parking a vehicle (other than a light rail vehicle) on a tram line.

PROVISION IN RESPECT OF FIXED CHARGE PENALTY OFFENCES – SECTION 103 OF THE ROAD TRAFFIC ACT 1961

The statutory basis for fixed charge offences is set out in section 103 of the Road Traffic Act 1961.[1]

It applies to such summary Road Traffic Act offences under:

(a) the Road Traffic Acts 1961-2006 and The Roads Act 1993;[2]

(b) the Roads Transport Act 1933;[3]

(c) Road Traffic Regulations made under the Road Traffic Acts or the European Community Act 1972;[4]

---

[1] As substituted by s.11, Road Traffic Act 2002 and amended by s.14, Road Traffic Act 2006.

[2] S.103(1)(a), Road traffic Act 1961 as substituted by s.14(a), Road Traffic Act 2006.

[3] *Ibid.*, s.103(1)(b)(i) as substituted by s.14(a), Road Traffic Act 2006.

[4] *Ibid.*, s.103(1)(b)(ii) as substituted by s.14(a), Road Traffic Act 2006.

(d) article 4, European Communities (Installation and Use of Speed Limitation Devices in Motor Vehicles) Regulations 2005[5] and articles 5, 6, 7, 8 or 9, European Communities (Compulsory use of Safety Belts and Child Restraint Systems in Motor Vehicles) Regulations 2006;[6]

(e) section 73 of the Finance Act.[7]

As may be declared by the Minister by way of regulations as fixed charge offences[8] and allows:

(a) a Garda, who has reasonable grounds for believing a fixed charge offence has been/is being committed, to serve an identified person using vehicle[9] and/or registered owner[10] of vehicle with a fixed charge notice, either personally or by post;[11]

(b) a Traffic Warden, who has reasonable grounds for believing a fixed charge offence has been/is being committed, to serve (including affixing notice to vehicle) an identified person using vehicle and/or registered owner of vehicle with a fixed charge notice, either personally or by post– provided same offence is not a penalty point offence.[12]

Where a registered owner (individual or body corporate) receives notice but was not driving, not capable of driving, or not otherwise using vehicle at time of alleged offence,[13] the registered owner must:

(a) give or send to a Garda/traffic warden within 28 days, details of a nominate user and using the prescribed form their full name and address;[14] or

(b) give or send to the Garda/traffic warden within a specified time period all the information within their knowledge or

---

[5] See S.I. No.831/2005 and s.103(1)(c) as substituted by s.14(a), Road Traffic Act 2006.
[6] See S.I. No.240/2006 and s.103(1)(d) – as substituted by s.14(a), Road Traffic Act 2006.
[7] S.103(1)(e), Road Traffic Act 1961 – as substituted by s.14(a), Road Traffic Act 2006.
[8] *Ibid.*, s.103(1) – as substituted by s.14(a), Road Traffic Act 2006.
[9] *Ibid.*, s.103(2)(a).
[10] *Ibid.*, s.103(2)(b).
[11] *Ibid.*, s.103(2).
[12] *Ibid.*, s.103(3).
[13] *Ibid.*, s.103(4)(b).
[14] *Ibid.*, s.103(4)(i).

procurement as the Garda/warden might reasonably request for the purposes of establishing identify of and location of vehicle user.[15]

Not later than 28 days after the notice/information is received by the Garda/warden, the commissioner shall cause the identified vehicle user to be served with notice, either personally or by post.[16]

In any prosecution for a fixed charge offence, it is presumed until the contrary is shown that:

(a) a relevant fixed charge notice was served;[17] and

(b) payment, accompanied by duly completed notice if required, was not made.[18]

The above constitutes a summary of the provisions of section 103 of the Road Traffic Act 1961. Where an individual pays their fixed penalty fine within the statutory 56 days period and in the manner prescribed in section 103, no prosecution will be initiated against that individual.[19]

Generally, practitioners won't be dealing with fixed charge penalty point offences unless their client has been summoned to court. There are two main circumstances in which a practitioner might find themselves representing a defendant summoned to court. Either their client has not paid their Fixed Penalty fine, but does not contest the summons before court; or they have not paid the fixed charge penalty because they wish to contest the alleged offence.

(A) Fixed penalty fine not paid – charge not contested

There may be a number of reasons why this has not happened.

(1) The defendant states that they did not receive the fixed penalty notice–incorrect address

A fixed charge penalty notice is issued by the Garda National Processing Office in Capel Street, Dublin to the registered owner (in the case of an offence caught on camera) or to the driver in all other

---

[15] *Ibid.*, s.103(4)(ii).
[16] *Ibid.*, s.103(5).
[17] *Ibid.*, s.103(10)(a) as amended by s.14(f), Road Traffic Act 2006.
[18] *Ibid.*, s.103(10)(b) as amended by s.14(f), Road Traffic Act 2006.
[19] *Ibid.*, s.103(7)(d).

cases. If the address of the registered owner of vehicle is incorrect, then this may explain why they did not receive fixed charge notice (FCN). However, practitioners should advise their clients that there is a clear duty on the owner to advise the Motor Taxation Office of any change of address: the FCN will generally be sent to the address of Registered Owner, unless another address is given to the Garda/warden.

If the registered owner changes their address, then they have an obligation under Article 9 of the Road Vehicles (Registration and Licensing) Regulations 1992[20] to notify the Motor Tax Office of their new address. Failure to comply with regulations is a summary offence contrary to section 12 (4) of the Roads Act 1920 (as amended) and carries a penalty of up to €1,269.74.[21]

In the circumstances, the fact that FCN was not sent to the correct address is merely an explanation rather than a defence. However, if the defendant is indicating that they had not updated their address by mistake and that, if they had received FCN they would have paid same, the court will be likely take this into consideration.

(2) The defendant states that they did not receive the fixed penalty notice–correct address

In other circumstances, the defendant may indicate that, though the address is correct, they simply never received the FCN. While there is a presumption in law that a FCN was served, when same FCN is served in compliance with statutory procedure set out, District Court Judges frequently make inquiries as to how FCN was served on the defendant.

Where there is a communal post box, or a series of post boxes in apartments building, difficulties can arise, in establishing that FCN was actually delivered to correct post box. Some District Court Judges have, if not satisfied on the evidence before court that FCN was properly served, or if they accept the defendant's evidence that they did not receive FCN, chosen to strike out summons.

However, some recent unreported decisions in Circuit Court appear to have severely limited the scope of any defence of claiming non-receipt of FCN by ruling that proof of posting of the notice as distinct from proof of receipt, is sufficient to establish service of

---

[20] S.I. No.385/1992.
[21] S.63, Finance Act 1993 increases penalty to £1,000 – converted to euro as €1,269.74.

FCN: and that, in the circumstances, it is not a defence to state that FCN was not received, where there is proof that FCN was posted to correct address.

Practitioners should be cognisant of the provisions of Part 3 of the Road Traffic Act 2010[22] (see below) which further clarifies the position in respect of the service of a FCN.

(3) The defendant received penalty notice but failed to pay FCN or nominate vehicle user within specified time

In other cases, the defendant receives the FCN but does not successfully or correctly pay fine within the designated time period. The court is likely to give a defendant credit in circumstances where they did make attempts to pay the fine, even if those attempts were unsuccessful. If a defendant is indicating to the court that they are accepting that the offence took place, and that they would have paid the FCN, had they received same, or that they did unsuccessfully attempted to pay same, then provided they do not have any previous convictions for similar offences, the court is likely to deal with matter quite leniently and may allow the defendant to pay a charitable contribution in lieu of a criminal conviction. In circumstances where the matter is struck out payment of a charitable contribution the defendant will not accrue any penalty points which might otherwise have applied. However, if they are convicted and fined, penalty points will be imposed.

(B) Fixed penalty fine not paid – charge contested

The second set of circumstances in which a defendant may find themselves before a court for a penalty point offence that might otherwise be dealt with by way of a fixed charge penalty is when the defendant contests the alleged offence and wishes to challenge the matter in the District Court.

In those circumstances, matters will proceed to trial. Without setting out in detail the general rules of evidence, as in all cases, it will be for the prosecution to prove all necessary elements of the offence.[23] Again, practitioners should be aware of the particular applicability of section 21, Road Traffic Act 2002 and section 35, Road Traffic Act 1994 (see below) to the prosecution of these offences.

---

[22] When same ss.34–49 come into operation.
[23] See Chapter 1 in respect of the Prosecution of Offences.

PART THREE – PROVISIONS IN RESPECT OF FIXED CHARGE OFFENCES – ROAD TRAFFIC ACT 2010

Section 103 of the Road Traffic Act 1961[24] is repealed and replaced by the provisions contained in sections 34 – 49 of the Road Traffic Act 2010.[25] Practitioners therefore need to be cognisant of the new provisions in respect of Fixed Charge Penalties, the main provisions, are summarised below.

FIXED CHARGE OFFENCES – SECTION 34 OF THE ROAD TRAFFIC ACT 2010

The statutory basis for fixed charge offences is set out in section 34 of the Road Traffic Act 2010 and applies to such summary Road Traffic offences[26] under:

(a) the Road Traffic Acts 1961-2010 and the Roads Act 1993 to 2007;[27]

(b) the Roads Transport Act 1933[28] and Road Traffic Regulations made under the Road Traffic Acts or the European Community Act 1972;[29]

(c) sections 34 and 39 of the Taxi Regulation Act 2003;[30]

(d) article 4 of the European Communities (Installation and Use of Speed Limitation Devices in Motor Vehicles) Regulations 2005;[31]

(e) articles 5, 6, 7, 8 or 9 of the European Communities (Compulsory use of Safety Belts and Child Restraint Systems in Motor Vehicles) Regulations 2006;[32] and

(f) section 73 of the Finance Act[33] and section 139 of the Finance Act 1992.[34]

---

[24] As amended by s.11, Road Traffic Act 2002, ss.18, 19 and 20, Road Traffic Act 2004 and s.14, Road Traffic Act 2006 – all of which are also repealed upon commencement of Pt.III, Road Traffic Act 2010.

[25] When same sections come into operation.

[26] Only summary road traffic offences can be prescribed by the minister as fixed charge offences.

[27] S.34(a), Road Traffic Act 2010.

[28] *Ibid.*, s.34(b)(i).

[29] *Ibid.*, s.34(b)(ii).

[30] *Ibid.*, s.34(c).

[31] See S.I. No.831/2005 and s.34(d), Road Traffic Act 2010.

[32] See S.I. No.240/2006 and s.34(e), Road Traffic Act 2010.

[33] S.34(f)(i), Road Traffic Act 2010.

[34] *Ibid.*, s.34(f)(ii), Road Traffic Act 2010.

As may be declared by the Minister by way of regulations as fixed charge offences.[35]

Fixed Charge Notice Service –
Section 35 of the Road Traffic Act 2010

Where a Garda has reasonable grounds for believing a fixed charge offence has been/is being committed,[36] that Garda (or Traffic Warden[37]/Transport Officer[38] or other Authorised Person[39]) may serve a Fixed Charge Notice (FCN), or cause a FCN to be served on an identified person using vehicle[40] and/or registered owner[41] of vehicle with a fixed charge notice, either personally or by post.[42]

A fixed penalty notice may be served on an individual by means of personal service,[43] by delivering it to the person, or leaving it at the address:

(i)   where they ordinarily reside;[44]

(ii) they gave to the Gardaí at the time of the alleged offence;[45]

(iii) of the registered owner of the vehicle.[46]

Or by postal service,[47] posting it to the address:

(i)   where they ordinarily reside;[48]

(ii) they gave to the Gardaí at the time of the alleged offence;[49]

(iii) of the registered owner of the vehicle.[50]

Where a registered owner (individual or body corporate) receives notice but was not driving, not capable of driving, or not otherwise

---

[35] S.34, Road Traffic Act 2010.
[36] S.35(1), Road Traffic Act 2010.
[37] *Ibid.*, s.35(4).
[38] *Ibid.*, s.35(5)(a).
[39] *Ibid.*, s.35(5)(b).
[40] *Ibid.*, s.35(1)(a).
[41] *Ibid.*, s.35(1)(b).
[42] *Ibid.*, s.35(1).
[43] *Ibid.*, s.35(3)(a).
[44] *Ibid.*, s.35(3)(a)(I).
[45] *Ibid.*, s.35(3)(a)(II).
[46] *Ibid.*, s.35(3)(a)(III).
[47] *Ibid.*, s.35(3)(b).
[48] *Ibid.*, s.35(3)(b)(I).
[49] *Ibid.*, s.35(3)(b)(II).
[50] *Ibid.*, s.35(b)(III).

using vehicle at time of alleged offence,[51] the registered owner must:

(a) give or send to a Garda/traffic warden within 28 days, details of a nominate user and using the prescribed form their full name and address;[52] or

(b) give or send to the Garda/traffic warden within a specified time period all the information within their knowledge or procurement as the Garda/warden might reasonably request for the purposes of establishing identify of and location of vehicle user.[53]

In any prosecution, it shall be presumed until the contrary is shown that the registered owner did not provide such name and address,[54] however, it is a defence to a prosecution under section 35(6), if an individual can demonstrate that the information concerned was not within their knowledge or procurement and that they had taken all reasonable steps to obtain same information.[55] The ordinary 6 months time period within which to institute summary proceedings does not apply to an offence contrary to section 35(6), and summary proceedings many be brought at any time within two years of the date of the offence.[56]

Not later than 28 days after the notice/information is received by the Garda/warden, the commissioner shall cause the identified vehicle user to be served with notice, either personally or by post.[57]

FIXED CHARGE NOTICE SERVICE – SECTION 36 OF THE ROAD TRAFFIC ACT 2010

Section 36 of the Road Traffic Act 2010[58] sets that a FCN:

(a) shall be in the prescribed form;[59]

(b) contains details of the manner of payment of FCN;[60]

---

[51] *Ibid.*, s.35(6)(b).
[52] *Ibid.*, s.35(6)(i).
[53] *Ibid.*, s.35(6)(ii).
[54] *Ibid.*, s.35(7).
[55] *Ibid.*, s.40(3).
[56] *Ibid.*, s.40(7).
[57] *Ibid.*, s.35(9).
[58] When same section comes into operation.
[59] S.36(1)(a), Road Traffic Act 2010 and subsequent Regulations, when same are commenced.
[60] *Ibid.*, s.36(1)(b).

(c) specifies the person and place payment to be made to, and if payment must be accompanied by a completed notice;[61]

(d) if penalty point offence, require that certain details of driving licence/permit be provided;[62]

(e) that penalty points will be endorsed on same licence/permit, on receipt of payment of following conviction.[63]

A FCN shall contain a statement containing/referring to the following information:[64]

(a) the individual has committed the specified offence;[65]

(b) that individual may pay FCN within 28 days;[66]

(c) that if they do not pay within 28 days, the fine can still be paid within the subsequent 28 days, however the fine to be paid will increase by 50%;[67]

(d) that a prosecution will not be initiated, if FCN paid;[68]

(e) where FCN served on registered owner, they shall pay the fine within 56 day period, or if not driving, not capable of driving, or not otherwise using vehicle at time of alleged offence,[69] send to a Garda/traffic warden within 28 days, either the details of a nominate user and using the prescribed form their full name and address:[70] or all the information within their knowledge or procurement as the Garda/warden might reasonably request for the purposes of establishing identify of and location of vehicle user;[71]

(f) that if registered owner complies by either paying fine,[72] or complying with nomination provisions of section 35(6), Road Traffic Act 2010, a prosecution will not be initiated against them.[73]

---

[61] *Ibid.*, s.36(1)(c).
[62] *Ibid.*, s.36(1)(d).
[63] *Ibid.*, s.36(1)(e).
[64] *Ibid.*, ss.36(2) and 36(3).
[65] *Ibid.*, ss.36(2)(a) and 36(3)(a).
[66] *Ibid.*, s.36(2)(b) and s.36(3)(b).
[67] *Ibid.*, ss.36(2)(c) and 36(3)(c), Road Traffic Act 2010.
[68] *Ibid.*, s.36(2)(d).
[69] *Ibid.*, s.36(3)(d).
[70] *Ibid.*, s.36(3)(d)(i).
[71] *Ibid.*, s.36(3)(d)(ii).
[72] *Ibid.*, ss.36(3)(e) and 36(3)(f).
[73] *Ibid.*, s.36(3)(g).

Legal Presumptions Under Part Three –
Section 38 of the Road Traffic Act 2010

In any prosecution for a fixed charge offence under Part 3 of the Road Traffic Act 2010, it is presumed until the contrary is shown that the relevant Fixed Charge Notice (FCN) was duly served.[74] If being served personally on an individual or affixed to vehicle, it is presumed FCN was so served or affixed; if served by post, service is presumed where there is proof of posting or delivery of notice. It is further presumed in any prosecution, until the contrary is shown that the alleged fixed charge fine payment, accompanied by duly completed notice if required, was not made.[75]

A document purporting to be a certificate or receipt of posting, or delivery, issued by An Post, or any other postal service is admissible as proof of the posting or delivery, until contrary is shown.[76] The registered owner of the vehicle, who does not nominate another individual, or otherwise comply with provisions of section 35(6) of the Road Traffic Act 2010, shall be presumed to have been driving or otherwise using vehicle until contrary is shown.[77]

Gardaí may request, or cause a notice to be created requesting that the Registered Owner provide certain information, or produce certain documentation (such as approved policy of insurance), and if the Registered Owner fails, within 28 days of receiving such a notice, to provide such information, or provides false or misleading information, they commit an offence and are liable upon summary conviction to pay a fine of up to €5,000.[78]

The ordinary 6 months' time period within which to institute summary proceedings does not apply to an offence contrary to section 38(4), and summary proceedings many be brought at any time within two years of the date of the offence.[79]

Offences in Relation to Fixed Charge Notices –
Section 40 of the Road Traffic Act 2010

Practitioners should note that it is an offence for any person, other than the person to whom the notice applies, to remove or interfere

---

[74] *Ibid.*, s.38(1)(a).
[75] *Ibid.*, s.38(1)(b).
[76] *Ibid.*, s.38(2).
[77] *Ibid.*, s.38(2).
[78] *Ibid.*, s.38(4) – see also ss.38(3)(b), 35(1) and 35(6).
[79] *Ibid.*, s.40(7).

with a FCN affixed to a vehicle.[80] It is also and offence for a person to fail to comply with the provisions in respect of section 35(6) of the Road Traffic Act 2010 in respect of nominating another person and such individuals are liable upon summary conviction to a fine of up to €1,000.[81]

It is further an offence, if a person, in nominating another person, or otherwise under the provisions of section 35(6), provides a Garda/traffic warden with information which is false or misleading and such individuals are liable upon summary conviction to a fine of up to €2,000.[82]

PAYMENT OF FIXED CHARGE ON SERVICE OF SUMMONS – SECTION 40 OF THE ROAD TRAFFIC ACT 2010

Practitioners should take particular cognisance of the provisions of section 44 of the Road Traffic Act 2010.[83] These provisions should further reduce the number of fixed charge offences coming before the court by allowing a person who has received a summons in respect of a fixed charge offence to pay the amount specified on the fixed charge notice attached to the court summons.

A person served with a summons in respect of fixed charge offence may pay a fixed charge in the amount stated in the FCN served with the summons.[84] This payment should be made, in the manner specified in the notice, no later than seven days before the date same person is summoned to appear in court. If the FCN attached to the summons is paid, in the manner specified, proceedings will be discontinued and the defendant will no longer be require to attend court.[85]

A FCN summons may be served by Court Services,[86] and the fixed charge fine shall be 100% greater[87] than the prescribed amount stated in the FCN originally served on that individual.[88] Where a person is served with a summons in respect of a fixed charge offence, it is not a defence for same person to give evidence that they were not served with the original FCN.[89]

---

[80] *Ibid.*, s.40(1).
[81] *Ibid.*, s.40(2).
[82] *Ibid.*, s.40(6).
[83] When same provisions come into operation.
[84] S.44(1), Road Traffic Act 2010.
[85] *Ibid.*, s.44(1).
[86] *Ibid.*, s.44(2).
[87] *Ibid.*, s.44(3)
[88] *Ibid.*, ss.35 and 44(3).
[89] *Ibid.*, s.44(7).

In practical terms, this means that where an individual receives a summons to attend court in respect of any fixed charge, and they advise that they were not served with the original FCN, they have a further opportunity to pay a fine and avoid attending court. Practitioners need to advice clients who receive such a summons that unless they are contesting the alleged offence, they should avail of the opportunity to pay the prescribed fine, no less than seven days before their summons date.

GENERAL PENALTY – SECTION 102 OF THE ROAD TRAFFIC ACT 1961

Practitioners should note that when reference is made to the general penalty, this means the penalty imposed under section 102 of the Road Traffic Act 1961, as amended,[90] namely:

First Offence – fine of up to €1,000.[91]

Second Offence (under same section) – fine of up to €2,000.[92]

Third/Subsequent Offence (under same section within 12 consecutive months) – fine of up to €2,000 and/or a term of imprisonment of up to three months.[93]

FIXED CHARGE OFFENCES

These 28 fixed charge offences are as follows:

(1) Illegally parking vehicle in disabled parking bay – article 44(1), Road Traffic (Traffic and Parking) Regulations.[94]

Enforcement – Gardaí and traffic wardens.

Fixed Charge Penalty: €80 (paid in 28 days);[95] €120 (paid in subsequent 28 days).[96]

---

[90] See Table contained in s.18, Road Traffic Act 2006 and see also S.I. No.86/2007 – Road Traffic Act 2006 (Commencement) Order 2007.
[91] Reference 20 – Pt.1 – Table – s.18, Road Traffic Act 2006.
[92] *Ibid.*, Reference 21 – Pt.1.
[93] *Ibid.*, Reference 21 – Pt.1.
[94] Art.44, S.I. No.182/1997 – Regulations enacted under s.35, Road Traffic Act 1994.
[95] See s.103(7)(b), Road Traffic Act 1961 as inserted by s.14(c), Road Traffic Act 2006. See art.5(a)(ii) and Sch.1 Pt.2 of S.I. No.135/2006 – Road Traffic Acts 1961 to 2005 (fixed charge offences) Regulations 2006.
[96] See s.103(7)(c), Road Traffic Act 1961 and art.5(a)(ii) and Sch.1 Pt.2 of S.I. No.135/2006 – Road Traffic Acts 1961 to 2005 (fixed charge offences) Regulations 2006.

Upon Conviction: General Penalty under section 102 of the Road Traffic Act 1961.[97]

(2) Failure by driver to have tax disc fixed and displayed on windscreen of vehicle – section 73 of the Finance Act 1976.

Section 73(1) sets out that it is an offence: to fail to display a tax disc on any vehicle which is being used, parked or kept in any public place, if same vehicle is one for which Motor Tax must be paid and displayed.

Enforcement – Gardaí and Traffic Wardens.

Fixed Charge Penalty: €60 (paid in 28 days):[98] €90 (paid in subsequent 28 days).[99]

Penalty (on conviction): fine of up to €1,269.74.[100]

(3) Failure by driver to have insurance disc fixed and displayed on windscreen – article 5 of the Road Traffic (Insurance Disc) Regulations,[101] as substituted by article 4 of the Road Traffic (Insurance Disc) (Amendment) Regulations 1986.[102]

Enforcement – Gardaí only.

Fixed Charge Penalty: €60 (paid in 28 days):[103] €90 (paid in subsequent 28 days).[104]

Upon Conviction: General Penalty under section 102 of the Road Traffic Act 1961.[105]

(4) Illegally parking vehicle in a taxi rank – article 36(2)(e) of the Road Traffic (Traffic and Parking) Regulations.[106]

---

[97] **First conviction** – fine up to €1,000; **Second conviction** – fine up to €2,000; **Third conviction** – fine up to €1,000 and/or imprisonment for up to 3 months. See also s.18, Road Traffic Act 2006.

[98] See art.5(b)(iii), S.I. No.135/2006.

[99] See s.103(7)(c), Road Traffic Act 1961 and art.5(b)(iii), S.I. No.135/2006.

[100] See s.76, Finance Act 1976 as amended by s.63, Finance Act 1993 to increase penalty to £1,000 – converted to euro as €1,269.74.

[101] S.I. No.355/1984.

[102] S.I. No.227/1986.

[103] Art.5(b)(i) and Sch.2, Pt.1 of S.I. No.135/2006.

[104] See s.103(7)(c), Road Traffic Act 1961 and art.5(b)(i) and Sch.2, Pt.1 of S.I. No.135/2006.

[105] **First conviction** – fine up to €1,000; **Second conviction** – fine up to €2,000; **Third conviction** – fine up to €1,000 and/or imprisonment for up to 3 months. See also s.18, Road Traffic Act 2006.

[106] Art.36(2)(e), S.I. No.182/1997 – Regulations enacted under s.35, Road Traffic Act 1994.

Enforcement – Gardaí and traffic wardens.

Fixed Charge Penalty: €40 (paid in 28 days):[107] €60 (paid in subsequent 28 days).[108]

Upon Conviction: General Penalty under section 102 of Road Traffic Act 1961.[109]

(5) Taxis illegally standing for hire in places other than at taxi rank – section 84 of the Road Traffic Act 1961.[110]

Enforcement – Gardaí and traffic wardens.

Fixed Charge Penalty: €40 (paid in 28 days):[111] €60 (paid in subsequent 28 days).[112]

Upon Conviction: General Penalty under section 102 of the Road Traffic Act 1961.[113]

(6) Illegally parking/using vehicle in a local authority car park – bye Laws enacted under section 101(7) of the Road Traffic Act 1961.[114]

Enforcement – traffic wardens only.

Fixed Charge Penalty: €40 (paid in 28 days):[115] €60 (paid in subsequent 28 days).[116]

Upon Conviction: General Penalty under section 102 of the Road Traffic Act 1961.[117]

---

[107] Art.5(c)(ii) and Sch.3, Pt.2 of S.I. No.135/2006.

[108] See s.103(7)(c), Road Traffic Act 1961 and art.5(c)(ii) and Sch.3, Pt.2 of S.I. No.135/2006.

[109] **First conviction** – fine up to €1,000; **Second conviction** – fine up to €2,000; **Third conviction** – fine up to €1,000 and/or imprisonment for up to 3 months. See also s.18, Road Traffic Act 2006.

[110] As substituted by s.15, Road Traffic Act 2002 and s.29, Road Traffic Act 2004.

[111] Art.5(c)(i) and Sch.3, Pt.1 of S.I. No.135/2006.

[112] See s.103(7)(c), Road Traffic Act 1961 and art.5(c)(i) Sch.3, Pt.1 of S.I. No.135/2006.

[113] **First conviction** – fine up to €1,000; **Second conviction** – fine up to €2,000; **Third conviction** – fine up to €1,000 and/or imprisonment for up to 3 months. See also s.18, Road Traffic Act 2006.

[114] As amended by s.6, Road Traffic Act 1968 and s.49, Road Traffic Act 1994.

[115] Art.5(c)(ii) and Sch.3, Pt.2 of S.I. No.135/2006.

[116] See s.103(7)(c), Road Traffic Act 1961 and art.5(c)(ii) and Sch.3, Pt.2 of S.I. No.135/2006.

[117] **First conviction** – fine up to €1,000; **Second conviction** – fine up to €2,000; **Third conviction** – fine up to €1,000 and/or imprisonment for up to 3 months. See also s.18, Road Traffic Act 2006.

(7) Illegally parking where a time restriction applies – article 37(1) of the Road Traffic (Traffic and Parking) Regulations 1997.[118]

Enforcement – Gardaí and traffic wardens.

Fixed Charge Penalty: €40 (paid in 28 days):[119] €60 (paid in subsequent 28 days).[120]

Upon Conviction: General Penalty under section 102 of the Road Traffic Act 1961.[121]

(8) Illegally parking a vehicle where local authority 'pay parking' applies – bye Laws enacted under section 36 of the Road Traffic Act 1994.[122]

Enforcement – traffic wardens only.

Fixed Charge Penalty: €40 (paid in 28 days):[123] €60 (paid in subsequent 28 days).[124]

Upon Conviction: General Penalty under section 102 of the Road Traffic Act 1961.[125]

(9) Illegally parking vehicle in a bus lane or bus only street – article 39(2) [bus lane] and Article 39(3) [bus only street] – Road Traffic (Traffic and Parking) Regulations.[126]

Enforcement – Gardaí and traffic wardens.

Fixed Charge Penalty: €40 (paid in 28 days):[127] €60 (paid in subsequent 28 days).[128]

---

[118] Art. 37(1), S.I. No.182/1997 – Regulations enacted under s.35, Road Traffic Act 1994.
[119] Art.5(c)(ii) and Sch.3, Pt.2 of S.I. No.135/2006.
[120] See s.103(7)(c), Road Traffic Act 1961 and art.5(c)(ii) and Sch.3, Pt.2 of S.I. No.135/2006.
[121] **First conviction** – Fine up to €1,000; **Second conviction** – Fine up to €2,000; **Third conviction** – Fine up to €1,000 and/or imprisonment for up to 3 months. See also s.18, Road Traffic Act 2006.
[122] As amended by s.12(1), Roads Act 2007.
[123] Art.5(c)(ii) and Sch.3, Pt.2 of S.I. No.135/2006.
[124] See s.103(7)(c), Road Traffic Act 1961 and art.5(c)(ii) and Sch.3 Pt.2 of S.I. No.135/2006.
[125] **First conviction** – Fine up to €1,000; **Second conviction** – Fine up to €2,000; **Third conviction** – Fine up to €1,000 and/or imprisonment for up to 3 months. See also s.18, Road Traffic Act 2006.
[126] Art.39, S.I. No.182/1997 – Regulations enacted under s.35, Road Traffic Act 1994.
[127] Art.5(c)(ii) and Sch.3 Pt.2 of S.I. No.135/2006.
[128] See s.103(7)(c), Road Traffic Act 1961 and art.5(c)(ii) and Sch.3 Pt.2 of S.I. No.135/2006.

Upon Conviction: General Penalty under section 102 of the Road Traffic Act 1961.[129]

(10) Illegally parking/stopping a vehicle at school entrances – article 41(1), Road Traffic (Traffic and Parking) Regulations.[130]

Enforcement – Gardaí and traffic wardens.

Fixed Charge Penalty: €40 (paid in 28 days):[131] €60 (paid in subsequent 28 days).[132]

Upon Conviction: General Penalty under section 102 of the Road Traffic Act 1961.[133]

(11) Illegally parking a vehicle (other than goods vehicle – 30 minutes maximum) in a loading bay during period of operation – Article 38(1)(b) of the Road Traffic (Traffic and Parking) Regulations.[134]

Enforcement – Gardaí and traffic wardens.

Fixed Charge Penalty: €40 (paid in 28 days):[135] €60 (paid in subsequent 28 days).[136]

Upon Conviction: General Penalty under section 102 of the Road Traffic Act 1961.[137]

(12) Illegally parking a HGV or bus in an area where weight restrictions apply – article 38 (1) (b) of the Road Traffic (Traffic and Parking) Regulations 1997.[138]

---

[129] **First conviction** – fine up to €1,000; **Second conviction** – fine up to €2,000; **Third conviction** – fine up to €1,000 and/or imprisonment for up to 3 months. See also s.18, Road Traffic Act 2006.

[130] Art.41, S.I. No.182/1997 – Regulations enacted under s.35, Road Traffic Act 1994.

[131] Art.5(c)(ii) and Sch.3, Pt.2, S.I. No.135/2006.

[132] See s.103(7)(c), Road Traffic Act 1961 and art.5(c)(ii) and Sch.3 Pt.2 of S.I. No.135/2006.

[133] **First conviction** – fine up to €1,000; **Second conviction** – fine up to €2,000; **Third conviction** – fine up to €1,000 and/or imprisonment for up to 3 months. See also s.18, Road Traffic Act 2006.

[134] Art.38, S.I. No.182/1997 – Regulations enacted under s.35, Road Traffic Act 1994.

[135] Art.5(c)(ii) and Sch.3 Pt.2, S.I. No.135/2006.

[136] See s.103(7)(c), Road Traffic Act 1961 and art.5(c)(ii) and Sch.3 Pt.2, S.I. No.135/2006.

[137] **First conviction** – fine up to €1,000; **Second conviction** – fine up to €2,000; **Third conviction** – fine up to €1,000 and/or imprisonment for up to 3 months. See also s.18, Road Traffic Act 2006.

[138] Art.38, S.I. No.182/1997 – Regulations enacted under s.35, Road Traffic Act 1994.

Enforcement – Gardaí and traffic wardens.

Fixed Charge Penalty: €40 (paid in 28 days):[139] €60 (paid in subsequent 28 days).[140]

Upon Conviction: General Penalty under section 102 of the Road-Traffic Act 1961.[141]

(13) Illegally parking a vehicle in a pedestrianised street during period of operation – article 45(2) of the Road Traffic (Traffic and Parking) Regulations 1997.[142]

Enforcement – Gardaí and traffic wardens.

Fixed Charge Penalty: €40 (paid in 28 days):[143] €60 (paid in subsequent 28 days).[144]

Upon Conviction: General Penalty under section 102 of the Road Traffic Act 1961.[145]

(14) Illegally parking vehicle (other than a bus) at a bus stop – article 36(2)(e) of the Road Traffic (Traffic and Parking) Regulations 1997.[146]

Enforcement – Gardaí and traffic wardens.

Fixed Charge Penalty: €40 (paid in 28 days):[147] €60 (paid in subsequent 28 days).[148]

Upon Conviction: General Penalty under section 102 of the Road Traffic Act 1961.[149]

---

[139] Art.5(c)(ii) and Sch.3, Pt.2, S.I. No.135/2006.

[140] See s.103(7)(c), Road Traffic Act 1961 and art.5(c)(ii) and Sch.3, Pt.2, S.I. No.135/2006.

[141] **First conviction** – fup to €1,000; **Second conviction** – fine up to €2,000; **Third conviction** – fine up to €1,000 and/or imprisonment for up to 3 months. See also s.18, Road Traffic Act 2006.

[142] Art.45, S.I. No.182/1997 – Regulations enacted under s.35, Road Traffic Act 1994.

[143] Art.5(c)(ii) and Sch.3, Pt.2, S.I. No.135/2006.

[144] See s.103(7)(c), Road Traffic Act 1961 and art.5(c)(ii) and Sch.3, Pt.2, S.I. No.135/2006.

[145] **First conviction** – fine up to €1,000; **Second conviction** – fine up to €2,000; **Third conviction** – fine up to €1,000 and/or imprisonment for up to 3 months. See also s.18, Road Traffic Act 2006.

[146] Art.45, S.I. No.182/1997 – Regulations enacted under s.35, Road Traffic Act 1994.

[147] Art.5(c)(ii) and Sch.3, Pt.2 of S.I. No.135/2006.

[148] See s.103(7)(c), Road Traffic Act 1961 and art.5(c)(ii) and Sch.3, Pt.2 of S.I. No.135/2006.

[149] **First conviction** – fine up to €1,000; **Second conviction** – fine up to €2,000; **Third**

(15) Illegally parking a bus outside area allocated for buses at bus stop/stand Bye laws made under section 86 of the Road Traffic Act 1961).

Enforcement – Gardaí and traffic wardens.

Fixed Charge Penalty: €40 (paid in 28 days):[150] €60 (paid in subsequent 28 days).[151]

Upon Conviction: General Penalty under section 102 of the Road Traffic Act 1961.[152]

(16) Failure to remove a vehicle parked on a cycle track before appointed commencement of operation – article 14(6) of the Road Traffic (Traffic and Parking) Regulations 1997.[153]

Enforcement – Gardaí and traffic wardens.

Fixed Charge Penalty: €40 (paid in 28 days):[154] €60 (paid in subsequent 28 days).[155]

Upon Conviction: General Penalty under section 102 of the Road Traffic Act 1961.[156]

(17) Parking vehicle where prohibited: article 36 of the Road Traffic (Traffic and Parking) Regulations 1997.[157]

Double Yellow Lines – article 36(2)(a) of the Road Traffic (Traffic and Parking) Regulations 1997.

No Parking Sign – article 36(2)(b) of the Road Traffic (Traffic and Parking) Regulations 1997.

---

conviction – fine up to €1,000 and/or imprisonment for up to 3 months. See also s.18, Road Traffic Act 2006.

[150] Art.5(c)(i) and Sch.3, Pt.1, S.I. No.135/2006.

[151] See s.103(7)(c), Road Traffic Act 1961 and art.5(c)(ii) and Sch.3, Pt.2 of S.I. No.135/2006.

[152] **First conviction** – fine up to €1,000; **Second conviction** – fine up to €2,000; **Third conviction** – fine up to €1,000 and/or imprisonment for up to 3 months. See also s.18, Road Traffic Act 2006.

[153] Art.14(6), S.I. No.182/1997 as amended by S.I. No.274/1998 – regulations enacted under s.35, Road Traffic Act 1994.

[154] Art.5(c)(ii) and Sch.3, Pt.2, S.I. No.135/2006.

[155] See s.103(7)(c), Road Traffic Act 1961 and art.5(c)(ii) and Sch.3, Pt.2 of S.I. No.135/2006.

[156] **First conviction** – fine up to €1,000; **Second conviction** – fine up to €2,000; **Third conviction** – fine up to €1,000 and/or imprisonment for up to 3 months. See also s.18, Road Traffic Act 2006.

[157] Art.36, S.I. No.182/1997 as amended by S.I. No.274/1998 – regulations enacted under s.35, Road Traffic Act 1994.

Cycle Track – article 36(2)(m) of the Road Traffic (Traffic and Parking) Regulations 1997.

Within 5m of a Road Junction – article 36(2)(c) of the Road Traffic (Traffic and Parking) Regulations 1997.

Continuous White Lines – article 36(2)(d) of the Road Traffic (Traffic and Parking) Regulations 1997.

Taxi Only Stands – article 36(2)(e) of the Road Traffic (Traffic and Parking) Regulations 1997.

Obstructing Emergency Service Stations – article 36(2)(f) of the RoadTraffic (Traffic and Parking) Regulations 1997.

Obstructing Driveways – article 36(2)(g) of the Road Traffic (Traffic andParking) Regulations 1997.

Within 15m of Pedestrian Crossing/Traffic Lights – article 36(2)(h) of the Road Traffic (Traffic and Parking) Regulations 1997.

Enforcement – Gardaí and traffic wardens.

Fixed Charge Penalty: €40 (paid in 28 days):[158] €60 (paid in subsequent 28 days).[159]

Upon Conviction: General Penalty under section 102 of the Road Traffic Act 1961.[160]

(18) Stopping/parking a vehicle in a clearway during period stated in traffic sign – article 40(2) of the Road Traffic (Traffic and Parking) Regulations 1997.[161]

Enforcement – Gardaí and traffic wardens.

Fixed Charge Penalty: €40 (paid in 28 days):[162] €60 (paid in subsequent 28 days).[163]

Upon Conviction: General Penalty under section 102 of the Road Traffic Act 1961.[164]

---

[158] Art.5(c)(ii) and Sch.3, Pt.2, S.I. No.135/2006.
[159] See s.103(7)(c), Road Traffic Act 1961 and art.5(c)(ii) and Sch.3, Pt.2, S.I. No.135/2006.
[160] **First conviction** – fine up to €1,000; **Second conviction** – fine up to €2,000; **Third conviction** – fine up to €1,000 and/or imprisonment for up to 3 months. See also s.18, Road Traffic Act 2006.
[161] Art.36, S.I. No.182/1997 – Regulations enacted under s.35, Road Traffic Act 1994.
[162] Art.5(c)(ii) and Sch.3, Pt.2, S.I. No.135/2006.
[163] See s.103(7)(c), Road Traffic Act 1961 and art.5(c)(ii) and Sch.3, Pt.2, S.I. No.135/2006.
[164] **First conviction** – fine up to €1,000; **Second conviction** – fine up to €2,000; **Third**

(19) Illegally stopping/parking a vehicle on any part of a motorway – article 33(1)(c) of the Road Traffic (Traffic and Parking) Regulations 1997.[165]

Enforcement – Gardaí and traffic wardens.

Fixed Charge Penalty: €80 (paid in 28 days):[166] €120 (paid in subsequent 28 days).[167]

Upon Conviction: General Penalty section 102 of the Road Traffic Act 1961.[168]

(20) Failure to obey traffic direction given by Gardaí – article 19 of the Road Traffic (Traffic and Parking) Regulations 1997.[169]

Enforcement – Gardaí only.

Fixed Charge Penalty: €80 (paid in 28 days):[170] €120 (paid in subsequent 28 days).[171]

Upon Conviction: General Penalty section 102 of the Road Traffic Act 1961.[172]

(21) Failure by a passenger aged 17 or over to comply with requirements regarding use of front and rear seatbelts – EC (Compulsory use of Safety Belts and Child Restraint Systems in Motor Vehicles) Regulations 2006.[173]

Enforcement – Gardaí only.

---

conviction – fine up to €1,000 and/or imprisonment for up to 3 months. See also s.18, Road Traffic Act 2006.

[165] Art.33, S.I. No.182/1997 – Regulations enacted under s.35, Road Traffic Act 1994.

[166] Art.5(a)(ii) and Sch.1, Pt.2, S.I. No.135/2006.

[167] See s.103(7)(c), Road Traffic Act 1961 and art.5(a)(ii) and Sch.1, Pt.2, S.I. No.135/2006.

[168] **First conviction** – fine up to €1,000; **Second conviction** – fine up to €2,000; **Third conviction** – fine up to €1,000 and/or imprisonment for up to 3 months. See also s.18, Road Traffic Act 2006.

[169] Art.19, S.I. No.182/1997 – Regulations enacted under s.35, Road Traffic Act 1994.

[170] Art.5(a)(ii) and Sch.1, Pt.2, S.I. No.135/2006.

[171] See s.103(7)(c), Road Traffic Act 1961 and art.5(a)(ii) and Sch.1, Pt.2, S.I. No.135/2006.

[172] **First conviction** – fine up to €1,000; **Second conviction** – fine up to €2,000; **Third conviction** – fine up to €1,000 and/or imprisonment for up to 3 months. See also s.18, Road Traffic Act 2006.

[173] Art.33, S.I. No.240/2006 – Regulations made under s.3, European Communities Act 1972.

Fixed Charge Penalty: €60 (paid in 28 days):[174] €90 (paid in subsequent 28 days).[175]

Upon Conviction: General Penalty under section 102 of the Road Traffic Act 1961.[176]

(22) Illegally entering a road with a HGV or bus where weight restrictions apply – article 17 of the Road Traffic (Traffic and Parking) Regulations 1997.[177]

Enforcement – Gardaí only.

Fixed Charge Penalty: €60 (paid in 28 days):[178] €90 (paid in subsequent 28 days).[179]

Upon Conviction: General Penalty under section 102 of the Road Traffic Act 1961.[180]

(23) Failure by a driver to give appropriate signals by the use of indicators or specified hand signals when intending to slow down, stop, or change course – article 18 of the Road Traffic (Traffic and Parking) Regulations/1997.[181]

Enforcement – Gardaí Only.

Fixed Charge Penalty: €60 (paid in 28 days):[182] €90 (paid in subsequent 28 days).[183]

Upon Conviction: General Penalty under section 102 of the Road Traffic Act 1961.[184]

---

[174] Art.5(b)(i) and Sch.2, Pt.1, S.I. No.135/2006 – as amended by S.I. No.240/2006.
[175] See s.103(7)(c), Road Traffic Act 1961 and art.5(b)(i) and Sch.2, Pt.1 of S.I. No.135/2006 – as amended by S.I. No.240/2006.
[176] **First conviction** – fine up to €1,000; **Second conviction** – fine up to €2,000; **Third conviction** – fine up to €1,000 and/or imprisonment for up to 3 months. See also s.18, Road Traffic Act 2006.
[177] Art.17, S.I. No.182/1997 – Regulations enacted under s.35, Road Traffic Act 1994.
[178] Art.5(b)(ii) and Sch.2, Pt.2, S.I. No.135/2006 – as amended by S.I. No.240/2006.
[179] See s.103(7)(c), Road Traffic Act 1961 and art.5(b)(ii) and Sch.2, Pt.2 of S.I. No.135/2006 – as amended by S.I. No.240/2006.
[180] **First conviction** – fine up to €1,000; **Second conviction** – fine up to €2,000; **Third conviction** – fine up to €1,000 and/or imprisonment for up to 3 months. See also s.18, Road Traffic Act 2006.
[181] Art.18, S.I. No.182/1997 – Regulations enacted under s.35, Road Traffic Act 1994.
[182] Art.5(b)(ii) and Sch.2, Pt.2, S.I. No.135/2006 – as amended by S.I. No.240/2006.
[183] See s.103(7)(c), Road Traffic Act 1961 and art.5(b)(ii) and Sch.2, Pt.2 of S.I. No.135/2006 – as amended by S.I. No.240/2006.
[184] **First conviction** – fine up to €1,000; **Second conviction** – fine up to €2,000; **Third conviction** – fine up to €1,000 and/or imprisonment for up to 3 months. See also

(24) Wholly or partly entering a yellow box unless the driver can clear the area – article 29 of the Road Traffic (Traffic and Parking) Regulations 1997.[185]

Enforcement – Gardaí only.

Fixed Charge Penalty: €60 (paid in 28 days):[186] €90 (paid in subsequent 28 days).[187]

Upon Conviction: General Penalty under section 102 of the Road Traffic Act 1961.[188]

(25) Driving a vehicle (other than a bicycle or operational taxi) in a bus lane during period of operation – article 32(3) of the Road Traffic (Traffic and Parking) Regulations 1997.[189]

Enforcement – Gardaí only.

Fixed Charge Penalty: €60 (paid in 28 days):[190] €90 (paid in subsequent 28 days).[191]

Upon Conviction: General Penalty under section 102 of the Road Traffic Act 1961.[192]

(26) Making a U-Turn on a dual carriageway where no U-turn sign is displayed – article 35 of the Road Traffic (Traffic and Parking) Regulations 1997.[193]

Enforcement – Gardaí only.

Fixed Charge Penalty: €60 (paid in 28 days):[194] €90 (paid in subsequent 28 days).[195]

---

s.18, Road Traffic Act 2006.

[185] Art 29, S.I. No.182/1997 – Regulations enacted under s.35, Road Traffic Act 1994.

[186] Art.5(b)(ii) and Sch.2, Pt.2 of S.I. No.135/2006 – as amended by S.I. No.240/2006.

[187] See s.103(7)(c), Road Traffic Act 1961 and art.5(b)(ii) and Sch.2, Pt.2 of S.I. No.135/2006 – as amended by S.I. No.240/2006.

[188] **First conviction** – fine up to €1,000; **Second conviction** – fine up to €2,000; **Third conviction** – fine up to €1,000 and/or imprisonment for up to 3 months. See also s.18, Road Traffic Act 2006.

[189] Art.32, S.I. No.182/1997 – Regulations enacted under s.35, Road Traffic Act 1994.

[190] Art.5(b)(ii) and Sch.2, Pt.2 of S.I. No.135/2006 – as amended by S.I. No.240/2006.

[191] See s.103(7)(c), Road Traffic Act 1961 and art.5(b)(ii) and Sch.2, Pt.2 of S.I. No.135/2006 – as amended by S.I. No.240/2006.

[192] **First conviction** – fine up to €1,000; **Second conviction** – fine up to €2,000; **Third conviction** – fine up to €1,000 and/or imprisonment for up to 3 months. See also s.18, Road Traffic Act 2006.

[193] Art.35, S.I. No.182/1997 – Regulations enacted under s.35, Road Traffic Act 1994.

[194] Art.5(b)(ii) and Sch.2, Pt.2 of S.I. No.135/2006 – as amended by S.I. No.240/2006

[195] See s.103(7)(c), Road Traffic Act 1961 and art.5(b)(ii) and Sch.2, Pt.2 of S.I. No.135/2006 – as amended by S.I. No.240/2006.

Upon Conviction: General Penalty under section 102 of the Road Traffic Act 1961.[196]

(27) Driving a vehicle (other than a light rail vehicle) on a tram line – article 8(2) of the Road Traffic (Traffic and Parking) (Amendment) Regulations 2003.[197]

Enforcement – Gardaí only.

Fixed Charge Penalty: €60 (paid in 28 days):[198] €90 (paid in subsequent 28 days).[199]

Upon Conviction: General Penalty under section 102 of the Road Traffic Act 1961.[200]

(28) Stopping/parking a vehicle (other than a light rail vehicle) on a tram line – article 10 of the Road Traffic (Traffic and Parking) (Amendment) Regulations 2003.[201]

Enforcement – Gardaí and traffic wardens.

Fixed Charge Penalty: €60 (paid in 28 days):[202] €90 (paid in subsequent 28 days).[203]

Upon Conviction: General Penalty under section 102 of the Road Traffic Act 1961.[204]

EVIDENCE IN RESPECT OF A CONSTITUENT OF THE OFFENCE BY MEANS OF AN ELECTRONIC OR OTHER APPARATUS – SECTION 21 OF THE ROAD TRAFFIC ACT 2002

Whilst the most obvious application of the provisions of section 21 might relate to the prosecution of speeding offences, section 21 of the

---

[196] **First conviction** – fine up to €1,000; **Second conviction** – fine up to €2,000; **Third conviction** – fine up to €1,000 and/or imprisonment for up to 3 months. See also s.18, Road Traffic Act 2006.

[197] Art.8, S.I. No.98/2003 – Regulations enacted under s.35, Road Traffic Act 1994.

[198] Art.5(b)(ii) and Sch.2, Pt.2 of S.I. No.135/2006 – as amended by S.I. No.240/2006.

[199] See s.103(7)(c), Road Traffic Act 1961 and art.5(b)(ii) and Sch.2, Pt.2 of S.I. No.135/2006 – as amended by S.I. No.240/2006.

[200] **First conviction** – fine up to €1,000; **Second conviction** – fine up to €2,000; **Third conviction** – fine up to €1,000 and/or imprisonment for up to 3 months. See also s.18, Road Traffic Act 2006.

[201] Art.8, S.I. No.98/2003 – Regulations enacted under s.35, Road Traffic Act 1994.

[202] Art.5(b)(ii) and Sch.2, Pt.2 of S.I. No.135/2006 – as amended by S.I. No.240/2006.

[203] See s.103(7)(c), Road Traffic Act 1961 and art.5(b)(ii) and Sch.2, Pt.2 of S.I. No.135/2006 – as amended by S.I. No.240/2006.

[204] **First conviction** – fine up to €1,000; **Second conviction** – fine up to €2,000; **Third**

Road Traffic Act 2002[205] can be summarised as follows:

Prima facie proof of constituent of offence may be established by tendering evidence obtained by means of:

- an electronic or other apparatus (including a camera) capable of providing a permanent record; or

- an electronic or other apparatus (including a radar gun) not capable of producing a permanent record;

- there is no requirement to prove that an electronic or other apparatus was accurate or in good working order.[206]

EVIDENCE IN RESPECT OF SPEED AND CERTAIN OTHER OFFENCES – SECTION 80 OF THE ROAD TRAFFIC ACT 2010

Practitioners should note that section 80 of the Road Traffic Act 2010[207] repeals and replaces section 21 of the Road Traffic Act 2002. The provisions contained in the new section 80 are however broadly similar to the provisions set out above.[208]

RULES OF THE ROAD

Guidance in respect of most of the Road Traffic Act offences can be found in the Rules of the Road. It is not a statutory offence to break any of these guidelines/rules. They are a useful explanatory note on how the offences operate. All licensed drivers are supposed to be familiar with the Rules of the Road and a court is likely to take a very dim view of anyone who comes before the court pleading a defence to any charges on the basis of a driving practice which contradicts these Rules of the Road.

---

conviction – fine up to €1,000 and/or imprisonment for up to 3 months. See also s.18, Road Traffic Act 2006.

[205] See s.15 Road Traffic Act 2004 and s.17 Road Traffic Act 2006.

[206] See Chapter 3 – Speeding Offences for further information in respect of the provisions of s.21, Road Traffic Act 2002.

[207] When same s. comes into operation.

[208] See Chapter 3 – Speeding Offences for further information in respect of the provisions of s.21, Road Traffic Act 2002 and s.80, Road Traffic Act 2010.

CHAPTER 12

Penalty Point Offences

There are presently 42 penalty point offences in operation in Ireland. Whilst the majority are fixed penalty offences,[1] some require a mandatory court appearance. In respect of these offences, an individual will receive either a charge sheet or more usually a summons and will be required to attend court. However, in addition to any other penalties that may be imposed by the court, these offences carry the additional punitive sanction of penalty points.

This chapter will deal with:

(a) the provisions in respect of penalty point offences;

(b) the new/additional provisions contained in the Road Traffic Act 2010;

(c) all penalty point offences requiring a mandatory court appearance;

(d) all penalty point offences which are fixed charge penalty offences and the various penalties that apply under the fixed charge penalty notice provisions and upon conviction.

Sections 2–7 of the Road Traffic Act of 2002 (as amended) set out a system whereby certain designated road traffic offences would carry penalty points. These penalty points are recorded on a person's licence record and remain so recorded for a period of three years.[2] If over the course of this three year period, an individual accrues 12 or more penalty points, then they will receive an automatic six month driving disqualification.[3] This disqualification is carried out by

---

[1] See Chapter 11 for more information in respect of same.
[2] S.4, Road Traffic Act 2002.
[3] *Ibid.*, s.3(1).

means of an administrative scheme,[4] and will not ordinarily involve any court appearance. An individual who accrues penalty points is notified of the endorsement of same penalty points on their licence and of the date of the removal of penalty points.[5] An individual who is disqualified by reason of accruing 12 penalty points in a three year period is also notified of same disqualification in writing, the date of the removal of same disqualification.[6]

Where an individual is notified of a penalty point disqualification, they are obliged within 14 days of date of notice to return their licence to the licensing authority.[7] Failure to return same licence is an offence[8] and carries a general penalty under section 102 of the Road Traffic Act 1961 (as amended[9]), namely:

General Penalty Under Section 102

First Offence – fine of up to €1,000.[10]

Second Offence (under same section) – fine of up to €2,000.[11]

Third/Subsequent Offence (under same section within 12 consecutive months) – fine of up to €2,000 and/or a term of imprisonment of up to three months.[12]

Practitioners should also be aware of the provisions of section 2(8) of the Road Traffic Act 2002 which states that:

'Where, upon being convicted of a penalty point offence, a court imposes an ancillary disqualification order for this penalty point offence, the penalty points in respect of the offence which would otherwise have accrued shall not be endorsed on the licence record.'[13]

This section appears to apply only to the situation where an individual is convicted of a road traffic offence (which is a penalty point offence), and upon conviction receives an ancillary disqualification under section 27 of the Road Traffic Act 1961 (as amended). In these

---

[4] *Ibid.*, ss.3 and5(1).
[5] *Ibid.*, ss.4(b) and 5(1).
[6] *Ibid.*, s.3(2)(b).
[7] *Ibid.*, s.5(1).
[8] *Ibid.*, s.5(3).
[9] General penalty under s.102 was raised to €1000 and €2000 on 5 March 2007. See – S.I. No.86/2007 — Road Traffic Act 2006 (Commencement) Order 2007.
[10] S.102(a), Road Traffic Act 1961, as amended by s.18(1) – Table – Pt.1 – Reference 20.
[11] *Ibid.*, s.102(b) as amended by s.18(1) – Table – Pt.1 – Reference 21.
[12] *Ibid.*, s.102(c) as amended by s.18(1) – Table – Pt.1 – Reference 22.
[13] S.2(8), Road Traffic Act 2002.

circumstances, the penalty points which would ordinarily have been imposed upon conviction will not be imposed.

Section 2(8) does not apply to any RTA offence for which the disqualification imposed by a court is consequential (i.e. mandatory) – Like dangerous driving[14] or driving without insurance.[15] Apart from the limited circumstances where section 2(8) applies, section 6 of the Road Traffic Act 2002 sets out that where during the three year period where penalty points have been endorsed on a person's licence record: or during the 6 month automatic disqualification period a person receives for accruing 12 or more penalty points,[16] an individual receives:

(a) a consequential disqualification;[17]

(b) an ancillary disqualification;[18]

(c) a special disqualification;[19] or

(d) disqualification pursuant to the European Convention of Driving Disqualifications,[20]

no part of these disqualification or cessation periods shall be reckonable as part of the three year endorsement or six month disqualification period under the penalty point system. When an individual's licence is restored, the three year endorsement period or six month period will resume as though it was not interrupted and continue until it has expired.[21]

PRODUCTION OF DRIVING LICENCE IN COURT – SECTION 22 OF THE ROAD TRAFFIC ACT 2002

Section 22 of the Road Traffic Act 2002[22] states that where a defendant is before the court charged with any road traffic offence under

---

[14] S.53, Road Traffic Act 1961 (as amended). See also Chapter 8 .

[15] *Ibid.*, s.56, Road Traffic Act 1961 (as substituted by s.34, Road Traffic Act 2004). Practitioners should note a first conviction will not necessarily result in mandatory disqualification – see Chapter 6.

[16] S.6, Road Traffic Act 2002.

[17] S.26, Road Traffic Act 1961.

[18] *Ibid.*, s.27.

[19] *Ibid.*, s.28.

[20] As amended by s.5m Road Traffic Act 2004. See also Sch.2, Road Traffic Act 2002 and S.I. No.11/2010 – Road Traffic Act 2002 (S.9)(Commencement) Order 2010 and Chapter 2.

[21] S.6, Road Traffic Act 2002.

[22] As substituted by s.21, Road Traffic Act 2004.

Road Traffic legislation, except for an offence under:

(a) section 84,[23] section 85,[24] or section 101 of Road Traffic Act 1961;

(b) section 35 of Road Traffic Act 1961 (as it relates to parking of vehicles) or section 36 of Road Traffic Act 1994,

the defendant shall, on the date they are first due to attend court, or at the discretion of the judge a later date, produce to the court their driving licence/permit AND furnish a copy of same licence/permit to court. It further states that court will record whether both licence and copy of licence/permit have been produced.

Any individual who fails to comply with the provisions of this section is guilty of an offence.[25]

Penalties

In respect of offences under section 22, the penalties are as follows:

First Offence – fine of up to €1,000.[26]

Second Offence (under same section) – fine of up to €2,000.[27]

Third/Subsequent Offence (under same section within 12 consecutive months) – fine of up to €2,000 and/or a term of imprisonment of up to three months.[28]

Disqualification:

Ancillary Disqualification: whilst a conviction under section 22 does not carry a mandatory disqualification, it is open to the court to make an ancillary disqualification order on the particular facts of the case.

PRODUCTION OF DRIVING LICENCE IN COURT – SECTION 63 OF THE ROAD TRAFFIC ACT 2010

Practitioners should note that section 63 of the Road Traffic Act 2010[29] amends section 22(1) of the Road Traffic Act 2002,[30] so that

---

[23] Inserted by s.15, Road Traffic Act 2002.
[24] Inserted by s.16, Road Traffic Act 2002.
[25] S.22(2), Road Traffic Act 2002.
[26] S.102(a), Road Traffic Act 1961, as amended by s.18(1) – Table – Pt.1 – Reference 20.
[27] *Ibid.*, s.102(b) as amended by s.18(1) – Table – Pt.1 – Reference 21.
[28] *Ibid.*, s.102(c) as amended by s.18(1) – Table – Pt.1 – Reference 22.
[29] When same section comes into operation.
[30] As inserted by s.21, Road Traffic Act 2004.

where a defendant is before the court charged with any road traffic offence under Road Traffic Act 1961–2010, except for an offence under:

(a) section 84,[31] section 85[32] or section 101 of Road Traffic Act 1961.

(b) section 35 of Road Traffic Act 1961 (as it relates to parking of vehicles); section 36 or section 36A of Road Traffic Act 1994,

the defendant shall, on the date they are first due to attend court, or at the discretion of the judge a later date, produce to the court their driving licence/permit AND a copy of same licence/permit to be furnished to court. It further states that court will record whether both licence and copy of licence/permit have been produced.

Any individual who fails to comply with the provisions of this section is guilty of an offence.[33]

Penalties

In respect of offences under Section 63, the penalties are as follows:

First Offence – fine of up to €1,000.[34]

Second Offence (under same section) – fine of up to €2,000.[35]

Third/Subsequent Offence (under same section within 12 consecutive months) – fine of up to €2,000 and/or a term of imprisonment of up to three months.[36]

Disqualification:

Ancillary Disqualification: whilst a conviction under section 63 does not carry a mandatory disqualification, it is open to the court to make an ancillary disqualification order on the particular facts of the case.

PART FIVE – AMENDEMENTS TO PROVISIONS IN RESPECT OF PENALTY POINT OFFENCES – ROAD TRAFFIC ACT 2010

Part Five of the Road Traffic Act 2010[37] makes a number of amendments to extend the scope of existing penalty point offences.

---

[31] Inserted by s.15, Road Traffic Act 2002.
[32] Inserted by s.16, Road Traffic Act 2002.
[33] S.22(2), Road Traffic Act 2002, as amended by s.21, Road Traffic Act 2004.
[34] S.102(a), Road Traffic Act 1961, as amended by s.18(1) – Table – Pt.1 – Reference 20.
[35] *Ibid.*, s.102(b) as amended by s.18(1) – Table – Pt.1 – Reference 21.
[36] *Ibid.*, s.102(c) as amended by s.18(1) – Table – Pt.1 – Reference 22.
[37] When same sections come into effect.

Practitioners therefore need to be cognisant of the new provisions which are summarised below.

**ENDORSEMENT OF PENALTY POINTS –
SECTION 53 OF THE ROAD TRAFFIC ACT 2010**

Section 53 of the Road Traffic Act 2010[38] provides for the amendment of sections 1 and 2 of the Road Traffic Act 2002 to allow for the endorsement of penalty points where a licence record does not exist,[39] and in respect of foreign driving licence holders who have committed penalty point offences in Ireland.[40] The section also provides for the transfer of any penalty points accumulated from such a new record to a pre-existing record, where such pre existing record is subsequently identified,[41] with the individual being so notified. Where the accumulation of the existing and newly transferred penalty points equals or exceeds 12 points, that individual will strand disqualified under section 3 of the Road Traffic Act 2002.[42]

Section 53 also creates a new section 2(10) of the Road Traffic Act 2010, allowing a vehicle insurer (with the approval of the minister) to have access to and inspect and examine any endorsements on the entry of licence record of an individual. They vehicle insurer may also obtain Copies of such entries as may reasonably be required for the purposes of renewing approved policies of insurance.[43]

Section 65 of the Road Traffic Act 2010[44] expands the definition of Driving licence under section 3(1) of the Road Traffic Act 1961 and will allow for to be record the imposition of penalty points upon drivers who:

(a) hold a full Irish driving licence; or

(b) drivers who hold a provisional licence or learners permit; or

(c) do not hold a current licence;[45] or

(d) hold a full foreign driving licence issued by a EU Member State the European Economic Area (EEA);[46]

---

[38] When same section come into operation.
[39] S.53(2)(a), Road Traffic Act 2010.
[40] *Ibid.*, s.53(2)(c), Road Traffic Act 2010.
[41] S.2(7), Road Traffic Act 2002 as substituted by s.53(3), Road Traffic Act 2010.
[42] *Ibid.*, s.2(7) as substituted by s.53(3), Road Traffic Act 2010.
[43] *Ibid.*, s.2(10) as added by s.53(3), Road Traffic Act 2010.
[44] When same section comes into operation.
[45] S.53(2)(a), Road Traffic Act 2010.
[46] See provisions of s.56, Road Traffic Act 2010 in terms of expanding the definition

(e) on foreign licences recognised by an order made under section
23A of the Road Traffic Act 1961.[47]

The First Schedule of the Road Traffic Act 2002 sets out the full list
of offences to which penalty points may be imposed. Practitioners
should note that penalty points will not operate in respect of an
offence, simply because they are listed in the First Schedule of the
Road Traffic Act. Same provision is not operational unless and until
the penalty point provision in respect of that specific scheduled
offence has been enacted by way of regulation.[48]

AMENDMENT OF FIRST SCHEDULE OF PENALTY POINTS – SECTION 54 OF THE ROAD TRAFFIC ACT 2010

Section 54 of the Road Traffic Act 2010[49] makes a number of amendments to the First Schedule of the Road Traffic Act 2002. It is
important for practitioners to note that these new penalty point
offences will only come into operation on the date stated in the
enabling regulation(s), until then, the current penalty point offences
will continue in place.

This is particularly relevant where an individual finds themselves
before the court on a Careless Driving charge. Section 54 (a) substitutes the Careless Driving offence in the First Schedule to the Road
Traffic Act 2002[50] for the new Careless driving (tried summarily)
offence contained at section 69 of the Road Traffic Act 2010[51] – with
new penalty point offence carrying only three and not five penalty
points.

---

of driving licence within the meaning of the Road Traffic Acts 1961–2010 and also
Chapter 4.

[47] Namely – Australia, Gibraltar, Guernsey, Iceland, Isle of Man, Japan, Jersey,
Liechtenstein, Norway, South Africa, South Korea and Switzerland See S.I.
No.527/2007, Road Traffic (Recognition of Foreign Driving Licences) Order 2007.

[48] See S.I. No.491/2002 – Road Traffic Act 2002 (Commencement) Order 2002; S.I.
No.214/2003 – Road Traffic Act 2002 (Commencement) Order 2003; S.I. No.321/
2003 – Road Traffic Act 2002 (Commencement)(No.2) Order 2003; S.I. No.248/
2004 – Road Traffic Act 2002 (Commencement of Certain Provisions) Order 2004;
S.I. No.134/2006 – Road Traffic Act 2002 (Commencement of Certain Provisions)
Order 2006; S.I. No.443/2006 – Road Traffic Act 2002 (Commencement of Cer-
tain Provisions relating to Driving while Holding Mobile Phone) Order 2006; S.I.
No.149/2009 – Road Traffic Act 2002 (Commencement of Certain Provisions)
(Penalty Points) Order 2009.

[49] When same section comes into operation.

[50] No.9 of Pt.1, Sch.1, Road Traffic Act 2002.

[51] When same section comes into operation.

The original First Schedule, Part 5 of the Road Traffic Act 2002 is substituted by a new Part Five which deals with offence of the holder of a learner permit driving without a qualified driver.[52] Penalty points which apply[53] are as follows:

Upon Payment of Fixed Charge Notice: **one point**

Upon Summary Conviction: **three points**

A new Part Nine is inserted after Part 8 of the First Schedule[54] and deals with the offences of:

(a) Using a vehicle which exceeds the maximum possible width;

Upon Payment of Fixed Charge Notice: **one point**

Upon Summary Conviction: **three points**

(b) Using a vehicle which exceeds the maximum possible length;

Upon Payment of Fixed Charge Notice: **one point**

Upon Summary Conviction: **three points**

(c) Using a vehicle with defective or worn tyres;

Upon Payment of Fixed Charge Notice: **two points**

Upon Summary Conviction: **four points**

Practitioners should also note that section 55 of the Road Traffic Act 2010[55] amends section 1(1) of the Road Traffic Act 2002, so that section 1(1) of the Probation of Offenders Act 1907, which allows the court to find the facts proved but not impose a criminal conviction does not apply to penalty point offences.

PENALTY POINT OFFENCES – MANDATORY COURT APPEARANCE

There are presently 10 penalty point offences which cannot be dealt by way of a fixed penalty notice and require a Defendant to attend court, namely:

(a) **Driving whilst Unfit** – section 48 of the Road Traffic Act 1961;

(b) **Driving without Insurance** – section 56 of the Road Traffic Act 1961;

(c) **Careless Driving** – section 52 of the Road Traffic Act 1961;

---

[52] Art.17, S.I. No.537/2006 – Road Traffic (Licensing of Drivers) Regulations 2006.
[53] When same section comes into operation.
[54] Pt.8 having been inserted by s.16(e), Road Traffic Act 2006.
[55] When same section comes into operation.

(d) **Breach of duties at scene of accident** – section 106 of the Road Traffic Act 1961;

(e) **Parking vehicle in a dangerous position** – section 55 of the Road Traffic Act 1961;

(f) **Driving dangerously defective vehicle** – section 54 of the Road Traffic Act 1961;

(g) **Using vehicle without a test certificate** – section 18 of the Road Traffic Act 1961;

(h) **Driving vehicle without remedying dangerous defect** – section 20 of the Road Traffic Act 1961;

(i) **Using vehicle without certificate of road worthiness** – regulation 19, S.I. No.771/2004;

(j) **Bridge strike** – section 138(3) of the Railway Safety Act 2005 (tried summarily).

DRIVING WHILST UNFIT[56] – SECTION 48 OF THE ROAD TRAFFIC ACT 1961

Penalties

In respect of offences under section 48 of the Road Traffic Act 1961 the penalties are as follows:

First Offence: fine of up to €1,000 and/or a term of imprisonment of up to one month.[57]

Second/Subsequent Offence: (under same section) – fine of up to €2,000 and/or a term of imprisonment of up to three months.[58]

Penalty Points: three (upon conviction[59]).
This offence does not carry the option of paying a fixed penalty notice. Section 2(8) of the Road Traffic Act 2002 applies if the court imposes an ancillary disqualification order under section 27 of the Road Traffic Act 1961. In those circumstances, penalty points will not be endorsed on the licence record.

---

[56] See Chapter 8 for more information in respect of this offence.

[57] S.48(2), Road Traffic Act 1961, as substituted by s.3, Road Traffic (Amendment) Act 1984 – penalties increased by s.18, Table, Pt.1, Reference 6, Road Traffic Act 2006.

[58] *Ibid.*, s.48(2) as substituted by s.3, Road Traffic (Amendment) Act 1984 – penalties increased by s.18, Table, Pt.1, Reference 6, Road Traffic Act 2006.

[59] See Reference 8, Pt.1, Sch.1, Road Traffic Act 2002 and S.I. No.134/2006 – Road Traffic Act 2002 (Commencement of Certain Provisions) Order 2006 which came into effect on 3 April 2006.

Disqualification:

Ancillary Disqualification: a first conviction under section 48 does not carry a mandatory disqualification. It is open to the court to make an ancillary disqualification order on the particular facts of the case.

Mandatory Disqualification: if a defendant is convicted of a second or subsequent conviction under this section within a three year period, a consequential disqualification period of not less than one year will apply.[60]

Penalty Point Disqualification: if a defendant accrues 12 penalty points upon conviction for this offence, then they will be disqualified under the administrative procedure set out under section 3 of the Road Traffic Act 2002.

Special Disqualification Order: this can be made by the District Court under section 28 of the Road Traffic Act 1961 upon an application by Garda. Grounds upon which such an application would be made are that the licence holder is by reason of a disease, or a mental or physical disability, either unfit or incompetent to driver. If granted, the order will remain in place until the disqualified person produces a valid certificate of fitness and/or competency.

OBLIGATION TO BE INSURED OR GUARANTEED[61] – SECTION 56 OF THE ROAD TRAFFIC ACT 1961

Penalties

In respect of offences under section 56 of the Road Traffic Act, the penalties are as follows:

Summary Conviction: fine of up to €5,000 and/or a term of imprisonment of up to six months.[62]

There is also a provision under section 6(4), Criminal Justice Act 1993 to make a compensation order in respect of loss or injury determined to have been caused as a result of a breach of section 56(3).

---

[60] S.26(7), Road Traffic Act 1961, as substituted by s.26, Road Traffic Act 1994 and amended by s.6(1)(e), Road Traffic Act 2006. See also s.3, Sch.2, Road Traffic Act (as amended).

[61] See Chapter 6 for more information in respect of this offence.

[62] See s.56(4), Road Traffic Act 1961as substituted by s.34, Road Traffic Act 1994 and s.18, Road Traffic Act 2006.

Penalty Points: five (upon conviction).[63]

There is no option to pay a fixed penalty notice. In most cases, a consequential disqualification order is imposed instead of penalty points. Practitioners should note that section 2(8) of the Road Traffic Act 2002 does not apply to section 56 offences as any disqualification imposed is consequential.

Disqualification:

Consequential Disqualification:

First Offence – two years.[64]

In the circumstances where it is a first offence under section 56 a court may decline to make a consequential disqualification order, or make a disqualification order of less than two years,[65] but only where a special reason has been provided to the court to justify not applying the consequential disqualification order. If a disqualification order is not imposed of a first offence, than penalty points are imposed instead.

Second or Subsequent Offence (within three years) not less than four years.[66] Obviously, it is open to the court to impose a longer disqualification period on the particular facts of the case.

Penalty Point Disqualification: if a defendant accrues 12 penalty points upon conviction for this offence, then they will be disqualified under the administrative procedure set out under section 3 of the Road Traffic Act 2002.

CARELESS DRIVING[67] – SECTION 52 OF THE ROAD TRAFFIC ACT 1961

Penalties

In respect of offences under section 52, the penalties are as follows:

Summary Conviction – fine of up to €2,000 and/or a term of imprisonment of up to three months.[68]

---

[63] See Reference 12, Pt.1, Sch.1, Road Traffic Act 2002 and also S.I. No.214/2003 – Road Traffic Act 2002 (Commencement) Order 2003. which came into effect on 1 June 2003.
[64] See s.26(5)(a), Road Traffic Act 1961 as substituted by s.26, Road Traffic Act 1994 and amended by s.6, Road Traffic Act 2006.
[65] *Ibid.*, s 26(5)(b) as substituted by s.26, Road Traffic Act 1994 and amended by s.6, Road Traffic Act 2006.
[66] *Ibid.*, s.26(5)(a) as substituted by s.26, Road Traffic Act 1994 and amended by s.6, Road Traffic Act 2006.
[67] See Chapter 8 for more information in respect of this offence.
[68] S.52(2), Road Traffic Act 1961 as amended by s.18, Table, Pt.1 Reference 11, Road

Penalty Points: five (upon conviction).[69]

The offence does not carry the option of paying a fixed penalty notice. Section 2(8) of the Road Traffic Act 2002 applies if the court imposes an ancillary disqualification order under section 27 of the Road Traffic Act 1961. In those circumstances, penalty points will not be endorsed on licence record.

Disqualification:

Ancillary Disqualification: a first conviction under section 52 does not carry a mandatory disqualification. It is open to the court to make an ancillary disqualification order on the particular facts of the case.

Mandatory Disqualification: if a defendant is convicted of a third or subsequent conviction under this section within a three year period, a consequential disqualification period of not less than one year will apply.[70]

Penalty Point Disqualification: if a defendant accrues 12 penalty points upon conviction for this offence, then they will be disqualified under the administrative procedure set out under section 3 of the Road Traffic Act 2002.

BREACH OF DUTIES AT THE SCENE OF AN ACCIDENT[71] – SECTION 106 OF THE ROAD TRAFFIC ACT 1961

Penalties

In respect of offences under section 106, the penalties are as follows:

Summary Conviction:

Where injury caused to person – fine of up to €2,000 and/or a term of imprisonment of up to six months.[72]

Where no injury caused to person – fine of up to €1,500 and/or a term of imprisonment of up to three months.[73]

Traffic Act 2006.

[69] See Reference 8, Pt.1, Sch.1, Road Traffic Act 2002 and also S.I. No.248/2004 – Road Traffic Act 2002 (Commencement of Certain Provisions) Order 2004 which came into effect on 4 June 2004.

[70] S.26(7), Road Traffic Act 1961, as substituted by s.26, Road Traffic Act 1994 and amended by s.6(1)(e), Road Traffic Act 2006. See also s.7, Sch.2, Road Traffic Act (as amended).

[71] See Chapter 7 for more information in respect of this offence.

[72] S.103(3)(a), Road Traffic Act 1961 as amended by s.18, Road Traffic Act 2006.

[73] *Ibid.*, s.103(3)(b) as amended by s.18, Road Traffic Act 2006.

Penalty Points: five (upon conviction)[74]

The offence does not carry the option of paying a fixed penalty notice. Section 2(8) of the Road Traffic Act 2002 applies if the court imposes an ancillary disqualification order under section 27 of the Road Traffic Act 1961. In those circumstances, penalty points will not be endorsed on licence record.

Disqualification:

Consequential Disqualification will be made in circumstances where the defendant failed to stop (subsection (1)(a), or remain at the scene of an accident (subsection (1)(b), and where an injury was caused to another person: and an MPV was involved in occurrence of same injury same injury: and the convicted person was driving the vehicle which caused the injury.

First Offence: minimum four years' disqualification.

Second/Subsequent Offence (same section): minimum six years' disqualification.

Where a consequential disqualification is imposed under above criteria, the court shall, or may (where court has discretion not to impose additional certificate condition on grounds of 'special reasons') disqualify an individual for a specified period set above AND until a certificate of competency and/or fitness is produced. In those circumstances, the disqualification is not lifted upon the expiration of specified period alone, this is only the first condition: an individual must, upon the expiration of the specified period, or at such later date as possible produce the required certificate before licence can be restored.

Ancillary Disqualification: where an offence under this section does not carry a mandatory disqualification it is open to the court to make an ancillary disqualification order on the particular facts of the case.

Penalty Point Disqualification: if a defendant accrues 12 penalty points upon conviction for this offence, then they will be disqualified under the administrative procedure set out under section 3 of the Road Traffic Act 2002.

---

[74] See Reference 14, Pt.1, Sch.1, Road Traffic Act 2002 and also S.I. No.134/2006 – Road Traffic Act 2002 (Commencement of Certain Provisions) Order 2006 which came into effect on 3 June 2006.

Parking a Vehicle in a Dangerous Position[75] – Section 55 of the Road Traffic Act 1961

Penalties

In respect of offences under section 55, the penalties are as follows:

Summary Conviction:

First Offence – where any part of offence occurred during lighting-up hours and contravened legal lighting requirements– a fine of up to €2,000 and/or a term of imprisonment of up to three months:[76] in all other cases – a fine of up to €1,000 and/or a term of imprisonment of up to one month.[77]

Second/Subsequent Offence – fine of up to €2,000 and/or a term of imprisonment of up to three months.[78]

Penalty Points: five (upon conviction).[79]

This offence does not carry the option of paying a fixed penalty notice. Section 2(8) Road Traffic Act 2002 applies if the court imposes an ancillary disqualification order under section 27 of the Road Traffic Act 1961. In those circumstances, penalty points will not be endorsed on licence record.

Disqualification:

Ancillary Disqualification: a first conviction under section 55 does not carry a mandatory disqualification. However, it is open to the court to make an ancillary disqualification order (section 27 of the Road Traffic Act 1961) on the particular facts of the case.

Mandatory Disqualification: if a defendant is convicted of a second or subsequent offence (where any part of second offence occurred during lighting-up hours and contravened legal lighting/reflector requirements under this section) within a three year period, a consequential

---

[75] See Chapter 8 for more information in respect of this offence.
[76] S.55(2)(a), Road Traffic Act 1961 as amended by s.18, Table, Pt.1, Reference 15, Road Traffic Act 2006.
[77] *Ibid.*, s.55(2)(a) as amended by s.18, Table, Pt.1, Reference 16, Road Traffic Act 2006.
[78] *Ibid.*, s.55(2)(a)as amended by s.18, Table, Pt.1, Reference 15, Road Traffic Act 2006.
[79] See Reference No.11 of Pt.1, Sch.1, Road Traffic Act 2002 and also S.I. No.134/2006 — Road Traffic Act 2002 (Commencement of Certain Provisions) Order 2006 which came into effect on 3 June 2006.

disqualification period of not less than one year will apply.[80]

Penalty Point Disqualification: if a defendant accrues 12 penalty points upon conviction for this offence, then they will be disqualified under the administrative procedure set out under section 3 of the Road Traffic Act 2002.

Driving a Dangerously Defective Vehicle[81] – Section 54 of the Road Traffic Act 1961

Penalties

In respect of offences under section 54, the penalties are as follows:

Summary Conviction – fine of up to €2,000 and/or a term of imprisonment of up to three months.[82]

Penalty Points: five (upon conviction).[83]
This offence does not carry the option of paying a fixed penalty notice. Section 2(8) of the Road Traffic Act 2002 applies if the court imposes an ancillary disqualification order under section 27 of the Road Traffic Act 1961. In those circumstances, penalty points will not be endorsed on licence record.

Disqualification:

Ancillary Disqualification: a first conviction under section 54 does not carry a mandatory disqualification. It is open to the court to make an ancillary disqualification order on the particular facts of the case.

Mandatory Disqualification: if a defendant is convicted of a second or subsequent conviction under this section within three years, a consequential disqualification period of not less than one year will apply.[84]

---

[80] S.26(7), Road Traffic Act 1961, as substituted by s.26, Road Traffic Act 1994 and amended by s.6(1)(e), Road Traffic Act 2006. See also s.3, Sch.2, Road Traffic Act (as amended).

[81] See Chapter 8 for more information in respect of this offence.

[82] S.54(4), Road Traffic Act 1961 as amended by s.6, Road Traffic Act 1968 and s.18, Table, Pt.1, Reference 14, Road Traffic Act 2006.

[83] See Reference 11, Pt.1, Sch.1, Road Traffic Act 2002 and also S.I. No.149/2009 – Road Traffic Act 2002 (Commencement of Certain Provisions) (Penalty Points) Order 2009 which came into effect on 1 May 2009.

[84] S.26(7), Road Traffic Act 1961, as substituted by s.26, Road Traffic Act 1994 and amended by s.6(1)(e), Road Traffic Act 2006. See also s.3, Sch.2, Road Traffic Act (as amended).

Penalty Point Disqualification: if a defendant accrues 12 penalty points upon conviction for this offence, then they will be disqualified under the administrative procedure set out under section 3 of the Road Traffic Act 2002.

USING A VEHICLE WITHOUT A TEST CERTIFICATE[85] – SECTION 18 OF THE ROAD TRAFFIC ACT 1961

Section 18 of the Road Traffic Act 1961,[86] provides that it is an offence for any class of vehicle to which section 18 applies to be used in a public place without a valid test certificate.

Penalties

In respect of offences under section 18(1), the penalties are as follows:

Summary Conviction – fine of up to €2,000 and/or a term of imprisonment of up to three months.[87]

Penalty Points: five (upon conviction).[88]
This offence does not carry the option of paying a fixed penalty notice. Section 2(8) of the Road Traffic Act 2002 applies if the court imposes an ancillary disqualification order under section 27 of the Road Traffic Act 1961. In those circumstances, penalty points will not be endorsed on licence record.

Disqualification:

Ancillary Disqualification: a first conviction under section 18 does not carry a mandatory disqualification. It is open to the court to make an ancillary disqualification order on the particular facts of the case.

Mandatory Disqualification: if a defendant is convicted of a second or subsequent conviction under this section within a three year period, a consequential disqualification period of not less than one year will apply.[89]

---

[85] See Chapter 5 for further information in respect of this offence.
[86] As amended by s.8, Road Traffic Act 1968 and s.23, Road Traffic Act 2002.
[87] S.18(2), Road Traffic Act 1961 as amended by s.18, Road Traffic Act 2006 – Table – Pt.1 – Reference 3.
[88] See Reference 2, Pt.1, Sch.1, Road Traffic Act 2002 and also S.I. No.149/2009 – Road Traffic Act 2002 (Commencement of Certain Provisions) (Penalty Points) Order 2009 which came into effect on 1 May 2009.
[89] S.26, Road Traffic Act 1961, as substituted by s.26, Road Traffic Act 1994 and amended by s.6(1)(e), Road Traffic Act 2006.

Penalty Point Disqualification: if a defendant accrues 12 penalty points upon conviction for this offence, then they will be disqualified under the administrative procedure set out under section 3 of the Road Traffic Act 2002.

Driving a Vehicle Without Remedying Dangerous Defects[90] – Section 20(10) of the Road Traffic Act 1961

Penalties

In respect of offences under section 20 (10) the penalties are as follows:

Summary Offence: (under same section) – fine of up to €2,000 and/or a term of imprisonment of up to three months.[91]

Penalty Points: three (upon conviction).[92]
This offence does not carry the option of paying a fixed penalty notice. Section 2(8) of the Road Traffic Act 2002 applies if the court imposes an ancillary disqualification order under section 27 of the Road Traffic Act 1961. In those circumstances, penalty points will not be endorsed on the licence record.

Disqualification:

Ancillary Disqualification: a first conviction under section 20 does not carry a mandatory disqualification. It is open to the court to make an ancillary disqualification order on the particular facts of the case.

Mandatory Disqualification: if a defendant is convicted of a second or subsequent conviction under this section within a three year period, a consequential disqualification period of not less than one year will apply.

Penalty Point Disqualification: if a defendant accrues 12 penalty points upon conviction for this offence, then they will be disqualified under the administrative procedure set out under section 3 of the Road Traffic Act 2002.

---

[90] See Chapter 8 for further information in respect of same.
[91] S.10(a), Road Traffic Act 1961 as amended by s.18, Table, Pt.1, Reference 4, Road Traffic Act 2006.
[92] See Reference 3, Pt.1, Sch.1, Road Traffic Act 2002 and also S.I. No.149/2009 – Road Traffic Act 2002 (Commencement of Certain Provisions) (Penalty Points) Order 2009 which came into effect on 1 May 2009.

USING A VEHICLE WITHOUT A CERTIFICATE OF ROAD WORTHINESS[93] – ARTICLE 19, S.I. NO. 771/2004-EUROPEAN COMMUNITIES (VEHICLE TESTING) REGULATIONS 2004

Regulation 19 clearly sets out that it is a criminal offence to:

Drive or otherwise cause to be used (in a public place) a vehicle to which these Regulations apply unless there is in force in respect of the vehicle a Certificate of Roadworthiness.

Penalties

In respect of offences under these regulations, the penalties are as follows:

Summary Offence: fine of up to €3,000 and/or a term of imprisonment of up to three months.[94]

Penalty Points: five (upon conviction).[95]
The offence does not carry the option of paying a fixed penalty notice. Section 2(8) of the Road Traffic Act 2002 applies if the court imposes an ancillary disqualification order under section 27 of the Road Traffic Act 1961. In those circumstances, penalty points will not be endorsed on the licence record.

Disqualification:

Ancillary Disqualification: whilst a first conviction under regulation 19 does not carry a mandatory disqualification, it is open to the court to make an ancillary disqualification order (section 27 of the Road Traffic Act 1961).

Mandatory Disqualification: if a defendant is convicted of a second or subsequent conviction under this section within a three year period, a consequential disqualification period of not less than one year will apply.[96]

Penalty Point Disqualification: if a defendant accrues 12 penalty points upon conviction for this offence, then they

---

[93] See Chapter 5 for further information in respect of this offence.
[94] Art.22, S.I. No.771/2004 – European Communities (Vehicle testing) Regulations 2004.
[95] See Reference 1, Pt.8, Sch.1, Road Traffic Act 2002 as inserted by s.16, Road Traffic Act 2006 and also S.I. No.149/2009 – Road Traffic Act 2002 (Commencement of Certain Provisions) (Penalty Points) Order 2009 which came into effect on 1 May 2009.
[96] S.26, Road Traffic Act 1961, as substituted by s.26, Road Traffic Act 1994 and amended by s.6(1)(e), Road Traffic Act 2006.

will be disqualified under the administrative procedure set out under section 3 of the Road Traffic Act 2002.

BRIDGE STRIKE – SECTION 138(3)
OF THE RAILWAY SAFETY ACT 2005 (TRIED SUMMARILY)

It is an offence under section 138 of the Railway Safety Act 2005 for an individual:

(a) to drive or attempt to drive a vehicle under the structure, where the height of the vehicle, including its load, is equal to or exceeds the height indicated in the traffic sign, so as to strike the structure;[97]

(b) having struck a structure, to fail to immediately contact the owner/person in charge of structure (where a contact number has been conspicuously displayed) and, if unable to make immediate contact with owner, fails to immediately notify the Gardaí.[98]

Penalties

In respect of offences under section 138(3), the penalties are as follows:

Summary Offence: fine of up to €5,000 and/or a term of imprisonment of up to six months.

Indictable Offence: fine of up to €50,000 and/or a term of imprisonment of up to three years.

Summary Conviction: offence contrary to subsection (4) – fine of up to €1,000.

Penalty Points: three (upon summary conviction).[99]
The offence does not carry the option of paying a fixed penalty notice. Section 2(8) of the Road Traffic Act 2002 only applies if the court imposes an ancillary disqualification order under section 27 of the Road Traffic Act 1961. In those circumstances, penalty points will not be endorsed on the licence record.

---

[97] S.138(2), Railway Safety Act 2005.
[98] *Ibid.*, s.138(4).
[99] See Reference 19, Pt.1, Sch.1, Road Traffic Act 2002 as inserted by s.16, Road Traffic Act 2006 and also S.I. No.149/2009 – Road Traffic Act 2002 (Commencement of Certain Provisions) (Penalty Points) Order 2009 which came into effect on 1 May 2009.

Disqualification:

Ancillary Disqualification: a summary conviction under section 138 does not carry a mandatory disqualification, but it is open to the court to make an ancillary disqualification order on the particular facts of the case.

Mandatory Disqualification: if a defendant is convicted of an indictment of an offence contrary to section 138(3), a consequential disqualification period of not less than four years will apply in respect of a first conviction, and not less than six years in respect of a second or subsequent conviction.[100]

Penalty Point Disqualification: if a defendant accrues 12 penalty points upon conviction for this offence, then they will be disqualified under the administrative procedure set out under section 3 of the Road Traffic Act 2002.

PENALTY POINT OFFENCES – FIXED CHARGE

The majority of penalty point offences are fixed charge offences.[101] This means that they carry a fixed financial penalty which if paid within a certain period of time does not result in the individual receiving a court summons. However, if the fixed charge is not paid with the time period set out in the fixed charge notice, a court summons will issue. The penalty points a driver will receive on payment of a fixed charge notice are generally speaking about half the points they will receive if they are summoned to court.

There are presently 32 penalty point offences which are dealt with by way of a fixed charge notice. Before examining these penalty point offences in turn, practitioners should be aware of the applicability of section 21 of the Road Traffic Act 2002 in relation to the prosecution of these offences.

EVIDENCE IN RESPECT OF A CONSTITUENT OF THE OFFENCE BY MEANS OF AN ELECTRONIC OR OTHER APPARATUS – SECTION 21 OF THE ROAD TRAFFIC ACT 2002

Whilst the most obvious application of the provisions of section 21 might relate to the prosecution of speeding offences, section 21 of the

---

[100] S.26(4)(a)(vi), Road Traffic Act 1961 as substituted by s.26, Road Traffic Act 1994 and amended by s.6(1)(a), Road Traffic Act 2006.
[101] See also Chapter 11.

Road Traffic Act 2002[102] can be summarised as follows:[103]

Prima facie proof of constituent of offence may be established by tendering evidence obtained by means of:

(a) electronic or other apparatus (including a camera) capable of providing a permanent record;[104] or

(b) electronic or other apparatus (including a radar gun) not capable of producing a permanent record.[105]

There is no requirement to prove that the electronic or other apparatus was accurate or in good working order.[106]

EVIDENCE IN RESPECT OF SPEED AND CERTAIN OTHER OFFENCES – SECTION 81 OF THE ROAD TRAFFIC ACT 2010

Practitioners should note that section 81 of the Road Traffic Act 2010[107] repeals and replaces section 21 of the Road Traffic Act 2002. The provisions contained in the new section 81 are however broadly similar to the provisions set out above.[108]

RULES OF THE ROAD

Guidance in respect of most of the following offences can be found in the Rules of the Road. It is not a statutory offence to break any of these guidelines/rules, but it is a useful explanatory note on how the following offences operate. All licensed drivers are supposed to be familiar with the Rules of the Road and a court is likely to take a very dim view of anyone who comes before the court pleading a defence to any of these charges on the basis of a driving practice which contradicts these Rules of the Road.

GENERAL PENALTY – SECTION 102 OF THE ROAD TRAFFIC ACT 1961

Practitioners should note that when reference is made to the general penalty applying, this means the penalty imposed under section 102

---

[102] See s.15, Road Traffic Act 2004 and s.17, Road Traffic Act 2006.
[103] See Chapter 3, for further information in respect of s.21, Road Traffic Act 2002.
[104] S.21(1)(a), Road Traffic Act 2002.
[105] *Ibid.*, s.21(1)(b).
[106] *Ibid.*, s.21(1).
[107] When same section comes into operation.
[108] Again Chapter 3, for further information in respect of the provisions of s.80, Road Traffic Act 2010.

Road Traffic Act 1961, as amended,[109] namely:

Penalties

First Offence – fine of up to €1,000.[110]

Second Offence (under same section) – fine of up to €2,000.[111]

Third/Subsequent Offence (under same section within 12 consecutive months) – fine of up to €2,000 and/or a term of imprisonment of up to three months.[112]

(1) SPEEDING[113] – SECTION 47 OF THE ROAD TRAFFIC ACT 1961[114]

Section 47 of the Road Traffic Act 1961, sets out the offence of:

(a) driving a vehicle at a speed in excess of the speed limit which applies in respect of that vehicle;[115] or

(b) applies to the road on which vehicle is being driven, if that speed limit is lower than speed limit applying to the vehicle.[116]

Penalties

In respect of offences under section 47(2), the penalties are as follows:

Fixed Charge Penalty: €80 (paid in 28 days):[117] €120 (paid in subsequent 28 days).[118]

Upon Conviction: General Penalty under section 102 of the Road Traffic Act 1961.[119]

---

[109] See Table contained in s.18, Road Traffic Act 2006 and see also S.I. No.86/2007 – Road Traffic Act 2006 (Commencement) Order 2007.

[110] Reference 20 – Pt.1 – Table contained in s.18, Road Traffic Act 2006.

[111] Reference 21 – Pt.1 – Table contained in s.18, Road Traffic Act 2006.

[112] Reference 21 – Pt.1 – Table contained in s.18, Road Traffic Act 2006.

[113] For further information on this charge, see Chapter 3 on Speeding Offences.

[114] As substituted by s.11, Road Traffic Act 2004.

[115] S.47(1)(a), Road Traffic Act 1961, as substituted by s.11, Road Traffic Act 2004.

[116] *Ibid.*, s.47(1)(b) as substituted by s.11, Road Traffic Act 2004.

[117] See s.103(7)(b), Road Traffic Act 1961 as inserted by s.14(c), Road Traffic Act 2006. See art.5(a)(ii) and Sch.1, Pt.1,S.I. No.135/2006 – Road Traffic Acts 1961 to 2005 (Fixed Charge Offences) Regulations 2006.

[118] See s.103(7)(c), Road Traffic Act 1961 and art.5(a)(ii) and Sch.1, Pt.1, S.I. No.135/2006 – Road Traffic Acts 1961 to 2005(Fixed Charge Offences) Regulations 2006.

[119] **First conviction** – fine up to €1,000; **Second conviction** – fine up to €2,000; **Third conviction** – fine up to €1,000 and/or imprisonment for up to 3 months. See also s.18, Road Traffic Act 2006.

Penalty Points: two (payment of fixed charge): four (upon conviction).[120] Section 2(8) of the Road Traffic Act 2002 applies if court imposes an ancillary disqualification order under section 27 of the Road Traffic Act 1961. In those circumstances penalty points will not be endorsed on licence record.

Disqualification: whilst a conviction under section 47 does not carry a mandatory disqualification, it is open to the court to make an ancillary disqualification order (section 27 of the Road Traffic Act 1961) on the particular facts of the case.

Penalty Point Disqualification: if a defendant accrues 12 penalty points upon conviction for this offence, then they will be disqualified under the administrative procedure set out under section 3 of the Road Traffic Act 2002.

(2) FAILURE BY A DRIVER TO COMPLY WITH FRONT SEAT BELT REQUIREMENTS – ARTICLE 6 OF THE ROAD TRAFFIC (CONSTRUCTION, EQUIPMENT AND USE OF VEHICLES)(AMENDMENT)(NO.3) REGULATIONS 1991[121]

Article 6 of the Road Traffic (Construction, Equipment and Use of Vehicles) (Amendment) (No. 3) Regulations, 1991 sets out that it is an offence for any driver to fail to comply with front seat belt requirements. It is the responsibility of the driver to ensure that any passenger under 17, occupying a front seat is wearing the appropriate seat belt or child restraint.[122]

Practitioners should note that whilst there are newer regulations set out in EC (Compulsory Use of Safety Belts and Child Restraint Systems in Motor Vehicles) Regulations 2006, and that the seat belt and/or child restraints used must as of 1 May 2008 comply with the provisions of the 2006 regulations,[123] the penalty point provisions in respect of same are not yet operational and the fixed charge offence and penalty point provisions currently in operation relate to offences

---

[120] See Reference 7, Pt.1, Sch.1, Road Traffic Act 2002 and also S.I. No.491/2002 – Road Traffic Act 2002 (Commencement) Order 2002 which came into effect on 31 October 2002.

[121] See S.I No.359/1991 – Road Traffic (Construction, Equipment and Use of Vehicles) (Amendment) (No.3) Regulations, 1991 and S.I. No.240 of 2006 – European Communities (Compulsory use of Safety Belts and Child Restraint Systems in Motor Vehicles) Regulations 2006 Regulations made under s.3, European Communities Act 1972.

[122] Art.6(3), S.I. No.359/1991.

[123] Art.3, S.I. No.240/2006.

under the 1991 Regulations. Practitioners should however familiarise themselves with the regulations contained in both the Road Traffic (Construction, Equipment and Use of Vehicles) (Amendment) (No. 3) Regulations, 1991 and the EC (Compulsory use of Safety Belts and Child Restraint Systems in Motor Vehicles) Regulations in respect of various seatbelt requirements.

Penalties

In respect of offences under article 6 of S.I. No.359/1991, the penalties are as follows:

Fixed Charge Penalty: €60 (paid in 28 days):[124] €90 (paid in subsequent 28 days).[125]

Upon Conviction: general Penalty under section 102 of the Road Traffic Act 1961.[126]

Penalty Points: two (payment of fixed charge): four (upon conviction).[127] Section 2(8) of the Road Traffic Act 2002 applies if the court imposes an ancillary disqualification order under section 27 of the Road Traffic Act 196. In those circumstances, penalty points will not be endorsed on the licence record.

Disqualification:

Ancillary Disqualification: a conviction under article 20 does not carry a mandatory disqualification. However, it is open to the court to make an ancillary disqualification order under section 27 of the Road Traffic Act 1961 on the particular facts of the case.

Penalty Point Disqualification: if a defendant accrues 12 penalty points upon a conviction for this offence, then they will be disqualified under the administrative procedure set out under section 3 of the Road Traffic Act 2002.

---

[124] See s.103(7)(b), Road Traffic Act 1961 as inserted by s.14(c), Road Traffic Act 2006. See art.5(b)(i) and Sch.2, Pt.1, S.I. No.135/2006 – Road Traffic Acts 1961 to 2005(Fixed Charge Offences) Regulations 2006.

[125] See s.103(7)(c), Road Traffic Act 1961 and art.5(b)(i) and Sch.2, Pt.1, S.I. No.135/2006 – Road Traffic Acts 1961 to 2005 (Fixed Charge Offences) Regulations 2006.

[126] **First conviction** – fine up to €1,000; **Second conviction** – fine up to €2,000; **Third conviction** – fine up to €1,000 and/or imprisonment for up to 3 months. See also s.18, Road Traffic Act 2006.

[127] See Reference 15, Pt.2, Sch.1, Road Traffic Act 2002 and also S.I. No.321/2003 – Road Traffic Act 2002 (Commencement)(No.2) Order 2003 which came into effect on 25 August 2003.

(3) Failure by a Driver to Comply with Front Seat Belt Requirements – Article 7 – Road Traffic (Construction, Equipment and Use of Vehicles)(Amendment)(No.3) Regulations 1991[128]

Article 7 of the Road Traffic (Construction, Equipment and Use of Vehicles) (Amendment) (No. 3) Regulations 1991 sets out that it is an offence for any driver to permit a person under 17 to occupy a rear seat when not wearing an appropriate seat belt or child restraint. It is the responsibility of the driver to ensure that any passenger under 17, occupying a rear seat is wearing the appropriate seat belt or child restraint.[129]

Again, as with an offence under article 6 of the 1991 regulations, the seat belt and/or child restraints used, must as of 1 May 2008 comply with the provisions of the subsequent 2006 regulations,[130] however the penalty point provisions in respect of same are not yet operational and the fixed charge offence and penalty point provisions currently in operation relate to offences under the 1991 Regulations.

Penalties

In respect of offences under article 7 of S.I. No.359/1991, the penalties are as follows:

Fixed Charge Penalty: €60 (paid in 28 days):[131] €90 (paid in subsequent 28 days).[132]

Upon Conviction: General Penalty under section 102 of the Road Traffic Act 1961.[133]

Penalty Points: two (payment of fixed charge): four (upon conviction).[134] Section 2(8) of the Road Traffic Act 2002 applies if the

---

[128] See S.I. No.359/1991 – Road Traffic (Construction, Equipment and Use of Vehicles) (Amendment) (No.3) Regulations, 1991 and S.I. No.240/2006 – European Communities (Compulsory use of Safety Belts and Child Restraint Systems in Motor Vehicles) Regulations 2006 regulations made under s.3, European Communities Act 1972.

[129] Art.6(3) of S.I. No.359/1991.

[130] Art.3 of S.I. No.240/2006.

[131] See s.103(7)(b), Road Traffic Act 1961 as inserted by s.14(c), Road Traffic Act 2006. See art.5(b)(i) and Sch.2, Pt.1, S.I. No.135/2006 – Road Traffic Acts 1961 to 2005 (Fixed Charge Offences) Regulations 2006.

[132] See s.103(7)(c), Road Traffic Act 1961 and art.5(b)(i) and Sch.2, Pt.1, S.I. No.135/2006 – Road Traffic Acts 1961 to 2005 (Fixed Charge Offences) Regulations 2006.

[133] **First conviction** – fine up to €1,000; **Second conviction** – fine up to €2,000; **Third conviction** – fine up to €1,000 and/or imprisonment for up to 3 months. See also s.18, Road Traffic Act 2006.

[134] See Reference 16. Pt.2, Sch.1, Road Traffic Act 2002 and also S.I. No.321/2003 –

court imposes an ancillary disqualification order under section 27 of the Road Traffic Act 196. In those circumstances, penalty points will not be endorsed on the licence record.

Disqualification:

Ancillary Disqualification: a conviction under article 20 does not carry a mandatory disqualification. However, it is open to the court to make an ancillary disqualification order under section 27 of the Road Traffic Act 1961 on the particular facts of the case.

Penalty Point Disqualification: if a defendant accrues 12 penalty points upon a conviction for this offence, then they will be disqualified under the administrative procedure set out under section 3 of the Road Traffic Act 2002.

(4) USING A MOBILE PHONE WHILST DRIVING – SECTION 3 OF THE ROAD TRAFFIC ACT 2006

Under section 3 of the Road Traffic Act 2006 it is an offence to hold a mobile phone whilst driving in a public place.[135] This is an increasingly common offence and is generally dealt with by way of a fixed penalty notice, unless an individual wishes to contest same charge. It is not, however, an offence for Gardaí, and members of the ambulance service or fire brigade acting in the course of their duties to hold a phone in relation to the performance of their duties.[136]

It is a defence if a defendant can demonstrate that they were using their mobile to call the Gardaí, ambulance, fire or emergency services or was involved in, or acting in response to, a genuine emergency.[137] It may also be a defence if an individual can show that they were using an appropriate hands-free mobile phone device.[138]

Practitioners should see also be aware of regulations set out in Fixed Charge Offence) (Holding Mobile Phone while Driving) Regulations 2006.[139] It is also a more general defence if a defendant can demonstrate that they were not holding a mobile phone at the time

---

Road Traffic Act 2002 (Commencement)(No.2) Order 2003 which came into effect on 25 August 2003.

[135] S.3(1), Road Traffic Act 2006.

[136] *Ibid.*, s.3(2).

[137] *Ibid.*, s.3(7).

[138] For definition of same, s.3(9), Road Traffic Act 2006.

[139] S.I. No.444/2006 – Road Traffic Acts 1961 to 2006 (Fixed Charge Offence) (Holding Mobile Phone While Driving) Regulations 2006.

of the alleged offence, or more generally that they were not driving the vehicle in question at the time of the alleged offence.

Penalties

In respect of offences under section 3, the penalties are as follows:

Fixed Charge Penalty: €60 (paid in 28 days):[140] €90 (paid in subsequent 28 days).[141]

Upon Conviction: fine of up to €2,000.[142]

Penalty Points: two (payment of fixed charge): four (upon conviction).[143] Section 2(8) of the Road Traffic Act 2002 applies if the court imposes an ancillary disqualification order under section 27 of the Road Traffic Act 1961. In those circumstances, penalty points will also not be endorsed on the licence record.

Disqualification:

Ancillary Disqualification: a conviction under section 3 does not carry a mandatory disqualification. However, it is open to the court to make an ancillary disqualification order under section 27 of the Road Traffic Act 1961 on the particular facts of the case.

Penalty Point Disqualification: if a defendant accrues 12 penalty points upon conviction for this offence, then they will be disqualified under the administrative procedure set out under section 3 of the Road Traffic Act 2002.

(5) Dangerous Overtaking – Article 10 of the Road Traffic (Traffic And Parking) Regulations 1997[144]

Article 10 provides that a driver shall not overtake or attempt to overtake:

(a) if to do so would endanger or inconvenience any other person;[145]

---

[140] Art.5, S.I. No.444/2006.
[141] S.103(7)(c), Road Traffic Act 1961 as inserted by s.11, Road Traffic Act 2002.
[142] S.3(8), Road Traffic Act 2006.
[143] See Reference 18, Pt.1, Sch.1, Road Traffic Act 2002 as inserted by s.16(2), Road Traffic Act 2006 and also S.I. No.443/2006 – Road Traffic Act 2002 (Commencement of Certain Provisions relating to Driving while Holding Mobile Phone) Order 2006 which came into effect on 1 September 2006.
[144] S.I. No.182/1997 – Road Traffic (Traffic and Parking) Regulations, 1997 – Regulations enacted under s.35, Road Traffic Act 1994.
[145] Art.10(1), S.I. No.182/1997.

(b) the roadway ahead is not free from approaching traffic; pedestrians and/or obstructions, and is not sufficiently long and wide to permit overtaking without danger or inconvenience;[146]

(c) on a stretch of roadway where overtaking is prohibited (traffic sign RUS 014);[147]

(d) on the left unless turning left/going straight ahead and overtaken vehicle has signalled to turn right;[148]

(e) on the left unless overtaking vehicle has signalled intention of turning left at next road junction; and[149]

(f) on the left unless overtaking vehicle in separate traffic lane and traffic lane to right is moving more slowly than left lane.[150]

Penalties

In respect of offences under article 10, the penalties are as follows:

Fixed Charge Penalty: €80 (paid in 28 days):[151] €120 (paid in subsequent 28 days).[152]

Upon Conviction: general penalty under section 102 of the Road Traffic Act 1961.[153]

Penalty Points: two (payment of fixed charge): five (upon conviction).[154] Section 2(8) of the Road Traffic Act 2002 applies if the court imposes an ancillary disqualification order under section 27 of the Road Traffic Act 1961 – in those circumstances, penalty points will not be endorsed on the licence record.

Disqualification:

> **Ancillary Disqualification:** a conviction under article 10 does not carry a mandatory disqualification. However, it is open

---

[146] *Ibid.*, art.10(2).
[147] *Ibid.*, art.10(3).
[148] *Ibid.*, art.10(5)(a).
[149] *Ibid.*, art.10(5)(b).
[150] *Ibid.*, art.10(5)(c).
[151] Art.5(a)(ii) and Sch.1, Pt.2, S.I. No.135/2006.
[152] See s.103(7)(c), Road Traffic Act 1961 and art.5(a)(ii) and Sch.1, Pt.2, S.I. No.135/2006.
[153] **First conviction** – fine up to €1,000; **Second conviction** – fine up to €2,000; **Third conviction** – fine up to €1,000 and/or imprisonment for up to 3 months. See also S.18, Road Traffic Act 2006.
[154] See Reference 4, Pt.4, Sch.1, Road Traffic Act 2002 and also S.I. No.134/2006 – Road Traffic Act 2002 (Commencement of Certain Provisions) Order 2006 which came into effect on 3 April 2006.

to the court to make an ancillary disqualification order under section 27 of the Road Traffic Act 1961 on the particular facts of the case.

Penalty Point Disqualification: if a defendant accrues 12 penalty points upon conviction for this offence, then they will be disqualified under the administrative procedure set out under section 3 of the Road Traffic Act 2002.

(6) Failure to Act in Accordance with a Garda Signal – Article 19 of the Road Traffic (Traffic and Parking) Regulations 1997[155]

A description of Garda signals is set out in Table C of the Second Schedule of these regulations. They are:

(a) Extending the right arm and hand at full length above the shoulder. Drivers and pedestrians approaching Gardaí from the front must halt;

(b) Extending the left arm and hand horizontally from the shoulder. Drivers and pedestrians approaching the Gardaí from behind must halt;

(c) Extending the right arm and hand at full length above the shoulder, and at the same time extending the left arm and hand horizontally from the shoulder. Drivers and pedestrians approaching Gardaí from the front and behind must halt;

(d) Garda beckons with his/her hand and forearm. Drivers and pedestrians approaching Gardaí from the front or from the right or left, or are stopped or halted by the Garda, shall proceed as beckoned;

(e) Garda points towards a particular traffic lane. Drivers shall move into that traffic lane.

Penalties

In respect of offences under article 19, the penalties are as follows:

Fixed Charge Penalty: €80 (paid in 28 days):[156] €120 (paid in subsequent 28 days).[157]

---

[155] S.I. No.182/1997 – Road Traffic (Traffic and Parking) Regulations, 1997 as inserted by art.4, S.I. No.98/2003 Regulations enacted under s.35, Road Traffic Act 1994.
[156] Art.5(a)(ii) and Sch.1, Pt.2, S.I. No.135/2006.
[157] See s.103(7)(c), Road Traffic Act 1961 and art.5(a)(ii) and Sch.1, Pt.2, S.I. No.135/2006.

Upon Conviction: general penalty under section 102 of the Road Traffic Act 1961.[158]

Penalty Points: one (payment of fixed charge): three (upon conviction).[159] Section 2(8) of the Road Traffic Act 2002 applies if the court imposes an ancillary disqualification order under section 27 of the Road Traffic Act 1961 – in those circumstances, penalty points will not be endorsed on the licence record.

Disqualification:

Ancillary Disqualification: a conviction under article 19 does not carry a mandatory disqualification. However, it is open to the court to make an ancillary disqualification order under section 27 of the Road Traffic Act 1961 on the particular facts of the case.

Penalty Point Disqualification: if a defendant accrues 12 penalty points upon conviction for this offence, then they will be disqualified under the administrative procedure set out under section 3 of the Road Traffic Act 2002.

(7) Failure to Stop a Vehicle Before a Stop Sign/Line – Article 20 of the Road Traffic (Traffic and Parking) Regulations 1997[160]

A driver of a vehicle shall stop vehicle in advance of:

(a) Stop Line (traffic sign RRM 017);[161]

(b) Stop Sign (traffic sign RUS 027).[162]

Where both a stop sign and line are present, the stop line carries greater importance.[163] It may be a defence to show same sign/line was not present at the time of the incident or was obscured from view.

---

[158] **First conviction** – fine up to €1,000; **Second conviction** – fine up to €2,000; **Third conviction** – fine up to €1,000 and/or imprisonment for up to 3 months. See also s.18, Road Traffic Act 2006.

[159] See Reference 11, Pt.4, Sch.1, Road Traffic Act 2002 and also S.I. No.134/2006 – Road Traffic Act 2002 (Commencement of Certain Provisions) Order 2006 which came into effect on 3 April 2006.

[160] S.I. No.182/1997 – Road Traffic (Traffic and Parking) Regulations, 1997 – Regulations enacted unders.35, Road Traffic Act 1994.

[161] Art.20(1), S.I. No.182/1997.

[162] *Ibid.*, art.20(1).

[163] *Ibid.*, art.20(2).

In respect of offences under article 20, the penalties are as follows:

Fixed Charge Penalty: €80 (paid in 28 days):[164] €120 (paid in subsequent 28 days).[165]

Upon Conviction: General Penalty under section 102 of the Road Traffic Act 1961.[166]

Penalty Points: two (payment of fixed charge): four (upon conviction.[167] Section 2(8) of the Road Traffic Act 2002 applies if the court imposes an ancillary disqualification order under section 27 of the Road Traffic Act 1961 – in those circumstances, penalty points will not be endorsed on the licence record.

Disqualification:

Ancillary Disqualification: a conviction under article 20 does not carry a mandatory disqualification. However, it is open to the court to make an ancillary disqualification order under section 27 of the Road Traffic Act 1961 on the particular facts of the case.

Penalty Point Disqualification: if a defendant accrues 12 penalty points upon conviction for this offence, then they will be disqualified under the administrative procedure set out under section 3 of the Road Traffic Act 2002.

(8) Failure to Yield the Right of Way at a Yield Sign/Line – Article 21 of the Road Traffic (Traffic and Parking) Regulations 1997[168]

'A driver of a vehicle approaching a traffic junction where there is a:

(a) yield Line (traffic sign RRM 018); or a

(b) yield Sign (traffic sign RUS 026);

shall yield right of way to traffic on a major road.'

It may be a defence to show same sign/line was not present at the time of the incident or was obscured from view.

---

[164] Art.5(a)(ii) and Sch.1, Pt.2, S.I. No.135/2006.

[165] See s.103(7)(c), Road Traffic Act 1961 and art. 5(a)(ii) and Sch.1, Pt.2, S.I. No.135/2006.

[166] **First conviction** – fine up to €1,000; **Second conviction** – fine up to €2,000; **Third conviction** – fine up to €1,000 and/or imprisonment for up to 3 months. See also s.18, Road Traffic Act 2006.

[167] See Reference 12, Pt.4, Sch.1, Road Traffic Act 2002 and also S.I. No.134/2006 – Road Traffic Act 2002 (Commencement of Certain Provisions) Order 2006 – which came into effect on 3 April 2006.

[168] S.I. No.182/1997 – Road Traffic (Traffic and Parking) Regulations, 1997 – Regulations enacted under s.35, Road Traffic Act 1994.

Penalties

In respect of offences under article 21, the penalties are as follows:

Fixed Charge Penalty: €80 (paid in 28 days):[169] €120 (paid in subsequent 28 days).[170]

Upon Conviction: General Penalty under section 102 of the Road Traffic Act 1961.[171]

Penalty Points: two (payment of fixed charge): four (upon con- viction.[172] Section 2(8) of the Road Traffic Act 2002 applies if the court imposes an ancillary disqualification order under section 27 of the Road Traffic Act 1961 – in those circumstances, penalty points will not be endorsed on the licence record.

Disqualification:

Ancillary Disqualification: a conviction under article 21 does not carry a mandatory disqualification. However, it is open to the court to make an ancillary disqualification order under section 27 of the Road Traffic Act 1961 on the particular facts of the case.

Penalty Point Disqualification: if a defendant accrues 12 penalty points upon conviction for this offence, then they will be disqualified under the administrative procedure set out under section 3 of the Road Traffic Act 2002.

(9) CROSSING A CONTINUOUS WHITE LINE – ARTICLE 25 OF THE ROAD TRAFFIC (TRAFFIC AND PARKING) REGULATIONS 1997[173]

A driver shall not cross a white line where:

(a) a continuous white line (traffic sign RRM 001) appears on a roadway;[174]

---

[169] Art.(a)(ii) and Sch.1, Pt.2, S.I. No.135/2006.
[170] See s.103(7)(c), Road Traffic Act 1961 and art.5(a)(ii) and Sch. 1, Pt.2, S.I. No.135/2006.
[171] **First conviction** – fine up to €1,000; **Second conviction** – fine up to €2,000; **Third conviction** – fine up to €1,000 and/or imprisonment for up to 3 months. See also s.18, Road Traffic Act 2006.
[172] See Reference 13, Pt.4, Sch.1, Road Traffic Act 2002 and also S.I. No.134/2006 – Road Traffic Act 2002 (Commencement of Certain Provisions) Order 2006 which came into effect on 3 April 2006.
[173] S.I. No.182/1997 – Road Traffic (Traffic and Parking) Regulations 1997 – Regulations enacted under s.35, Road Traffic Act 1994.
[174] Art.25(1), S.I. No.182/1997.

(b) two parallel continuous white lines (traffic sign RRM 001) appear on a roadway;[175]

(c) a broken white line (traffic sign RRM 002) appears on a roadway, unless it can be crossed without danger to other traffic or pedestrians;[176] or

(d) a continuous white line and a broken white line appear parallel on a roadway, unless a broken traffic line is nearer and it can be crossed without danger to other traffic or pedestrians.[177]

The above does not preclude a driver from crossing over a continuous/broken white line for the purposes of entering/leaving land or a premises on the right side of the roadway.[178]

Penalties

In respect of offences under article 25, the penalties are as follows:

Fixed Charge Penalty: €80 (paid in 28 days):[179] €120 (paid in subsequent 28 days).[180]

Upon Conviction: General Penalty under section 102 of the Road Traffic Act 1961.[181]

Penalty Points: two (payment of fixed charge): four (upon conviction.[182] Section 2(8) of the Road Traffic Act 2002 applies if the court imposes an ancillary disqualification order under section 27 of the Road Traffic Act 1961 – in those circumstances, penalty points will not be endorsed on licence record.

Disqualification:

Ancillary Disqualification: a conviction under article 25 does not carry a mandatory disqualification. However, it is open

---

[175] *Ibid.*

[176] *Ibid.*, art.25(2).

[177] *Ibid.*, art.25(3).

[178] *Ibid.*, art.25(4).

[179] Art.5(a)(ii) and Sch.1, Pt.2, S.I. No.135/2006.

[180] See s.103(7)(c), Road Traffic Act 1961 and art.5(a)(ii) and Sch.1, Pt.2, S.I. No.135/2006.

[181] **First conviction** – fine up to €1,000; **Second conviction** – fine up to €2,000; **Third conviction** – fine up to €1,000 and/or imprisonment for up to 3 months. See also s.18, Road Traffic Act 2006.

[182] See Reference 17 of Pt.4, Sch.1, Road Traffic Act 2002 and also S.I. No.134/2006 – Road Traffic Act 2002 (Commencement of Certain Provisions) Order 2006 which came into effect on 3 April 2006.

to the court to make an ancillary disqualification order under section 27 of the Road Traffic Act 1961 on the particular facts of the case.

Penalty Point Disqualification: if a defendant accrues 12 penalty points upon conviction for this offence, then they will be disqualified under the administrative procedure set out under section 3 of the Road Traffic Act 2002.

(10) ENTRY BY A DRIVER INTO A HATCHED MARKED AREA – ARTICLE 26 OF THE ROAD TRAFFIC (TRAFFIC AND PARKING) REGULATIONS 1997[183]

Where traffic sign number RRM 021 [hatched markings] has been provided in an area of roadway, a vehicle shall not enter the area.

Penalties

In respect of offences under article 26, the penalties are as follows:

Fixed Charge Penalty: €80 (paid in 28 days):[184] €120 (paid in subsequent 28 days).[185]

Upon Conviction: General Penalty under section 102 of the Road Traffic Act 1961.[186]

Penalty Points: one (payment of fixed charge): three (upon conviction).[187] Section 2(8) of the Road Traffic Act 2002 applies if the court imposes an ancillary disqualification order under section 27 of the Road Traffic Act 1961 – in those circumstances, penalty points will not be endorsed on the licence record.

Disqualification:

Ancillary Disqualification: a conviction under article 26 does not carry a mandatory disqualification. However, it is open to the court to make an ancillary disqualification order

---

[183] S.I. No.182/1997 – Road Traffic (Traffic and Parking) Regulations, 1997 – Regulations enacted under s.35, Road Traffic Act 1994.

[184] Art.5(a)(ii) and Sch.1, Pt.2, S.I. No.135/2006.

[185] See s.103(7)(c), Road Traffic Act 1961 and art.5(a)(ii) and Sch.1, Pt.2, S.I. No.135/2006.

[186] First conviction fine up to €1,000; **Second conviction** – fine up to €2,000; **Third conviction** – fine up to €1,000 and/or imprisonment for up to 3 months See also s.18, Road Traffic Act 2006.

[187] See Reference 18, Pt.4, Sch.1, Road Traffic Act 2002 and also S.I. No.134/2006 – Road Traffic Act 2002 (Commencement of Certain Provisions) Order 2006 which came into effect on 3 April 2006.

under section 27 Road Traffic Act 1961 on the particular facts of the case.

Penalty Point Disqualification: if a defendant accrues 12 penalty points upon conviction for this offence, then they will be disqualified under the administrative procedure set out under section 3 of the Road Traffic Act 2002.

(11) Failure to Comply with Traffic Lane Markings – Article 27 of the Road Traffic (Traffic and Parking) Regulations 1997[188]

'Where:

(a) a broken white line indicates a boundary of a traffic lane (traffic sign RRM 003) appears on a roadway;

(b) a maintain direction sign (traffic sign RRM 004) appears on a road-way;

(c) a must turn left sign (traffic sign RRM 005) appears on a road-way; or

(d) must turn right sign (traffic sign RRM 006);

the traffic must proceed in the direction indicated by arrows on sign.[189]'

Penalties

In respect of offences under article 27, the penalties are as follows:

Fixed Charge Penalty: €80 (paid in 28 days):[190] €120 (paid in subsequent 28 days).[191]

Upon Conviction: General Penalty under section 102 of the Road Traffic Act 1961.[192]

Penalty Points: one (payment of fixed charge): three (upon conviction).[193] Section 2(8) of the Road Traffic Act 2002 applies if

---

[188] S.I. No.182/1997 – Road Traffic (Traffic and Parking) Regulations, 1997 – Regulations enacted under s.35, Road Traffic Act 1994.

[189] Art.27(2), S.I. No.182/1997.

[190] Art.5(a)(ii) and Sch.1, Pt.2, S.I. No.135/2006.

[191] See s.103(7)(c), Road Traffic Act 1961 and art.5(a)(ii) and Sch.1, Pt.2, S.I. No.135/2006.

[192] **First conviction** – fine up to €1,000; **Second conviction** – fine up to €2,000; **Third conviction** – fine up to €1,000 and/or imprisonment for up to 3 months. See also s.18, Road Traffic Act 2006.

[193] See Reference 19, Pt.4, Sch.1, Road Traffic Act 2002 and also S.I. No.134/2006 –

the court imposes an ancillary disqualification order under section 27 of the Road Traffic Act 1961 – in those circumstances, penalty points will not be endorsed on the licence record.

Disqualification:

Ancillary Disqualification: a conviction under article 27 does not carry a mandatory disqualification. However, it is open to the court to make an ancillary disqualification order under section 27 of the Road Traffic Act 1961 on the particular facts of the case.

Penalty Point Disqualification: if a defendant accrues 12 penalty points upon conviction for this offence, then they will be disqualified under the administrative procedure set out under section 3 of the Road Traffic Act 2002.

(12) FAILURE TO OBEY TRAFFIC LIGHTS – ARTICLE 30 OF THE ROAD TRAFFIC (TRAFFIC AND PARKING) REGULATIONS 1997[194]

'(1) Where a traffic light is provided a driver shall not:

(a) cross the stop line associated with same traffic light when that traffic light is red.

(b) cross the stop line associated with same traffic light when that traffic light is (non-flashing) amber unless vehicle is so close to traffic lights that it cannot safely stop before passing traffic light/traffic light stop line.'

(2) Where a traffic light is provided a driver may:

(a) cross the stop line associated with same traffic light when that traffic light is green provided that no other user is endangered by so crossing and driver complies with rules in respect of yielding and not entering box junctions;

(b) cross the stop line associated with same traffic light, if traffic light is an arrow light, only when that traffic light arrow is green;

(c) cross the stop line associated with same traffic light when that traffic light is intermittent flashing amber light provided right of way is first yielded to any pedestrians who have commenced crossing;

Road Traffic Act 2002 (Commencement of Certain Provisions) Order 2006 which came into effect on 3 April 2006.

[194] S.I. No.182/1997 – Road Traffic (Traffic and Parking) Regulations, 1997 – Regulations enacted under s.35, Road Traffic Act 1994.

(d) where there is a Traffic light in advance of a yield Line or yield Sign, or both, driver may proceed when lower amber light is flashing intermittently provided they have first yielded right of way.'

In respect of offences under article 30, the penalties are as follows:

Fixed Charge Penalty: €80 (paid in 28 days):[195] €120 (paid in subsequent 28 days).[196]

Upon Conviction: General Penalty under section 102 of the Road Traffic Act 1961.[197]

Penalty Points: two (payment of fixed charge): five (upon conviction).[198] Section 2(8) of the Road Traffic Act 2002 applies if the court imposes an ancillary disqualification order under section 27 of the Road Traffic Act 1961. In those circumstances, penalty points will not be endorsed on the licence record.

Disqualification:

Ancillary Disqualification: a conviction under article 30 does not carry a mandatory disqualification. However, it is open to the court to make an ancillary disqualification order under section 27 of the Road Traffic Act 1961 on the particular facts of the case.

Penalty Point Disqualification: if a defendant accrues 12 penalty points upon conviction for this offence, then they will be disqualified under the administrative procedure set out under section 3 of the Road Traffic Act 2002.

(13) FAILURE TO OBEY TRAFFIC LIGHTS AT A RAILWAY CROSSING – ARTICLE 31 OF THE ROAD TRAFFIC (TRAFFIC AND PARKING) REGULATIONS 1997[199]

'A driver or pedestrian approaching a railway level crossing shall

---

[195] Art.5(a)(ii) and Sch.1, Pt.2, S.I. No.135/2006.

[196] See s.103(7)(c), Road Traffic Act 1961 and art.5(a)(ii) and Sch.1, Pt.2, S.I. No.135/2006.

[197] **First conviction** – fine up to €1,000; **Second conviction** – fine up to €2,000; **Third conviction** – fine up to €1,000 and/or imprisonment for up to 3 months. See also s.18, Road Traffic Act 2006.

[198] See Reference 21, Pt.4, Sch.1, Road Traffic Act 2002 and also S.I. No.134/2006 – Road Traffic Act 2002 (Commencement of Certain Provisions) Order 2006 which came into effect on 3 April 2006.

[199] S.I. No.182/1997 – Road Traffic (Traffic and Parking) Regulations, 1997 – Regulations enacted unders.35, Road Traffic Act 1994.

not:

(a) proceed past stop line, barrier, half barrier, or otherwise past traffic light signal while red light are flashing;[200]

(b) proceed past stop line, barrier, half barrier, or otherwise past traffic light signal when same traffic light is a non flashing amber light unless vehicle is so close to traffic lights that it cannot safely stop before passing traffic light/traffic light stop line;[201]

(c) enter, either totally or partially, a yellow box (traffic sign RRM 020) unless vehicle can clear area without stopping, notwithstanding colour of any traffic light sign covering yellow box.[202]'

Penalties

In respect of offences under article 31, the penalties are as follows:

Fixed Charge Penalty: €80 (paid in 28 days):[203] €120 (paid in subsequent 28 days).[204]

Upon Conviction: General Penalty under section 102 Road Traffic Act 1961.[205]

Penalty Points: two (payment of fixed charge): five (upon con- viction).[206] Section 2(8) of the Road Traffic Act 2002 applies if the court imposes an ancillary disqualification order under section 27 of the Road Traffic Act 1961. In those circumstances, penalty points will not be endorsed on the licence record.

Disqualification:

Ancillary Disqualification: a conviction under article 3 one does not carry a mandatory disqualification. However, it is open to the court to make an ancillary disqualification

---

[200] Art.31(1), S.I. No.182/1997.
[201] *Ibid.*, art.31(2).
[202] *Ibid.*, art.31(3).
[203] Art.5(a)(ii) and Sch.1, Pt.2, S.I. No.135/2006.
[204] See s.103(7)(c), Road Traffic Act 1961 and art.5(a)(ii) and Sch.1, Pt.2, S.I. No.135/2006.
[205] **First conviction** – fine up to €1,000; **Second conviction** – fine up to €2,000; **Third conviction** – fine up to €1,000 and/or imprisonment for up to 3 months. See also s.18, Road Traffic Act 2006.
[206] See Reference 22, Pt.4, Sch.1, Road Traffic Act 2002 and also S.I. No.134/2006, Road Traffic Act 2002 (Commencement of Certain Provisions) Order 2006 which came into effect on 3 April 2006.

order under section 27 of the Road Traffic Act 1961 on the particular facts of the case.

Penalty Point Disqualification: if a defendant accrues 12 penalty points upon conviction for this offence, then they will be disqualified under the administrative procedure set out under section 3 of the Road Traffic Act 2002.

(14) Driving a Vehicle Against the Flow of Traffic – Article 33(1)(A) of the Road Traffic (Traffic and Parking) Regulations 1997[207]

'A driver shall not drive against the flow of traffic on a motorway.'

Penalties

In respect of offences under article 33(1)(a), the penalties are as follows:

Fixed Charge Penalty: €80 (paid in 28 days):[208] €120 (paid in subsequent 28 days).[209]

Upon Conviction: General Penalty under section 102 of the Road Traffic Act 1961.[210]

Penalty Points: two (payment of fixed charge): four (upon conviction).[211] Section 2(8) of the Road Traffic Act 2002 applies if the court imposes an ancillary disqualification order under section 27 of the Road Traffic Act 1961. In those circumstances, penalty points will not be endorsed on the licence record.

Disqualification:

Ancillary Disqualification: a conviction under article 33 does not carry a mandatory disqualification. However, it is open to the court to make an ancillary disqualification order

---

[207] S.I. No.182/1997 – Road Traffic (Traffic and Parking) Regulations, 1997 – Regulations enacted under s.35, Road Traffic Act 1994.

[208] Art.5(a)(ii) and Sch.1, Pt.2, S.I. No.135/2006.

[209] See s.103(7)(c), Road Traffic Act 1961 and art.5(a)(ii) and Sch.1, Pt.2, S.I. No.135/2006.

[210] **First conviction** – fine up to €1,000; **Second conviction** – fine up to €2,000; **Third conviction** – fine up to €1,000 and/or imprisonment for up to 3 months. See also s.18, Road Traffic Act 2006.

[211] See Reference 23, Pt.4, Sch.1, Road Traffic Act 2002 and also S.I. No.134/2006 – Road Traffic Act 2002 (Commencement of Certain Provisions) Order 2006 which came into effect on 3 April 2006.

under section 27 of the Road Traffic Act 1961 on the particular facts of the case.

Penalty Point Disqualification: if a defendant accrues 12 penalty points upon conviction for this offence, then they will be disqualified under the administrative procedure set out under section 3 of the Road Traffic Act 2002.

(15) DRIVING A VEHICLE ON THE HARD SHOULDER OF A MOTORWAY – ARTICLE 33(1)(B) OF THE ROAD TRAFFIC (TRAFFIC AND PARKING) REGULATIONS 1997[212]

'A driver shall not drive against the flow on or across any part of a motor- way which is not a carriageway.'

This prohibition does not apply to any part of a motorway which is provided for the parking of vehicles or the provision of services or amenities.

Penalties

In respect of offences under article 33(1)(b) the penalties are as follows:

Fixed Charge Penalty: €80 (paid in 28 days):[213] €120 (paid in subsequent 28 days).[214]

Upon Conviction: General Penalty under section 102 of the Road Traffic Act 1961 applies.[215]

Penalty Points: one (payment of fixed charge): three (upon conviction.[216] Section 2(8) of the Road Traffic Act 2002 applies if the court imposes an ancillary disqualification order under section 27 of the Road Traffic Act 1961. In those circumstances, penalty points will not be endorsed on the licence record.

---

[212] S.I. No.182/1997 – Road Traffic (Traffic and Parking) Regulations, 1997 – Regulations enacted under s.35, Road Traffic Act 1994.
[213] Art.5(a)(ii) and Sch.1, Pt.2, S.I. No.135/2006.
[214] See s.103(7)(c), Road Traffic Act 1961 and art.5(a)(ii) and Sch.1, Pt.2, S.I. No.135/2006.
[215] **First conviction** – fine up to €1,000; **Second conviction** – fine up to €2,000; **Third conviction** – fine up to €1,000 and/or imprisonment for up to 3 months. See also s.18, Road Traffic Act 2006.
[216] See Reference 24, Pt.4, Sch.1, Road Traffic Act 2002 and also S.I. No.134/2006 – Road Traffic Act 2002 (Commencement of Certain Provisions) Order 2006 which came into effect on 3 April 2006.

Disqualification:

Ancillary Disqualification: a conviction under article 33 does not carry a mandatory disqualification. However, it is open to the court to make an ancillary disqualification order under section 27 of the Road Traffic Act 1961 on the particular facts of the case.

Penalty Point Disqualification: if a defendant accrues 12 penalty points upon conviction for this offence, then they will be disqualified under the administrative procedure set out under section 3 of the Road Traffic Act 2002.

(16) Driving a HGV/Bus on the Outside Lane of a Motorway – Article 33(1)(D) of the Road Traffic (Traffic and Parking) Regulations 1997[217]

A driver of HGV or Bus (or other vehicle prescribed by regulation under section 4 of the Road Traffic Act 2004) shall not drive on the outside of a lane or motorway.

Penalties

In respect of offences under article 33(1)(d), the penalties are as follows:

Fixed Charge Penalty: €80 (paid in 28 days):[218] €120 (paid in subsequent 28 days).[219]

Upon Conviction: General Penalty under section 102 Road Traffic Act 1961 applies.[220]

Penalty Points: one (payment of fixed charge): three (upon conviction.[221] Section 2(8) of the Road Traffic Act 2002 applies if the court imposes an ancillary disqualification order under

---

[217] S.I. No.182/1997 – Road Traffic (Traffic and Parking) Regulations, 1997 – Regulations enacted under s.35, Road Traffic Act 1994.

[218] Art.5(a)(ii) and Sch.1, Pt.2, S.I. No.135/2006.

[219] See s.103(7)(c), Road Traffic Act 1961 and art.5(a)(ii) and Sch.1, Pt.2, S.I. No.135/2006.

[220] **First conviction** – fine up to €1,000; **Second conviction** – fine up to €2,000; **Third conviction** – fine up to €1,000 and/or imprisonment for up to 3 months. See also s.18, Road Traffic Act 2006.

[221] See Reference 25, Pt.4, Sch.1, Road Traffic Act 2002 and also S.I. No.134/2006 – Road Traffic Act 2002 (Commencement of Certain Provisions) Order 2006 which came into effect on 3 April 2006.

section 27 of the Road Traffic Act 1961. In those circumstances, penalty points will not be endorsed on the licence record.

Disqualification:

Ancillary Disqualification: a conviction under article 33 does not carry a mandatory disqualification. However, it is open to the court to make an ancillary disqualification order under section 27 of the Road Traffic Act 1961 on the particular facts of the case.

Penalty Point Disqualification: if a defendant accrues 12 penalty points upon conviction for this offence, then they will be disqualified under the administrative procedure set out under section 3 of the Road Traffic Act 2002.

(17) FAILURE TO DRIVE ON THE LEFT SIDE OF ROAD – ARTICLE 9 OF THE ROAD TRAFFIC (TRAFFIC AND PARKING) REGULATIONS 1997[222]

'Save where otherwise required by these regulations, a vehicle shall be driven on left hand side or roadway in such a manner as to:

(a) allow, without danger or inconvenience to traffic or pedestrians, approaching traffic to pass on right; or

(b) allow, without danger or inconvenience to traffic or pedestrians, overtaking traffic to overtake on right.'

Penalties

In respect of offences under article 9, the penalties are as follows:

Fixed Charge Penalty: €60 (paid in 28 days):[223] €90 (paid in subsequent 28 days).[224]

Upon Conviction: General Penalty under section 102 of the Road Traffic Act 1961 applies.[225]

---

[222] S.I. No.182/1997 – Road Traffic (Traffic and Parking) Regulations, 1997 – Regulations enacted under s.35, Road Traffic Act 1994.

[223] Ar.5(b)(ii) and Sch.1, Pt.2, S.I. No.135/2006.

[224] See s.103(7)(c), Road Traffic Act 1961 and art.5(b)(ii) and Sch.1, Pt.2, S.I. No.135/2006.

[225] **First conviction** – fine up to €1,000; **Second conviction** – fine up to €2,000; **Third conviction** – fine up to €1,000 and/or imprisonment for up to 3 months. See also s.18, Road Traffic Act 2006.

Penalty Points: one (payment of fixed charge): three (upon conviction.[226] Section 2(8) of the Road Traffic Act 2002 applies if the court imposes an ancillary disqualification order under section 27 of the Road Traffic Act 1961. In those circumstances, penalty points will not be endorsed on the licence record.

Disqualification:

> **Ancillary Disqualification:** a conviction under article 9 does not carry a mandatory disqualification. However, it is open to the court to make an ancillary disqualification order under section 27 of the Road Traffic Act 1961 on the particular facts of the case.

> **Penalty Point Disqualification:** if a defendant accrues 12 penalty points upon conviction for this offence, then they will be disqualified under the administrative procedure set out under section 3 of the Road Traffic Act 2002.

(18) FAILURE TO OBEY REQUIREMENTS AT JUNCTIONS – ARTICLE 11 OF THE ROAD TRAFFIC (TRAFFIC AND PARKING) REGULATIONS 1997[227]

'Where a driver is approaching a road junction they shall:

(a) drive on left hand side of roadway if intending to turn left at a junction;

(b) drive close to centre of roadway if intending to turn right at a junction;

(c) drive on right hand side of one way roadway (wide enough for two lanes of traffic) if intending to turn right at a junction.'

Penalties

In respect of offences under article 11, the penalties are as follows:

Fixed Charge Penalty: €60 (paid in 28 days):[228] €90 (paid in subsequent 28 days).[229]

---

[226] See Reference 3, Pt.4, Sch.1, Road Traffic Act 2002 and also S.I. No.134/2006 – Road Traffic Act 2002 (Commencement of Certain Provisions) Order 2006 which came into effect on 3 April 2006

[227] S.I. No.182/1997 – Road Traffic (Traffic and Parking) Regulations, 1997 – Regulations enacted under s.35, Road Traffic Act 1994.

[228] Art.5(b)(ii) and Sch.1, Pt.2, S.I. No.135/2006.

[229] See s.103(7)(c), Road Traffic Act 1961 and art.5(b)(ii) and Sch.1, Pt.2, S.I. No.135/2006.

Upon Conviction: General Penalty under section 102 of the Road Traffic Act 1961 applies.[230]

Penalty Points: one (payment of fixed charge): three (upon conviction.[231] Section 2(8) of the Road Traffic Act 2002 applies if the court imposes an ancillary disqualification order under section 27 of the Road Traffic Act 1961. In those circumstances, penalty points will not be endorsed on the licence record.

Disqualification:

Ancillary Disqualification: a conviction under article 9 does not carry a mandatory disqualification. However, it is open to the court to make an ancillary disqualification order under section 27 of the Road Traffic Act 1961 on the particular facts of the case.

Penalty Point Disqualification: if a defendant accrues 12 penalty points upon conviction for this offence, then they will be disqualified under the administrative procedure set out under section 3 of the Road Traffic Act 2002.

(19) Failure to Obey Requirements Regarding Reversing of Vehicles – Article 12 of the Road Traffic (Traffic and Parking) Regulations 1997[232]

'A driver shall not reverse:

(a) onto a major road from another road;[233]

(b) from a place adjacent to a public road onto that public road unless it is clear to driver that to so reverse would not endanger other traffic or pedestrians;[234]

(c) in other circumstances, unless before reversing, driver has ensured that to so reverse would not endanger other traffic or pedestrians.'[235]

---

[230] **First conviction** – fine up to €1,000; **Second conviction** – fine up to €2,000; **Third conviction** – fine up to €1,000 and/or imprisonment for up to 3 months. See also s.18, Road Traffic Act 2006.

[231] See Reference 5, Pt.4, Sch.1, Road Traffic Act 2002 and also S.I. No.134/2006 – Road Traffic Act 2002 (Commencement of Certain Provisions) Order 2006 which came into effect on 3 April 2006.

[232] S.I. No.182/1997 – Road Traffic (Traffic and Parking) Regulations, 1997 – Regulations enacted under s.35, Road Traffic Act 1994.

[233] Art.12(1), S.I. No.182/1997.

[234] *Ibid.*, art.12(2).

[235] *Ibid.*, art.12(3).

Penalties

In respect of offences under article 12, the penalties are as follows:

Fixed Charge Penalty: €60 (paid in 28 days):[236] €90 (paid in subsequent 28 days).[237]

Upon Conviction: General Penalty under section 102 of the Road Traffic Act 1961 applies.[238]

Penalty Points: one (payment of fixed charge): three (upon conviction.[239] Section 2(8) of the Road Traffic Act 2002 applies if the court imposes an ancillary disqualification order under section 27 of the Road Traffic Act 1961. In those circumstances, penalty points will not be endorsed on the licence record.

Disqualification:

Ancillary Disqualification: a conviction under article 12 does not carry a mandatory disqualification. However, it is open to the court to make an ancillary disqualification order under section 27 of the Road Traffic Act 1961 on the particular facts of the case.

Penalty Point Disqualification: if a defendant accrues 12 penalty points upon conviction for this offence, then they will be disqualified under the administrative procedure set out under section 3 of the Road Traffic Act 2002.

(20) Driving on a Footpath – Article 13 of the Road Traffic (Traffic and Parking) Regulations 1997[240]

'A vehicle shall not be driven, wholly or partly along or across a footpath unless:

(a) the vehicle is being so driven for the purposes of entering or exiting a place adjacent to the footpath.'

---

[236] Art.5(b)(ii) and Sch.1, Pt.2, S.I. No.135/2006.

[237] See s.103(7)(c), Road Traffic Act 1961 and art.5(b)(ii) and Sch.1, Pt.2, S.I. No.135/2006.

[238] **First conviction** – fine up to €1,000; **Second conviction** – fine up to €2,000; **Third conviction** – fine up to €1,000 and/or imprisonment for up to 3 months. See also s.18, Road Traffic Act 2006.

[239] See Reference 6, Pt.4, Sch.1, Road Traffic Act 2002 and also S.I. No.134/2006, Road Traffic Act 2002 (Commencement of Certain Provisions) Order 2006 which came into effect on 3 April 2006.

[240] S.I. No.182/1997 – Road Traffic (Traffic and Parking) Regulations, 1997 – Regulations enacted under s.35, Road Traffic Act 1994.

Penalties

In respect of offences under article 13, the penalties are as follows:

Fixed Charge Penalty: €60 (paid in 28 days):[241] €90 (paid in subsequent 28 days).[242]

Upon Conviction: General Penalty under section 102 of the Road Traffic Act 1961 applies.[243]

Penalty Points: one (payment of fixed charge): three (upon conviction.[244] Section 2(8) of the Road Traffic Act 2002 applies if the court imposes an ancillary disqualification order under section 27 of the Road Traffic Act 1961. In those circumstances, penalty points will not be endorsed on the licence record.

Disqualification:

Ancillary Disqualification: a conviction under article 13 does not carry a mandatory disqualification. However, it is open to the court to make an ancillary disqualification order under section 27 of the Road Traffic Act 1961 on the particular facts of the case.

Penalty Point Disqualification: if a defendant accrues 12 penalty points upon conviction for this offence, then they will be disqualified under the administrative procedure set out under section 3 of the Road Traffic Act 2002.

(21) Driving on a Cyclepath – Article 14(5)(A) of the Road Traffic (Traffic and Parking) Regulations 1997[245]

'(1) A vehicle (other than a mechanically-propelled wheelchair) shall not be driven, wholly or partly along or across a cycle path

---

[241] Art.5(b)(ii) and Sch.1, Pt.2, S.I. No.135/2006.

[242] See s.103(7)(c), Road Traffic Act 1961 and art.5(b)(ii) and Sch.1, Pt.2, S.I. No.135/2006.

[243] **First conviction** – fine up to €1,000; **Second conviction** – fine up to €2,000; **Third conviction** – fine up to €1,000 and/or imprisonment for up to 3 months. See also s.18, Road Traffic Act 2006.

[244] See Reference.7, Pt.4, Sch.1, Road Traffic Act 2002 and also S.I. No.134/2006 – Road Traffic Act 2002 (Commencement of Certain Provisions) Order 2006 which came into effect on 3 April 2006.

[245] Art.14(5)(a), S.I. No.182/1997 – Road Traffic (Traffic and Parking) Regulations, 1997 as inserted by art.6 of S.I. No.274/1998 – Road Traffic (Traffic and Parking) (Amendment) Regulations, 1998 regulations enacted under s.35, Road Traffic Act 1994.

unless:

(a) the vehicle is being so driven for the purposes of entering or exiting a place adjacent to the footpath.'[246]

Article 14 sets out a comprehensive list of regulations in respect of the operation of cycle tracks, however, only an offence of driving a mechanically-propelled vehicle (MPV) on a cycle path is currently a penalty point offence.

Penalties

In respect of offences under article 14, the penalties are as follows:

Fixed Charge Penalty: €60 (paid in 28 days):[247] €90 (paid in subsequent 28 days).[248]

Upon Conviction: General Penalty under section 102 of the Road Traffic Act 1961 applies.[249]

Penalty Points: one (payment of fixed charge): three (upon conviction.[250] Section 2(8) of the Road Traffic Act 2002 applies if the court imposes an ancillary disqualification order under section 27 of the Road Traffic Act 1961. In those circumstances, penalty points will not be endorsed on the licence record.

Disqualification:

Ancillary Disqualification: a conviction under article 14 does not carry a mandatory disqualification. However, it is open to the court to make an ancillary disqualification order under section 27 of the Road Traffic Act 1961 on the particular facts of the case.

Penalty Point Disqualification: if a defendant accrues 12 penalty points upon conviction for this offence, then they

---

[246] Art.15(5)(a), S.I. No.182/1997.

[247] Art.5(b)(ii) and Sch.1, Pt.2, S.I. No.135/2006.

[248] See s.103(7)(c), Road Traffic Act 1961 and art.5(b)(ii) and Sch.1, Pt.2, S.I. No.135/ 2006.

[249] **First conviction** – fine up to €1,000; **Second conviction** – fine up to €2,000; **Third conviction** – fine up to €1,000 and/or imprisonment for up to 3 months. See also s.18, Road Traffic Act 2006.

[250] See Reference 8, Pt.4, Sch.1, Road Traffic Act 2002 and also S.I. No.134/2006 – Road Traffic Act 2002 (Commencement of Certain Provisions) Order 2006 which came into effect on 3 April 2006.

will be disqualified under the administrative procedure set out under section 3 of the Road Traffic Act 2002.

(22) Failure to Turn Left When Entering a Roundabout – Article 15 of the Road Traffic (Traffic and Parking) Regulations 1997[251]

Article 15 states that it is an offence for any driver entering a roundabout to fail to turn left on to same roundabout.

Penalties

In respect of offences under article 15, the penalties are as follows:

Fixed Charge Penalty: €60 (paid in 28 days):[252] €90 (paid in subsequent 28 days).[253]

Upon Conviction: General Penalty under section 102 of the Road Traffic Act 1961 applies.[254]

Penalty Points: one (payment of fixed charge): three (upon conviction.[255] Section 2(8) of the Road Traffic Act 2002 applies if the court imposes an ancillary disqualification order under section 27 of the Road Traffic Act 1961. In those circumstances, penalty points will not be endorsed on the licence record.

Disqualification:

Ancillary Disqualification: a conviction under article 9 does not carry a mandatory disqualification. However, it is open to the court to make an ancillary disqualification order under section 27 of the Road Traffic Act 1961 on the particular facts of the case.

Penalty Point Disqualification: if a defendant accrues 12 penalty points upon conviction for this offence, then they

---

[251] S.I. No.182/1997, Road Traffic (Traffic and Parking) Regulations, 1997 – Regulations enacted under s.35, Road Traffic Act 1994.

[252] Art.5(b)(ii) and Sch.1, Pt.2, S.I. No.135/2006.

[253] See s.103(7)(c), Road Traffic Act 1961 and art.5(b)(ii) and Sch.1, Pt.2, S.I. No.135/2006.

[254] **First conviction** – fine up to €1,000; **Second conviction** – fine up to €2,000; **Third conviction** – fine up to €1,000 and/or imprisonment for up to 3 months. See also s.18, Road Traffic Act 2006.

[255] See Reference 9, Pt.4, Sch.1, Road Traffic Act 2002 and also S.I. No.134/2006 – Road Traffic Act 2002 (Commencement of Certain Provisions) Order 2006 which came into effect on 3 April 2006.

will be disqualified under the administrative procedure set out under section 3 of the Road Traffic Act 2002.

(23) DRIVING ON THE MEDIAN STRIP – ARTICLE 15 OF THE ROAD TRAFFIC (TRAFFIC AND PARKING) REGULATIONS 1997[256]

Article 16 provides that a vehicle may not be driven wholly or partly along or across a median strip. This provision amounts to a total prohibition on driving on a median strip and does not contain any defences or exceptions. A median strip is defined as 'any area between two carriageways which is a not a traffic line'.

Penalties

In respect of offences under article 16, the penalties are as follows:

Fixed Charge Penalty: €60 (paid in 28 days):[257] €90 (paid in subsequent 28 days).[258]

Upon Conviction: General Penalty under section 102 of the Road Traffic Act 1961 applies.[259]

Penalty Points: one (payment of fixed charge): three (upon conviction.[260] Section 2(8) of the Road Traffic Act 2002 applies if the court imposes an ancillary disqualification order under section 27 of the Road Traffic Act 1961. In those circumstances, penalty points will not be endorsed on the licence record.

Disqualification:

Ancillary Disqualification: a conviction under article 9 does not carry a mandatory disqualification. However, it is open to the court to make an ancillary disqualification order under section 27 of the Road Traffic Act 1961 on the particular facts of the case.

---

[256] S.I. No.182/1997 – Road Traffic (Traffic and Parking) Regulations, 1997 – Regulations enacted under s.35, Road Traffic Act 1994.

[257] Art.5(b)(ii) and Sch.1, Pt.2, S.I. No.135/2006.

[258] See s.103(7)(c), Road Traffic Act 1961 and art.5(b)(ii) and Sch.1, Pt.2, S.I. No.135/2006.

[259] **First conviction** – fine up to €1,000; **Second conviction** – fine up to €2,000; **Third conviction** – fine up to €1,000 and/or imprisonment for up to 3 months. See also s.18, Road Traffic Act 2006.

[260] See Reference 10, Pt.4, Sch.1, Road Traffic Act 2002 and also S.I. No.134/2006 – Road Traffic Act 2002 (Commencement of Certain Provisions) Order 2006 which came into effect on 3 April 2006.

Penalty Point Disqualification: if a defendant accrues 12 penalty points upon conviction for this offence, then they will be disqualified under the administrative procedure set out under section 3 of the Road Traffic Act 2002.

(24) Failing to Stop for a Traffic Warden Sign – Section 96 of the Road Traffic Act 1961[261]

Section 96 creates an offence of failing to stop for a traffic warden sign. In any prosecution under this section, it is presumed unless shown to the contrary that the school warden was acting in accordance with section 96 and all regulations including article 44 of the Road Traffic (Signs) Regulations 1997 in respect of uniform requirements. The powers conferred on a school warden are exercisable only upon the wearing a prescribed uniform of a hat and coat of reflective material.

Penalties

In respect of offences under section 96, the penalties are as follows:

Fixed Charge Penalty: €80 (paid in 28 days):[262] €120 (paid in subsequent 28 days).[263]

Upon Conviction: General Penalty under section 102 of the Road Traffic Act 1961 applies.[264]

Penalty Points: one (payment of fixed charge): four (upon conviction).[265] Section 2(8) of the Road Traffic Act 2002 applies if the court imposes an ancillary disqualification order under section 27 of the Road Traffic Act 1961. In those circumstances, penalty points will also not be endorsed on the licence record.

Disqualification:

Ancillary Disqualification: a conviction under section three does not carry a mandatory disqualification. However, it

---

[261] As amended by s.6, Road Traffic Act 1968.

[262] Art.5(a)(i) and Sch.1, Pt.1, S.I. No.135/2006.

[263] S.103(7)(c), Road Traffic Act 1961 and art.5(b)(ii) and Sch.1, Pt.1, S.I. No.135/ 2006.

[264] **First conviction** – fine up to €1,000; **Second conviction** – fine up to €2,000; **Third conviction** – fine up to €1,000 and/or imprisonment for up to 3 months. See also s.18, Road Traffic Act 2006.

[265] See Reference 13, Pt.1, Sch.1, Road Traffic Act 2002 and also S.I. No.134/2006 – Road Traffic Act 2002 (Commencement of Certain Provisions) Order 2006 which came into effect on 3 April 2006.

is open to the court to make an ancillary disqualification order under section 27 of the Road Traffic Act 1961 on the particular facts of the case.

Penalty Point Disqualification: if a defendant accrues 12 penalty points upon conviction for this offence, then they will be disqualified under the administrative procedure set out under section 3 of the Road Traffic Act 2002.

(25) Failure to Stop When So Required by a Member of the Gardaí – Section 109 of the Road Traffic Act 1961[266]

Section 109 provides that any individual driving a car in a public place:

'(a) Shall stop their vehicle upon request of the Gardaí, and

(b) remain stationary for such period as reasonably necessary for the Gardaí to discharge duties.'

The Supreme Court has held that the power conferred upon the Gardaí under this section is not a statutory power requiring motorists to stop.[267] There is a general duty for a motorist to stop when requested: but they can subsequently challenge the Garda's grounds for stopping them or ask for an explanation as to why they were asked to stop: it may therefore be an arguable defence to a charge of having failed to remain stationary to demonstrate to the court that when an defendant asked a Garda for the reason they had been stopped, the Garda failed to given them a reasonable explanation.

Penalties

In respect of offences under section 109, the penalties are as follows:

Fixed Charge Penalty: €80 (paid in 28 days):[268] €120 (paid in subsequent 28 days).[269]

General Penalty under section 102 of the Road Traffic Act 1961 applies.[270]

---

[266] As amended by s.6, Road Traffic Act 1968.
[267] See *DPP (Stratford) v. Fagan* [1994] 3 I.R. 265.
[268] Art.5(a)(i) and Sch.1, Pt.1, S.I. No.135/2006.
[269] S.103(7)(c), Road Traffic Act 1961 and art.5(b)(ii) and Sch.1, Pt.1, S.I. No.135/2006.
[270] **First conviction** – fine up to €1,000; **Second conviction** – fine up to €2,000; **Third**

Penalty Points: one (payment of fixed charge): five (upon conviction).[271] Section 2(8) of the Road Traffic Act 2002 applies if the court imposes an ancillary disqualification order under section 27 of the Road Traffic Act 1961. In those circumstances, penalty points will not be endorsed on the licence record.

Disqualification:

Ancillary Disqualification: a conviction under section 109 does not carry a mandatory disqualification. However, it is open to the court to make an ancillary disqualification order under section 27 of the Road Traffic Act 1961 on the particular facts of the case.

Penalty Point Disqualification: if a defendant accrues 12 penalty points upon conviction for this offence, then they will be disqualified under the administrative procedure set out under section 3 of the Road Traffic Act 2002.

(26) FAILURE TO LEAVE APPROPRIATE DISTANCE BETWEEN YOU AND THE CAR IN FRONT – ARTICLE 7 OF THE ROAD TRAFFIC (TRAFFIC AND PARKING) REGULATIONS 1997[272]

Article 7 sets out the offence of driving a vehicle in a public place at a speed exceeding that which will enable its driver to bring it to a halt within the distance which the driver can see to be clear. This general speed restriction applies to driving any vehicle in a public place. A vehicle must be driven a safe breaking distance behind any vehicle in front. Article 7 applies irrespective of whatever maximum speed limit may apply.

Penalties

In respect of offences under article 7, the penalties are as follows:

Fixed Charge Penalty: €80 (paid in 28 days):[273] €120 (paid in subsequent 28 days).[274]

---

conviction – fine up to €1,000 and/or imprisonment for up to 3 months. See also s.18, Road Traffic Act 2006.

[271] See Reference 15, Pt.1, Sch.1, Road Traffic Act 2002 and also S.I. No.134/2006 – Road Traffic Act 2002 (Commencement of Certain Provisions) Order 2006 which came into effect on 3 April 2006.

[272] S.I. No.182/1997 – Road Traffic (Traffic and Parking) Regulations, 1997 – Regulations enacted under s.35, Road Traffic Act 1994.

[273] Art.5(a)(ii) and Sch.1, Pt.2, S.I. No.135/2006.

[274] See s.103(7)(c), Road Traffic Act 1961 and art.5(a)(ii) and Sch.1, Pt.2, S.I. No.135/2006.

Upon Conviction: General Penalty under section 102 of the Road Traffic Act 1961.[275]

Penalty Points: two (payment of fixed charge): four (upon conviction).[276] Section 2(8) of the Road Traffic Act 2002 applies if the court imposes an ancillary disqualification order under section 27 of the Road Traffic Act 1961 – in those circumstances, penalty points will not be endorsed on the licence record.

Disqualification:

Ancillary Disqualification: a conviction under article 7 does not carry a mandatory disqualification. However, it is open to the court to make an ancillary disqualification order under section 27 of the Road Traffic Act 1961 on the particular facts of the case.

Penalty Point Disqualification: if a defendant accrues 12 penalty points upon conviction for this offence, then they will be disqualified under the administrative procedure set out under section 3 of the Road Traffic Act 2002.

(27) FAILURE TO YIELD – ARTICLE 8 OF THE ROAD TRAFFIC (TRAFFIC AND PARKING) REGULATIONS 1997[277]

'Save as otherwise indicated to elsewhere in these regulations, a driver of a vehicle shall yield right of way when:

(a) starting from a stationary position to other traffic and pedestrians;[278]

(b) approaching a junction to another vehicle or pedestrian already turning/crossing a junction;[279]

(c) entering a public road from another place other than public road to vehicles and pedestrians already proceeding along road in either direction;[280]

---

[275] **First conviction** – fine up to €1,000; **Second conviction** – fine up to €2,000; **Third conviction** – fine up to €1,000 and/or imprisonment for up to 3 months. See also s.18, Road Traffic Act 2006.

[276] See Reference 1, Pt.4, Sch.1, Road Traffic Act 2002 and also S.I. No.134/2006 – Road Traffic Act 2002 (Commencement of Certain Provisions) Order 2006 which came into effect on 3 April 2006.

[277] S.I. No.182/1997 – Road Traffic (Traffic and Parking) Regulations, 1997 – Regulations enacted under s.35, Road Traffic Act 1994.

[278] Art.8(2), S.I. No.182/1997.

[279] *Ibid.*, art.8(3).

[280] *Ibid.*, art.8(4).

(d) approaching a junction along a road other than a major road to vehicles and pedestrians already proceeding along major road in either direction irrespective of traffic sign indicating later road is major;[281]

(e) approaching a junction along a major road to vehicles and pedestrians approaching a junction from the right;[282]

(f) approaching a junction intending to turn right to vehicles approaching on same road from the opposite direction intending to turn left or drive straight ahead;[283]

(g) intending to drive from one traffic lane to another to any traffic on that other lane.'[284]

Penalties

In respect of offences under article 8, the penalties are as follows:

Fixed Charge Penalty: €80 (paid in 28 days):[285] €120 (paid in subsequent 28 days).[286]

Upon Conviction: General Penalty under section 102 of the Road Traffic Act 1961.[287]

Penalty Points: two (payment of fixed charge): four (upon conviction).[288] Section 2(8) of the Road Traffic Act 2002 applies if the court imposes an ancillary disqualification order under section 27 of the Road Traffic Act 1961 – in those circumstances, penalty points will not be endorsed on licence record.

Disqualification:

Ancillary Disqualification: a conviction under article 7 does not carry a mandatory disqualification. However, it is open to the court to make an ancillary disqualification order

---

[281] *Ibid.*, art.8(5).
[282] *Ibid.*, art.8(6).
[283] *Ibid.*, art.8(7).
[284] A *Ibid.*, art.8(8).
[285] Art.5(a)(ii) and Sch.1, Pt.2, S.I. No.135/2006.
[286] See s.103(7)(c), Road Traffic Act 1961 and art.5(a)(ii) and Sch.1, Pt.2, S.I. No.135/2006.
[287] **First conviction** – fine up to €1,000; **Second conviction** – fine up to €2,000; **Third conviction** – fine up to €1,000 and/or imprisonment for up to 3 months. See also s.18, Road Traffic Act 2006.
[288] See Reference 2, Pt.4, Sch.1, Road Traffic Act 2002 and also S.I. No.134/2006 – Road Traffic Act 2002 (Commencement of Certain Provisions) Order 2006 – which came into effect on 3 April 2006.

under section 27 of the Road Traffic Act 1961 on the particular facts of the case.

Penalty Point Disqualification: if a defendant accrues 12 penalty points upon conviction for this offence, then they will be disqualified under the administrative procedure set out under section 3 of the Road Traffic Act 2002.

(28) DRIVING WITHOUT REASONABLE CONSIDERATION[289] – SECTION 51(A) OF THE ROAD TRAFFIC ACT 1961[290]

Penalties

In respect of offences under section 51(a), the penalties are as follows:

Fixed Charge Penalty: €80 (paid in 28 days):[291] €120 (paid in subsequent 28 days).[292]

Upon Conviction: General Penalty under section 102 of the Road Traffic Act 1961.[293]

Penalty Points: two (payment of fixed charge): four (upon conviction).[294] Section 2(8) of the Road Traffic Act 2002 applies if the court imposes an ancillary disqualification order under section 27 of the Road Traffic Act 1961 – in those circumstances, penalty points will not be endorsed on the licence record.

Disqualification:

Ancillary Disqualification: a conviction under section 51(a) does not carry a mandatory disqualification. However, it is open to the court to make an ancillary disqualification order under section 27 of the Road Traffic Act 1961 on the particular facts of the case.

Penalty Point Disqualification: if a defendant accrues 12 penalty points upon conviction for this offence, then they will be dis-

---

[289] See Chapter 8 for more information in respect of this offence.

[290] As inserted by s.49, Road Traffic Act 1968.

[291] Art.5(a)(i) and Sch.1, Pt.1, S.I. No.135/2006.

[292] See s.103(7)(c), Road Traffic Act 1961 and art.5(a)(i) and Sch.1, Pt.1, S.I. No.135/2006.

[293] **First conviction** – fine up to €1,000; **Second conviction** – fine up to €2,000; **Third conviction** – fine up to €1,000 and/or imprisonment for up to 3 months. See also s.18, Road Traffic Act 2006.

[294] See Reference 17, Pt.1, Sch.1, Road Traffic Act 2002 as inserted by s.22, Road Traffic Act 2004 and also S.I. No.134/2006 – Road Traffic Act 2002 (Commencement of Certain Provisions) Order 2006 which came into effect on 3 April 2006.

qualified under the administrative procedure set out under section 3 of the Road Traffic Act 2002.

(29) FAILURE TO COMPLY WITH MANDATORY TRAFFIC SIGNS AT JUNCTIONS – ARTICLE 22 OF THE ROAD TRAFFIC (TRAFFIC AND PARKING) REGULATIONS 1997[295]

'Where at any junction:

(a) a must maintain direction sign (traffic sign RUS 004/RUS 004A); or

(b) a must turn right sign (traffic sign RUS 005/RUS 005A); or

(c) a must turn left sign (traffic sign RUS 006/RUS 006A);

are provided, Traffic (other than a light rail vehicle) must proceed in the direction indicated by arrows on sign.'

Penalties

In respect of offences under article 22, the penalties are as follows:

Fixed Charge Penalty: €60 (paid in 28 days):[296] €90 (paid in subsequent 28 days).[297]

Upon Conviction: General Penalty under section 102 of the Road Traffic Act 1961 applies.[298]

Penalty Points: one (payment of fixed charge): three (upon conviction.[299] Section 2(8) of the Road Traffic Act 2002 applies if the court imposes an ancillary disqualification order under section 27 of the Road Traffic Act 1961. In those circumstances, penalty points will not be endorsed on the licence record.

Disqualification:

Ancillary Disqualification: a conviction under article 22 does not carry a mandatory disqualification. However, it is open to the

---

[295] S.I. No.182/1997 – Road Traffic (Traffic and Parking) Regulations, 1997 – Regulations enacted under s.35, Road Traffic Act 1994.
[296] Article 5(b)(ii) and Sch.2, Pt.2, S.I. No.135/2006.
[297] See s.103(7)(c), Road Traffic Act 1961 and art.5(b)(ii) and Sch. 2, Pt.2, S.I. No.135/2006.
[298] **First conviction** – fine up to €1,000; **Second conviction** – fine up to €2,000; **Third conviction** – fine up to €1,000 and/or imprisonment for up to 3 months. See also s.18, Road Traffic Act 2006.
[299] See Reference 14, Pt.4, Sch.1, Road Traffic Act 2002 and also S.I. No.134/2006 – Road Traffic Act 2002 (Commencement of Certain Provisions) Order 2006 – which came into effect on 3 April 2006.

court to make an ancillary disqualification order under section 27 of the Road Traffic Act 1961 on the particular facts of the case.

Penalty Point Disqualification: if a defendant accrues 12 penalty points upon conviction for this offence, then they will be disqualified under the administrative procedure set out under section 3 of the Road Traffic Act 2002.

(30) FAILURE TO COMPLY WITH PROHIBATORY TRAFFIC SIGNS AT JUNCTIONS – ARTICLE 23 OF THE ROAD TRAFFIC (TRAFFIC AND PARKING) REGULATIONS 1997[300]

'Where the following prohibitory traffic signs appear:

(a) a must not maintain direction sign (traffic sign RUS 011); or

(b) a must not turn right sign (traffic sign RUS 012);[301] or

(c) a must not turn left sign (traffic sign RUS 013);[302]

traffic must not proceed in the direction indicated by arrows on sign.[303]

Where the following prohibitory traffic signs appear:

(d) a must not maintain direction sign (traffic sign RUS 011) and a must not turn right sign (traffic sign RUS 012);[304] or

(e) a must not maintain direction sign (traffic sign RUS 011) and a must not turn left sign (traffic sign RUS 013);[305]

traffic must not proceed in either of the directions indicated by arrows on signs.'

The above traffic signs may be accompanied by information plates advising time periods in which the restrictions apply, or classes of vehicles to which restrictions will not apply. It is therefore a defence to a charge under article 23 to demonstrate that at the time of the alleged offence, the prohibitory traffic sign was not in operation, or it did not apply to the class of vehicle being driver by the defendant.

---

[301] S.I. No.182/1997 – Road Traffic (Traffic and Parking) Regulations, 1997 – Regulations enacted under s.35, Road Traffic Act 1994.
[302] Art.23(1), S.I. No.182/1997.
[303] *Ibid.*, 23(1).
[3034] *Ibid.*, 23(1).
[305] *Ibid.*, 23(2).
[305] *Ibid.*, 23(2).

Penalties

In respect of offences under article 23, the penalties are as follows:

Fixed Charge Penalty: €60 (paid in 28 days):[306] €90 (paid in subsequent 28 days).[307]

Upon Conviction: General Penalty under section 102 of the Road Traffic Act 1961 applies.[308]

Penalty Points: one (payment of fixed charge): three (upon conviction.[309] Section 2(8) of the Road Traffic Act 2002 applies if the court imposes an ancillary disqualification order under section 27 of the Road Traffic Act 1961. In those circumstances, penalty points will not be endorsed on the licence record.

Disqualification:

Ancillary Disqualification: a conviction under article 23 does not carry a mandatory disqualification. However, it is open to the court to make an ancillary disqualification order under section 27 of the Road Traffic Act 1961 on the particular facts of the case.

Penalty Point Disqualification: if a defendant accrues 12 penalty points upon conviction for this offence, then they will be disqualified under the administrative procedure set out under section 3 of the Road Traffic Act 2002.

---

(31) Failure to Comply with Keep Left/Right Signs – Article 24 of the Road Traffic (Traffic and Parking) Regulations 1997[310]

'Where the following traffic signs appear:

(a) a must keep left sign (traffic sign RUS 001/RUS 001A) – approaching traffic must stay left of same sign;[311]

---

[306] *Ibid.*, 5(b)(ii) and Sch.2, Pt.2, S.I. No.135/2006.

[307] See s.103(7)(c), Road Traffic Act 1961 and art.5(b)(ii) and Sch.2, Pt.2, S.I. No.135/2006.

[308] **First conviction** – fine up to €1,000; **Second conviction** – fine up to €2,000; **Third conviction** – fine up to €1,000 and/or imprisonment for up to 3 months. See also s.18, Road Traffic Act 2006.

[309] See Reference 15, Pt.4, Sch.1, Road Traffic Act 2002 and also S.I. No.134/2006 – Road Traffic Act 2002 (Commencement of Certain Provisions) Order 2006 – which came into effect on 3 April 2006.

[310] S.I. No.182/1997 – Road Traffic (Traffic and Parking) Regulations, 1997 – Regulations enacted under s.35, Road Traffic Act 1994.

[311] Art.24(1), S.I. No.182/1997.

(b) a must keep right sign (traffic sign RUS 002) – approaching traffic must stay right of same sign;[312]

(c) a must pass either side sign (traffic sign RUS 003);[313]

approaching traffic must stay either left or right of same sign.'

Penalties

In respect of offences under article 24, the penalties are as follows:

Fixed Charge Penalty: €60 (paid in 28 days):[314] €90 (paid in subsequent 28 days).[315]

Upon Conviction: General Penalty under section 102 of the Road Traffic Act 1961 applies.[316]

Penalty Points: one (payment of fixed charge): three (upon conviction.[317] Section 2(8) of the Road Traffic Act 2002 applies if the court imposes an ancillary disqualification order under section 27 of the Road Traffic Act 1961. In those circumstances, penalty points will not be endorsed on the licence record.

Disqualification:

Ancillary Disqualification: a conviction under article 24 does not carry a mandatory disqualification. However, it is open to the court to make an ancillary disqualification order under section 27 of the Road Traffic Act 1961 on the particular facts of the case.

Penalty Point Disqualification: if a defendant accrues 12 penalty points upon conviction for this offence, then they will be disqualified under the administrative procedure set out under section 3 of the Road Traffic Act 2002.

---

[312] *Ibid.*, 24(2).
[313] *Ibid.*, 24(3).
[314] Art.5(b)(ii) and Sch.2, Pt.2, S.I. No.135/2006.
[315] See s.103(7)(c), Road Traffic Act 1961 and art.5(b)(ii) and Sch.2, Pt.2, S.I. No.135/2006.
[316] **First conviction** – fine up to €1,000; **Second conviction** – fine up to €2,000; **Third conviction** – fine up to €1,000 and/or imprisonment for up to 3 months. See also s.18, Road Traffic Act 2006.
[317] See Reference 16, Pt.4, Sch.1, Road Traffic Act 2002 and also S.I. No.134/2006 – Road Traffic Act 2002 (Commencement of Certain Provisions) Order 2006 – which came into effect on 3 April 2006.

(32) ILLEGAL ENTRY INTO ONE WAY STREET – ARTICLE 28 OF THE ROAD TRAFFIC (TRAFFIC AND PARKING) REGULATIONS 1997[318]

'Where a No Entry line (RRM 019) is provided across the entrance to a road, a driver must not proceed beyond that sign and must not enter road.'

Penalties

Fixed Charge Penalty: €60 (paid in 28 days):[319] €90 (paid in subsequent 28 days).[320]

Upon Conviction: General Penalty under section 102 of the Road Traffic Act 1961 applies.[321]

Penalty Points: one (payment of fixed charge): three (upon conviction.[322] Section 2(8) of the Road Traffic Act 2002 applies if the court imposes an ancillary disqualification order under section 27 of the Road Traffic Act 1961. In those circumstances, penalty points will not be endorsed on the licence record.

Disqualification:

Ancillary Disqualification: a conviction under article 24 does not carry a mandatory disqualification. However, it is open to the court to make an ancillary disqualification order under section 27 of the Road Traffic Act 1961 on the particular facts of the case.

Penalty Point Disqualification: if a defendant accrues 12 penalty points upon conviction for this offence, then they will be disqualified under the administrative procedure set out under section 3 of the Road Traffic Act 2002.

---

[318] S.I. No.182/1997 – Road Traffic (Traffic and Parking) Regulations, 1997 – Regulations enacted under s.35, Road Traffic Act 1994.

[319] Art.(b)(ii) and Sch.2, Pt.2, S.I. No.135/2006.

[320] See s.103(7)(c), Road Traffic Act 1961 and art.5(b)(ii) and Sch.2, Pt.2, S.I. No.135/2006.

[321] **First conviction** – fine up to €1,000; **Second conviction** – fine up to €2,000; **Third conviction** – fine up to €1,000 and/or imprisonment for up to 3 months. See also s.18, Road Traffic Act 2006.

[322] See Reference 20, Pt.4, Sch.1, Road Traffic Act 2002 and also S.I. No.134/2006 – Road Traffic Act 2002 (Commencement of Certain Provisions) Order 2006 – which came into effect on 3 April 2006.

Mandatory Disqualification Table – Road Traffic Acts 1961–2006

Road Traffic Legislation	Road Traffic Offence	Circumstances	Minimum Duration
Section 18(2), Road Traffic Act 1961.	Using vehicle without Test certificate.	Second or subsequent offence with 3-year period.	1 year.
Section 20(10),Road Traffic Act 1961.	Driving vehicle before remedying dangerous defect.	Second or subsequent offence with 3-year period.	1 year.
Section 38(2), Road Traffic Act 1961.	Driving while disqualified s38(5)(a).	Each offence.	1 year.
Section 48, Road Traffic Act 1961.	Driving while unfit.	Second or subsequent offence with 3-year period.	1 year.
Section 49(1), Road Traffic Act 1961.	Driving/attempting to drive under influence of drink/drug.	First offence.	4 years.
Section 49(1), Road Traffic Act 1961.	Driving/attempting to drive under influence of drink/drug.	Second or subsequent offence.	6 years.
Sections 49(2), 49(3), and 49(4), Road Traffic Act 1961.	Drink driving/attempting to drive (Lowest Category) (80–100mg/100ml).	First offence.	1 years.
Sections 49(2), 49(3), and 49(4), Road Traffic Act 1961.	Drink driving/attempting to drive (Lowest Category) (80–100mg/100ml).	Second or subsequent offence.	2 years.
Sections 49(2), 49(3), and 49(4), Road Traffic Act 1961.	Drink driving/attempting to drive (Middle Category) (100–150mg/100ml).	First offence.	2 years.

(Continued)

(Continued)

Road Traffic Legislation	Road Traffic Offence	Circumstances	Minimum Duration
Sections 49(2), 49(3), and 49(4), Road Traffic Act 1961.	Drink driving/attempting to drive (Middle Category) (100–150mg/100ml).	Second or subsequent offence.	4 years.
Sections 49(2), 49(3), and 49(4), Road Traffic Act 1961	Drink driving/attempting to drive (Highest Category) (exceeding 150mg/100ml)	First offence.	3 years.
Sections 49(2), 49(3), and 49(4), Road Traffic Act 1961.	Drink driving/attempting to drive (Highest Category) (exceeding 150mg/100ml).	Second or subsequent offence.	6 years.
Section 50(1), Road Traffic Act 1961.	Being in charge with the intent to drive	First offence.	2 years.
Section 50(1), Road Traffic Act 1961.	Being in charge with the intent to drive.	Second or subsequent offence.	4 years.
Sections 50(2), 50(3), 50(4), Road Traffic Act 1961.	Being in charge with the intent to drive (Lowest Category) (80–100mg/100ml).	First offence.	1 year.
Sections 50(2), 50(3), 50(4), Road Traffic Act 1961.	Being in charge with the intent to drive (Lowest Category) (80–100mg/100ml).	Second or subsequent offence.	2 years.
Sections 50(2), 50(3), 50(4), Road Traffic Act 1961.	Being in charge with the intent to drive (Middle Category) (100–150mg/100ml).	First offence.	2 years.
Sections 50(2), 50(3), 50(4), Road Traffic Act 1961.	Being in charge with the intent to drive (Middle Category) (100–150mg/100ml).	Second or subsequent offence.	4 years.

(Continued)

(Continued)

Road Traffic Legislation	Road Traffic Offence	Circumstances	Minimum Duration
Sections 50(2), 50(3), 50(4), Road Traffic Act 1961.	Being in charge with the intent to drive (Highest Category) (exceeding 150mg/100ml).	First offence.	3 years.
Sections 50(2), 50(3), 50(4), Road Traffic Act 1961.	Being in charge with the intent to drive (Highest Category) (exceeding 150mg/100ml).	Second or subsequent offence.	6 years.
Section 13, Road Traffic Act 1994.	Failure/refusal to provide specimen at Garda station.	First offence.	4 years.
Section 13, Road Traffic Act 1994.	Failure/refusal to provide specimen at Garda station.	Second or subsequent offence.	6 years.
Section 14, Road Traffic Act 1994.	Failure/refusal to accompany member to Garda Síochána station.	First offence.	4 years.
Section 14, Road Traffic Act 1994.	Failure/refusal to accompany member to Garda Síochána station.	Second or subsequent offence.	6 years.
Section 15, Road Traffic Act 1994.	Failure/refusal to provide blood or urine specimen while in hospital.	First offence.	4 years.
Section 15, Road Traffic Act 1994.	Failure/refusal to provide blood or urine specimen while in hospital.	Second or subsequent offence.	6 years.
Section 52, Road Traffic Act 1961.	Careless driving.	Third or subsequent offence within 3 .years.	1 year.
Section 5, Road Traffic Act 1961.	Dangerous driving (Tried on Indictment).	First offence.	4 years.

(Continued)

(Continued)

Road Traffic Legislation	Road Traffic Offence	Circumstances	Minimum Duration
Section 53, Road Traffic Act 1961.	Dangerous driving (Tried on Indictment).	Second or subsequent offence.	6 years.
Section 53, Road Traffic Act 1961.	Dangerous driving (Summary).	First offence.	2 years.
Section 53, Road Traffic Act 1961.	Dangerous driving (Summary).	Second or subsequent offence.	4 years.
Section 54, Road Traffic Act 1961.	Driving dangerously defective vehicle.	Second or subsequent offence within 3 years.	1 year.
Section 55, Road Traffic Act 1961.	Dangerous parking (at night).	Second or subsequent offence within 3 years.	1 year.
Section 56, Road Traffic Act 1961.	Using uninsured vehicle.	First offence (unless special circumstances).	2 years(can impose disqualification of less than 2 years or no disqualification at all).
Section 56, Road Traffic Act 1961.	Using uninsured vehicle.	Second or subsequent offence within 3 years.	4 years.
Section 106, Road Traffic Act 1961.	Breach of duties at scene of accident/fail to stop/remain at scene of accident – driver of vehicle which injures person/property.	First offence.	4 years.

(Continued)

(Continued)

Road Traffic Legislation	Road Traffic Offence	Circumstances	Minimum Duration
Section 106, Road Traffic Act 1961.	Breach of duties at scene of accident/fail to stop/remain at scene of accident – driver of vehicle which injures person/property.	Second or subsequent offence.	6 years.
Section 106, Road Traffic Act 1961.	Breach of duties at scene of accident (other than above).	Second or subsequent offence within 3 years.	1 year.
Section 106, Road Traffic Act 1961.	Breach of duties at scene of accident.	First offence.	4 years.
Section 112, Road Traffic Act 1961.	Unauthorised taking of vehicle.	Each offence.	1 year.
Section 138(3), Railway Safety Act 2005.	Bridge strikes (on Indictment).	First offence.	4 years.
Section 138(3), Railway Safety Act 2005.	Bridge strikes (on Indictment).	Second or subsequent offence.	6 years.
Regulation 19(1), EC (Vehicle Testing) Regulation – S.I. No.771/2004.	Driving vehicle without a certificate of road worthiness.	Second or subsequent offence within 3 years.	1 year.

Mandatory Disqualification Table

Proposed Disqualification Periods upon Commencement of Provisions of Road Traffic Act 2010

Road Traffic Legislation	Road Traffic Offence	Circumstances	Minimum Duration
Section 18(2), Road Traffic Act 1961.	Using vehicle without test certificate.	Second or subsequent offence with 3-year period.	1 year.
Section 20(10), Road Traffic Act 1961.	Driving vehicle before remedying dangerous defect.	Second or subsequent offence with 3-year period.	1 year.
Section 38(2), Road Traffic Act 1961.	Driving while disqualified s38(5)(a).	Each offence.	1 year.
Section 48, Road Traffic Act 1961.	Driving while unfit.	Second or subsequent offence with 3-year period.	1 year.
Section 4(1), Road Traffic Act 2010.	Driving/attempting to drive under influence of drink/drug.	First offence.	4 years.
Section 4(1), Road Traffic Act 2010.	Driving/attempting to drive under influence of drink/drug.	Second or subsequent offence.	6 years.
Sections 4(2), 4(3), 4(4), Road Traffic Act 2010.	Drink driving/attempting to drive (less than 80mg/100ml).	First offence (fixed penalty fine) 'Specified person'.	No disqualification, 3 penalty points **3 months' disqualification.**
Sections 4(2), 4(3), 4(4), Road Traffic Act 2010.	Drink driving/attempting to drive (less than 80mg/100ml).	Second or subsequent offence (drink driving offence).	1 year.

(Continued)

(Continued)

Road Traffic Legislation	Road Traffic Offence	Circumstances	Minimum Duration
Sections 4(2), 4(3), 4(4), Road Traffic Act 2010.	Drink driving/attempting to drive (80–100mg/100ml).	First offence.	1 year.
Sections 4(2), 4(3), 4(4), Road Traffic Act 2010.	Drink driving/attempting to drive (80–100mg/100ml).	Second or subsequent offence (drink driving offence).	2 years.
Sections 4(2), 4(3), 4(4), Road Traffic Act 2010.	Drink driving/attempting to drive (100–150mg/100ml).	First offence.	2 years.
Sections 4(2), 4(3), 4(4), Road Traffic Act 2010.	Drink driving/attempting to drive (100–150mg/100ml).	Second or subsequent offence (drink driving offence).	4 years.
Sections 4(2), 4(3), 4(4), Road Traffic Act 2010.	Drink driving/attempting to drive (exceeding 150mg/100ml).	First offence.	3 years.
Sections 4(2), 4(3), 4(4), Road Traffic Act 2010.	Drink driving/attempting to drive (exceeding 150mg/100ml).	Second or subsequent offence (drink driving).	6 years.
Section 5(1), Road Traffic Act 2010	Being in charge with the intent to drive.	First offence.	4 years.
Section 5 (1), Road Traffic Act 2010.	Being in charge with the intent to drive .	Second or subsequent offence (drink driving).	6 years.
Sections 5(2), 5(3), 5(4), Road Traffic Act 2010.	Being in charge with the intent to drive (less than 80mg/100ml).	First offence (fixed penalty fine) **'Specified Person.'**	No disqualification, 3 penalty points **3 months' disqualification.**
Sections 5(2), 5(3), 5(4), Road Traffic Act 2010.	Being in charge with the intent to drive (less than 80mg/100ml).	First offence (upon conviction).	6 Months.
Sections 5(2), 5(3), 5(4), Road Traffic Act 2010.	Being in charge with the intent to drive (less than 80mg/100ml).	Second or subsequent offence (drink driving offence).	1 year.

(Continued)

(Continued)

Road Traffic Legislation	Road Traffic Offence	Circumstances	Minimum Duration
Sections 5(2), 5(3), 5(4), Road Traffic Act 2010.	Being in charge with the intent to drive (80- 100mg/100ml).	First offence.	1 year.
Sections 5(2), 5(3), 5(4), Road Traffic Act 2010.	Being in charge with the intent to drive (80- 100mg/100ml).	Second or subsequent offence (drink driving offence).	2 years.
Sections 5(2), 5(3), 5(4), Road Traffic Act 2010.	Being in charge with the intent to drive (100-150mg/100ml).	First offence.	2 years.
Sections 5(2), 5(3), 5(4), Road Traffic Act 2010.	Being in charge with the intent to drive (100-150mg/100ml).	Second or subsequent offence (drink driving offence).	4 years.
Sections 5(2), 5(3), 5(4), Road Traffic Act 2010.	Being in charge with the intent to drive (exceeding 150mg/100ml).	First offence.	3 years.
Sections 5(2), 5(3), 5(4), Road Traffic Act 2010.	Being in charge with the intent to drive (exceeding 150mg/100ml).	Second or subsequent offence (drink driving offence).	6 years.
Section 12, Road Traffic Act 2010.	Failure/refusal to provide specimen at Garda Station.	First offence.	4 years.
Section 12, Road Traffic Act 2010.	Failure/refusal to provide specimen at Garda Station	Second or subsequent offence (drink driving offence).	6 years.
Section 14, Road Traffic Act 2010.	Failure/refusal to provide blood or urine specimen while in hospital.	First offence.	4 years.
Section 14, Road Traffic Act 2010.	Failure/refusal to provide blood or urine specimen while in hospital.	Second or subsequent offence (drink driving offence).	6 years.
Section 52, Road Traffic Act 1961 (as amended by section 69, Road Traffic Act 2010).	Careless driving (Tried on Indictment).	First offence.	4 years.

(Continued)

(Continued)

Road Traffic Legislation	Road Traffic Offence	Circumstances	Minimum Duration
Section 52, Road Traffic Act 1961 (as amended by section 69, Road Traffic Act 2010).	Careless driving (Tried on Indictment).	Second or subsequent offence.	6 years.
Section 52, Road Traffic Act 1961 (as amended by section 69, Road Traffic Act 2010).	Careless driving (Tried summarily).	First offence **(unless special circumstances).**	2 years **(can impose disqualification of less than 2 years or no disqualification).**
Section 52, Road Traffic Act 1961 (as amended by section 69, Road Traffic Act 2010).	Careless driving (Tried summarily).	Second or subsequent offence.	4 years.
Section 53, Road Traffic Act 1961 (as amended by section 69, Road Traffic Act 2010).	Dangerous driving (Tried on Indictment).	First offence.	4 years.
Section 53, Road Traffic Act 1961 (as amended by section 69, Road Traffic Act 2010).	Dangerous driving (Tried on Indictment).	Second or subsequent offence.	6 years.
Section 53, Road Traffic Act 1961 (as amended by section 69, Road Traffic Act 2010).	Dangerous driving (Tried summarily).	First offence.	2 years.

(Continued)

(Continued)

Road Traffic Legislation	Road Traffic Offence	Circumstances	Minimum Duration
Section 53, Road Traffic Act 1961 (as amended by section 69, Road Traffic Act 2010).	Dangerous driving (Tried summarily).	Second or subsequent offence.	4 years.
Section 54, Road Traffic Act 1961 (as amended by section 69, Road Traffic Act 2010).	Driving dangerously defective vehicle.	Second or subsequent offence within 3 years.	1 year.
Section 55, Road Traffic Act 1961 (as amended by section 69, Road Traffic Act 2010).	Dangerous parking (at night).	Second or subsequent offence within 3 years.	1 year.
Section 56, Road Traffic Act 1961.	Using uninsured vehicle.	First offence **(unless special circumstances).**	2 years **(can impose disqualification of less than 2 years or no disqualification).**
Section 56, Road Traffic Act 1961	Using uninsured vehicle.	Second or subsequent offence within 3 years.	4 years.
Section 106, Road Traffic Act 1961.	Breach of duties at scene of accident/fail to stop/remain at scene of accident – driver of vehicle which injures person/property.	First offence.	4 years.

(Continued)

(Continued)

Road Traffic Legislation	Road Traffic Offence	Circumstances	Minimum Duration
Section 106, Road Traffic Act 1961.	Breach of duties at scene of accident/fail to stop/remain at scene of accident – driver of vehicle which injures person/property.	Second or subsequent offence.	6 years.
Section 106, Road Traffic Act 1961.	Breach of duties at scene of accident (other than above).	Second or subsequent offence within 3 years.	1 year.
Section 106, Road Traffic Act 1961.	Breach of duties at scene of accident	First offence.	4 years
Section 112, Road Traffic Act 1961.	Unauthorised taking of vehicle.	Each offence.	1 year.
Section 138(3), Railway Safety Act 2005.	Bridge strikes (on Indictment).	First offence.	4 years.
Section 138(3), Railway Safety Act 2005.	Bridge strikes (on Indictment).	Second or subsequent offence.	6 years.
Regulation 19(1), EC (Vehicle Testing) Regulation – S.I. No.771/2004.	Driving vehicle without a certificate of road worthiness.	Second or subsequent offence within 3 years.	1 year.

Index